D0795545

WebDAV

Next-Generation Collaborative Web Authoring

Prentice Hall PTR Series in Computer Networking and Distributed Systems

Radia Perlman, Series Editor

WebDAV
Next-Generation Collaborative Web Authoring

Lisa Dusseault

PRENTICE
HALL
PTR

PRENTICE HALL
Professional Technical Reference
Upper Saddle River, New Jersey 07458
www.phptr.com

Library of Congress Cataloging-in-Publication Data

Dusseault, Lisa
    WebDAV: next-generation collaborative Web authoring / Lisa Dusseault.
        p. cm. -- (Prentice Hall PTR series in computer networking and distributed systems)
    Includes bibliographical references and index.
    ISBN 0-13-065208-3
    1. WebDAV (Standard) 2. Web site development--Standards. 3. Internet programming.
    4. Client/server computing. I. Title. II. Series.

    TK5105.5863.D87 2003
    005.2'76--dc21

                                                                            2003050879

Editorial/Production Supervision: *Techne Group*

Executive Editor: *Mary Franz*

Editorial Assistant: *Noreen Regina*

Marketing Manager: *Curt Johnson*

Manufacturing Buyer: *Maura Zaldivar*

Cover Design Director: *Jerry Votta*

Full-Service Production Manager: *Anne R. Garcia*

© 2004 Pearson Education, Inc.
Publishing as Prentice Hall Professional Technical Reference
Upper Saddle River, NJ 07458

PRENTICE
HALL
PTR

Prentice Hall PTR offers excellent discounts on this book when ordered in quantity for bulk purchases or special sales. For more information, please contact: U.S. Corporate and Government Sales, 1-800-382-3419, corpsales@pearsontechgroup.com. For sales outside of the U.S., please contact: International Sales, 1-317-581-3793, international@pearsontechgroup.com.

Company and product names mentioned herein are the trademarks or registered trademarks of their respective owners.

All rights reserved. No part of this book may be reproduced, in any form or by any means, without permission in writing from the publisher.

Printed in the United States of America

First Printing

ISBN 0-13-065208-3

Pearson Education Ltd.
Pearson Education Australia PTY, Limited
Pearson Education Singapore, Pte. Ltd.
Pearson Education North Asia Ltd.
Pearson Education Canada, Ltd.
Pearson Educación de Mexico, S.A. de C.V.
Pearson Education—Japan
Pearson Education Malaysia, Pte. Ltd.

About Prentice Hall Professional Technical Reference

With origins reaching back to the industry's first computer science publishing program in the 1960s, and formally launched as its own imprint in 1986, Prentice Hall Professional Technical Reference (PH PTR) has developed into the leading provider of technical books in the world today. Our editors now publish over 200 books annually, authored by leaders in the fields of computing, engineering, and business.

Our roots are firmly planted in the soil that gave rise to the technical revolution. Our bookshelf contains many of the industry's computing and engineering classics: Kernighan and Ritchie's *C Programming Language*, Nemeth's *UNIX System Administration Handbook*, Horstmann's *Core Java*, and Johnson's *High-Speed Digital Design*.

PH PTR acknowledges its auspicious beginnings while it looks to the future for inspiration. We continue to evolve and break new ground in publishing by providing today's professionals with tomorrow's solutions.

CONTENTS

Chapter 2

Chapter 3

Chapter 5
WebDAV Modifications to HTTP   107

Chapter 9
Putting the Pieces Together — 213

Chapter 15
Designing WebDAV Applications   **391**

Appendix A
Microsoft and Windows Tips   **409**

Appendix B
HTTP Status Codes 421

Preface

WebDAV is a protocol that allows Web authoring tools and many other document-oriented applications to save documents directly to a Web server and manage the content on the server. Many Internet clients and servers as well as office productivity applications already implement WebDAV. This book explains what WebDAV is, how it works, and how to use it both in Web authoring tools and in custom document-based applications.

Readers

This book assumes only a minimum level of familiarity or comfort with the way the Internet and the World Wide Web work. Readers might want to start with a good Internet book ([Stevens98]) or a good HTTP book ([Krishnamurthy01] or [Gourley02]) to familiarize themselves with the architecture of the World Wide Web and the protocols and practices that make it work.

This book can be used in many ways:

- IT planners can use this book to understand whether WebDAV might serve as a suitable document management standard, before making important software purchasing decisions.
- Software implementors who are interested in implementing WebDAV or in adding WebDAV functionality can use this book to learn practical details about WebDAV that aren't in the standard specifications and to learn about resources for the task.
- Custom application designers can use this book to understand how to design an application to use the WebDAV document model. This allows the custom

application to work seamlessly with WebDAV-capable content applications such as Office 2000.

- Webmasters can use this book to understand how they can simplify and streamline their publication and authoring processes using WebDAV-enabled server software and existing HTML-authoring products. Like custom application designers, they will find out how document management can be customized to allow a custom publishing process or workflow process.

Organization of the Book

This book is divided into five main sections.

Introductory Material   Chapter 1, *Introduction*, introduces WebDAV, and why and how it was developed. Chapter 2, *History of Web and Collaborative Authoring*, gives more depth on the technologies that existed prior to WebDAV (FTP, HTTP), and the drawbacks that the WebDAV designers knew they needed to overcome. Chapter 3, *HTTP Mechanics*, provides a review of HTTP that is only necessary if you're not already familiar with HTTP.

How WebDAV Works   Chapter 4, *Data Model*, provides an overview of WebDAV functionality by explaining the data model, which is crucial to understanding how WebDAV works. Chapter 5, *WebDAV Modifications to HTTP*, explains how WebDAV extends HTTP methods. Chapters 6, 7, and 8 describe the practical aspects of how the core WebDAV protocol works. These chapters will be useful to developers of WebDAV-enabled software and custom applications. Chapter 9, *Putting the Pieces Together*, pulls this material together into extended examples.

WebDAV Extensions   Chapter 11, *Versioning*, and Chapter 12, *Multifile Versioning*, introduce the WebDAV versioning standard DeltaV in sufficient depth to enable the reader to read the DeltaV specifications and be able to put details into context. Chapter 13, *Access Control*, introduces the Access Control specification, which is soon to be a standard.

Software and Custom Applications   Chapter 10, *WebDAV Products and Tools*, introduces a number of client and server software packages that support WebDAV. Chapter 14, *Custom WebDAV Applications*, and Chapter 15, *Designing WebDAV Applications*, discuss what custom applications can do with WebDAV, and how to design such custom applications.

Reference Appendixes   *Microsoft and Windows Tips* and *HTTP Status Codes*.

Typographical Conventions

In this book, certain fonts and character types are used to set off certain kinds of words. Here are the conventions and an example of each:

- HTTP and WebDAV method names are presented in CAPS (COPY).
- Property names and status codes are shown in Helvetica (creationdate).

- Headers, XML tags, and code samples are presented in fixed-width `Courier New` (`response`). **`Bold Courier`** is sometimes used within code samples to draw attention to the most salient parts of the example.

Icons Used

Three icons are used to draw the reader's attention to various sections.

A "curves ahead" sign shows something that might be tricky to understand or implement.

An exclamation mark indicates that there's an important recommendation or note in the text. It might be simple, but it's important.

A bomb icon shows a place where the specification is unclear, problematic, or tricky.

References

Many of the references in this book are in a standard recognizable style including the primary author's last name and year of publication:

[Stevens98]

However, I use an odd reference style for IETF standards, because those standards are more commonly known by their IDs or names than by their authors or dates. IETF standards are each issued a Request for Comments (RFC) number:

[RFC2518]

This approach is intended to give the reader a quick idea whether the reference is a protocol standard or some other document.

Acknowledgments

The technical reviewers for this book included Greg Stein, Jim Whitehead, Yaron Goland, Geoff Clemm, Brian Korver, Elias Sinderson, Andrew Sieja, and Terence Spies. I would never have gotten started without Greg and Jim in particular and their planning and early involvement. Kevin Dick, Andrew McGregor, and Terence Spies also advised me on what material to include. However, all errors and omissions are my fault and not theirs!

Peter Raymond and Rick Rupp of Merant provided very helpful explanations and diagrams of baselines and configurations. Keith Ito's Tracer tool was used to produce the traces. Thanks also to Gary Gershon who contributed some advice for Chapter 15.

The WebDAV mailing lists and the WebDAV and Delta V working group members were important sources of information on various implementations and issues. For example, Stephan Eissing provided useful information on how various client programs do "safe save."

Radia Perlman showed such complete confidence that I would produce something worthwhile that she asked me to put this book in her series before I'd written a word. Her support and advice were crucial. Thanks also to my editors, Mary Franz and her assistant Noreen Regina of Prentice Hall, particularly for being patient with me.

I can't imagine having to write a book without Google. I used it regularly to look up even information I thought I knew.

My quilting and karate buddies and other friends kept me sane. My parents brought me to the point where I wanted to write a book, and could.

Eric Rescorla inspired this effort and supported it from start to finish, reviewing every word several times over and directing me to explain and organize material better than I thought I could. I couldn't have done it without him.

Introduction

The World Wide Web has created an explosion in the availability of information, making vast amounts of content accessible from any computer connected to the Internet. Users can navigate between related sites or search for information in massive public indexes. Sites are available in hundreds of human languages and host all kinds of files, from plain text to sounds, images, and movies.

This wide interoperability and broad access was made possible through the use of two standards: Pages are formatted in *HyperText Markup Language* (HTML) and retrieved with *HyperText Transfer Protocol* (HTTP). These two standards can be implemented on almost any computing platform, from PCs to cell phones. A Web site creator can make a site public using free software, a cheap computer, and an Internet connection. As soon as the Web site is connected to the Internet, it can potentially be accessed by anybody with an Internet connection. Thus, the World Wide Web is more open than any other content or publishing system humankind has known.

The Web was intended from the start to be an editable medium as well as a browsable one. When Tim Berners-Lee wrote the first Web client at the European Particle Physics Laboratory (CERN), it was intended as a tool for collaborating scientists to put text online and link to each other's text without having to work through a centralized database of any kind. Thus, the first client could edit pages as easily as viewing them.

When the Web escaped its research laboratory creche and took over the Internet, most Web clients could browse but not edit. Browsing was considered the most crucial feature to making the Web useful, and browsing is much easier than editing.[1] The early emphasis on browsing led to a standardized HTTP protocol that lacked important authoring features: There was no way to rename or copy Web pages. There was no way to create folders to contain Web pages. There wasn't even a standard way to list the names of the Web pages inside a specified folder. Proprietary protocols soon emerged to fill the gap, but for nearly 10 years, no standard Web authoring protocol was available.

Web-based Distributed Authoring and Versioning (WebDAV) is the first standard protocol to address Web authoring [RFC2518]. It builds on and extends HTTP to bring the same benefits to authoring that the Web has already brought to viewing content. Web site authors can use Web-DAV to remotely yet securely update their Web pages. Collaborators can use WebDAV to jointly author an electronic document without overwriting each other's changes or wondering which email or directory contains the authoritative version. Client software on all kinds of platforms can interact with WebDAV resources on a variety of servers. The Web is finally becoming a true authoring medium.

1.1   What Is Authoring?

Web authoring is the process of creating, updating, and managing content on a Web server. A basic Web server offers a set of text files formatted in HTML. These files contain links to other files. The content hosted by a Web server can also include non-HTML documents as well as images, programs, music, and video.

Web authoring frequently takes place remotely; the user creates content on a client machine and then transfers that content to the Web server. To offer that functionality, the Web server must provide a way for clients to create new Web pages and give the Web pages names and locations. Clients must be able to see a Web page's current content and provide new content to the server to replace old content. Clients must also be able to delete obsolete Web pages.

Web authoring frequently involves more than one author. A Web site may be managed by a team of people collaborating on the same files, contributing individual expertise to create a rich set of pages. Multiple authors frequently try to update the same pages within a short period, and without knowing that others are working on the same pages. Multiple authors make an authoring solution more difficult, yet teams of Web content authors are common.

Originally, HTTP attempted to solve the authoring problem with a few simple operations: the ability to download, upload, or delete a Web page. Although these operations provided some authoring functionality, many problems were left unsolved. Some of the most pressing were:

- No method for creating a new folder/directory. Web pages, like files on any file system, are typically organized in directories.
- No methods defined to move, copy, or rename Web pages.

---

1.   A more complete and nuanced explanation of the development of early Web clients can be found in *Weaving the Web* [Berners-Lee00].

- No way for clients to request a standardized (software-parsable) listing of a folder's contents.
- No way for two authors working on the same content to easily coordinate their changes.

Because these problems are in practice quite frustrating, basic HTTP has hardly ever been used for authoring without custom extensions.

1.1.1   The Bad Old Days

The first Web sites were necessarily created with text editors because no specialized tools existed. If the Web author happened not to be working directly on the Web server machine, *File Transfer Protocol* (FTP) [RFC959] would commonly be used to transmit the finished HTML file to the Web server. However, FTP was a standard in 1985, long before the Web came along, so it wasn't designed for authoring Web sites. It doesn't handle multiple authors gracefully, it doesn't use the same namespace as HTTP, and its directory listing format isn't well standardized. Obviously, something new was needed.

The first generation of popular Web authoring software consisted of HTML editors. These tools greatly improved the ability to change a local HTML file, but the process of getting the changed files to a remote server remained difficult. Many HTML editors did not attempt to do this at all, instead requiring the user to transfer the files separately to the Web server.

1.1.2   Usable but Proprietary Software

The second generation of Web authoring software attempted to solve the problem of putting the files on the Web server (as well as HTML editing) but did so with proprietary or awkward methods. Each major authoring package had significant incompatibilities with other software.

- Vermeer FrontPage, which became Microsoft FrontPage, used a proprietary protocol to remotely manage pages. A couple of non-Microsoft servers work with the FrontPage protocol, but few non-Microsoft client implementers have adopted it.
- Macromedia Dreamweaver and Allaire's ColdFusion provided some distributed authoring capabilities (including the ability to lock Web pages for single-author edits in Dreamweaver), but through proprietary protocols or protocol extensions only.
- Netscape Navigator Gold had the capability to place files on the server, using either FTP or the HTTP PUT request. This solution worked well enough for single-author Web sites but didn't work well with multiple authors because both FTP and HTTP PUT overwrite other authors' changes.

Professional Web development teams sometimes use source control repositories known as *Configuration Management* (CM) systems. Concurrent Versioning System (CVS) on Unix and Microsoft SourceSafe are both CM servers. CM servers typically support either proprietary or custom protocols, which are difficult for any other product to pick up and support. Although CM provides excellent functionality for multiple authors and even allows recovery of older versions of any document, it is unwieldy for Web site development. For example, it is frequently difficult or undesirable to host the Web site directly from the files in the CM repository. Therefore, any time the Web site is tested or released, its latest pages must be copied to a Web server.

1.1.3   Web Authoring via Web Forms

A number of Internet services and sites (today including MSN, AOL, GeoCities, and Yahoo!) host small personal Web sites for a large number of members. To manage changes submitted by all these users, these services use custom-built HTML forms to allow Web page editing.

An HTML form is a text file formatted in HTML with HTML tags identifying fields for a user to fill in and usually text explaining to the user what information to enter into each field. All Web browsers are capable of displaying basic HTML forms with a standard set of fields, collecting the user input, and returning the field values in a standard format to the server.

HTML forms are the lowest common denominator tool for solving the Web site authoring problem. A Web-based user interface does not require special software downloads. For example, in 2003 Yahoo! GeoCities hosted PageWizards [GeoCities02], [GeoCities03]. A PageWizard was a series of forms that walked the user through a number of steps to end up with a finished personal Web site.

Web-based user interfaces have some serious drawbacks:

- Users have very little control over their content because the content can't be accessed directly. For example, users can't back up their Web sites or synchronize them with local working copies.
- These interfaces are usually designed for use by one author only and cannot handle multiple authors managing the same content.
- Web interfaces are slow because the entire page and even images are transmitted to the client with each page refresh or page change.
- Web interfaces have very poor capabilities for text editing, so frequently authors want to use their own text editing tool.
- Using a text editing tool together with the Web-based authoring interface requires multiple steps and is error-prone, as I'll explain in the next section.

1.1.4   Multiple Stages Multiply Errors

The authoring systems we've discussed so far (proprietary, CM, and Web form based) all had clear interoperability problems, so many Web sites continued to use FTP for authoring. Every site had different conventions for relating FTP locations to Web locations, so it was difficult for authors to figure out where to put files on the FTP server. If the site required authorization, users could find it frustrating to log in to the FTP server as well as the Web server, possibly with different passwords. However, these are only minor frustrations compared to losing all the work you've done in a day—a potential outcome when an updated file is overwritten accidentally.

When authoring requires downloading and uploading files using different pieces of software in several stages, errors multiply. The stages include:

1. Browse to the correct file on the Web or FTP server. Save the file locally, choosing a name and location.
2. Edit the file, making sure all links will work even when the file is in a different location.
3. Open another piece of software, such as an FTP client.
4. Open a connection to the correct server.
5. Navigate to the correct remote location.
6. Browse the local file system looking for the changed file that was just saved, and upload it.

Saving to the local file system can be a problem because the local file system might have different file-naming rules than the server. Unix has always allowed file extensions like ".html," but Windows file systems used to restrict the extension to three characters. Unix treats names with different capitalization as different file names, but Windows does not, so a Windows user could upload `index.HTM` instead of `index.htm`. Because of the lost update problem, sites frequently have backup directories, but the user then has to choose between multiple locations of the same file. Files named `default.htm` and `index.htm` are so common, the wrong one may be updated.

These mistakes may not seem too likely when considered theoretically, but I make them often enough, particularly if my work is interrupted. My most common error is to save a file to two different local directories on different occasions, creating two local copies. When I upload the file to a server, I sometimes upload the wrong copy. I've also made backups of files and then overwritten the copy that had my recent changes with the copy from backup. Most memorably, I did that with the references file for this book after a month of improvements. I know I'm sometimes careless, but I also know that other users make the same mistakes, aided by software that doesn't make it easy enough to do things properly.

1.2   Third-Generation Web Authoring

The third generation of Web authoring software is based on WebDAV, the first open standard for Web authoring. This generation started in 1998 when WebDAV became a Proposed Standard. By 2002, WebDAV-based Web authoring had achieved wide interoperability, availability, and deployment. HTML authoring tools released after the year 2000 commonly support WebDAV to save content to any given Web server. As a result, the Web can finally be as empowering for individual content creators as it is for content consumers.

The name "WebDAV" stands for "Web-based Distributed Authoring and Versioning." Versioning automatically preserves past versions of Web pages on the server, and WebDAV designers wanted to allow the client to access and restore past versions of Web pages. Because it's rather complicated, versioning was not standardized in the original WebDAV specification, but it was standardized separately three years later. Versioning is important for large, complicated Web sites and for Web-based source code repositories, but it is not needed in all Web authoring scenarios. For example, Photoshop and many other Adobe applications support WebDAV but not versioning, yet users still get the benefit of sharing files and coordinating multiple authors online.

WebDAV works transparently with existing Web content by extending HTTP. HTTP allows reading or browsing documents on the Internet, but it doesn't do a good job of allowing authoring. WebDAV adds new functionality within the HTTP framework in a way that interacts seamlessly with existing HTTP clients and servers and existing Web content.

WebDAV has already achieved wide deployment on many platforms, in software from many vendors. It can be found in modern versions of Web servers such as Apache and Microsoft Internet Information Server (IIS). It can be found in Web browsers such as Microsoft Internet Explorer (IE). Desktop applications, namely Microsoft Office 2000 and Adobe software, including Photoshop, Acrobat, and GoLive, are adopting WebDAV. Finally, WebDAV client functionality is being implemented in modern operating systems at the file system level, in Windows XP and Mac OS X.

The Internet Engineering Task Force (IETF, *www.ietf.org*) standardized WebDAV after years of design work and discussion coordinated through an IETF Working Group. The WebDAV Working Group completed initial design work in 1998 and submitted a draft for approval. In February 1999, WebDAV was accepted as a standards-track specification and given the identification RFC2518. This book focuses on the functionality defined in the original WebDAV RFC.

IETF Documents

"RFC" stands for "Request For Comments" and identifies a document published by the IETF. RFCs are most often named by their RFC number, rather than author and year, so I've taken the same approach in references in this book.

1.3 WebDAV History

The design of WebDAV took nearly three years and the combined efforts of many individuals. This section gives a brief overview of that history and can be skipped if the reader wants to get on with the technical details.

1.3.1 The WebDAV Working Group

The history of WebDAV begins with HTTP, originally put together by Tim Berners-Lee while at CERN. Although Berners-Lee intended HTTP to handle authoring as well as browsing, in practice the functionality didn't allow interoperable multi-author access to write Web pages. While the Web was in its infancy, the focus and priorities of Web client and server implementers and protocol designers were mostly on making Web browsing work interoperably. Once the basic framework was in place, however, various members of the community started thinking about making authoring work as well.

IETF and W3C

The IETF was started in 1986 as a loose collection of government researchers. It quickly expanded to include all who were interested in participating. By the time the Web protocols needed standardization in 1993, the IETF was the obvious place to bring open protocols for change control. Two working groups were formed to develop the Uniform Resource Locator (URL) specification and HTTP standards. However, the IETF rejected the idea of working on a document format or markup language like HTML, preferring to stick with addressing and protocols.

In 1994, Tim Berners-Lee began the World Wide Web Consortium (W3C), primarily to keep HTML change control from slipping into the hands of any single company, but also to work on other Web-related technology. This included the *Platform for Internet Content Selection* (PICS) ratings technology, *Portable Network Graphics* (PNG), and most famously, *Extensible Markup Language* (XML). Many protocols in the IETF, like WebDAV, now use XML to marshal data extensibly within a protocol.

In the summer of 1996, several people meeting regularly at the IETF meetings and at the W3C realized that they shared a common set of goals. An informal Distributed Authoring design group was formed using the still-extant mailing list w3c-dist-auth@w3.org for communication. Early participants included employees from various large and small software companies, representatives of the W3C, and hypertext researchers, including grad students.

These ad-hoc participants requested a *Birds Of a Feather* (BOF) meeting at the 37th IETF conference on December 11, 1996. A BOF is the preliminary step to forming an IETF Working Group—the IETF uses the informal meeting to gauge the level of interest and discuss how reachable the goals of the working group will be. The attendees of this BOF overwhelmingly approved the formation of a working group within the Applications Area, with Jim Whitehead (then a graduate student at the University California at Irvine) as chairman. By this time, the team had already produced several versions of several draft documents. Many features were considered for inclusion in the core protocol or for publication as separate proposals. Access control and versioning were at one time part of the core protocol, but these turned out to be large and complicated features that needed to be dealt with on their own.

As with most standards, WebDAV was influenced by several parties with different viewpoints. It's interesting to see how these parties affected the development of the standard. The W3C, Microsoft, Netscape, and a group of graduate students at UC Irvine all influenced WebDAV significantly in its early development.

1.3.2 Suggested Requirements

The first WebDAV Working Group document to gain IETF approval was a Requirements draft, which became an Informational RFC in February 1998 [RFC2291]. Informational RFCs are permanent documents published by the IETF but not intended to be implemented as standards. The WebDAV requirements RFC is a short (21 pages) specification defining terms and outlining required features. The features were:

1. Properties
2. Links
3. Locking and reservations
4. Ability to retrieve the source code of a dynamically generated Web page (as opposed to the processed output for the page)
5. Partial write (upload only a specified range of bytes when creating or changing a file)
6. Copy, move, and rename
7. Ability to create a collection and list its members
8. Versioning and variants
9. Access control

By mid-1998, it became clear that links, versioning and variants, and access control were all such challenging areas that they required independent standardization work. Eventually, the group pared the requirements list down to a minimal feature list including properties, locking, move/copy/ rename, and handling collections. All other features were postponed.

1.3.3 W3C Pressure

The initial goal for the Distributed Authoring Working Group was provided by Dan Connolly of the W3C to "make Web editing as reliable as browsing, and nearly as ubiquitous." Henrik Frystyk and Roy Fielding were also early key contributors, and Tim Berners-Lee (at the time, director of the W3C) took an interest. The W3C XML proposals (including the XML standard but also the namespaces proposal still in process in 1998) became a big part of WebDAV's design.

However, some of the ideas proposed by W3C members were unacceptable to corporate interests.

- The W3C control model usually involved a dumb server and smart clients. In this model, clients would be entirely responsible for lock semantics and enforcement, perhaps by setting some "lock" property to an appropriate value. Other clients would voluntarily respect this value and refrain from modifying the resource. This model was unacceptable to commercial server developers who must make their servers work reliably under all conditions, including while handling queries from malicious or simply buggy client software. When the server enforces lock semantics, a bug-ridden client is more likely to hurt only its own users.

- A proposed data model for properties defined each property as a resource, so that a property could have its own properties and so on. This is rather similar to the model adopted by the W3C's standard for Resource Description Framework (RDF). RDF covers some of the same territory as WebDAV in that it has a standard for expressing metadata for Web resources. This model proved unacceptable to many software companies with Web servers that stored Web pages in the file system, because their architecture could not easily be adapted to efficiently store and retrieve data with such a complex model. WebDAV ultimately used a data model that is a blend of existing file system and simple database data models.
- Tim Berners-Lee wanted URL paths to remain entirely arbitrary, as HTTP URL paths are. The WebDAV Working Group decided not to follow this example. Instead, WebDAV requires that the URL for a WebDAV resource contain the URL to its parent. For example, the parent of `http://www.example.com/hr/index.html` must be the collection `http://www.example.com/hr/`.

1.3.4 Corporate Pressure

Corporate pressure is always present in standards work. The IETF is composed of individual members who freely participate in working groups and pay only nominal fees to attend the optional conferences (unlike the W3C, which has corporations as paying members). However, trips to IETF conferences are expensive, and employees frequently attend at the request and expense of their employers. Perhaps this is for the best, because corporate adoption is often essential for the success of a standard protocol.

Yaron Goland of Microsoft contributed an early list of features that would be required for Microsoft's Web editing products to support a standard protocol. This list included file and directory properties, move/copy, and lock/unlock. Netscape submitted a proposal to use new HTTP methods and headers to implement the WebDAV functionality.

The first concrete proposal for a Web authoring standard came from Yaron Goland and Jim Whitehead. Asad Faizi, from the Netscape enterprise server group, soon published an Internet Draft loosely describing the Netscape solution. Neither group was aware of the other's work before this. Each group justified its decisions in various ways. Usually, designers presented their proposals in theoretical terms because it's considered bad form in the IETF for attendees to blatantly push their employer's solution for commercial reasons.

It should be noted that not all IETF participants from one company agree with each other. Some observers were surprised to see Microsoft server implementers (Alex Hopmann, myself) and client implementers (Yaron Goland, Josh Cohen) disagreeing with each other strongly. Still, the starkest disagreements were between companies. Microsoft and Netscape each had proprietary solutions for the functionality proposed for WebDAV, so both companies had vested interests in making WebDAV resemble their own solutions. The employees from each company tended to see their model as the natural and superior solution.

Participation from vendors with proprietary solutions can sometimes delay the process, but it can also sometimes speed it. Implementers without versioning support were happy to allow versioning to be moved to another draft when the core draft became too lengthy. This suggestion was naturally opposed by participants from source-code control software vendors such as Perforce. In the end, the decision to postpone versioning clearly sped the standardization of WebDAV. It also kept barriers to implementation low, allowing early implementation of Web-DAV in both Microsoft software and open-source projects.

The proposal from Asad Faizi was merged with design ideas from Yaron Goland and Jim Whitehead. Early contributions from two Novell employees (Steve Carter and Del Jensen) led them to be added as authors as well. This became the WebDAV protocol specification with five authors, which eventually became RFC2518.

1.3.5   The Final Draft

The WebDAV Working Group completed its initial design work in early 1998 and submitted it to the IETF for approval. In February 1999, it was accepted as an IETF Proposed Standard (what the IETF calls the first tier of standard document maturity).

A few WebDAV implementations existed even before the specification was approved. This is generally encouraged by the IETF because it shows both the need for the protocol and the feasibility of its design. Those that were known to exist when the Proposed Standard was published were:

- UC Irvine students (under the guidance of Jim Whitehead) developed the WebDAV Explorer client.
- Joe Orton, then from the University of York, released the Sitecopy client.
- Jim Davis of Xerox produced a Python-based WebDAV client.
- Cyberteams ran a WebDAV server publicly for interoperability testing.
- Greg Stein's WebDAV module for Apache was released and running on the site *www.webdav.org*.
- Microsoft implemented an early version of the draft to work with IIS 4.0 and made this module available as an extension to the server.

In 1999, the working group's attention turned to various extensions to WebDAV including versioning and access control. Access control became a major focus of the WebDAV group, resulting in submission of a draft to the Internet Engineering Steering Group (IESG) as a proposed standard in late 2002. However, the IESG suggested some simplifications, and as of early 2003 an updated draft had not yet been resubmitted.

There was sufficient interest in versioning to form a standalone working group, so that group could attract a different membership and stay focused on versioning features. To create this working group, WebDAV participants organized the DeltaV BOF in Oslo in July 1999. The first working group meeting was in San Diego in December 2000, under the chairmanship of Jim

Amsden. DeltaV finished its work in the fall of 2001, and the DeltaV standard was approved in March 2002 [RFC3253].

1.3.6 Today

Work on WebDAV extensions continues, as client and server implementers demand more features within the WebDAV framework. The WebDAV Working Group is an open group, which anybody can join merely by joining the mailing list and to which anybody can contribute by writing their proposals in email or in a draft submitted to the IETF.

In addition to working on extensions to RFC2518, the working group is responsible for advancing WebDAV along the standards track, when and if the protocol shows the required maturity. A new RFC number is issued for each step in this track. Implementations may be compliant with RFC2518 but not with the successor to RFC2518; however, the working group attempts to keep changes to a minimum and to maximize interoperability, even between versions.

WebDAV interoperability events have been held yearly since 2001. These events attracted 20 to 30 client and server implementers and have been a great experience for improving interoperability and understanding the actual application of the standard. Interoperability events may require registration and a modest attendance fee, but additional implementers are always welcome.

1.4 Requirements and Scenarios

The first step in technical design is defining and understanding requirements, and this step can be retraced to provide a better understanding of an existing design. The requirements relate closely to the technology comparisons in the next chapter, and scenarios help put everything in context, so it's useful to introduce them now.

Some WebDAV requirements were drawn from existing practice. For example, since Front Page had a proprietary way to copy, move, and rename Web pages, and so did all the other proprietary solutions, WebDAV had to match this existing functionality.

Other requirements were drawn from *scenarios*, which are stories about how people interact with their software, their documents, and their collaborators. Scenarios help us understand which features are useful and which aren't. If a compelling story can't be told for how a feature is used and why the feature can't easily be done in some other fashion, then it's a good bet the requirement can be cut from the list.

When a protocol can be simplified by cutting requirements or reducing options, good designers do so in order to make it more easily implementable and interoperable (and incidentally to reduce the design period from infinite duration to just a few years). What remains is the minimum requirements list.

These few scenarios illustrate the kinds of situations that the core WebDAV protocol had to handle and from which the minimum requirements were derived.

- Several members of a project team share a task checklist spreadsheet. Since anybody can update task status in the spreadsheet, users should not be allowed to accidentally overwrite each other's changes. The group leader needs to know when the spreadsheet was last updated and by whom. The project team also has a large number of directories with specifications. It's convenient to keep file and directory names short, but short names can make it hard to find the right file. To solve this problem, their files and directories can all have descriptions and project names, stored as properties.

- A quilt guild shares digital images of its members' quilts online. The images are stored in a common location. Guild members use a wide variety of software on different operating systems, so they need a publishing solution that doesn't depend on one software platform. The users have access to the Internet through various routes— corporate accounts, university accounts, and home-based ISP access.

- A Web site design firm is employed to design, implement, and maintain Web sites for their clients. The desktop computers used by the design firm and the Web servers they work on aren't on the same local network (the servers are often at high-availability hosting sites or at the client premises). Proprietary protocols could be used to maintain and extend these remote servers, but each customer might use a different proprietary Web management system. It's far easier if the remote servers all support an Internet standard protocol. Standard authentication and access control are essential in this scenario because a diverse and changing list of people are authorized to modify any given site.

Most Internet users can identify with the frustrations of having been in these situations. Most have also endured the inadequacies of sending files over email or using FTP. These difficulties dictate a set of requirements.

- WebDAV had to define folders, or directories, since HTTP does not specify how to view directories. Standard directory listings would allow the quilters' software to navigate and present information compatibly.

- WebDAV had to define how metadata, or information about Web server files, could be represented and accessed. Metadata is what allows a project team leader to see when a task list was last updated and who updated it; it allows custom properties such as descriptions and project names to be associated with each document.

- WebDAV had to protect a document from other changes during editing. CM software, file systems, and even databases protect files (or rows) with locks. Locks prevent project team members from accidentally losing each other's changes to task lists.

- WebDAV had to use HTTP addresses to name editable resources, because there was no other way for new Web users, like the quilters, to make changes to the correct Web pages.

- WebDAV had to be an Internet protocol, one that was likely to be allowed by many ISPs and that could be supported on many platforms. This allows Web site design firms to use common tools to edit customers' Web sites remotely.

This isn't a very detailed or exhaustive list of requirements, but rather a list designed to illustrate the problem space. This list of requirements was also generated with the benefit of hindsight, which is why they so neatly define WebDAV. When the working group discussed requirements, many more were brought up and their importance was hotly debated. The process of defining a standard is much messier than the result, as the history of the working group demonstrated.

1.5   Extended Example, Concepts, and Terminology

This section introduces an extended example, used throughout this book to illustrate WebDAV with a consistent set of users and files. Our users are Alice, Bob, and Carl, who all work in a Web content publishing team within the HR department of a mid-sized corporation. Whenever the HR department needs to share files internally or publish content to the rest of the company, this team gets involved. The company has bet heavily on the Web for internal information exchange, so this process always involves Web publishing. Since the company is not very large, the HR department's processes are still somewhat ad hoc.

The extended example can be broken down into three sections, illustrating WebDAV first in terms of distributed authoring, then for a simple publishing process, and finally for the quick creation of a custom application.

1.5.1   Distributed Web Authoring

The original purpose of WebDAV was to allow several people who use Web authoring tools to collaborate on a set of Web pages. Alice, Bob, and Carl use WebDAV most frequently to collaboratively author Web content.

Alice is the manager of a content publishing team within the HR department. Her team maintains the internal HR Web site, which consists mostly of a set of documents for employee reference, and writes and updates those documents. The story in Table 1–1 illustrates how typical Web authoring tasks map to the basic WebDAV terminology.

Figure 1–1 shows the relationships among collections, resources, and URLs. In WebDAV, the information about what collection each resource is in makes up the path part of the URL. Since the `hr/` collection contains the resource `index.html`, `hr/` must appear in the path of the URL for `index.html`.

1.5.2   Simple Publishing Process

Sometimes, multiple authors working together need a process to help them coordinate their work. Publishing processes and simple workflow processes can easily be applied to WebDAV

Table 1–1   Example Illustrating Basic WebDAV Terminology

What the User Does	What Is Happening in WebDAV Terms
Alice needs to post information on ergonomics for employees. This is a new project, so there isn't even a place to put such information. Alice wants to create a new folder under the hr folder, so she uses Windows Explorer to navigate to the hr folder on the WebDAV server.	The folder is called a **collection**. A WebDAV collection contains other WebDAV resources. Collections are not expected to have document bodies, but they do have properties. A collection is a type of **resource**. A resource might also be any type of file. Files usually have a document body or content, such as the HTML code for a Web page. Resources can be created, moved, copied, and deleted.
Alice lists the files inside the hr folder.	Every resource in every WebDAV collection has a set of **properties**. Among other things, properties allow the client to get a listing of folder contents. Each property has a name and a value. For example, every file has the property named **getlastmodified** with a timestamp value. A resource may have only the minimum required set of properties (fewer than 10), or it may have hundreds of user-writable custom properties.
Alice creates a new folder in hr called ergonomics.	WebDAV defines a method specifically for creating collections.
Alice then **copies** a file from another folder to use as a template. Once the file is copied to the ergonomics folder, she **renames** it posture.doc.	WebDAV supports **copy** and **rename** (rename is done with the **move** command). Properties are moved or copied with the resource.
The new file has the **URL** http://www.example.com/hr/ergonomics/posture.doc.	Every WebDAV resource gets its own Uniform Resource Locator (**URL**), which is an address to locate the resource. It is an HTTP URL so that the resource can be accessed via any Web browser. When WebDAV is used, the URL for any resource must consist of the URL for its parent collection plus the name of the resource. See Figure 1–1.
Alice opens the file using Word to edit it (she is composing a guide on posture for computer users). Word downloads and automatically **locks** the file.	Files can be opened by downloading them with a normal HTTP GET request. This doesn't protect the files from being edited by other users. WebDAV supports locking with explicit **lock** requests. When a file is locked, no other user can lock the file or edit it. The file is protected from lost updates.

Table 1–1   Example Illustrating Basic WebDAV Terminology *(Continued)*

What the User Does	What Is Happening in WebDAV Terms
Alice asks Bob to add new material to the posture guide. Bob tries to do this while Alice still has the file open in Word, and his client software lets him know that the file is read-only.	Since the file is currently locked, Bob's software correctly opens the file but notifies Bob that he won't be allowed to save the file. Only Alice can make changes to the file until her Word client releases the lock. Even if Bob's software attempted to overwrite the file, the server would prevent this change.
Bob checks the file and sees that Alice still has the file locked. Now he can remind Alice to close the file and save her changes before he begins.	Currently, lock information is organized as a property, which can be directly queried on a resource. Bob can see whether the file is currently locked, and if it is locked, who imposed the lock.
	Web Folders wouldn't allow Bob to view the lock information, but other WebDAV clients do.

resources. These applications are similar to the basic distributed authoring scenario as far as most interactions go, but some custom behavior is usually added.

For Alice, Bob, and Carl, "publishing" simply means posting Web pages where everybody else in the company can see them. In the Web world, this is also called **going live**. If only the HR department employees can see a Web page, it's not live yet. Nobody wants to publish pages before they're ready or publish the wrong set of pages and have inconsistent information. Some process is needed to control publishing and improve reliability. Alice's team uses a simple publishing process, and WebDAV makes it possible.

Alice's coworker Carl wrote a dynamic page to serve as the main navigation page for the HR Web site. It's a simple page with a little scripting to automatically include links to documents that are in a published state, but it omits documents that are still drafts. The script finds

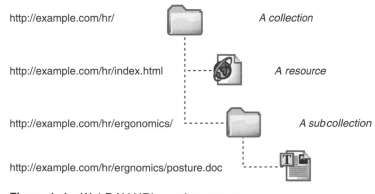

http://example.com/hr/   A collection

http://example.com/hr/index.html   A resource

http://example.com/hr/ergonomics/   A subcollection

http://example.com/hr/ergnomics/posture.doc

Figure 1–1   WebDAV URLs and resources.

out which documents to link to by looking in certain collections for resources with a WebDAV property named publish. If the value of the publish property is "true," the page includes a link to that document. The navigation page doesn't have to be altered often, because new documents automatically get included if the publish value is true. The team can focus on creating new content, rather than always updating the navigation page.

Even after a document is published in this scenario, it can still be altered. WebDAV can also be used to move or rename the document (without losing the value of the publish property) or update its content or properties.

1.5.3   Custom Application Example

Custom applications can easily be built on top of WebDAV. Because WebDAV's data model includes a document body, it is suitable for any file-based application. Resources can have property names and property values, so many database-like applications can also be mapped onto the WebDAV model.

Our sample custom application is a repository for employee photos. Carl is responsible for the development and maintenance of a simple Web-based organization chart including employee photos. All the photo image files are stored as WebDAV resources in a WebDAV `employees/` collection, and some properties like date-taken are created and given values at this time.

Each resource representing an employee has properties for the employee's first name, last name, start date, division, manager, employees, and the date the photo was taken. The body or content of each resource is a GIF (Graphics Interchange Format) file, an image of the employee.

Carl's Web pages use this data to allow any employee to browse the organization chart. This application automatically constructs Web pages for the chart. Each page shows an employee's full name, photo, and division name, and contains links to similar pages for his or her manager and subordinates.

Another Web page, only accessible to the HR department, allows employee information to be updated. Updating the photos is even easier; since the photos are simply WebDAV resources in a collection, a WebDAV-enabled image-editing tool can be used to save the photos directly to the image folder. The image folder can be sorted based on the date-taken property, to see which employees need an updated photo.

1.6   What WebDAV Is and Is Not

So far, we've covered what WebDAV is for and why it was developed, but we should also discuss some common conceptions and misconceptions up front.

WebDAV Is HTTP: True   It's a set of extensions to HTTP/1.1 as defined in RFC2068 (although the authoritative reference for HTTP/1.1 as of this printing is RFC2616). WebDAV uses the HTTP/1.1 version tag in the header line of every request. WebDAV also makes extensive use of the HTTP/1.1 methods GET, PUT, and DELETE. Thus, WebDAV cannot be separated from HTTP. It also cannot be considered to be "layered" on top of HTTP as protocols such as SOAP are.

> **Layering on HTTP**
>
> Although HTTP was never intended to be a transport protocol, it has come to be used as such because it's the only protocol that is allowed through many corporate firewalls and the only way to reach users behind those firewalls. Thus, applications that have little to do with the Web and nothing to do with hypertext use HTTP requests, typically the POST method, to send their messages over the Internet. Typically, most of the information is carried in the request body. Sometimes, important features of HTTP such as caching must be entirely disabled or worked around. These protocols cannot be considered to be part of HTTP, because they do not act on HTTP resources.

WebDAV Is an API: False   Some confusion has arisen here because many industry standards, such as CORBA or the Document Management Alliance (DMA) standard, are Application Programming Interface (API) standards. APIs are usually tied to specific platforms, but protocols like WebDAV almost never are. APIs can embody specific architectural decisions, such as how to store properties, whereas protocols allow the implementation to store information any way as long as it is marshaled interoperably. A well-designed protocol can be implemented in any programming language or style. A protocol should have a longer shelf life and broader interoperability than an API because the same protocol can be reimplemented on the new device or cool programming language of the day.

> **Document Management API**
>
> A document management API standard does exist. The Document Management Alliance (now part of AIIM International) controls the DMA standard and defines the API [ODMA97]. Like WebDAV, DMA provides a common model for document management. Like WebDAV, DMA is intended to promote interoperability between vendors of client and server systems. Unlike WebDAV, the standard interface through which DMA exposes its model is an API. This results in a standard more useful for corporate, intranet use. Note that WebDAV is compatible with DMA (as DMA participants pointed out in an email to the WebDAV mailing list). In other words, WebDAV can be used as the protocol where DMA is used as the programming model.

Another distinction is that APIs are usually the interface between two pieces of software running on the same machine or within the same local network. Although many languages provide remote procedure call mechanisms today, APIs still can't take the place of protocols, because APIs are seldom designed to take network latency into account or to operate with firewalls. WebDAV was designed from the start as an Internet protocol, intended to work with high latencies, busy servers, firewalls, and proxies.

Finally, although WebDAV is not an API, several toolkits exist with APIs to help implementers add WebDAV support more quickly and easily to both client and server applications.

WebDAV Is a Document Management System: False   You can find document management systems for sale as large software packages. Some of these systems may support WebDAV, which could be an important factor in purchasing decisions. These systems might include client software as well as server software and provide tools for administering the document repository. WebDAV has been adopted as a component by some, but any protocol is only one piece of a complex document management system.

WebDAV Is a Server-to-Server Protocol: False   WebDAV does not define how servers talk to each other or interact. Thus, a client wanting to copy a file from one server to another will likely have to download the file contents from one server and upload the contents to the other server. Individual server implementations may be able to talk to other servers, but this is either done with a protocol other than WebDAV or with one server behaving as a client making requests of the other.

WebDAV Is a Network File System for the Internet: True   WebDAV allows the major elements of directory and file navigation as well as directory and file manipulation—all using HTTP.

WebDAV Is an Appropriate Successor to FTP: True   WebDAV provides the major advantages of FTP and can entirely replace FTP for some purposes, such as authoring or uploading Web sites. For Web site authoring in particular, WebDAV offers important advantages over FTP:

- A WebDAV address for a resource is the same as the HTTP address. An FTP address must be different and has to be known by the author.
- WebDAV offers more flexible security options. HTTP offers several ways for both clients and servers to authenticate or identify themselves.
- WebDAV has a standardized directory listing format. FTP directory listings can be in any format, making it hard for clients to know how to parse the data and present it in any way other than plain text.
- WebDAV provides locks to prevent overwrites from multiple authors.
- WebDAV has support for metadata. FTP only shows the basic file properties listed by the remote file system and can't edit property values at all. WebDAV allows the client to set and retrieve whatever basic or custom properties it wants.

Chapter 2, *History of Web and Collaborative Authoring*, covers in more detail how Web site authoring worked before WebDAV, including how FTP has been used.

WebDAV Is a Microsoft Technology: False   WebDAV was designed and standardized through the IETF, an open Internet standards body. Microsoft employees participated in the design and standardization process from the early stages. Once the protocol became a standard, Microsoft followed its embrace and extend strategy. A number of Microsoft-designed extensions to WebDAV are known to exist (many are described in this book), and although those extensions may be Microsoft-specific, the basic WebDAV protocol is not.

In its technical and marketing material, Microsoft sometimes refers to "Microsoft Web-DAV." Although this phrase does refer to a protocol mostly compatible with the IETF-defined WebDAV standard, it presumably gives Microsoft some leeway when an incompatibility or missing requirement is identified. The concept has found its way into other literature as well, possibly confusing readers (and software reviewers) into believing that WebDAV is a Microsoft technology. For example, *PC Magazine* [Simone00] stated that Adobe GoLive supported "Microsoft's Web Distributed Authoring and Versioning"—a misnomer in several ways, since the actual expansion of the WebDAV acronym is "Web-*based* Distributed Authoring and Versioning."

WebDAV Is a Standard: True The WebDAV specification has been approved as an IETF standards-track document and assigned an RFC number (RFC2518). The IETF has three levels of standardization for the standards track, in order to indicate relative maturity and stability. WebDAV is at the first of those three levels, called Proposed Standard. At this stage, most software vendors feel comfortable implementing a standard. In the future, WebDAV may progress to Draft Standard, like HTTP/1.1 [RFC2616], or even Internet Standard, like *Transmission Control Protocol* (TCP) [RFC793].[2]

WebDAV Is a Web Service: Maybe It depends on how you define a Web Service. A Web Service might be defined as an application that provides semantic services whose abilities can be discovered on-the-fly by a client given an HTTP URL. A Web Service might be defined as an application that uses HTTP for transport and XML for marshaling semantic information. Both of these definitions imply that WebDAV is a Web Service.

However, if a Web Service can only be an application that advertises its services using Web Service Description Language (WSDL) and is accessed using Simple Object Access Protocol (SOAP) over HTTP, then WebDAV is *not* a Web Service.

1.7 Roles for WebDAV

Although WebDAV is a useful protocol for distributed authoring of Web pages, and clearly WebDAV has a larger role to play, there are different ideas of what that larger role is.

CM Interoperability CM systems include a wide variety of enterprise and group-oriented software. The lines are blurry here, because some products are sold as "document management," others "knowledge management," others "file management" or even "team portal," and each name implies a different level of functionality and complexity. Some examples include Microsoft Sharepoint Server, Adobe InDesign and GoLive, and Lotus Notes.

---

2.   The current status of all IETF RFCs can be viewed in the RFC Index at *www.ietf.org/iesg/1rfc_index.txt*. There is also an RFC series document that provides more information on the IETF process and standard levels [RFC2026].

CM systems have more features than file systems do. They've been around for many years but for most of that time have been unable to interoperate with each other or with most other software. Until recently, CM users usually had to install a special client software program and use it separately from their productivity applications. Most of these systems now support Web interfaces, so client software doesn't have to be installed locally. Some even extend productivity applications such as Office with custom add-ins. However, no matter what, using the CM interface requires actions different from normal local authoring.

WebDAV could become a common-denominator protocol, allowing authoring applications to save to CM systems even when the authoring application is from a different vendor. WebDAV could also be useful for administrators to migrate documents into or out of CM systems or to link multiple systems.

Common-Denominator Information Retrieval   Microsoft's   take   on   WebDAV clearly encompasses the CM interoperability view but takes it further, to data not traditionally viewed as simple standalone electronic documents. Microsoft's presentations make it clear that Microsoft views HTTP and HTTP-based protocols as the key to client/server interoperability. It's the common way for clients to interoperate with information on a server, even if that information is also available via other specialized methods or protocols. The content stored this way is by no means limited to Web pages and Office documents. Already, it includes email messages, newsgroup postings, address book information, shared and personal calendars, appointments, and tasks. Figure 1–2 shows a few of the clients and servers that may already use WebDAV to interoperate.

One drawback to this approach is that WebDAV doesn't offer the complete set of functionality each application requires. For example, the calendar server products Microsoft and Lotus offer both send appointment reminders from the server to the client, but HTTP and WebDAV do not handle server-initiated messages.

Networked File System Access   Many people now view WebDAV as a nascent protocol for a networked file system, one that is suitable for use on or with the Web [Stein02].

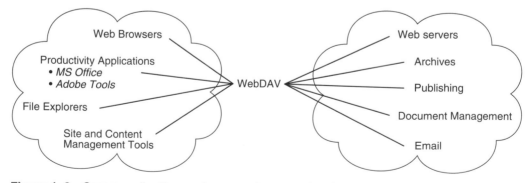

Figure 1–2   Common client/server language for managing documents.

Microsoft's Web Folders feature exemplifies this approach, treating the WebDAV repository just like a networked file share. Oracle's Internet File System (IFS) provides a common repository for hosting many kinds of files and supporting several Internet protocols, including WebDAV. Universities are providing students with personal file space on WebDAV servers rather than on traditional network file servers.

In many ways, WebDAV is more suitable for truly remote file systems than the protocols that were originally designed for intranets. The Internet tends to be a high-latency environment compared to intranets; each request takes longer to arrive at its destination, even if the bandwidth is equal. Protocols designed for low-latency intranet environments tend to use many interchanges to accomplish a task. For example, Microsoft's protocol for accessing file shares (SMB) performs a number of round-trip operations to change a file. This can take several seconds if the client has to wait for several server responses. The same operation is done with a single PUT request in HTTP.

On the other hand, WebDAV is missing one or two features commonly implemented by networked file systems, such as server-to-server copy. Most important, WebDAV client implementations aren't yet as mature or as fully integrated into the operating system as the networked file system client implementations.

Source Control Systems   WebDAV can be the standard access protocol for versioning systems, including source code repositories [Stein99], [Whitehead01]. Many Web sites today are developed with the assistance of a source control system, so DeltaV was designed to handle this task. DeltaV can also be used to access any kind of source code, such as the files that are compiled to build a software product.

1.8 Summary

When the Web was originally designed, it was good for reading but not writing. This meant that Web sites had to be authored with a series of nonstandard ad hoc tools. WebDAV provides a standard mechanism for authoring Web-based data. WebDAV provides a full suite of remote document access capabilities, including file storage, directory management, and support for collaborative authoring.

WebDAV is built on HTTP. WebDAV adds new functionality to HTTP but doesn't change existing functionality. This means that ordinary Web browsers can read data on WebDAV servers. It's also easy for implementers to add WebDAV functionality to existing Web clients and servers.

WebDAV was developed by the IETF's WebDAV Working Group. Work on the WebDAV began in 1996, and RFC2518, defining the first version of WebDAV, was published in 1998. WebDAV is currently a Proposed Standard and is being refined for promotion to Draft Standard.

WebDAV solves the problems of concurrent editing. Before WebDAV, it was difficult for people to collaborate on Web-based documents, because there was no standard way to coordinate their changes. WebDAV solves this problem with the introduction of locks.

WebDAV handles metadata. WebDAV provides a standardized way for clients to discover properties such as size, file type, and creation date. Clients can also attach arbitrary properties such as comments or search keywords to resources.

WebDAV can be used for more than just Web sites. WebDAV turns HTTP into a general Web-based network file system. This makes it relatively easy to build other kinds of networked applications such as document management and source control systems on top of WebDAV.

CHAPTER 2

History of Web and Collaborative Authoring

There's a lot of background to cover in order to understand a protocol like WebDAV. First, WebDAV extends HTTP, so it's important to understand HTTP. Second, the WebDAV designers were familiar with many existing proprietary authoring protocols as well as email protocols and FTP, so WebDAV was designed with their features and flaws in mind. These older protocols point up WebDAV's advantages. This chapter also contrasts the way in which WebDAV solves certain problems with the way the problems were solved (or not solved) elsewhere.

I'll cover Web site authoring solutions first because WebDAV was designed to do Web site authoring. However, I'll also compare email, FTP, and HTTP/1.1 (without WebDAV extensions) because those three protocols combined to form the only standards-based Internet collaborative Web authoring "solution" before WebDAV.

2.1   A Brief History of Web Authoring

For years, authors have struggled with downloading documents via HTTP, uploading documents via FTP, and exchanging documents via email. The "Stone Age" of Web authoring was the time before any Web authoring tools existed. The only Web software available was the Web browser (HTTP client) and the HTTP server. These were only available on Unix operating systems initially, although Windows-based browsers emerged quickly. Many Web pages were authored in the same location where they were published (in place) using text editors. This approach meant that authors of Web sites had to have Unix user accounts on the Web server.

2.1.1   HTTP Editing

Tim Berners-Lee wanted users to be able to edit documents as easily as they could browse documents on the Web. To this end, HTTP includes two methods that theoretically allow Web pages to be updated: PUT, to create or change a file, and DELETE, to remove a file. Some Web servers allowed these two methods, which meant that the user could theoretically update existing pages.

Soon, however, authors turned from HTTP to other mechanisms (such as FTP and local file copying). HTTP didn't work for these authors for a number of reasons.

- At the time, HTTP didn't have an authentication model administrators trusted. Without that, allowing changes was too insecure. Many administrators disabled PUT and DELETE completely.
- HTTP did not have a concept of collections, so there was no way to decide where to put a new Web page.
- Early HTTP browsers focused on browsing and did not support editing. Text editors did not support HTTP. Thus, files had to be edited using one tool and uploaded to the server using another tool.

2.1.2   Editing via Remote Login

Unix users commonly make changes to a file on another machine by logging in to the remote server and launching a text editor remotely. The rlogin command allows login from a Unix workstation to a Unix server. The Telnet protocol can be used to log in to any server supporting that standard, using client software freely available for any platform. Once logged in to the remote server, the user can issue commands on the remote server, such as a command to rename a file on the remote server.

The first problem is that although remote login is an easy way to move and copy a remote file, it is not easy to edit the file. To edit the file, the Unix user has to launch a text-editing tool installed on the remote server. Since Telnet and rlogin support text exchange only, this capability is limited to tools that have text-only user interfaces, such as *vi* or *emacs*. Finally, the user has to have a system account to log in to the remote server, and that account must be granted access to both the file and the editing tool.

A similar but somewhat better option for Unix workstation users was to mount a Unix-based Web server's file system via *Network File System* (NFS), *Andrew File System* (AFS), or something similar. Then the pages could be edited as if they were local. In that situation, Graphical User Interface (GUI) text editors could be used.

Note with all these approaches, the author had to find out manually where the Web content was stored in the file system namespace. For example, my first Web home page in 1993 could be downloaded at the address:

```
http://www.csclub.uwaterloo.ca/~ldusseault/index.html
```

but I had to log in to `csclub.uwaterloo.ca` remotely from a student lab and then navigate to and edit the page at the location `/home/users/ldusseault/web/index.html`.

Windows users worked the same way. In universities and many companies, even if the desktop machines ran Windows, Web developers had to have Unix accounts on the Unix Web server. Just like Unix users, Windows users had to Telnet to the Web server to edit pages. To edit my Web pages in 1993, I used Telnet from a Windows desktop (or a dumb Unix terminal) to connect to the Unix server. I used *vi* to edit pages within the Telnet window and a Web browser named Cello to view the results. Luckily, I had learned to use *vi* before, so I already knew some of the esoteric incantations and input modes.

At first, none of the tools used to edit Web pages had any functionality related to either the HTTP protocol or the HTML format, and these tools could not understand HTTP URLs. General-purpose editing tools like *vi* require authors to know all the codes for HTML elements as well as where to find Web page source files on the file system.

2.1.3   Editing and Copying

Editing pages in place can lead to publicly embarrassing errors. Since HTML pages were edited without the assistance of a tool that understood HTML, it was all up to the author to create syntactically correct HTML. Errors inevitably happen, and if a Web page is edited in place it can't be tested without also making the errors publicly visible until they're fixed. My Web pages had a small enough readership (two or three?) that I could afford to experiment directly, but authors of more professional Web sites preferred to author and test in one location and then copy the finished product to the Web publishing location.

Editing and then copying sounds simple, but it typically involves the following steps, each step using different tools:

1. Edit the page using a text editor. Save locally or to an unpublished local network location.
2. Load the page in progress into a browser to see the effect of your changes. Go back to step 1 if it doesn't look good.
3. When you're satisfied, manually copy the page to the Web content location. This step frequently involved FTP or a file system remote copy command. Recall that this step still required knowing the server's file system path to the live Web content, which is different from the HTTP path and different again from the file system path where the test pages are stored. Make sure that all the necessary files are copied, including images. Make sure that all the links still work, because the paths have just changed! Go back to step 1 if links are broken.

2.1.4   HTML Editing Tools

It wasn't very long before software developers released tools to make it easier to work with HTML. Some early tools were quite primitive—essentially text editors decorated with extra buttons for functions such as Paragraph or Header 1. The extra buttons would insert HTML tags like <P> or <H1> at the cursor location. All this did to help the author was make it possible for him or her to edit HTML without memorizing the magic characters for each tag; the author still had to know what each tag did and how to make sure its syntax stayed correct through text changes. Some specialized HTML text editors allowed the author to preview the appearance of the page so that he or she didn't have to open a separate Web browser to view it. However, these tools were still fundamentally text editors because the author had to return to the plain-text display to make any edits.

The next step in Web authoring tools was WYSIWYG (What You See Is What You Get). WYSIWYG tools show the Web page exactly as it ought to appear to browsers and allow the author to edit and manipulate text within the WYSIWYG view. FrontPage, Word, and GoLive are examples of applications that author Web pages in WYSIWYG style now.

Many authoring tools did, and still do, treat Web pages as individual resources without taking into account the relationships between them. To add a link, the author might have been required to type in the entire link manually. This method is error-prone because it's too easy to mistype a file name or the name of an anchor (a location within a file that can be linked directly). If the target of the link was renamed, moved, or deleted, the link broke, and there was no way to discover broken links except through manual testing. Therefore, in addition to sophisticated Web page authoring tools, link and site management tools emerged. This kind of preliminary Web management eventually grew into another tool category, culminating in features such as the ability to view a map of the entire Web site.

By 1996, when preliminary work on the WebDAV protocol began, graphical Web authoring tools included SoftQuad HotMetal Pro 2.0, Quarterdeck WebAuthor 2.0, Adobe PageMill 1.0, and InContext Spider 1.1. These tools focused first on editing and only later on site management tasks such as link checking or automatic link fixup.

2.2 Network-Enabled Web Authoring Tools

Between 1995 and 1998 developers began to build networking capabilities into Web authoring tools. This trend was driven by a few common factors.

2.2.1 Networking Changes

During this time, network access began to change. Companies started bringing Internet access to employee desktops. Universities had long had Internet access (yes, even before the Web), but the way the Internet was accessed on campuses changed. No longer was the Internet tied mostly to Unix servers and Unix clients: Microsoft embraced the Internet and in 1995 brought out Windows-based Web servers and clients, extending the set of tools already available to Windows users. Macintosh users gained access to Web tools in a similar timeframe. With increased network access and the growth of the Web as an industry, it became possible to consider Web-specific remote authoring capabilities.

The growth of the Web and of Internet access made it difficult to continue with Telnet, FTP, and NFS. Authors of Web sites increasingly used Windows, not Unix. Telnet tools existed for Windows and Macintosh, but users had to go out of their way to install and learn to use Telnet.

NFS support was rare on Windows and Macintosh desktops. FTP was the only viable upload tool, and then only if the Web server had FTP. Although it sounds odd to Unix users, in 1995 some Windows Web servers did not support FTP at all.

2.2.2 Growth in Team Sizes

The economic importance of the Web soon meant that sites were no longer authored by a programmer or two but by teams of specialized experts. Coordinating the efforts of a medium-sized team with only FTP to update the Web site was challenging.

For example, in 1996 I worked on a Microsoft Web development team building a technology showcase site. The team of 14 included four Web development engineers who wrote HTML and scripting code, three graphical designers, two text writers/editors, a producer, two program managers, a tester, and a team manager, all using Windows, of course. Most of these contributors never learned to use Telnet, FTP, or any of the command-line tools so familiar to Unix users at the time. The team employed many authoring and image manipulation tools, everything from Windows Notepad to Adobe Photoshop.

None of the tools used by this Web site team worked together or had remote authoring capability. The Web site was produced in stages: Contributors saved their work locally and then copied the files manually (with Windows network file sharing) to the correct location on a staging server. This step often resulted in mistakes such as misnaming files, forgetting to copy or create files, putting files in the wrong directories, or overwriting or deleting the wrong files. On the staging server, some testing was done before the whole site was copied to a production server, but it was difficult to coordinate changes on the staging server. I recall bitter arguments between developers when they accidentally (or as was alleged, intentionally) overwrote each other's work and lost updates.

2.2.3 Early Networked Tools

Only a few tools supported remote authoring in 1996. All of them did remote authoring based on HTTP, but each client tool could only talk to the corresponding server because all the HTTP extensions were different.

- FrontPage, acquired by Microsoft through its purchase of Vermeer in January 1996, interoperated with a Web server running FrontPage Server Extensions (FPSE).
- AOLPress, formerly GNNPress and NaviPress, could author on AOLServer (formerly GNNServer and NaviServer).
- Netscape Composer could author on Netscape Enterprise Server.
- W3C's Amaya browser used W3C's Jigsaw server.

2.2.4 Connected, But Not Interoperable

Although these solutions had much in common, they did not interoperate or even provide the same features or use the same data model. Each used a proprietary protocol (FPSE, AOLServer

Extensions, Netscape Extensions) or an open but insufficiently powerful standard protocol (HTTP, FTP) with nonstandard extensions. For a time, the divisions were strictly along product lines; no two Web servers from different software companies supported the same protocol mechanisms for authoring. Then an FPSE module for Apache made it possible for Windows FrontPage clients to do remote authoring on Unix-based servers for the first time [FrontPage03]. However, most client implementors were reluctant to support the Microsoft-controlled FrontPage protocol, so these client applications were still not supported by a FrontPage site.

By 1996 most vendors of image-processing, Web publishing, and office document applications were considering adding Web authoring capabilities to their products. Some of these products were used as part of the Web site design process, and others were being used to share documents in a corporate office setting (where the Web was used even for intranet-only sites because it could be accessed from any operating system). However, without a standard, it was difficult to choose an approach or figure out how to interoperate with various Web servers.

2.3   The Standards Revolution in Web Authoring

Finally, in late 1996, vendors of many of these noninteroperable tools managed to get together and launch a concerted effort to develop a joint standard. Their desire was to eventually be able to use any Web or office productivity authoring tool for remote authoring on any Web server. To make this goal a reality, convergence on a single protocol was needed.

One possibility was to pick one of the existing protocols, give it a solid specification, resolve any outstanding issues, and then declare that protocol the Web authoring standard. However, political and technical obstacles combined to make this approach undesirable for each pre-existing solution. If an existing proprietary protocol were used, it would provide significant advantages to the company owning the protocol. It would also require that the company relinquish its intellectual property rights over the protocol, since only an open standard would achieve broad interoperability. Since 1996 was the height of the war over browser market share, there was no way Microsoft would agree to use a Netscape standard, or vice versa.

From a technical perspective, existing protocols were a poor choice anyway. The next sections analyze each of these protocols to show why.

2.3.1   FrontPage Server Extensions

FPSE add FrontPage authoring capability to an existing Web server [FrontPage02]. The extensions accept POST requests to do operations that can't normally be done in HTTP, such as setting permissions and configuring WebBots. There are a number of problems with FPSE as a standard protocol, although it's evidently successful as a Windows solution.

- Protocol operations are tightly tied to FrontPage features. For example, there are operations to apply a theme (a common look and feel for a Web site) and to list which code libraries are currently in use on the server side. Some operations did not generalize well to other authoring tools. However, part of the reason that FrontPage continues to use FPSE is because WebDAV does not provide these operations.

- FrontPage computes and verifies links when changes are made. Not all Web authoring applications interoperate well with this feature, and it is time-consuming for the server.
- The protocol uses the POST method with a body containing commands to be executed on the server. POST is used even to upload file bodies, an operation for which HTTP PUT already exists. There is opposition to the use of POST to "tunnel" arbitrary commands to the server as FrontPage does (see the sidebar, *Why Not Use POST?*).
- FrontPage can grant authoring privileges to a specific directory but not to a specific file. FrontPage was designed more for Web site development process in which a few people are responsible for maintaining large areas of content, whereas general collaborative authoring scenarios require more granular permissions models.
- Some protocol operations are addressed to the FrontPage Server Extensions CGI scripts, while the Web resource being operated on is named inside the POST body. This is not a recommended use of the Web namespace. Instead, the IETF encourages protocol operations to address the URLs of the entities that are being operated on.
- Some protocol operations are addressed to special files created on the server to make FrontPage run. For example:

```
GET http://www.example.com/_vti_inf.html
```

Of course, there were also political pressures to prevent adoption of a pre-existing Microsoft protocol or architecture. Nobody wanted to give Microsoft a big head start by adopting a Microsoft model.

Why Not Use POST?

Many applications standards developers at the IETF oppose use of the HTTP POST method to tunnel new protocol semantics. One reason for using multiple methods with meaningful names is that firewall administrators can block certain HTTP methods that might be harmful (e.g., PUT or DELETE) while allowing others like GET. Another objection is aesthetic: HTTP uses methods to convey the basic purpose of the request, and it's not very elegant to abandon that channel of communication.

2.3.2 AOLPress

The AOLPress Extensions were a strong early influence on the WebDAV protocol, since they demonstrated that remote Web authoring was possible using new HTTP methods. These included methods for overwrite prevention (LOCK/UNLOCK) and namespace manipulation (MKDIR, BROWSE). Versioning information was accessed using HTTP headers (`Content-Version`, `Derived-From`). However, this protocol didn't meet all of WebDAV's requirements:

- It had no metadata (property) support.
- Directory listing capabilities were very limited. The BROWSE method returns a simple list of lines containing {mime type} {resource name} pairs. Subcollections are indicated with a nonstandard MIME type (`application/x-navidir`). The model is not easily extensible, so it's hard to add extra properties to directory listings.
- The protocol had no support for copying or moving Web pages. Although GET and PUT can be used to copy a Web page, this is an expensive operation because the entire file must be transferred twice.

2.3.3 Netscape Extensions

Of the proprietary protocols, the Netscape Extensions came closest to meeting the requirements of WebDAV. This protocol had metadata operations (GETATTRIBUTES, SETATTRIBUTES), overwrite prevention (LOCK, UNLOCK), namespace management (MKDIR, RMDIR, DESTROY, COPY, MOVE), and version control (CHECKIN, CHECKOUT, DEFAULT, LABEL, REVLOG). It even supported basic linear versioning.

Assuming for the moment that political issues (caused by Netscape Extensions' origin at Netscape) could be swept away, could it have been standardized as is? There were a few technical shortcomings:

- The protocol was underspecified. It was discribed in only about 20 percent of the page count of the WebDAV protocol specification yet involved substantially more functionality. Under-specification generally leads to interoperability problems, since it forces implementers to make assumptions about many issues. For example, SETATTRIBUTES allowed multiple attributes to be set using a single method, but the specification provided no guidance on how to handle errors when some properties are successfully written and others are not.
- Attributes in the Netscape Extensions were ASCII text name/value pairs. This model would have required a centralized registration authority for properties to avoid conflicts.
- The ASCII attribute values provided a poor foundation for representing the wide range of characters found in current human languages. For example, they did not support any of the Unicode encodings, such as UTF-8 and UTF-16 (see the sidebar, *Unicode, UTF-8, and UTF-16*), and there were no provisions for character set labeling or human language labeling.
- While Netscape Extensions provided locking, they do not specify the exact semantics of that lock. It was unclear what methods LOCK affects. Presumably, PUT is prevented by a lock, but the specification was silent on LOCK's impact on DESTROY, RMDIR, SETATTRIBUTES, CHECKIN, and LABEL. It was also unclear whether the lock is associated with a specific person, client, or network connection. No standard error code indicated that an operation failed because a resource is locked.

While the Netscape Extensions protocol was a useful source of ideas for the WebDAV protocol, lack of detail in many areas limited its impact.

Unicode, UTF-8, and UTF-16

The Unicode Standard (*www.unicode.org/*) has become the primary international character coding system, supporting most of the characters used in most human languages. No other single encoding system supports so many characters from so many languages. Modern distributed authoring systems require excellent internationalization support, so Unicode is a natural choice.

Although some systems (such as the Java programming language) natively support Unicode, most Internet protocols and XML only support ASCII. The Internet has a long tradition of using ASCII. However, all is not lost: Two standard transformations reversibly express Unicode in an ASCII stream—UTF-8 [RFC2279] and UTF-16 [RFC2781]. Nearly all new IETF protocols support both UTF-8 and UTF-16 in order to handle internationalization well. Older protocols that do not support Unicode are considered flawed.

2.3.4 Amaya/Jigsaw

The Amaya editor and browser and its Jigsaw server counterpart were created by the W3C in 1997 as showcases and reference implementations for W3C innovations. The focus in Amaya was on its WYSIWYG HTML-editing environment and support for advanced (at the time) features like Cascading Style Sheets (CSS) and XML. Amaya was capable of using HTTP PUT to save to the Jigsaw server, and its implementors intended to do more. In the end, Jigsaw turned to WebDAV for remote authoring support, releasing a WebDAV package in 2000 and adding this functionality to the core product in the 2.2 release in 2001.

2.4 HTTP, Pre-WebDAV

The Web was always intended to be a read-and-write publishing medium. Tim Berners-Lee explained how users should be able to correct errors in Web pages or add to them simply by clicking in their browser window and beginning to edit. Why didn't the Web fulfill its writability promise for seven Web years (equivalent to 49 regular technology years)? Isn't it reasonable that once browsers became sophisticated enough to support remote editing with secure authentication, HTTP would take off as an authoring protocol as well?

To answer these questions, one has to consider HTTP's characteristics in rather specific terms. Chapter 4, *Data Model*, covers HTTP in enough detail to explain anything that might be confusing in the following section. However, even without being familiar with HTTP or having read Chapter 4, you should find the gist of the arguments clear.

2.4.1   Obvious Missing Features

A comparison of HTTP to WebDAV suggests that HTTP lacked important authoring features, because WebDAV added these features. Or is it so clear? The WebDAV Working Group argued at length about some seemingly obvious features, with the intent to keep the protocol as simple as it could be—but not too simple. Mercifully, I'll rehash the arguments quickly.

How to Create a Collection   There is no way to create a new collection in HTTP without WebDAV. The Web server administrator has to create a new collection in the underlying file system, probably by logging on to the Web server locally or remotely. Since not all Web authors have administrator privileges, this requirement can present a barrier.

Copy Operation   HTTP has the GET and PUT methods. By performing a GET on the source resource, then a PUT of the same content to a new location, the client can get the same result as a COPY method. The argument for defining an explicit COPY method lies in conserving both bandwidth and latency. For small files, the GET and the PUT are two roundtrips, or twice as much latency. For larger files, the GET and the PUT can consume vastly more bandwidth than the COPY request.

When to Conserve Bandwidth

Protocol designers that use binary representations to save every bit on the wire are disdainful of the way HTTP "wastes" bandwidth in verbose header names and values (and are absolutely horrified by WebDAV, with its use of XML bodies). However, HTTP message sizes only impact HTTP performance (compare to the Internet Protocol [IP], where wasting a bit affects every message on the Internet). HTTP could also try to conserve every bit, but it would then be impossible to implement due to complexity. So, why is bandwidth important to conserve in the COPY case?

One reason is that file bodies are enormous compared to the size of packets on the Internet. Web pages are often HTML, which isn't a very compact format, but still, HTML files are much smaller than image files or Microsoft Office documents. Other formats get even larger. Adobe authoring products have rather large file sizes, so PUT and GET requests are used very sparingly in these products: Files are saved by default to the local file system, and only when the user explicitly asks are they published to the Web.

Move and Rename   HTTP doesn't have a move or rename method, as most document management systems and file systems do. A client can perform a copy operation and then delete the original resource (assuming the COPY request is added to HTTP). However, this doesn't quite do the same thing a move operation would do. If a client tries to do a move operation without assistance from the server, metadata from the original resource is lost. For example, the creationdate property will be a new value if the resource is created from scratch with GET or

COPY. If the server supports a move operation, then the resource can keep the more useful value, the time when the resource was originally created.

Standardized Content Listings   There was no standard way to list collection contents in HTTP. Most Web servers create an HTML content listing when a user tries to download a collection using the GET method. However, each server has a different HTML format for this information, and many even contain different content. Clients do not attempt to parse those formats and thus cannot determine what resources exist in a collection.

2.4.2   ETags and the Lost Update Problem

When one user overwrites another user's changes by accident, this is called the **lost update** problem. The first user's update is the one that is lost (see Figure 2–1).

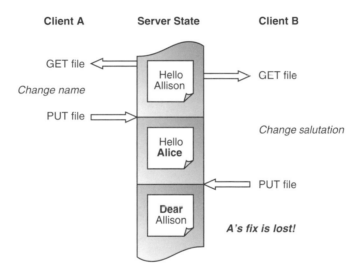

Figure 2–1   Lost update problem.

The HTTP Entity Tag, or ETag, feature was thought to have the potential to prevent the lost update problem, but ETags do not solve it satisfactorily. This section explains how ETags work, what the lost update problem is, and where ETags fall short in solving the problem.

The designers of HTTP went to a great deal of trouble to design mechanisms to tell when a file is changed. A client need not download a page if it has been downloaded before, saved in a local cache, and hasn't changed since. Avoiding these unnecessary downloads can make Web surfing much faster, and ETags help avoid unnecessary downloads.

ETags are used to compare two or more entities from the same resource. If a current ETag matches an earlier ETag from the same resource, then the resource has the same content it did before. For example, clients frequently compare an ETag saved for a cached file to the ETag for the server's latest version of that file. If the ETag is different, then the file must be downloaded again. If the ETag is the same, then the cached resource can be used.

It's also possible to use ETags to avoid the worst of the lost update problem. An authoring application that expects to be the only application changing a resource would simply do GET, allow the user to perform edits, and then do a PUT request to change the original resource. However, when there are other authors involved, the authoring application needs to check whether the resource has been changed since the GET operation, using ETags of course. ETags prevent accidental overwrites because they already exist to see if the resource has changed.

For details on how HTTP uses ETags, see the explanation of the `If-Match` header in Chapter 3, *HTTP Mechanics*. The W3C has a very good note [Nielsen99] on using ETags to detect the lost update problem.

However, ETags don't solve the "aggravated user" problem illustrated in Figure 2–2. A user can work for hours editing a Web page, only to find that the file has changed and she may have to start again with the latest content. From a distributed authoring point of view, that's not good enough. There must be a way for the user to block other users making changes for a while.

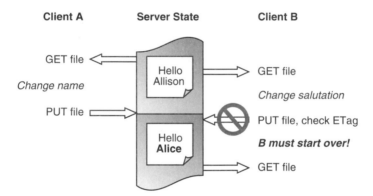

Figure 2–2   ETags prevent lost updates but not wasted time.

2.5   The File Transfer Protocol

FTP was an important component of the Web authoring process at first, as discussed in Section 2.1.3. Users edited and saved pages locally, and then the widely interoperable and standard FTP protocol was used to transfer the finished pages to a Web server.

FTP servers hosted massive amounts of data when HTTP was invented, and they still do today. Web pages have been able to link to FTP pages since the CERN project's early days because Tim Berners-Lee saw that the more information that was available through the Web (even if you were directed out of the Web), the more valuable it would be. It was natural to use FTP to fill in the gaps left by HTTP. Not only could users' FTP clients upload files to the FTP file space, these same clients could also upload files to the HTTP file space on the server. FTP supports creating, updating, moving, copying, and deleting files and folders, so it filled in most of the missing HTTP authoring features.

The primary advantage of this combination is the ubiquity of FTP servers and clients. Almost every server platform that supports HTTP also has an FTP server available today, and most client operating systems come with FTP client support (even if on Windows the FTP tool is obscure and seldom used).

Since FTP is a ubiquitous tool that supports remote file authoring, why not continue to use FTP to author Web sites? The WebDAV inventors took the trouble to invent WebDAV because FTP has many subtle drawbacks, some specifically related to Web authoring. Let's look at some of those concerns.

2.5.1   Missing Functionality

FTP does not solve the lost update problem. If the user uploads a file with a name identical to an existing file on the remote server, the remote file is overwritten. There's no way to mark the server's copy of the file to let other users know it's being edited.

FTP lacks metadata support. Document authoring systems require properties for bibliographic metadata such as the author of the document, subject, keywords, and a brief description.

2.5.2   Poor Navigation

FTP does not have a standard way to list directory contents. Directory listings look different on Windows and Unix servers, regardless of the user's client or operating system. Although graphical FTP clients exist, they may not work with all FTP servers, and they work better for browsing and downloading than for authoring. FTP was originally designed not for graphical clients but for command-line interfaces.

Addresses are file system paths, not Web URLs. Since FTP is designed for file transfer between file systems, it exposes the file system hierarchy. To upload files with FTP, users need to understand the mapping between FTP file paths and HTTP URLs on their Web server. There is no way to automatically discover this mapping. A Web site author has to know the mapping scheme, and these schemes may be nonintuitive and vary from server to server. A Web authoring protocol should natively use HTTP URLs to avoid address mapping confusion.

2.5.3   Some Performance Concerns

FTP is a stateful protocol able to handle fewer active users. FTP keeps the network connection open and persists state information such as the authentication credentials and the current working directory. In 1996, Internet servers could not support very many TCP connections. FTP users become accustomed to annoying "connection refused" messages on high-traffic systems.

FTP requires extra connections, reducing active user limits even more. FTP requires two TCP connections, a control channel and a data channel, to be held open for each session. The client must first establish the control connection, then select the file to download, and then establish the data connection. This takes longer than establishing an HTTP connection, since HTTP only requires one TCP connection to both identify the file and download it. Sometimes an entire HTTP transaction can be completed before an FTP session is fully established.

FTP Addresses

FTP sites commonly use a domain name beginning with "ftp." There are some conventions for naming FTP directories, such as putting general-use files under the directory "pub." Imagine the following addresses are each valid document addresses:

1. `ftp://ftp.example.com/pub/contrib/index.html`
2. `ftp://ftp.example.com/pub/doc/www/index.html`
3. `ftp://www.example.com/pub/doc/www/index.html`

What the user wants to do is edit a Web page with this address:

`http://www.example.com/index.html`

The client software has no way of knowing which FTP address, if any, can be used to update the correct Web page. The user must know what FTP server and path to use for each Web site.

2.5.4 Lessons Learned

FTP was intended for the transfer of files across the widely divergent storage systems available in the 1970s; storing metadata and fixing the lost update problem were simply not design goals. Hence, the lack of support for these features does not lessen the importance of FTP's achievements in interoperable cross-system file transfer. Although FTP wasn't seriously considered by experts in the area as a long-term standard Web authoring solution, it did serve as a conscious example for what a Web authoring protocol should do and how it might do it successfully.

FTP's Advantages

FTP does, of course, have some advantages over WebDAV for Web authoring. Its first advantage is its ubiquity.

Subtler, however, is the consideration that FTP clearly addresses the original file at all times. FTP servers never transform files. Web servers transform dynamic pages (such as Java Server Pages or Active Server Pages) that contain code for the server to execute. The contents of the downloaded Web page change for every viewer or even every download.

As we'll see much later, WebDAV attempts to deal with the problem of whether to retrieve the original source code or the dynamically generated output, but it fails to solve the entire problem. FTP works around the source-versus-output problem because it's a completely different protocol that always retrieves and updates the original.

2.6 WebDAV for Sharing Documents

So far, I've discussed how WebDAV can be useful for Web authoring tools. That's not the only way WebDAV is used, however. In addition to editing Web pages, WebDAV can be used to author any kind of electronic document, even one not ultimately intended for Web publishing. This usage is called **Web-based file sharing** or **Internet file sharing**. File sharing requires more restrictive permissions than the typical public Web page, because files are often shared among only a small set of people. Privacy becomes important.

To understand how good WebDAV is at wide-area file sharing, we need to compare it to the alternatives. Only two sets of protocols are commonly used for file sharing: the protocols used by networked file systems and the protocols used by email.

2.6.1 Networked File Systems

Networked file systems are very common today. They work very well within a corporate network. However, when wide-area file sharing is needed, companies increasingly look to WebDAV. This section explains why this is the case.

Networked file systems have existed for over 20 years. The most common today are *Server Message Block* (SMB), NFS, and *Andrew File System* (AFS, a successor to NFS). Although all of them can potentially be used over the Internet, each has drawbacks for Internet file sharing.

NFS   NFS is the Unix standard for networked file systems. It is a mature and open IETF standard [RFC3010]. The major stumbling block to wider adoption of NFS is lack of support by Microsoft client and application software. However, one could argue that there are good reasons that Microsoft does not support NFS—the protocol relies on clients to enforce access control settings. Thus, it's impossible to make some files on a shared file system accessible to anonymous users without opening up all files to possible attackers.

SMB and Samba   SMB is the standard networked file system protocol for Microsoft file systems. The earliest publication describing SMB came from IBM in 1985. SMB is broadly deployed and even offers some cross-platform interoperability: Samba is a popular SMB server for Unix, and there are various Unix SMB clients as well.

SMB has more flexible security than NFS does. However, like NFS, SMB was designed before the Internet and was intended to run over intranet protocols (NetBEUI or NetBIOS) rather than TCP [Vidstrom03]. With SMB, the client software uses Remote Procedure Calls (RPC) to ask the file system to open remote files and edit them, just as if the client software were making local procedure calls to the local file system.

The Andrew File System   AFS is the successor to NFS. Security is vastly improved over NFS, offering powerful file-level permissions enforceable by the server. However, AFS was not designed for high-latency situations. The system is instead designed to have servers close to the end user and to replicate data to those servers. On the Internet, where file sharing is ad hoc rather than controlled, AFS can be difficult to deploy, because servers must be configured to trust each other.

Roundtrips in Networked File Systems

The networked file systems described here were all designed for low-latency or local networks. Further, they were consciously modeled after local file system access. This design history partly explains the "chattiness" of the protocols, or the number of requests and responses required to complete a simple operation. For example, in SMB:

1. `negprot` command to negotiate protocol version
2. `sessetupX` command to log in and start session
3. `tcon` command to select ("connect" to) a share or tree
4. `open` a file
5. `read` a file

Thus, what would be a single GET roundtrip in HTTP is as long as five roundtrips in SMB for a new share. When the network latency involves noticeable fractions of seconds, as it does over many wide-area networks or the Internet, there is a noticeable delay in SMB operation.

2.6.2 Collaborative Authoring via Email

When multiple authors collaborate on a document, they need to exchange copies of the document. If these authors don't have access to the same networked file system, email becomes the medium of choice.

Email is probably the most pervasive networked system in existence. Almost every end-user computer in every network has access to a mail server that can forward email to and from the Internet. Users don't even have to be online constantly to use email—computers can connect to a network just long enough to download new mail and upload sent mail. Email clients all support MIME, handling any document type. For this reason, email has become a popular system for exchanging documents.

Email is so useful for exchanging documents that it will continue to be used no matter how good and widely deployed Web-based file sharing becomes. There is no expectation that WebDAV will replace email in any serious way. However, WebDAV can be used together with email to make file sharing more effective.

2.6.3 Email Attachment Semantics

Email applications typically send attachments by attaching the entire document. It is possible to send a link to a file rather than the entire file, but replacing attachments with links isn't trivial. First, there's no guarantee that users can put the file in a location where it will be readable by other users. Then, after that hurdle has been overcome (perhaps with a networked file system), there's the problem of accurately locating the file and of ensuring that all the recipients have the necessary software and permissions to access the shared file.

WebDAV is beginning to improve this situation. Users who have access to a WebDAV repository can upload files to a permanent shared location and then send the HTTP URL manually to a number of email recipients. There has been some work to extend email software to handle this process even more easily by automatically uploading the file and inserting links into email. One example using this technique is Xythos WebFile Client, which has extensions for some common email clients.

Why does it matter whether users send attachments by reference or by sending the entire file? There are a number of differences in behavior. One option isn't always the right one, so it seems reasonable to give users the choice. Some of the following considerations will affect users' choices:

Copy Proliferation   With email, a copy of the entire document is sent in every email to every recipient. Sometimes recipients save the document locally and keep a copy on their email server. If the document is mailed back with edits or later versions are mailed around again for comments, the number of copies becomes very large. Clearly, the first problem with this method is disk space, but there's a subtler problem with manageability of all these copies. For example, the author responsible for integrating changes can get confused by receiving and saving various copies with edits and comments from different people. It's hard to keep track of which is the official copy and which are copies generated from attachments returned by reviewers or co-authors. This is a clear win for sending links rather than attachments.

Visibility of Changes   When documents are sent via email, the entire document is usually included as an attachment. This is called *sending by value*, and it means that once the email is sent, the attachment cannot be changed. If the author decides to make a change, the document must be sent out again. Otherwise, users might review a version that isn't the latest version. In contrast, *sending by reference* means that all users will see the latest version of the file on the repository automatically. Sometimes that's a good thing, sometimes it's not.

Retrieval on Demand   Users want to be able to download according to their own choice. Email doesn't offer that option—users must wait for the file to be emailed to them even if they don't want it, or they must ask for the file to be mailed because it hasn't been. However, sending the entire file via email guarantees that the end user will receive the file (there's no second download step that requires network connectivity and no chance of a permissions error).

2.7   Summary

In the early days of Web authoring, only HTTP itself could be used, however insufficiently, for remotely changing a Web page. Since then, many other protocols have been put to use to allow remote Web authoring, but all have suffered from drawbacks.

Web authoring has improved greatly. Early Web browsers did only Web browsing because editing was much more complicated. When HTML editing tools became more sophisticated, the next step was supporting an Internet protocol so that the Web pages could be changed on the server.

Initially, most users used FTP. Users would edit files on their local machines and then use FTP to copy files manually to the server. However, FTP had some significant defects in addressing, navigation, and performance.

HTTP lacked important features. There was no standard way to create directories copy or move resources, list the contents of directories, or deal with file metadata. The lost update problem could be solved, but not without frustrating users who were unable to reserve files for the duration of an editing session.

Many vendors developed proprietary Web authoring protocols. Although some Web authoring systems with integrated HTML editing developed sophisticated remote authoring capability, these systems—FrontPage, AOLPress, Netscape, and Amaya—were not interoperable. Most used HTTP with different extensions or FTP with magic addresses.

WebDAV was developed as a standard alternative. None of the proprietary protocols was entirely satisfactory, and the existence of multiple competing protocols caused interoperability problems. The WebDAV Working Group took the best ideas from each proprietary protocol to build a single standard protocol.

HTTP Mechanics

W ebDAV depends on HTTP and the HTTP infrastructure. WebDAV follows the HTTP request and response syntax and uses HTTP methods (particularly GET, PUT, DELETE, OPTIONS) and HTTP error codes. Many HTTP headers are reused in WebDAV requests, and some WebDAV headers are added to HTTP requests. WebDAV requests and responses pass through proxies and firewalls that treat them as HTTP. WebDAV has many required features that are only documented in the HTTP specification, so it's important to understand HTTP.

Few good books thoroughly cover HTTP. *Web Protocols and Practice* [Krishnamurthy01] is the first exception. It starts with basic HTTP material and adds extensive detail on underlying protocols, caching, and performance concerns. *HTTP: The Definitive Guide* [Gourley02] covers the basics a little more fully and adds in-depth material on URLs, proxying, security, and Web hosting.

This chapter provides an overview of HTTP/1.1 for the purposes of WebDAV usage. HTTP/1.1 replaced HTTP/1.0 in 1997, and WebDAV extends HTTP/1.1, so I don't cover HTTP/1.0 features, for the most part. Not all HTTP features are discussed, and some are only briefly mentioned. Some HTTP methods must be used more carefully in a WebDAV repository; those complexities are covered in Chapter 5, *WebDAV Modifications to HTTP*. This chapter is not intended to exhaustively describe HTTP, so I've focused on explanations and simple examples rather than syntax, definitions, and corner cases.

3.1 URLs

A URL is an address to a digital resource, much like a street address to a house. Both kinds of addresses include specific information; a street address has a house number, and a URL has the resource name. Both kinds of addresses also include high-level information; a street address has the name of the city where the house is located, and a URL has the name of the server. To locate a house based on its street address, postal systems route a letter starting with the least specific information. For example, all letters to Norway get put into the same bag. Once the bag gets to Norway, the next step is to look at the city name, and so on.

Postal addresses aren't organized to be written down in the same order that they are handled. The country is near the bottom of the address, whereas the house number is near the top. In contrast, programmers and protocol designers think algorithmically. Knowing that addresses are always parsed starting with the most general information, programmers put that first. In a URL, the most general information is the name of the **protocol** to use to get the resource, which is officially called the **scheme**, then, increasing in specificity, the **server** address, then a TCP **port number**, and finally the **path** of the resource to ask for (see Figure 3–1). This structure holds for most URLs, including HTTP URLs.

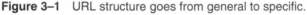

http://www.example.com:8080/hr/index.html

| Protocol | Server address | Port | Opaque "path" |

Figure 3–1   URL structure goes from general to specific.

To locate an HTTP resource from an HTTP URL, a client follows roughly these steps:

1. If the client recognizes the **protocol**, it should know how to parse the rest of the URL. URLs for other protocols might have different structures.
2. Find the **server** from its name. Domain names are resolved to an IP address through the Domain Name System (DNS) protocol [RFC1035].
3. Open a TCP connection to that IP address, requesting the **port**.
4. Using this TCP connection, send a request using the specified protocol. Ask for the resource by asking for the **path** part of the URL.

Domain Names

Domain names are ordered with the most specific piece first, the opposite order from URLs. IP addresses are ordered with the least specific piece first. Either way, address resolution is usually passed off to another module.

The server uses the path to identify the resource, and usually the path part is also least specific to most specific. The path might look like a file system path, as shown in the example in Figure 3–1, with directory names and a file name at the end. However, it might not look like that. The path part of the URL can be opaque or meaningless to the client. The client does not attempt to parse the path but merely provides the entire path to the server to identify the resource. Many e-commerce sites use URLs that are only meaningful to the software running on that server, such as:

```
http://store.example.com/
index.asp?id=CF52&addtocart=true&goBack=Yes
http://www.sharemation.com/_xy-29129_docstore1
```

WebDAV puts a few more constraints on URL structure than HTTP does, but that won't be covered until we get to WebDAV URLs (Chapter 5, *WebDAV Modifications to HTTP*).

3.1.1   Relative URLs

In addition to full URLs, HTTP also uses relative or partial URLs. Again, the concept is similar to street addresses. If you and I are standing in Conestogo, Ontario, and I tell you that I used to live at 39 King Street, it's clear from our location that I'm referring to the King Street in Conestogo and not one of the tens of thousands of other King Streets (the same street name appears in every town in the province).

HTTP requests frequently are sent to a relative address. Since TCP is used to establish a connection to the correct server and port, and the protocol is specified anyway, the relative address only has to include the path.

```
/hr/ergonomics/posture.doc
```

It's possible to construct even shorter relative addresses. If the client and server both agree they're talking about resources within `/hr/ergonomics/`, the relative address could just be `posture.doc`.

3.1.2   Links

Links allow Web browsers to find and identify URLs. A Web browser can't construct or make up HTTP URLs on its own—the browser has to find URLs. The most common way of finding a URL is to load another Web page with a link in it.

After the client downloads and displays the page, the user can see if the page contains links that would be useful for further navigation. A link in an HTML page can be a full or relative URL, associated with some text or an image (see Listing 3–1). The user clicks on the linked image or text to request the addressed resource. Linked text and images are organized together with ordinary text and images, all formatted with HTML tags.

A standard link contains no information other than the URL. The resource could be a Web page, an image, a text file, or a data file. Possibly the resource at the URL is unavailable, deleted, or never existed. The URL in the link could be a typo, but there's no way to know up front. The browser can't determine the size, type, or date last modified of the linked resource without querying that address on the server where it's hosted.

Listing 3–1   Simple HTML document with links.

```
<html>
Links:
<br>
<a href="/aboutus.html">About us</a>,
<a href="/events.html">Upcoming Events</a>,
<a href="http://other.example.com/index.html">Our Sponsor</a>
</html>
```

There are some great advantages to links and URLs, compared to the mechanisms in earlier systems such as FTP and Gopher. Thanks to the universality of URLs, networked information repositories can link to other repositories, even repositories run by other organizations on
distant machines, without any coordination required. Thanks to links in text, navigation can be
organized not just by the way files were stored but by arranging links in any helpful way. Links
can be embedded in paragraphs of text, listed as references or footnotes, or organized in hierarchical menus.

3.1.3   URL Escaping

URLs can contain only a limited number of characters from the base US-ASCII set. Any
unprintable characters from that set are excluded. Many more printable characters are reserved
for special purposes within the Uniform Resource Identifier (URI) or excluded altogether
[RFC2396] (see Table 3–1).

Table 3–1   Reserved and Excluded URI Characters

	;	semicolon
	/	slash
	?	question mark
	:	colon
	@	at sign
Reserved	&	ampersand
	=	equal sign
	+	plus sign
	$	dollar sign
	,	comma
	< >	angle brackets
	#	pound sign
Delimiters	%	percent sign
	"	double quote

Table 3–1   Reserved and Excluded URI Characters *(Continued)*

	{ }	curly braces
	|	pipe symbol
	\	backslash
Unwise	^	caret
	[ ]	square brackets
	'	single quote
Excluded		space, tab, etc.
		ASCII control characters (line feed, carriage return, etc.)

Many characters were excluded because URIs and URLs encompass existing addresses. SMTP mailbox addresses can appear in URLs, so @ must be reserved to act as a separator between the mailbox and the mail server (mailto:alice@mail.example.com). HTTP URLs use colon, slash, pound, question mark, and ampersand to delimit various parts of the URL.

Other characters are excluded because URLs must appear inside HTML pages and HTTP messages. Spaces are used as separator characters in HTTP messages. Angle brackets are used as control characters in HTML, and both single and double quotes are used to contain attribute values, as in the `href` attribute. Note the use of angle brackets and double quotes in the link examples in the previous section (Listing 3–1).

Characters that can't directly appear in URLs can be encoded by using % followed by two hexadecimal digits. For example, %20 replaces a single space in a URL.

In protocols and data formats (HTTP, SMTP, XML, or other), URLs always are formatted legally—that is, with excluded characters encoded. URLs appear unescaped only when displayed to users and never when saved or transmitted.

3.1.4   Requests to Directories

Often, the first HTTP request to a new server is to a URL with no path part:

```
http://www.example.com/
```

This address isn't usually the address of a page—the Web server considers it the address of the root directory of the Web content, but there's no standard way to return a directory in HTTP. Two kinds of responses are common.

First, the Web server might construct an HTML page on-the-fly, containing a simple list of the pages in the directory. This is very common, but there's no standard format for this kind of response.

Second, instead of returning information for the base directory, the server might return a default starting page. The administrator defines one or more default page names for the entire server. If a directory contains a page with that default name, the page is returned in response to a request for the directory. The page has its own URL, such as:

```
http://www.example.com/index.html
```

The response includes the URL of the default page (in the Location header; see Section 3.7.13) so that the client can use the "correct" URL in the future for requests such as PUT and DELETE.

The first mechanism is frequently used by Web servers hosting content with very few link-rich pages, such as Office documents, data files, or pictures. These servers return directory listings to allow users to navigate, just as in FTP. That's why Web servers have frequently replaced FTP servers—Web servers can easily handle the FTP navigation model as well as handle more sophisticated navigation.

The second mechanism is frequently used by Web servers where the content is compiled into carefully organized pages for navigation. The directories might contain resources that users shouldn't see out of context alone, such as partial image maps or footer HTML included in complete pages. On these servers, administrators might forbid directory content listings entirely.

3.2 Message Structure

HTTP's structure is based on years of text protocol design experience, particular email protocols. Three-digit error codes, including "200 OK," were used in email protocols in 1973 [RFC524]. Header names and values (separated by a carriage returns and a line feed, or CRLF) also appeared in early email protocols [RFC561], probably modeled on interoffice paper messages, where header lines ("To: Alice," "From:Bob," "Re:Staff Meeting") are followed by the message body. Multipart Internet Mail Extensions (MIME) first standardized some of the headers reused by HTTP, like `Content-Type` and `Content-Transfer-Encoding` ("`Transfer-Encoding`" in HTTP) [RFC1341].

3.2.1 HTTP Requests

An HTTP request must contain a request line with method, Request-URI, and protocol version. It can contain a number of headers, each new header on a new line. It must contain an empty line signaling the end of the headers. Finally, a request might have a body (see Figure 3–2).

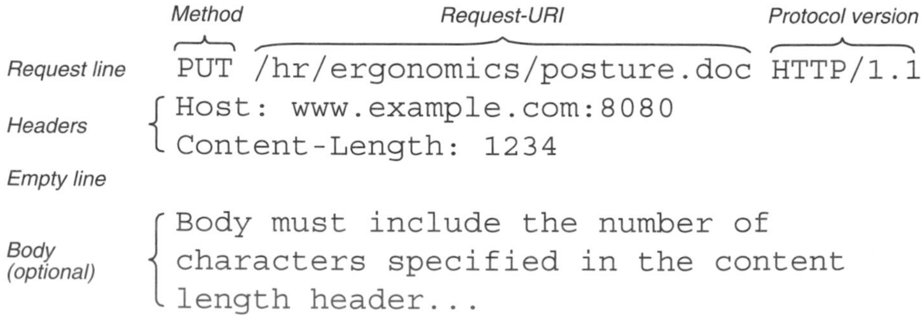

```
                    Method          Request-URI           Protocol version
Request line      PUT /hr/ergonomics/posture.doc HTTP/1.1
Headers           { Host: www.example.com:8080
                  { Content-Length: 1234
Empty line

Body              { Body must include the number of
(optional)        { characters specified in the content
                  { length header...
```

Figure 3–2 HTTP request structure.

The request method, URI, and protocol version appear on the first line of the request, separated from each other by spaces. Headers appear on subsequent lines, and an arbitrary number of headers might appear before the blank line that signals the end of the headers. Finally, if the request has a body, the body follows immediately after the blank line.

If a message has no body, it ends with a blank line. A GET request does not have a body, and it's the most common type of request used on the Web (see Listing 3–2).

Listing 3–2 Minimum GET request.

```
GET /index.html HTTP/1.1
Host: example.com.80
↵
```

The character ↵ is used in this book to explicitly show where an empty line must appear. It does not actually appear in protocol messages.

Note that much of this text is case-sensitive. In the first line, the method name, Request-URI,[1] and protocol version are case-sensitive. Header names are case-insensitive; however, it's good practice to capitalize header names exactly as they are defined in specifications, in case the recipient relies on consistent capitalization. Header values might or might not be case-sensitive, depending on the definition of the header.

The Request-URI (/index.html) begins with a slash because it is a relative URI. It must be combined with the host identified in the Host header to fully specify the location of the resource. However, Request-URIs need not be relative. In fact, RFC2616 mandates that Web proxies and servers *must* accept an absolute URI in the Request-URI, because it's more reliable to put the entire resource URL in the Request-URI than to split it up into two parts. Therefore, servers must also accept the GET request structure shown in Listing 3–3.

Listing 3–3 GET request showing host name in the Request-URI.

```
GET http://example.com:80/index.html HTTP/1.1
↵
```

HTTP/1.1 clients must send absolute URIs in requests to HTTP/1.1 proxies, whereas requests to Web servers can still use the old form of relative URIs.

1. If a domain name appears inside a Request-URI, that part is not case-sensitive, in accordance with the DNS standard.

3.2.2   Header Syntax

HTTP headers follow some basic syntax rules.

- The header name must begin immediately after a CRLF, without leading or trailing white space (spaces and/or indents) and without white space within the name. Some punctuation, spacing, and control characters are forbidden in header names, but all US-ASCII alphanumeric characters are allowed as well as the hyphen and underscore. Header names are case-sensitive.
- The header name is followed immediately by a colon, then some nonbreaking white space, and then the value of the header. The colon might also be followed immediately by the header value. If there is white space after the colon, the first non-white-space character indicates the beginning of the header value.
- Header values might continue on multiple lines. If a CRLF is followed by white space at the beginning of the next line, then the next line is actually part of the last header. The CRLF and all the leading white space can be replaced with a single space.[2]

Many headers can appear multiple times in a message. If the header appears multiple times, the recipient can combine the multiple values into one header, separating the values with commas. For example, the `Accept-Language` header contains a number of language codes in which the user finds it acceptable to receive documents. So, the following pair of headers:

```
Accept-Language: fr
Accept-Language: en
```

is equivalent to:

```
Accept-Language: fr, en
```

 This rule for combining headers has a couple of interesting consequences. First, a header syntax without comma-separated values cannot appear multiple times in an HTTP message, because when the receipient tries to combine the headers, the syntax will be invalid. Second, the order in which headers of the same name appear is important if the order of the comma-separated values is important. This presents an exception to the general rule that header order is not significant.

3.2.3   Required Request Headers

The `Host` header is required on every request, to identify the virtual server the requested resource is on.

---

2.   Remember this line continuation rule because I'll use it to format headers in examples so that the header is syntactically correct, even when it is longer than the page width. When I can't format the header correctly, I'll use a special symbol (↯) to show that the new line is part of the page formatting, not part of the message formatting.

Virtual Servers

A single Web server can be used to host several Web sites with different names. Multiple sites can share the same host machine but use different domain or IP addresses and port numbers. These might all be different virtual servers hosted by the same machine:

```
http://www.bettysbagels.com
http://www.joesjava.com
http://www.joesjava.com:8080
http://192.28.31.1
```

Clients must treat these as different servers because the /index.html resource might be a different resource on each virtual server. The client must include the host name and port either in an absolute URL (in the Request-URI) or in the Host header of every request so that the server software knows what virtual server is being addressed.

The Content-Type header is required in every message that contains a body. The Content-Type header shows the recipient what MIME type and character set were used for the body.

The Content-Length header is usually included to indicate the length of the body. When the Content-Length header is present, HTTP parsers stop reading the body when the number of bytes read equals the Content-Length. When the header is not present, the HTTP parser continues trying to read the body until one party times out the TCP connection. Section 3.2.8 describes some less common ways to indicate the length of the body.

3.2.4   HTTP Responses

HTTP responses have a slightly different structure for the first line of the message: first the protocol version, then a three-digit status code, and finally some status text. After that, headers and a body follow exactly as in request messages (see Figure 3–3).

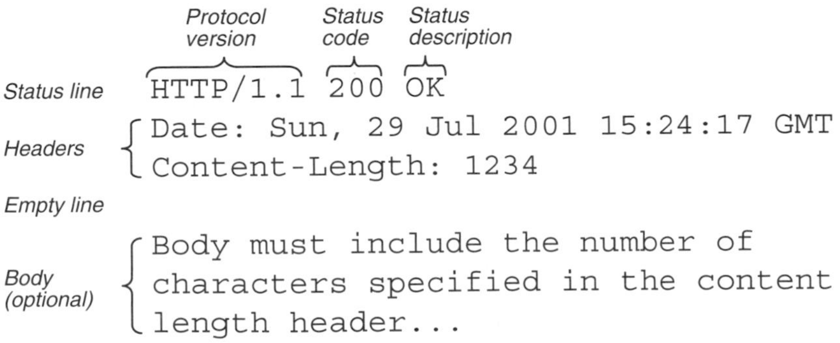

```
                       Protocol      Status   Status
                       version       code     description
                       ⏞             ⏞        ⏞
Status line            HTTP/1.1      200      OK

Headers          ⎰ Date: Sun, 29 Jul 2001 15:24:17 GMT
                 ⎱ Content-Length: 1234

Empty line

                 ⎧ Body must include the number of
Body             ⎨ characters specified in the content
(optional)       ⎩ length header...
```

Figure 3–3   HTTP response structure.

The 200 OK response is the most common HTTP response because it's used to send the content of a Web page when the client requests it using GET. Listing 3–4 is a more complete example of a possible response to the GET request in Listing 3–2.

Listing 3–4   Typical GET response.

```
HTTP/1.1 200 OK
Date: Sun, 29 Jul 2001 15:24:17 GMT
Content-Length: 25
Content-Type: text/html
Expires: Sun, 29 Jul 2001 19:24:17 GMT
Cache-control: private
↵
<body>Hello World!</body>
```

Responses should have the `Date` header showing the time the reply was generated. No other header is required on all responses. If the response has a body, it should include the `Content-Length` and `Content-Type` headers.

Listing 3–4 has two headers (`Expires` and `Cache-Control`) to specify how long and for whom the response body might be cached. Web pages are cached by most browsers so that if the user wants to look at the same page later, the page doesn't have to be downloaded again. Many proxy servers or intermediaries also have a common cache used for many different client connections. When one user requests a cachable file through the intermediary, it's cached so that the next user to request the same file can get a quick response. With the response headers given in Listing 3–4:

- Intermediaries and client caches are instructed to store and reuse the page only until the expiration time (the `Expires` header).
- Intermediaries are instructed to use the cached file only for the current user, not for any other user (the `Cache-control` value of `private`).

Intermediaries, Proxies, and Caches

HTTP has plenty of infrastructure besides just servers and clients, including several kinds of intermediaries. In this context, an intermediary is any HTTP entity between the client and the server. Typically, the client opens a TCP connection to the intermediary, and the intermediary opens its own TCP connection to the next intermediary or the final server. If an intermediary only exists to forward HTTP requests and responses, it is called a **proxy**. If it also caches responses, it is called a **caching proxy**. Extensive research and documentation exists on intermediaries and caching. See, for example, "Known HTTP Proxy/Caching Problems" [RFC3143] and *Web Protocols and Practice* [Krishnamurthy01].

A PUT response is quite similar. In a PUT interaction, the client sends content to overwrite a Web page, and the server responds with a status code to show whether the request succeeded. As with a GET interaction, the `Host` header must be on the request, and the `Date` header must be on the response. `Content-Type` and `Content-Length` now appear on the request because the request message, not the response, has a body (see Listing 3–5).

Listing 3–5   PUT request and response: Only the request message has a body.

Request:
```
PUT /index.html HTTP/1.1
Host: example.com:80
Content-Type: text/html
Content-Length: 33
⏎
<body>Hello World, part 2!</body>
```

Response:
```
HTTP/1.1 204 No Content
Date: Sun, 29 Jul 2001 15:24:07 GMT
⏎
```

A response with the 204 status code never has a response body, which is what "No Content" means. It is still a success response code (almost all 200 series responses are full successes), and the response body is not expected to be there in response to a PUT.

Normally, once a success or error response is sent, the server closes the TCP connection. This allows the server to go on and handle other clients with new TCP connections. The connection is reestablished for the next HTTP request. Section 3.5 covers alternatives to closing the connection.

3.2.5   Error Responses

Error responses are formatted in the same way as success responses; they just use different status codes. Many servers add a body to error responses in order to provide extra information. Typically, the error response body is formatted in HTML and is intended to be displayed. For example, if the client issues a request with an unknown method to a server running IIS 4.0, the server returns what appears in Listing 3–6.

3.2.6   Status Code Categories

So far, we've seen three different status codes. Servers use 200 OK to return a Web page, 204 No Content when a method is successful and the response has no body, and 501 Not Supported when the server does not support some required functionality requested by the client.

Listing 3–6 Sample error response with body.

```
HTTP/1.1 501 Not Supported
Server: Microsoft-IIS/4.0
Date: Sun, 29 Jul 2001 15:30:28 GMT
Connection: close
Content-Type: text/html
Content-Length: 121
↵
<html><head><title>Method Not Supported</title></head>
<body><h1>The specified method is not supported</h1>
</body></html>
```

In addition to these, HTTP defines some few dozen response status codes for different conditions and situations. Although status codes can be any three-digit number, only some ranges are defined. The status codes are grouped into several ranges, some of which have particular meaning:

- 000–099 codes are undefined and unused.
- 100–199 codes are used informationally or for ongoing communications—for example, a temporary response indicating that the real response is still coming although it hasn't been sent yet.
- 200–299 codes are used for success messages.
- 300–399 codes are used for redirecting requests to another location or authority.
- 400–499 codes are used for client errors. Users will be most familiar with code 404, used when a Web page is not found.
- 500–599 codes are used for server error. For example, 500 is used when unexpected errors occur in server code and the server's only option is to respond with a generic error.
- 600–999 are undefined and unused by HTTP and WebDAV.

3.2.7 Common Status Codes

Here is a quick run-through of the most common status codes and what they mean. Forty status codes are defined in RFC2616; only the most common are covered here.

- **200 OK:** A success response containing a body will use this status code, if no other status code is more informative.
- **201 Created:** When a new resource is created in response to a request, this status code is the most appropriate.
- **204 No Content:** A success response that does not contain a body will use this status code if no other status code is more informative.

- 400 Bad Request: Since a request can be improperly formatted in any number of ways, the 400 status code is common (especially when debugging client software).
- 401 Unauthorized: The user is not authorized to perform the requested action. The user could potentially authenticate him or herself and gain authorization to perform the action.
- 403 Forbidden: The server forbids this action. For example, the server could forbid the use of PUT altogether.
- 404 Not Found: Any time the request needs to find an existing resource, 404 Not Found might be returned if the resource does not exist.
- 409 Conflict: The request cannot be fulfilled as expected by the client. This definition is rather loose, and as a result, this status code is used widely when HTTP is extended.
- 412 Precondition Failed: The client added some preconditions to the request (see, for example, the HTTP `If-Match` and `If-None-Match` precondition headers in Section 3.7.6) and the preconditions were not met.
- 415 Unsupported Media Type: The server received a body on a request with a media type it could not handle. For example, a POST request with an unexpected body type could result in this error.
- 500 Internal Server Error: This error can occur any time the server encounters a bug or problem that is likely the fault of the server or the cause of which is unknown.
- 501 Not Implemented: A requested feature (usually the feature named in the method) is not implemented by the server.

Clients must be aware that there may be more than one problem with the request; however, the server can only return one status code and may choose any appropriate status code.

3.2.8 Message Length

HTTP/1.1 specifies five different ways the sender might indicate that the message is completed. All techniques must be supported in WebDAV implementations as well.

- `Content-Length` header: The body is complete when the specified number of octets are received.
- An empty body is expected when there is no `Content-Length` header, no `Content-*` header, and no other length header.
- `Transfer-Encoding` header indicates a different mechanism, and the mechanism is chosen with the value of this header.
- `Content-Type` header with MIME type "multipart/byteranges": Body length information is inside a multipart MIME envelope.
- When a `Content-Type` header value is shown but no `Content-Length` or `Transfer-Encoding` header: Body is complete when the TCP connection closes.

The message sender should indicate the correct body length through one of the first four mechanisms. Otherwise, HTTP messages are too subject to truncation attacks and transmission errors. It's easy for a hacker to force a TCP connection to be dropped, and without some indication of the expected body length, the recipient can't tell if the connection was finished or prematurely broken. Note that none of the methods described here reliably prevent truncation attacks, because with an unencrypted channel an attacker can modify several parts of the message, including header values. Only security protocols (typically S/MIME or SSL) protect the message from being tampered with.

Content-Length   The content length is measured in bytes or octets. If the sender somehow sends a content length that is too small, the recipient could cut off the message when the content length is reached. That could result in an unusable file, particularly with formats like Microsoft Word documents. Conversely, if the sender has a content length that is too long and the TCP connection isn't closed, the recipient will wait for the rest of the content. When the client sends a content length that is too long, it can seem like the server is hanging. Clearly, it's important to get this value right.

Responses Where Body Must Be Empty   Requests such as GET requests are expected not to have bodies, and the server can confirm that no body is expected by the absence of the Content-* headers. Responses in the 100–199 range, as well as 204 and 304 responses, are required to have empty bodies. No Content-Length header is required for these messages. Alternatively, the Content-Length header could have a value of 0, but this is rare.

Transfer-Encoding   When the Transfer-Encoding header is present, the length of the message is defined according to the transfer encoding mechanism. The Transfer-Encoding header takes precedence over the Content-Length header.

The only transfer encoding mechanism defined in RFC2616 is **chunked transfer encoding**. When chunked transfer encoding is used, the message body is still delivered as the body of a single message, but within the body the sender includes additional fields that are stripped out by the recipient. The additional fields allow the recipient to ensure that a complete message of the correct size has been received, even if the size isn't known by the sender until after the last byte is sent.

 Chunked transfer encoding must be supported by all HTTP/1.1 clients and servers, because chunked bodies may appear on both requests and responses.

Media Type Multipart/Byteranges   If the Content-Type response header shows that the media type is multipart/byteranges, then the length of the response body is included within the message body itself. Support for this mechanism is *not* required, so the server can only use it if the client advertises support for it by sending a Range header with multiple ranges. This mechanism cannot be used in requests.

Closing Connection   The server has the option of closing the connection when the response is finished. The close of the connection also indicates the end of the response if the body length wasn't specified in another way. This method isn't recommended, because connections can close accidentally. However, the client must deal with a closed connection gracefully when no `Content-Length` header is present.

More detail on any of these mechanisms can be found in the HTTP/1.1 specification or in a book on HTTP/1.1.

3.3 HTTP Methods

GET, PUT, DELETE, POST, HEAD, and OPTIONS are all HTTP methods useful in collaborative authoring. This section provides a brief overview of each, and the next chapter provides more details on how to use these methods in a WebDAV client or server implementation.

Web servers frequently contain both **static** and **dynamic** pages, and some HTTP methods handle these differently. A **static page** is one that is stored, byte for byte, the same way it is transmitted over HTTP. A **dynamic page** is one that is stored containing some source code. The server interprets the code and uses its output as part or all of the entity transmitted over HTTP. Originally, dynamic resources were C or Perl programs hosted out of a "cgi-bin" directory on the server (CGI is Common Gateway Interface [CGI96]). Links to CGI-generated resources may look like this:

> `http://example.com/cgi-bin/hrdata?empname=alice`

More recent technology allows HTML pages to contain embedded script that is evaluated by the server. On the server, these pages are stored in the same directories as static resources, and you can often tell this from the URL:

> `http://example.com/hr/info/empinfo.jsp?empname=alice`

In general, there's no reliable way for clients to tell if a resource is static or dynamic. The client can download any of these pages consistently but can't author dynamic resources.

3.3.1 GET

GET is the workhorse request of HTTP, the one request used to retrieve every static Web page, every dynamic Web page, every image, and every document. A GET request must include the name (full path) of the requested resource and the name of the host on which the resource appears (see Listing 3–7).

Listing 3–7 Simple GET request.

```
GET /index.html HTTP/1.1
Host: example.com:80
⏎
```

A GET request commonly includes some of the following information from the client:

- The languages the user prefers the response page to be in.
- The formats the client can handle. For example, the client may handle image/jpeg and image/bmp but not image/tiff.
- The encodings the client can handle. The client may be able to unzip large files compressed using the gzip format and can advertise this feature in an attempt to save bandwidth.
- The conditions that must be met in order for the server to process the operation. For example, the client could specify that the file must have been modified in the last day; otherwise, the server can ignore the request.
- The part of the response to return (the range).
- The browser software and version sending the request.
- The user's authentication information.

The response includes the requested resource. If the requested resource is a dynamic resource, the response is the output of the process that is responsible for generating the page. If the request is a static resource, the response typically includes the page in whatever format it is stored in. The static page in its stored format may first be transformed to a compressed format, a transfer encoding, or a `multipart/byteranges` format under certain circumstances.

The response must include the date and the content type (see Listing 3–8).

Listing 3–8 Simple GET response.

```
HTTP/1.1 200 OK
Date: Sun, 29 Jul 2001 15:24:17 GMT
Content-Length: 25
Content-Type: text/html

<body>Hello World!</body>
```

The response also commonly includes:

- The language of the response body
- The last-modified date of the resource
- How to cache, or not to cache, the response body
- The ETag for the resource (ETags are discussed in detail later; for now it's sufficient to think of it as an ID for the current version of the page)

The GET request and its response illustrate the extremely simple flow of basic HTTP. In one simple request, perhaps as short as two lines of text, the client asks for a useful resource.

In a single response, the server sends that resource. It's trivial to write a basic client application to download Web resources.

3.3.2   GET with File System Directories

Web servers construct directory URLs based on the directory path and name, just as with Web pages. The URL may or may not end with a / character, so either or both (or neither!) of these URLs may point to a directory:

```
http://www.example.com/hr
http://www.example.com/hr/
```

Section 3.1.4 explained that a GET to a file system directory can return two kinds of successful responses. The first, a dynamically generated content listing, is returned as `Content-Type: text/html`, which the browser displays as a Web page. The second, a default starting page usually called `index.html`, has the same content type. In fact, the browser can't tell the difference between a dynamically generated directory contents listing and an index page with links.

> **Hidden Pages**
>
> Even if the server administrator turns off the feature displaying directory contents as HTML, users can find and download publicly readable Web pages. A recent court case involved an unfortunate company with financial information publicly readable in a hidden page. Of course, a reporter guessed the name of the document and retrieved it [Delio02].

3.3.3   PUT

HTTP defines the PUT method to allow Web pages to be authored. When a client knows the URL to a Web page, image, or other document, it can send a PUT request to change the content of a document and set its content type (see Listing 3–9).

Clearly, the PUT request is core to WebDAV because it allows new Web resources to be created and existing resources to be updated. There are some subtleties that HTTP clients rarely have to handle without WebDAV, so I'll wait until Chapter 5 to deal with those.

When used to overwrite a resource, a PUT request may change some of the metadata of the existing resource as well as the body or entity. The client may send a new `Content-Type` value or a `Content-Language` value, as well as the new `Content-Length` value. The server must store this information in order to be able to respond to GET and HEAD requests with the same values.

PUT can reliably be used to edit static resources but not necessarily to edit dynamic resources. To see if a resource can be edited, the client must send an OPTIONS request and see if PUT is an allowed method on the resource (see Section 3.7.2).

Listing 3–9   Simple PUT request and response.

Request:
```
PUT /index.html HTTP/1.1
Host: example.com:80
Content-Type: text/html
Content-Length: 33
↵
<body>Hello World, part 2!</body>
```

Response:
```
HTTP/1.1 204 No Content
Date: Sun, 29 Jul 2001 15:24:07 GMT
↵
```

PUT isn't as useful in basic HTTP as it is with WebDAV functionality. Without an explicit way to identify and create collections, clients can't be sure how or where to create a new Web page. PUT is easier to use when combined with locking functionality—with locks, users can edit a file without worrying about other users changing the file. Many plain Web server administrators disable PUT since it isn't used, which does make security simpler.

3.3.4   DELETE

The DELETE request is defined in HTTP to delete resources (see Listing 3–10).

Listing 3–10   Simple DELETE example.

Request:
```
DELETE /index.html HTTP/1.1
Host: example.com:80
↵
```

Response:
```
HTTP/1.1 204 No Content
Date: Sun, 29 Jul 2001 16:28:27 GMT
↵
```

Like the PUT request, DELETE is not used much on servers that only support HTTP. Without all the functionality of file management, including copy, move, and create collections, DELETE just isn't sufficiently useful. As with PUT, plain Web server administrators often disable DELETE for added security.

Like PUT, DELETE can reliably be used with static resources, but not necessarily on dynamic resources. Servers can advertise which resources support DELETE with the `Allow` header on an OPTIONS response (see Section 3.7.2).

Again, there are more details to consider when DELETE is used in the context of Web-DAV, but we'll get to that in the next chapter.

3.3.5 POST

HTTP/1.1 specifies that the behavior of a POST request on an ordinary resource depends on the nature of the resource. If the resource identified by the URL is a program or script, it may be able to accept any kind of custom client request. The most common use of POST is to accept form submissions (see [Krishnamurthy01] Section 6.2).

In particular, when a Web form allows the Web client to upload a file to the server, the POST method is used to send the file. WebDAV doesn't mention forms and form-based uploads at all, but there's nothing to prevent a WebDAV server from hosting a file upload form. Doing so allows the repository to support file upload via ordinary Web browsers as well as WebDAV client software.

The most common way for a Web browser to upload a file to a Web server is to complete a file upload form on a Web site. The way this form is constructed by the server and handled by the client is defined in HTML 3.2 and 4.0. The form has to specify that POST will be used to submit the form, and the form must have an input element of type `file`. The form must also define what URL to upload the file to (the `action` attribute), and what encoding or `enctype` to use with the file body. The `multipart/form-data` encoding type is the MIME type specifically defined for uploading a file when a form is submitted [RFC2388] (see Listing 3–11).

Listing 3–11   Minimal form for file upload using POST.

```
<FORM NAME=fileUpload METHOD=POST
   ACTION='/xythoswfs/webui/lisa?action=upload'
   ENCTYPE='multipart/form-data'>
   <INPUT TYPE=FILE NAME=FILE1 ID=FILE1>
   <INPUT TYPE=HIDDEN NAME='targetpath' VALUE='/lisa'>
</FORM>
```

Browsers heavily restrict use of the `file` input type in order to maintain privacy. Typically, the user must select each file manually; there's no way to upload a collection with all its contents. The input field must appear in the form (not be hidden), and it can't be given a starting value. These restrictions help save the user from being tricked into uploading sensitive information to a server, but they also make forms hard to use in some situations, particularly when the user wants to upload multiple files.

When the user submits the form, the browser sends a POST request to the server. The POST request includes a body of type `multipart/form-data` [RFC2388]. This MIME type was specifically defined to allow file uploads through HTML form submission. The document type is a standard MIME multipart type with boundaries as defined in RFC2046. Each part of the multipart document has one or more headers that can appear in any order and cover multiple lines.

The document includes one part for each file uploaded. These parts each contain:

- The `Content-Disposition` header holding the name of the file input field and the name of the file uploaded
- The `Content-Type` header with the type of the file being uploaded
- A blank line to separate headers from the body
- The contents of the file being uploaded

In addition, the `multipart/form-data` document includes one part for each other piece of form data from the HTML form (whether radio buttons, checkboxes, text fields, or even hidden fields). In theory, these parts are supposed to contain the `Content-Type` header too, but in practice these parts each contain:

- The `Content-Disposition` header holding the name of the input field
- A blank line to separate headers from the body
- The body of the section consisting of the value assigned to the field in the form

Listing 3–12 could be the submission of a form by MS IE 6.0. Most of the request headers aren't relevant to this example, but they're shown for completeness.

Listing 3–12 POST request to upload file.

```
POST /xythoswfs/webui/lisa?action=upload HTTP/1.1
Accept: image/gif, image/x-xbitmap, image/jpeg, image/pjpeg,
   application/vnd.ms-excel, application/msword,
   application/vnd.ms-powerpoint, */*
Referer: http://www.example.com/xythoswfs/webui/lisa
Accept-Language: en-us
Content-Type: multipart/form-data;
   boundary=-------------------------7d312541017a
Accept-Encoding: gzip, deflate
User-Agent: Mozilla/4.0 (compatible; MSIE 6.0; Windows NT 5.1)
Host: www.example.com
Content-Length: 327
Connection: Keep-Alive
Cache-Control: no-cache
⏎
```

Listing 3–12   POST request to upload file. *(Continued)*

```
----------------------------7d312541017a
Content-Disposition: form-data; name="targetpath"
↵
/lisa
----------------------------7d312541017a
Content-Disposition: form-data; name="FILE1"; filename="C:\Documents ↯
and Settings\Lisa\My Documents\ip-address.txt"
Content-Type: text/plain
↵
198.144.203.248
----------------------------7d312541017a--
```

When this POST request is received by the server, the server must separate each part using the boundary string, and then parse and evaluate the MIME headers from each part. What the server does with the bodies received is completely up to the server. POST has no guaranteed semantics, and neither does the `multipart/form-data` MIME type. A server might store an uploaded file, translate it and display the translation, email it, or print it out.

The POST method is frequently used to upload files in Web authoring, as discussed in Section 1.1.3. Form uploads vary widely in their implementation, however, on both the server and the client side.

On the server side, since each site hosts its own forms, every form is different. A site can put any fields in the form (Listing 3–12 used the `targetpath` field to select where to upload the file). The client provides the local file name and sometimes the path in the POST body, but there's no standard way to choose the destination location and file name. There's no standard way to specify if the file uploaded should overwrite a previous file or not.

On the client side, Web browsers don't all implement the `multipart/form-data` type consistently with each other or with the specification, although most follow the lead of IE. For example:

- RFC2388 requires a `Content-Type` header in each part, but IE omits that header when sending a form value other than a file body, and so do other browsers.
- Mac OS uploads files encoded as Mac Binary.
- Netscape Navigator 4 on Macintosh escapes the name of the file that is uploaded. Most browsers don't escape the file name.
- Some browsers give the full name and location of the file, as IE does (even showing the drive letter, as in Listing 3–12). Other browsers only provide the file name.

The bottom line for form uploads is that the mechanism offers wide interoperability and customizability but has several costs compared to PUT:

- Each site must design and maintain its own forms and choose how to handle file names and target locations.
- A form is difficult to use for frequent or multiple file uploads.
- A form can't easily be used by an editing tool. Users make more mistakes manually selecting files to upload than when their editing tool can upload the file directly.

3.3.6 HEAD

HEAD requests allow the client to find out information about a resource without actually downloading the resource. A HEAD request returns the headers that a GET request (with the same options, to the same target) would have returned—but it does not return the body. Thus, a HEAD response is unique in that it contains statements about the body type and length without actually including a body (see Listing 3–13).

Listing 3–13   HEAD request and response.

Request:
```
HEAD /index.html HTTP/1.1
Host: nondav.example.com
↵
```

Response:
```
HTTP/1.1 200 OK
Date: Sat, 13 Oct 2001 19:11:04 GMT
Server: Apache/1.3.14 (Unix)
Last-Modified: Thu, 19 Oct 2000 03:28:13 GMT
ETag: "870be-8f0-39ee6a4d"
Accept-Ranges: bytes
Content-Length: 2288
Content-Type: text/html
↵
```

3.3.7 OPTIONS

The client uses the OPTIONS request to find out the features the server or a specified resource supports. Finding out the supported features of a resource is simple because the OPTIONS request can be addressed directly to that resource.

The response to OPTIONS varies depending on the target resource. Most Web resources support GET, HEAD, and OPTIONS. Some resources may support PUT and DELETE as well, and other resources may support POST. A client might go so far as to send an OPTIONS request for every resource it downloads, in order to see if the resource supports GET. In practice, however, clients don't go that far, because support for common methods (particularly GET) is rather predictable.

The example OPTIONS response is taken from a static resource on an Apache server. Static resources on this Apache server support only the GET, HEAD, OPTIONS, and TRACE methods (not PUT, DELETE, or POST). Other servers show very different OPTIONS responses (see Listing 3–14).

Listing 3–14   OPTIONS request to an individual resource and response.

Request:
```
OPTIONS /index.html HTTP/1.1
Host: nondav.example.com
↵
```

Response:
```
HTTP/1.1 200 OK
Date: Sat, 13 Oct 2001 15:26:52 GMT
Server: Apache/1.3.14 (Unix)
Content-Length: 0
Allow: GET, HEAD, OPTIONS, TRACE
↵
```

Although RFC2616 states that responses to OPTIONS requests are not cachable, this is generally interpreted as saying that proxies must not cache OPTIONS responses. In practice, clients can't afford to send OPTIONS requests before every WebDAV request, so client software often stores OPTIONS information temporarily.

One minor problem with OPTIONS is that it doesn't work on an unmapped URL. An OPTIONS request to a resource that doesn't exist returns 404 Not Found, not a successful OPTIONS response. Therefore, a client cannot see what methods may be used on unmapped URLs without trying those methods out. For example, it's impossible to confirm that PUT can be used to create a new resource in a given location.

3.3.8   OPTIONS *

Many clients send OPTIONS / requests in order to find out what features the server supports. This isn't quite the right way to do things, because OPTIONS introduces a magic Request-URI for this purpose. A Request-URI consisting of a single asterisk or * means that the request does not apply to a single resource but to the server itself. A response to OPTIONS * is theoretically different from the response to OPTIONS / (e.g., PUT may be supported for some resources on the server, but not on the root directory). However, both Apache 1.3 and Microsoft IIS 5.0 generate the same OPTIONS response to both / and *.

Ideally, OPTIONS * responses would show all the features that are supported anywhere on the server. Unfortunately, that isn't always possible. Sometimes features are implemented to extend an existing Web server, and the base HTTP engine isn't aware of all the extension features. For example, one of the quickest ways of implementing a WebDAV server is to start with a Web server that supports an extension mechanism such as Java Servlets and then write the extension code to apply only to requests addressed to the servlet. Thus, OPTIONS * requests might not show Web-DAV support, even if an OPTIONS request to /servlet/dav does show WebDAV support.

 WebDAV clients should not rely on OPTIONS * alone. Some features might be available or disabled only in certain sections of a repository. This kind of information can only be found through an OPTIONS request directed at a specific resource.

3.3.9 TRACE

The TRACE method is used to loop back the request message to the sender. This can be useful to see how firewalls, proxies, and/or cache servers are modifying the request as it is transmitted to the final recipient.

WebDAV servers should theoretically support TRACE since it is a required part of HTTP/1.1, but it is vestigial and has even been the subject of a minor security hole. The security hole allowed attackers to trick a client to get cookie values from a server not controlled by the attacker [Owen03].

3.3.10 CONNECT

SSL/TLS [RFC2246] can be used to protect the confidentiality of everything in an HTTP transaction, both request and response, including the method and target resource. However, HTTP proxies were originally designed to examine the HTTP request line and headers to know where to forward the request and how to cache it. Proxies aren't necessarily trustable intermediaries, so this is a breach of confidentiality. The CONNECT method is used to work around this problem.

The CONNECT method is reserved in HTTP/1.1, but it is specified in a separate standard [RFC2817]. When the proxy receives a CONNECT request, it connects to the server and then blindly proxies any data sent by the client to the server and from the server to the client. This allows the client and server to have an end-to-end encrypted connection, even when a proxy is in the way.

3.4 HTTP ETags

ETags identify a particular instance of an entity. An **entity** is the information transferred as the payload of a request or response. It's useful for the client to be able to ask a Web server if an entity that the client previously cached is still up to date. This is done by having the server provide ETags for all GET response bodies that can be cached, and the client sends the ETag back in requests for the same resource.

HTTP defines both strong and weak ETags. Two entities from the same URL with the same weak ETag should be mostly the same, whereas two entities from the same URL with the same strong ETag must be exactly the same. Clients can detect a weak ETag because it must begin with "W/". We'll ignore weak ETags for the rest of this book because WebDAV servers should and do generally implement strong ETags.

ETags are generated by the server and are opaque to the client. Whenever a cachable entity is downloaded, the server can provide an ETag in the `ETag` header (the format of the `ETag` header is simple—it contains one entity tag). Any Web resource cache should store ETags in order to do cache invalidation. When the ETag changes, the entity in the cache becomes obsolete and should be discarded or updated.

The primary use of ETags is to avoid downloading a file that hasn't changed since the last time it was downloaded. The alternative is generally to use the last-modified date of a resource to see if it has changed, but this approach is less reliable, and ETags should be used whenever they are available. The mechanism is simple:

1. The server provides the ETag to the client with the `ETag` header on every successful GET response. The `ETag` header simply includes the ETag value for the current instance of the resource.

2. The client returns the ETag to the server when it checks whether it needs to download the resource again. The client puts all possible matching ETags (if multiple instances for the same URL are cached) in the `If-None-Match` header. If any of these ETags match the server's instance, the server responds with **412 Precondition Failed**. If none of those ETags match the server's instance, the server responds with its instance body (see Listing 3–15).

Listing 3–15 Request for cached resource.

Request:
```
GET /index.html HTTP/1.1
Host: nondav.example.com
If-None-Match: "870be-8f0-39ee6a4d"
⏎
```

Response
```
HTTP/1.1 304 Not Modified
Server: Apache/1.3.14 (Unix)
Date: Tue, 15 Nov 1994 08:12:31 GMT
ETag: "870be-8f0-39ee6a4d"
⏎
```

The other header that uses ETags is `If-Match`, which has the opposite syntax: If the `If-Match` header is on a request, the server must only apply the operation if all the clauses in the header are "true" in that they match the resource being addressed.

 Both the `If-Match` and `If-None-Match` headers can take multiple values separated with commas. Both headers can also have the special value *, which matches any token. Thus, `If-Match: *` means that the request can succeed only if the addressed resource matches any token (that means it exists). `If-None-Match: *` is the opposite, meaning the server should apply the operation only if the addressed resource cannot match any token (that means it does not exist).

Unless there's a very strong reason not to (I can't think of any), WebDAV servers should support ETags and return the `ETag` header in response to every GET request. Not only are ETags useful for saving bandwidth, they are quite necessary to prevent all **lost update** cases. The WebDAV Working Group has repeatedly discussed making ETags required functionality for all WebDAV-compliant servers. The cases in which WebDAV uses ETags are discussed later.

If the server provides ETags, then clients *must* use ETags rather than dates to do cache validation and lost-update protection.

3.5 Beyond the Request/Response Model

HTTP/1.1 defines a few mechanisms that extend the basic model in which a single request triggers a single response and then the TCP connection is closed again. Most of these mechanisms involve keeping TCP connections alive for a number of message roundtrips. There are some startup costs to establishing a TCP connection, so these mechanisms can improve performance.

WebDAV defines another mechanism that extends the request/response model. The 102 Processing response is defined for WebDAV servers to use when the final response is delayed due to lengthy processing. This mechanism is defined in Section 5.2.

3.5.1 Keeping Connections Alive

The client uses the `Connection` request header (see Section 3.7.7) to indicate whether it prefers to maintain the TCP connection after the server's response. If the client sends the `Keep-Alive` header value, then the server can choose not to drop the connection when it has sent the response.

Keeping connections alive offers a couple of benefits:

- An ordinary TCP connection has some startup costs. Many books cover TCP performance considerations quite effectively, including books on HTTP ([Gourley02] and [Krishnamurthy01]) and, naturally, TCP references [Stevens98].
- A secure connection, such as a SSL or TLS connection, incurs even more startup costs. The first connection includes expensive key generation and certificate verification, and subsequent connections must at least restore the encryption context [Rescorla00].

3.5.2 Pipelining

When the connection is kept alive, the client can **pipeline** requests for improved performance. In pipelining, the client does not have to wait for the server's first response before sending a second request, so in theory the second response should arrive faster. The server must respond to each request in the order in which it is received. Note that pipelining doesn't have to be used all the time when a connection is kept alive. At any point, the client may decide to wait for a server's response before sending another request.

 The HTTP/1.1 specification requires that only *idempotent* requests should be pipelined together. In theory, an **idempotent request** is one in which multiple instances of the same request have the same effect as one instance of the request. In practice, a client implementer cannot tell when requests are going to be idempotent. For example, the client implementer could believe that using PUT to upload the same body over and over again is no different than uploading it once, and thus PUT is an idempotent request (and Section 9.6 of RFC2616 encourages this belief). However, if the server supports versioning and each PUT request creates a new version, the request is not strictly idempotent. Since in practice the client can't tell, the client might as well pipeline any set of requests for which the failure of one request won't affect whether or not the client attempts another request.

For example, the client might use pipelining with PUT requests to upload all the contents of a local directory to the server without waiting for intermediate success responses.

3.5.3 Predicting Success for Lengthy Requests

The latest specification for HTTP/1.1 [RFC2616] defines the Expect header so that a client can make sure that a lengthy request will be successful before sending the entire request. The client includes the Expect header in a normal request but pauses when it reaches the request body. The server sees the Expect header and responds to the request headers before waiting for the request body. This allows the server to say that it may allow the request (with a 100 Continue response), in which case the client can send the entire request body. If the request must fail, the server responds with an appropriate error response immediately. For example, if a lock would prevent the request from succeeding, the server responds with 423 Locked.

This mechanism is particularly useful with PUT requests because the client may send a large body with PUT. If the client is operating over a slow upload link, it can save a lot of time that would be wasted uploading a large file in a request doomed to fail.

Any WebDAV server should be prepared to receive the Expect header and send 100 Continue responses or a specific error. This applies not only to the PUT method but to any method that can take a body.

However, WebDAV clients cannot currently rely on using the Expect header. The client can't verify whether the server will support the Expect header before sending it. There's no way to tell the difference between a server supporting HTTP/1.1 as defined in RFC2068, which is obsolete, and a server supporting HTTP/1.1 as defined in RFC2616. Only RFC2616 defines the Expect header.

 An HTTP/1.1 server compliant with RFC2068 may respond to one of these requests as if the Expect header is not present. For example, the server could wait for the request body to appear and eventually time out the response. To work around this problem, the client could attempt the request with the Expect header, but if it doesn't receive a 100 Continue or an error response quickly, it would have to drop the TCP connection and try the request again without the `Expect` header and with the full request body present.

If the server notices but does not understand the entire `Expect` header, it responds with the 417 Expectation Failed error.

3.6   HTTP Security

Many security mechanisms exist for HTTP, typically designed originally to solve various e-commerce scenarios. HTTP is concerned with only a few major threats.

User Identification   Many Web servers need to identify users. Some sites limit access to resources, and these sites need to identify users to see if the operation is allowed (access control). Some sites store user preference information; MSN and Yahoo! build custom home pages for each logged-in user. Users are typically identified with a username and password. Certificates or public keys could also identify users, but not very many Internet users have these yet.

Server Identification   The most common scenario in which server identity must be securely established is e-commerce. Users send their credit card numbers to sites like Amazon.com to make purchases. It's very important that the server be truly Amazon.com and not a site run by an attacker impersonating a known site in order to gather and use credit card numbers. Servers are usually identified with certificates signed by trusted certificate authorities such as VeriSign.

Confidentiality   Information sent using HTTP should not always be publicly readable. In e-commerce, this includes messages containing credit card numbers from clients to servers and messages traveling from servers to clients and that contain order confirmations with home delivery addresses. In authoring/publishing scenarios, this information includes any message containing a resource body that isn't supposed to be publicly readable. Any information sent over TCP without encryption must be considered publicly readable, because it's quite easy to sniff network packets at some point between the client and the server.

Most of these threats can be addressed with a good transport security mechanism. Confidentiality is ensured with transport channel encryption (SSL/TLS). Message integrity, or tamper prevention, is ensured via signatures on transport layer messages. Server identification is handled via certficates exchanged when the transport channel is established.

The remaining threat is user identification, which is addressed with HTTP authentication within the HTTP message. There are several HTTP authentication mechanisms and a framework to allow clients and servers to choose one. Authentication works even better when combined with a transport security mechanism, because the transport security provides extra protection for confidentiality and message integrity, both of which help prevent impersonation attacks.

Transport security and HTTP authentication are both easy to provide. An HTTP or WebDAV implementer (or somebody designing a custom HTTP or WebDAV application) is unlikely to have to reimplement any of these security mechanisms.

3.6.1 Basic Authentication

The Basic authentication mechanism and the framework for choosing an authentication mechanism in HTTP are both defined in an RFC [RFC2617]. Basic authentication only addresses user identification, and it does so very poorly.

The Basic authentication challenge includes the `Basic` identifier string and optionally the realm or domain the user should log in to.

```
WWW-Authenticate: Basic realm="example.com"
```

The realm is provided so that the client can prompt the user to log in to the site. The client might connect to the site with an IP address and have no other way to identify the site. The client displays the realm string to help the user recall the username and password to enter to log in to that site. The client may also cache usernames and passwords along with the realm so that the user isn't continually prompted for the same password. The realm should be a domain name registered with the site host so that it doesn't overlap with other sites.

The client authenticates by sending the `Authorization` header on the request. The username and password are concatenated together, transformed using base 64 encoding, and included in the header value.

```
Authorization: BASIC bGlzYTpoZXN0
```

The Basic `Authorization` header value is always the same for a given username and password. That means that it's trivial for a hacker to reuse the header value on new HTTP requests, impersonating another user and gaining access to his or her resources. Even worse, it's trivial to capture TCP packets, unencode this header value, and recover the original username and password.

Since Basic authentication exposes the user's name and password over the wire, it isn't recommended for use over unprotected transport channels. Basic authentication is acceptable if it's used on messages that are encrypted within an SSL/TLS connection, using the server's public key to make the channel confidential.

What about sites that don't care about security? Some sites, like newspapers, only want the user to log in so that the site can track usage patterns or demographic information. The site administrators don't care if one user impersonates another, because their statistics don't have to be perfectly accurate. The site administrators don't care about access control, because all the articles are actually publicly readable. However, this setup does a great disservice to the site's users.

Since many users choose the same passwords for several sites, an attacker who has captured one Basic `Authorization` header can often use that to break into an account on a more secure site. Users have a hard time remembering many passwords, and so they reuse them frequently. Users also have a hard time distinguishing which connections are secure and which aren't, especially if sites change their policy. For that reason, any site using Basic authentication over a clear channel is exposing passwords that may not be unique and that may allow other sites to be attacked. This hurts users whose accounts are broken into as well as the other sites.

3.6.2   Digest Authentication

Digest authentication is the general recommendation for unencrypted HTTP authentication. Most Web servers and clients now support Digest, although there have been reported interoperability problems between MS IE and Apache and between Mozilla and MS IIS. Navigator is the only browser that does not support Digest in any recent version.

Digest addresses user identity and does a much better job of protecting against user impersonation. A Digest `Authentication` header value may not be reusable by an attacker. It uses a nonreversible digest algorithm (usually MD5 [RFC1321]), so an attacker cannot extract the username and password, even if the entire transaction is captured.

Digest authentication protects against **replay attacks** by using different seed or **nonce** values for each request. The header can't be copied and reused on a new HTTP request if the nonce changes.

Digest addresses the message-tampering threat as well, protecting against certain man-in-the-middle attacks. An attacker could capture the client's HTTP request with Digest authentication and modify the HTTP request before forwarding it to the server. This could be quite harmful in e-commerce if an attacker could replace an order for one gold coin with an order for 100 or have the delivery sent to another location. **Message integrity** protection prevents tampering with the message body. The client calculates a **checksum** for the original message body and sends it in the `Authorization` header for the server to compare. It's quite difficult to generate a bogus message body that has the same checksum as the original message. Message integrity does not provide confidentiality, however—Digest authentication does not involve any message body encryption. The headers and their values are also not protected by Digest.

As with Basic, Digest authentication is advertised in the `WWW-Authenticate` header when the server challenges the client to authenticate. The Digest challenge includes quite a bit of challenge information.

```
WWW-Authenticate: Digest realm="www.example.com",
    stale=false, nonce="ec2cc00f21f71acd35ab9be057970609",
    qop="auth", algorithm="MD5"
```

The client needs to use all the information in this challenge to correctly authenticate. Here is what each parameter means:

- As with Basic, the **realm** is used to prompt the user to log in to the correct server. The client may temporarily cache usernames and passwords by associating them with the realm.
- The **algorithm** tells the client how to compute the digest and the checksum. The MD5 algorithm is the only one defined.
- The **nonce** is a unique authentication challenge: The client must use the nonce when computing the digest. If the nonce changes in every authentication challenge, then the user is protected from replay attacks. When the nonce changes, the `Authentication` header value changes too, and a previously valid header value is no longer valid.
- The **qop** (quality of protection) value indicates that the server is merely looking for the client to authenticate. Another possibility is for the server to ask for message integrity as well as authentication (`qop=auth-int`).

- The **stale** directive advises the client on whether it's appropriate to prompt the user for the password again or use a cached value for the password. The server would send `stale=true` when it needs the client to rechallenge the user.

 WebDAV clients and servers *must* support Digest authentication. This really shouldn't be too hard, because many programming languages now have HTTP libraries supporting Digest authentication, and many Web servers can be extended while still using their Digest implementation.

- The Java 2 Platform now includes a Digest authentication implementation.
- Two modules for Python (httpx and urllib2) support Digest authentication.
- At least one library for C supports Digest (libwww and neon for clients).
- WebDAV libraries for various programming languages should also support Digest.
- Custom servers extending Apache can use the `mod_auth_digest` module.
- Custom servers extending IIS 5.0 can use the IIS 5.0 built-in Digest implementation.

Clients should support both Basic and Digest authentication, but clients should never choose Basic authentication if Digest is offered by the server. Many servers advertise both in order to support all kinds of unknown clients, so it's up to the client to choose the more secure mechanism. Even if the TCP connection is encrypted, that might only be true for the first hop, and information may be sent in the clear after that hop, exposing the user's password.

NTLM Authentication

The HTTP authentication framework is extensible. The server can extend the standard `WWW-Authenticate` header to advertise custom mechanisms, and the client can use the standard `Authorization` header to send authentication information other than Basic or Digest.

NTLM authentication is the Microsoft proprietary authentication solution and the most common nonstandard authentication mechanism. IIS 5.0 advertises support for NTLM authentication (perhaps along with Basic and Digest) when it challenges the client to authenticate. The NTLM mechanism is undocumented; however, it has been analyzed by independent experts. It is a challenge-response mechanism, more secure than Basic, but it seems to be less secure than Digest.

3.6.3 Transport Security

Many Internet application protocols use TCP as a transport layer by making a TCP connection and sending all data in TCP packets. There ought to be a way to provide confidentiality and server authentication for the transport layer so that all these application protocols can reuse the same secure connection technology. The only transport layer security mechanisms worth mentioning, used by practically all modern application protocols, are the SSL/TLS series of protocols.

Transport security typically solves several problems at the same time. These are the most common functions provided. Some of these functions can be turned off, but very frequently they all are used.

1. It authenticates the server through a certificate that includes the server's domain name and is signed by a trusted certificate authority. This is quite useful in e-commerce where users are loathe to send their credit cards to any old Web server.
2. It encrypts the entire communication channel so that all data on the channel is private.
3. It signs each message so that the recipient can make sure the message was not tampered with in transit.

Note that transport security doesn't address user identification very often, although it can in theory. With HTTP, it's often easiest for the administrator to configure HTTP authentication rather than configure transport layer client authentication.

The IETF recommends the Transport Layer Security (TLS) protocol [RFC2246]. TLS was standardized in January 1999 but is not as new as it appears, because it is a careful refinement of Secure Socket Layer 3 (SSL3). SSL3 itself is based on SSL2, which was published in 1995 [Hickman95]. SSL3 is the most widely implemented version as of 2002, but TLS is slowly replacing SSL3 [Rescorla01]. Since SSL/TLS handles upgrade cases, the application protocol rarely needs to worry about versions.

WebDAV client and server implementors should choose a SSL/TLS toolkit so that transport security doesn't have to be reimplemented. Open-source security toolkits are a great resource for impementors because with open source any independent expert can examine the source code to discover potential coding errors and security holes (and security experts aren't shy about reporting these). The most frequently used open-source toolkits are OpenSSL for C and PureTLS for Java. If a HTTP implementation plugs in to a toolkit correctly, then the best quality mechanism available to both client and server will be chosen automatically for each connection.

Newest and Best? Go with Tried and True

Security mechanisms and implementations should be reused wherever possible. A good security mechanism like TLS takes years of experience and refinements by experts. A new mechanism, even if it uses the newest, greatest cryptography, is likely to have all kinds of undiscovered problems. A good security implementation takes years of careful development work by rare and highly paid experts. The developer must pay careful attention to every possible threat and every coding error that could open a theoretically secure protocol to attack. A good security implementation may be in beta a long time as implementors slowly become more certain that holes have been plugged and changes do not open new holes.

WebDAV servers supporting SSL/TLS should also support the CONNECT method (described in Section 3.3.10). *SSL and TLS: Designing and Building Secure Systems* [Rescorla01] has detailed information on HTTP and SSL/TLS interactions, including CONNECT, proxy interactions, and various threats.

All WebDAV clients should support SSL and TLS because distributed authoring frequently requires much better authorization and confidentiality than regular Web browsing does. Some WebDAV repositories only support SSL or TLS connections, rejecting ordinary TCP connections altogether, so a client that doesn't support SSL/TLS can't interoperate with these repositories at all.

3.7 HTTP Headers

This section briefly covers every HTTP header mentioned in this book, plus a few bonus headers. You can skim through it now to familiarize yourself with the wealth of headers and what they can do, or refer back to this section later when you encounter an unfamiliar header.

In addition to the HTTP headers listed here, additional headers are defined in the HTTP/1.1 specification and elsewhere. Many clients and servers also use custom headers that aren't standardized and aren't even intended to be recognized. HTTP/1.1 specifies that unknown headers must be ignored (unless they begin with `Content-`). Examples are given for most headers.

3.7.1 Accept-Ranges Header

The `Accept-Ranges` header allows the server to advertise in an OPTIONS response whether it supports range requests and how it can measure ranges. The only value defined in the HTTP specification for this header is `bytes`, indicating that the server can accept byte-range requests and return partial resource contents.

When clients know that the server supports range requests, clients can download large files piece by piece. Since a dropped connection is more likely to occur in a long download than a short one merely due to increased time spent, this feature is frequently used to break a large download into chunks. Usually, if a ranged request fails, only that ranged request needs to be reissued, rather than all of them.

```
Accept-Ranges: bytes
```

Note that the `Accept-Ranges` header may have different values depending on what resource is the target of the OPTIONS request. A dynamically generated resource might not support byte-range requests, whereas a static resource in the same directory would.

The `Accept-Ranges` header also appears on other kinds of responses. Apache 1.3 sends the `Accept-Ranges` header in response to GET requests.

3.7.2 Allow Header

The `Allow` header is used mostly in OPTIONS responses. It can also be used in a PUT request and response, but it rarely is in practice. This header shows the list of methods that are currently supported by the resource addressed in the request. This value can change over time because as it may depend not only on the type of the resource but also on its current state.

```
Allow: GET, HEAD, OPTIONS, TRACE
```

When an OPTIONS * request is used to find out the server's general feature set, the `Allow` header in the response should include every method known to the server, if possible.

3.7.3 Authorization Header

The `Authorization` header allows the client to provide user authentication credentials to the server in an HTTP request.

The example of Basic syntax shows that the word *BASIC* comes first so the server knows how to interpret the header. In Basic syntax, the rest of the header value is simply the result of base-64 encoding the username and password concatenated together with : in between.

```
Authorization: BASIC bGlzYTp0ZXN0
```

The Digest syntax and mechanism are much more complicated. Both authentication mechanisms are described in a companion document to the HTTP specification, "HTTP Authentication: Basic and Digest Access Authentication" [RFC2617].

3.7.4 Accept-* Headers

With the OPTIONS response, we've already seen the major mechanisms allowing clients to get information about the supported features of a Web server. What we haven't seen yet is how servers learn about client support and user preferences. A series of headers on requests provides this kind of information (see Table 3–2). Usually, these headers appear on GET requests, but they can be used more widely whenever the client expects a response body (e.g., a POST request).

The `Accept-Ranges` header is defined in Section 3.7.1 because it usually appears in OPTIONS responses.

3.7.5 Content-* Headers

Whenever an HTTP message contains a body, it must use at least some headers to provide information about the body, most commonly `Content-Length` and `Content-Type` (see Table 3–3).

3.7.6 Conditional Headers

The conditional headers allow clients to put conditional statements on the request such that the server will process the request only if the conditions are met.

Accept Headers on Every Request
The designers of HTTP wanted the protocol to be *stateless*. A stateless protocol is one that never or rarely requires a server to cache or save information from one request to use in a later request. Since the server can't remember what functions the client supports, the client must put this information in every request. Putting extra information on every request trades off bandwidth for state. The designers of HTTP were gambling that the ability for servers to reply quickly and to many users made up for the "wasteful" use of bandwidth. The Accept headers are a good example of using bandwidth in an attempt to improve performance. On Web servers that use cookies extensively to look up state, the advantage may be lost. Still, it remains possible to write a very fast server that doesn't maintain any state, doesn't use cookies, and handles many requests flexibly according to the header values used.

Table 3–2 HTTP Accept-* Headers, Descriptions, and Examples

Accept-Charset	Lists the character sets that the client is capable of handling (comma-separated). Accept-Charset: iso-8859-5, unicode-1-1
Accept-Encoding	Lists the body encodings that the client is capable of handling (comma-separated). The only common values for this header denote the Unix "compress" encoding and the GNU "gzip" encoding, both of which provide compression. Note that Netscape 6.2 requests gzip encoding even though it does not handle the result properly by unzipping the response before handing it on to user or file system—but this has been fixed in later versions. Accept-Encoding: compress, gzip
Accept-Language	Lists the human languages that the user prefers or can handle, in comma-separated values. Usually this kind of information is derived from the locale of the client software or user preference settings, rather than functional capabilities of the client software. We show here an example that includes preference information, with French (fr) being the most preferred language, followed by English (en) and then German (de), as indicated by decreasing q values. The language code is separated from the q value by a semicolon. No q value implies a q value of 1 (maximum). Accept-Language: fr, de;q=0.5, en;q=0.7

If-Match, If-None-Match, and If-Range all compare ETag values known to the client to current ETag values for resources on the server. The client may store ETags in its resource cache or remember the ETag for a file that it is editing. These may only be used by the

Table 3–3   HTTP Content-* Headers, Descriptions, and Examples

Content-Type	The media type, MIME type, or file type of the response body. Usually text/html for Web pages. `Content-Type: text/html; charset=UTF-8` Legal MIME types and character sets are both defined by the Internet Assigned Numbers Association (IANA). The UTF-8 transformation for Unicode is defined in [RFC2279].
Content-Length	The length of the response body, an integer, the number of octets in the body. When no body is present, `Content-Length` may be 0, or the header may be omitted. See Section 3.2.8 for other cases concerning message length. `Content-Length: 1882`
Content-Language	Shows the language(s) that the body is in. If the sender does not know the language or considers that the content is appropriate for any preferred language, this header is omitted. `Content-Language: en-Us`
Content-Encoding	Lists any additional encodings on the body. For example, if the body was compressed, the server would list the compression algorithm used. This may include several sequential encodings in the order they were applied. If no encodings were used, this header is omitted. `Content-Encoding: gzip`
Content-Location	The preferred address or location for the resource. This may be an absolute URL or a relative URL (relative to the server/host that responds to the request). This is most useful for resources that have multiple variants—for example, documents that exist in several languages. `Content-Location: /hr/recruiting/job-1229-fr.txt`
Content-MD5	An MD5 digest of the response body, provided so that the client can check the integrity of the response. This could guard against transmission errors. `Content-MD5: Q2hlY2sgSW50ZWdyaXR5IQ==` The `Content-MD5` header is discussed in [RFC1864].
Content-Range	When a partial response body is sent, this indicates how much and what part of the body was sent. `Content-Range: 0-511`

client if the server supports ETags, of course. Servers usually indicate ETag support by returning the ETag in GET and PUT responses. These headers are useful for maintaining caches but absolutely essential in distributed authoring scenarios to avoid accidental overwrites.

`If-Modified-Since` and `If-Unmodified-Since` serve mostly the same purpose as `If-Match` and `If-None-Match`, but these headers use the last-modified timestamp instead and can only handle one value. Comparing timestamps is a less reliable technique (suffering from clock skew, time zone, and granularity problems [Krishnamurthy99]), but it was the only technique specified in HTTP/1.0 and the only technique supported on some Web servers. ETags and the headers to compare ETags were added in HTTP/1.1. For clients, these headers are a less reliable fallback mechanism if the server doesn't support ETags. The server will probably supply either the ETag or the Last-Modified date when responding to GET or PUT requests.

In each of the conditional headers, multiple values are separated by commas. For `If-Match` and `If-None-Match`, * is a special value indicating "any ETag." When a request fails due to a conditional header, the response is 412 Precondition Failed. `If-Range` is the exception (see Table 3–4).

Table 3–4 HTTP Conditional Headers, Descriptions, and Examples

If-Match	The server compares the requested resource to all ETags in the `If-Match` header. The request fails if the resource fails to match any of the ETags. This allows the client to upload a new instance of a page only if the page hasn't changed since the last instance was downloaded. `If-Match: "10880-22388"`
If-None-Match	The request fails if the requested resource matches any of the ETags in this header. `If-None-Match: *` is a special construct that will cause the request to fail if the requested resource already exists, because * can match any ETag. This header allows the client to download a resource only if the resource is different from any of the client's cached instances. `If-None-Match: "10880-22388", "10880-21271"`
If-Modified-Since	The request fails if the requested resource has not been modified since the date given in the header value. `If-Modified-Since: Sat, 29 Oct 1994 19:43:31 GMT`
If-Unmodified-Since	The request fails if the requested resource has been modified since the date given. `If-Unmodified-Since: Sat, 29 Oct 1994 19:43:31 GMT`
If-Range	This header is used with the `Range` header, when the client has part of a resource and wants to download the rest of the resource, but making sure that the part already received has not changed. This header can use either ETags like `If-Match` (preferred method) or dates like `If-Modified-Since`. A partial resource is returned if the condition succeeds (the part specified in the `Range` header). The entire resource is returned if the condition fails. `If-Range: "10880-22388"`

3.7.7   Connection Header

The client uses the Connection header to indicate whether it would like to maintain the TCP connection after the server's response. The reasons to do this are discussed in Section 3.5. The only valid values for the Connection header are:

```
Connection: Close
Connection: Keep-Alive
```

When the server sees Close in the Connection request header, it must close the connection after sending the response. The Keep-Alive value leaves the decision up to the server—it may keep the connection open as the client requests, or it may close it. If the server keeps the connection open after the first response, it can still decide to close the connection later, after any subsequent response.

3.7.8   User-Agent Header

The User-Agent header identifies the HTTP client software acting on behalf of the user. Web browsers usually show the version and platform of the browser software.

MSDAIPP User Agent

Some applications use a lower layer that translates application requests from some API into WebDAV requests. For example, Word and Excel send PUT requests with the same User-Agent value. The value identifies a software layer that makes HTTP requests based on ODBC calls.

```
User-Agent: Microsoft Data Access Internet Publishing
Provider DAV 1.1
```

Sometimes, HTTP servers use the value of the User-Agent header to decide what features the client can support and to customize the format or contents of a response. However, this practice is problematic for a couple of reasons:

- Client software can change behavior from one release to another, or even with security patches, but may not necessarily update the User-Agent string.
- When a server limits its features based on which User-Agent strings it receives, this encourages browsers to mimic other browsers in order to try to get a certain behavior out of the server. This can be seen in the many browsers that put MSIE *and* Mozilla in their User-Agent strings. What kind of browser advertises this User-Agent value[3]?

```
Mozilla/4.0 (compatible; MSIE 5.5; Windows NT 5.0)
```

---

3.   Both MSIE 5.5 and some versions of Mozilla use this exact User-Agent string with only the operating system varying.

- Many browsers allow users to change the value the `User-Agent` header returns [Mozdev03].

Because of these problems, whenever new client features must be identified, this should be done in other headers that can be standardized and used by other clients that support the same features.

3.7.9 Expect Header

The client uses the `Expect` header to verify if a request is likely to succeed before sending the whole body. See Section 3.5.3.

3.7.10 Cache Control Headers

Several headers exist in order to help keep caches up to date and performing well. These header values are used by caching software to decide whether to cache resources, for whom, and for how long. All of these headers are used in server responses (see Table 3–5).

Table 3–5   Cache Control Headers, Descriptions, and Examples

Cache-Control	This header can contain values like `no-cache` to help caches know whether to keep a cached response body. Other possible values are `private` to indicate that the resource isn't publicly readable and `public` to indicate the inverse. The full listing of possible values and what they mean can be found in the HTTP specification. `Cache-Control: no-cache`
Expires	The `Expires` header provides a date after which the document is considered "stale" and should not be used from a cache. Instead, the cache should fail the request or get a more recent copy from the server. `Expires: Thu, 01 Dec 1994 16:00:00 GMT`
Pragma	Although the `Pragma` header is obsolete (replaced by the more flexible `Cache-Control` header), it's still used on many servers to handle older clients and proxies. `Pragma: no-cache`

WebDAV servers may not find the HTTP cache control mechanisms sufficient, because WebDAV servers are more likely to have files with restricted permissions. A file that is publicly readable may later have its permissions changed, so it would be nice if the file wasn't cached anywhere. A file that is not publicly readable shouldn't be cached at an intermediary, because that intermediary can't be trusted to restrict permissions the same way the WebDAV server does. Thus, many WebDAV servers make every attempt to disable caching. This is most effectively done with the addition of two headers to responses with bodies. The two headers are both needed in practice to handle HTTP/1.0 and HTTP/1.1 software.

```
Cache-Control: no-cache
Pragma: no-cache
```

Even when the resource is publicly readable, it's hard for a WebDAV server to know how long the client can safely cache the resource, because a WebDAV resource may be changed at any moment.

3.7.11 Date

The Date header is required on most server responses and should contain the date the response was generated. The server may choose not to send the Date header with certain status codes (100, 101, 500, 503) or if it is unable to provide a reasonable approximation of the current time.

```
Date: Tue, 15 Nov 1994 08:12:31 GMT
```

3.7.12 Range

Clients can request only part of a resource body by specifying the range in bytes, provided the server supports this feature (as shown in OPTIONS response, discussed in Section 3.3.7). This can be useful to resume an interrupted download, as long as the client makes sure that the file being downloaded has not changed since the first byte range was downloaded.

The following example shows the client request for the tail end of a resource (bytes 93300 to the end of the document). The syntax also supports requests for a range of bytes at the beginning or middle of the resource contents.

```
GET /users/alice/report.doc HTTP/1.1
Bytes: 93300-
If-Match: "etag11083"
⏎
```

3.7.13 Location

The server uses the Location header to tell the client the real address of the resource. The most common use is when the client requests a URL that the server has mapped to another URL—for example, if the collection

```
http://www.example.com/hr/
```

maps to the default page

```
http://www.example.com/hr/index.html
```

When the client sends a GET request for the first URL, the server returns the body of the resource addressed by the second URL. The server also includes the Location header with the correct URL for the client to use in the future, particularly for PUT and DELETE requests:

```
Location: http://www.example.com/hr/index.html
```

WebDAV servers can also use this header in response to any method.

3.7.14 Server

The HTTP server can identify the software it is running by using a string in the `Server` header.

```
Server: Tomcat Web Server/3.3 Final ( JSP 1.1; Servlet 2.2 )
```

3.7.15 Upgrade

The `Upgrade` header is used to upgrade from HTTP/1.1 to another version of HTTP or even a completely unrelated protocol. It's not commonly used, partly because it was added with future versions of HTTP in mind, and we're not there yet. A server should ignore this header if it does not offer upgrade opportunities. The following example is completely fictitious:

```
Upgrade: HTTP/2.0, IRC/6.9, RTA/x11
```

3.7.16 WWW-Authenticate

The `WWW-Authenticate` header appears frequently on 401 Unauthorized responses. When the method fails because the user isn't authenticated, the server needs to challenge the client to authenticate. The server must provide some information in this challenge—at a minimum, the server needs to specify the authentication mechanisms it supports and the server the user should try to log in to. A sample Basic authentication challenge is shown here, and an example of a Digest authentication challenge appears in Section 3.6.2.

```
WWW-Authenticate: Basic realm="example.com"
```

3.8 Summary

HTTP is used to browse Web pages. HTTP is a client/server protocol with which Web browsers make requests to Web servers for resources stored on the server. HTTP resources can be static Web pages or dynamically generated pages, images, or any other kind of file. HTTP/1.0 was standardized by the IETF in 1996. HTTP/1.1 became a Proposed Standard in 1997 and was upgraded to Draft Standard in 1999 as RFC2616.

Every HTTP resource has a URL, or address. URLs are usually found in links in Web pages, but they're also passed around in email and even on paper. An HTTP URL has a path part that typically includes a path with directory names, but in an HTTP URL this path is supposed to be opaque to clients.

HTTP is a request/response protocol. An HTTP request is self-contained and normally generates a single self-contained response. A request always has a request line containing the method, request-URI for the resource being addressed, and the protocol version. A request may also have a number of headers and a body. The response is formatted similarly, with a response line, headers, and optional body.

HTTP defines eight methods: GET, PUT, POST, OPTIONS, HEAD, TRACE, DELETE, and CONNECT. In practice, however, only GET, POST, and CONNECT are widely used by ordinary browsers and servers. PUT and DELETE were designed to allow some limited authoring functionality, but in practice they are not well enough defined to be useful.

HTTP goes beyond request and response with a few interesting mechanisms. These mechanisms improve the performance of more advanced HTTP interactions. WebDAV clients and servers must also be aware of these mechanisms.

HTTP supports caching and proxy servers. A fair amount of the HTTP specification is designed to make sophisticated caching and proxying possible. Caches and proxies must be taken into account when WebDAV applications are being designed.

CHAPTER 4

Data Model

HTTP/1.1 has a simple data model: Ultimately, all Web objects are resources, which can be addressed by *Uniform Resource Identifiers* (URIs). WebDAV extends this data model while still keeping it rather simple.

- A collection is a special kind of resource that contains other resources. As a type of resource, a collection is addressable.
- All resources have properties with names and values, but properties are not independently addressable and do not have URIs.
- Any resource may be locked. Locks are not independently addressable either.

A data model allows clients to have assumptions about the way information will be organized on the server and to use these assumptions to access information on behalf of the user. A consistent data model helps keep protocol design focused and can improve interoperability.

This chapter covers all the components of the model and how they interact. After this, it will become much easier to understand what WebDAV protocol interactions do.

XML has been mentioned before now, but this chapter starts to refer to XML concepts like elements, attributes [Bray00], qualified names, and namespaces [Bray99]. XML is sufficiently human readable that the examples in this book should be digestible by anybody with a passing familiarity with XML, but some of the terminology may be a little daunting. There are many books on XML, both simple and complicated, and many Web sites, tutorials, and articles. For a complete primer, I recommend *XML: A Manager's Guide* [Dick03].

4.1 Basic Components

A **WebDAV resource** is an addressable Web object, such as a file or directory. An ordinary resource can be viewed as a file. It can have a content body of any MIME type [RFC2045], [RFC2046], including HTML-formatted text, other text, an image, an executable, or an Office document. It can have locks and properties. The specification for URI Syntax [RFC2396] defines a resource as "anything that has identity." HTTP/1.1 [RFC2616] defines a resource both as "a network data object or service" and "anything that has a URI." The WebDAV specification does not redefine a resource but works from these definitions.

A **collection** resource follows all the same rules as a regular resource: It has a URL and properties, and it can be locked. Normally, a collection has no content body or an undefined content body. A collection has added functionality because it can contain other resources. Collections can be nested to form a hierarchy or tree to organize resources.

Terminology: Resource and Collection

Although it's convenient to think of a **resource** as either a file or a directory, we use the word *resource* more frequently because it's well defined and because it includes both concepts. The word **collection** always refers to a WebDAV collection resource. **File** and **directory** are used to talk about file system objects outside of the context of WebDAV. The words **child** and **parent** indicate a direct relationship between a resource and the collection that contains it. **Descendants** covers all the resources inside a collection, whether they are directly inside the collection or within subcollections.

A **lock** is a restriction placed on a resource. Usually, it restricts users other than the owner of the lock from making any changes on the resource. A lock has a token to identify it, but that token is meaningful only in the context of the resource that is locked.

A **property** is a name/value pair on a resource. Any resource can have any set of properties. A property is not independently addressable, but each property has a qualified name that uniquely identifies it on the resource where it appears.

In all figures in this book, a couple of conventions are used to represent resources, locks, and properties. Figure 4–1 introduces most of those conventions.

Resources are represented with icons. Hierarchy is represented as a tree with dashed lines, sometimes arranged the same way an Explorer-style client displays hierarchy. Properties are represented as iconic tables to represent a list of property/value pairs. Locks are represented with a shaded box to show the scope of the lock.

A property name is actually an XML **qualified name**, which means that it combines a short, readable element name with a unique XML namespace.

Locks and properties are bound to individual resources. For example, to create a lock, the client must request that the resource be locked by giving the resource's address.

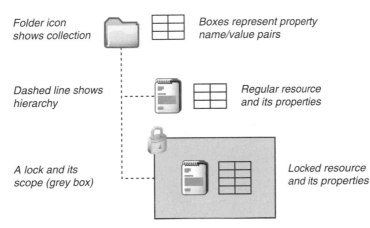

Folder icon
shows collection

Boxes represent property
name/value pairs

Dashed line shows
hierarchy

Regular resource
and its properties

A lock and its
scope (grey box)

Locked resource
and its properties

Figure 4–1   Figure conventions.

XML Names, Qualified Names, and Namespaces

The base XML recommendation [Bray00] defined **elements** and **element names**. An XML document can have an element named status with a text value:

```
<status>200</status>
```

An element name like "status" is such a common word that different applications quickly collide with each other. "Status" could mean response status, e-commerce order status, or a purchaser's credit status. The XML namespaces recommendation [Bray99] addresses this issue with **qualified names**, which are names distinguished with a unique **namespace**. The namespace can be very long in order to ensure uniqueness, so in any XML document each namespace may be given a nickname or **prefix**. Prefixes are completely arbitrary, so each prefix must be defined in the scope where it is used. Here, the prefix is a1 and the namespace is http://example.com/ expenses/.

```
<a1:status xmlns:a1='http://example.com/expenses/'>
<a1:paid-in-full/></a1:status>
```

A WebDAV **repository** is a collection of WebDAV resources hosted at the same server address. Within a repository, it's possible to move and copy files from one collection to another. This isn't a concept defined or required for the WebDAV specification, but it's very useful to talk about WebDAV behavior.

4.2 URLs and WebDAV Resources

Every WebDAV resource has an HTTP URL. Since WebDAV resources are also fully compliant HTTP resources, the same URL allows access for both ordinary Web browsers and WebDAV clients. The WebDAV client can discover WebDAV support by querying the resource with OPTIONS.

Figure 4–2 shows a simple WebDAV URL. It is also an HTTP URL; in fact, it is the same as the URL shown in Figure 3–1 in Chapter 3, *HTTP Mechanics*. The only difference is that now the client can interpret even more of the URL.

Figure 4–2 A simple URL.

HTTP treats the path part of the URL as an unstandardized string: Clients theoretically cannot make any assumptions about how the server handles or interprets the path `/hr/index.html`. In WebDAV, however, the path part of the URL includes the name of the resource and the collection hierarchy in which it appears. This was a de facto construction for most HTTP servers, but WebDAV makes it mandatory.

Collection names are separated with the forward slash (/) character. Each collection must be the parent of the collection or resource that appears after it in the URL. A WebDAV-compliant URL ending in a slash always refers to a collection (but not all collection URLs end in a slash).

Backward Slashes

Forward and backward slashes (/, \) are sometimes treated as synonyms in HTTP URLs. The backward slash is not allowed in URLs, but Windows users may be in the habit of typing backward slashes anyway. Client software may accept backward slashes users type in, but the software must convert to forward slashes before sending URLs in protocol messages.

4.2.1 Root URL

A WebDAV repository usually has some kind of root collection that contains all other collections. Of course, the root does not have a parent collection. A successful request to the repository's root URL should show that it is a collection and that it supports WebDAV.

Often, the URL to the root of a repository consists of the server URL and a path consisting only of /. For example:

```
http://www.example.com:8080/
```

In some cases, however, the root of the repository may include a path element. This method may be used at sites where several Web services are hosted, including perhaps regular Web files and other services as well as a WebDAV repository. The only way for this server to know when the WebDAV repository is being addressed is to include some string in the path to indicate which hosted application to address.

> ```
> http://multiapp.example.com/davdocs/
> ```

On this server, the path / is unlikely to be a WebDAV collection.

4.2.2 Path Hierarchy

After the WebDAV repository root, the URL path may have a number of collection names and finally may contain one file name. If a repository has two collections for two different departments, appearing right under the root directory, these might appear as:

> ```
> http://www.example.com/hr/
> http://www.example.com/finance/
> ```

Inside the hr collection is a default Web page and a few more collections.

> ```
> http://www.example.com/hr/index.html      file
> http://www.example.com/hr/ergonomics/     collection
> http://www.example.com/hr/benefits/       collection
> ...
> ```

The hierarchy that these addresses correspond to can be drawn without any further information (see Figure 4–3).

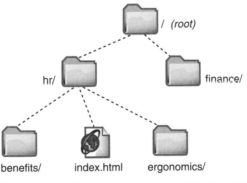

Figure 4–3   Hierarchy based on URL structure.

In this example, every resource we've shown is a collection, except for index.html. The client browsing this repository can tell what's a collection and what's not with the DAV:resourcetype property that exists on every resource.

4.2.3 URL Uniqueness

It is very common to see multiple URLs refer to the same Web resource. The classic example of this is a site with daily news or a daily comic, where on August 15, the page today.html is the same page as aug15.html, but on the following day, today.html is the same page as aug16.html.

WebDAV does not explicitly deal with multiple URLs to a single resource. If a server is configured so that the two URLs `aug15.html` and `today.html` bind to the same file [Clemm03], clearly a GET request to each URL will return the same content body. Other operations aren't so evident, and since WebDAV doesn't deal with multiple bindings, there is no required behavior. For example, the server must decide whether locking one URL will cause the other URL to also be locked.

It's also possible for one URL to refer to multiple resources. The page `userguide.doc` might have both French and English variants (variants are defined in RFC2616), both stored and mapped to the same URL. WebDAV does not deal with this issue, either. HTTP defines how the server knows which resource to return in response to a GET request, but there's no way to know how to author one of them using WebDAV. The WebDAV Working Group has discussed whether to address this topic, but more important features have come up so far.

4.3   Using the Hierarchy

Because the WebDAV data model includes the explicit idea of hierarchy, it's possible to apply some operations to a tree, some to a single node, and some to a node and its direct children. WebDAV achieves this goal by allowing the client to specify the **depth** to which the operation should be applied. Legal values for depth include only the three values 0, 1, and `infinity`. Some server implementations are case-sensitive and do not even accept `infinity`, which is a reasonable way to implement the `Depth` header, because HTTP header values may be case-sensitive and RFC2518 doesn't say otherwise for this specific header.

Any operation on a resource without children is always depth 0, even if the depth isn't specified. A depth infinity request that addresses a noncollection resource could be rejected with an error, although the WebDAV specification doesn't require this.

Depth is easiest to understand by looking at examples. These examples all take place on requests to the `hr/` collection (as shown in Figure 4–3).

Depth 0   Collections may be copied and locked with depth 0, but they may not be moved or deleted with depth 0, because moving or deleting only a collection (and not its children) leaves the namespace inconsistent due to orphaned resources without parents. The properties of a single collection can be queried with depth 0, in which case the server returns only the properties of that collection and none of its children.

In the example shown in Figure 4–4, the collection `hr/` is copied with depth 0 to the location `hrbackup/`, where no resource exists yet. A depth 0 copy operation must copy the collection properties to a new location, without copying any of its children. The collection `hrbackup/` will be created empty but with properties copied from `hr/`. Some server-managed properties (such as DAV:resourcetype and any permissions-related properties) should be copied with existing values to the new location. The server must change certain other server-managed properties (such as DAV:creationdate and DAV:getlastmodified) to appropriate new values to preserve the semantics of those properties.

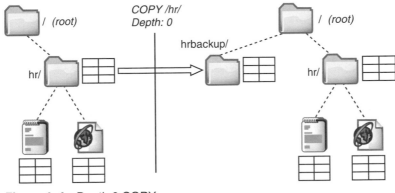

Figure 4–4   Depth 0 COPY.

A depth 0 collection copy is only of use to initialize certain property values and permissions. Effectively, the client is using an existing collection as a template for a new collection.

Depth Infinity   Depth infinity is the opposite of depth 0. With depth infinity, the scope of the request includes every resource starting from and including the resource addressed and all of its children recursively, both subcollections and noncollection children. The MOVE, DELETE, COPY, and LOCK operations all support depth infinity requests. Property discovery can also be done with depth infinity.

In the example in Figure 4–5, a depth infinity COPY covers a collection, its properties, its children, and all descendents. The new collection `hrbackup/` contains copies of all the descendants of `hr/`. All new resources must have property values copied from the original resources.

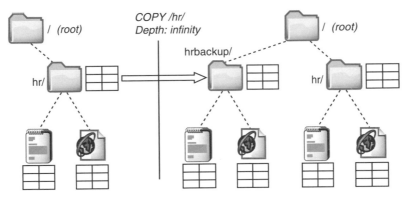

Figure 4–5   Depth infinity COPY.

Depth infinity copies may partially fail, in which case the server must return detailed information that allows the client to see which parts failed and why.

Depth 1   The depth value 1 is only allowed for PROPFIND requests, so the example illustrating depth 1 must be a property listing. This kind of request is made very frequently.

Every time an Explorer-like client interface displays a directory listing, it is displaying the results of a depth 1 property request. If the client *requested* the resource type property for the hr/ collection (as shown in Figure 4–3) in a depth 1 request, the answer would include:

```
http://www.example.com/hr/                    collection
http://www.example.com/hr/index.html
http://www.example.com/hr/ergonomics/         collection
http://www.example.com/hr/benefits/           collection
```

Note that the collection hr/ itself is also included in the depth 1 results because the resource addressed is also included in an operation of any depth. The children of the subfolders are not included as they would be in response to a depth infinity request. The file index.html has a blank resource type because it is not a collection, it is the standard resource type.

The reason depth 1 is forbidden on other requests is that there are namespace consistency and specification issues:

- A MOVE operation cannot handle depth 1, because it would leave the "grandchildren" of the moved directory orphaned of their parents.
- A DELETE operation cannot accept depth 1 for the same reason.
- A COPY operation could theoretically copy just the children of a folder and not the grandchildren, but it's not allowed by the specification. This was probably disallowed in order to simplify, because the designers didn't have a compelling use case for depth 1 copies.
- A LOCK operation could theoretically lock the directory and its direct children, but again, it's not allowed in WebDAV.

4.4 Metadata

Metadata is data about data. It's information about a resource, which is itself information. In WebDAV, all resources can have metadata.

Metadata is increasingly useful to the World Wide Web because it has grown larger and increasingly sophisticated. It's not always enough to have a Graphical Interchange Format (GIF) image on a Web site and the only information available about it is its name, lvrfplace.gif. Search engines should be able to find not only text documents with the words *living room* and *fireplace* but also images of a living room including a fireplace. Ideally, clients could find out more about the image, such as whether it's copyrighted and how much screen space to allocate to displaying it—all before downloading the image.

The data about the image is best made available separately from the image itself. If the information is only available inside the image file, the cost of downloading the entire file may be prohibitive for search engines or for browsers using slow links. Further, many file formats don't allow internal metadata. WebDAV solves this problem by providing a framework for metadata outside the file body. It also defines a basic schema (a set of property names and types) for all kinds of resources.

WebDAV also defines two methods to deal with properties: PROPFIND, to retrieve properties, and PROPPATCH, to change property values. Until Chapter 7, *Property Operations*, we'll simply take it for granted that these methods are used somehow to get or set property values.

The model for metadata is a flat property/value space. Every property on a resource must have a unique name. Properties cannot contain each other, nor can properties have properties.

Property Values   Property values are always Unicode strings, typically expressed in UTF-8 or UTF-16 characters. The client and server can also negotiate another character formatting. Just about any data type or structured object can be converted to and from a string format, so properties are pretty powerful.

Representing Unicode

Unicode is a code for representing alphabetic and other characters. It can represent most characters used by most written human languages. Although native Unicode environments exist, most Internet communication goes through some system at some point, which may not be native Unicode. However, nearly all systems support ASCII. UTF-8 and UTF-16 allow Unicode characters to be encoded in ASCII.

Both PROPFIND and PROPPATCH use XML message bodies to marshal the XML property names and string property values. String values are usually fairly easy to transmit as text inside an XML element. It's only tricky when the WebDAV property value is also structured as XML, but that topic is covered in detail in Section 7.1.8.

A property may exist but have an empty value. Sometimes this is because the mere existence of a property is used to convey information. A property with an empty value is different from a nonexistent property in that:

- A request for a nonexistent property will result in a 404 Not Found error response, whereas a request for an empty property will return a successful but empty result.
- A list of the names of all the properties that exist on a resource does include the names of properties with empty values.

The flexibility of unlimited properties on every resource, property names, namespaces, and the ability to define any data type (as long as it can be represented as a string) means that WebDAV metadata is very powerful. This is the fundamental reason that WebDAV can be used for so many applications.

4.4.1   Live and Dead Properties

The distinction between **live** and **dead** properties is rather arbitrary, but it matters because WebDAV defines them to behave differently in certain protocol operations. All the properties defined in the previous section are live properties.

WebDAV defines live and dead properties in RFC2518:

```
Live Property - A property whose semantics and syntax are
enforced by the server. For example, the live
"getcontentlength" property has its value, the length of the
entity returned by a GET request, automatically calculated by
the server.
Dead Property - A property whose semantics and syntax are not
enforced by the server. The server only records the value of a
dead property; the client is responsible for maintaining the
consistency of the syntax and semantics of a dead property.
```

By this definition, live properties include:

- Properties **calculated** by the server. The creationdate property is calculated by the server when the resource is created. On some WebDAV servers, the client may later explicitly set or override the value, but regardless, the server sets the value at one point.
- **Protected** properties. Clients aren't allowed to change the value of a protected property. The lockdiscovery property is protected because the only way clients can change LOCK information is through the LOCK and UNLOCK requests (and lockdiscovery is also calculated).
- Properties used as **configuration** information. These properties may be given values by clients, but the server may check the syntax and then use the value to change its behavior. For example, a current draft [Korver03] proposes a quota-assigned property. A server supporting this property may allow clients with sufficient authorization to set the value of the quota-assigned property on a resource, as long as the value is an integer. The server uses the value to limit the amount of storage used within that resource.
- Properties where the server verifies syntax or data type. Clients may provide values for use only by other clients, but the server helps enforce consistent syntax. For example, a custom server application might check the employee-start-date to make sure it is a valid date. On that server, the employee-start-date property is live, even though on any server not checking syntax, the property would be a dead property.

Dead properties are written and read by clients without any interference from the WebDAV server. The server doesn't care whether a dead property is set, what the value is, what the data type is, or how big the property is. An example could be the employee fullname property used in the employee directory scenario: Clients set the full name and dynamically generated Web pages display it, but the WebDAV server engine isn't involved except by storing and retrieving the value when asked.

4.4.2 Required Live Properties

WebDAV requires certain properties to exist on any resource (see Table 4–1). Some of these, like resourcetype, are crucial to doing WebDAV operations correctly. Others, like creationdate are more informational. Some are protected, which means clients may not set their values. These properties can be used to display file listings in Windows Explorer style (showing size, type, and last modified date) as well as other common displays. This makes it possible for a WebDAV collection to be displayed and used like a regular file system directory.

Table 4–1   WebDAV Required Properties

Property Name	Meaning	Found On	Protected
creationdate	The date and time a resource was created.	All resources	Yes
displayname	The name of the resource to be shown to users (may be empty).	All resources	Maybe
getcontentlanguage	The language (e.g., English, Spanish) of the resource. Equivalent to the value of the `Content-Language` header on a GET response.	All resources that respond to a GET request with a content body	Maybe
getcontentlength	The length of the resource. Equivalent to the value of the `Content-Length` header on a GET response.	All resources that respond to a GET request with a content body	Yes
getcontenttype	Content type (e.g. text, text/xml, application/ms-word). Equivalent to the value of the `Content-Type` header on a GET response. May include character set information as well.	All resources that respond to a GET request with a content body	Maybe
getetag	The ETag of the resource. Equivalent to the value of the `ETag` header on a GET response (see Chapter 2, Section 2.4.2).	All resources that respond to a GET request with a content body	Yes
getlastmodified	The date and time a resource body was last modified. Equivalent to the value of the **Last-Modified** header in response to a GET request.	All resources that respond to a GET request with a content body	Yes

Table 4–1   WebDAV Required Properties *(Continued)*

Property Name	Meaning	Found On	Protected
resourcetype	The type of resource (e.g., collection).	All resources	Yes
lockdiscovery	List of detailed information for each lock existing on the resource.	All locked resources	Yes
source	The location of the source code, for a resource that is dynamically generated.	Resources with dynamically generated content (on some servers)	Not specified
supportedlock	List of the kinds of locks that may be created on this resource.	All resources on a server that supports locking	Yes

These semantic descriptions are based on the assumption that the resource is static. A static resource has a well-defined getlastmodified value, but who knows what value to give that property on a dynamic resource, where the content is being regenerated for every GET request?

These properties are discussed in more detail in Chapter 7.

Relationship of Properties and Headers

Some WebDAV properties have a close relationship to HTTP headers. These properties begin with "get" because they have the same value as headers that may be used in the GET response in HTTP/1.1. For example, getcontentlength must have the same value as the `Content-Length` header in response to a GET request for the same resource.

4.4.3   MOVE, COPY, and Properties

The behavior of live and dead properties matters most for MOVE and COPY. Since dead properties aren't ever checked or set by the server, dead properties are always moved or copied as part of the resource. However, for live properties, the most appropriate behavior depends on the semantics of the property and on the operation.

- A calculated property like creationdate or lockdiscovery may have to be recalculated. The creationdate might stay the same after a MOVE, but a COPY creates a new resource and the creationdate property is probably given a new value.

- A configuration property like quota-assigned might even be removed—for example, if the resource is being moved to a section of the repository that doesn't enforce quota limits.
- A property with data-type enforcement like the employee-start-date example will probably be moved or copied just like a dead property.

In the absence of specific information about how to treat the property in COPY or MOVE, the server should try to copy or move the property value but still provide the same semantics or calculations.

4.4.4 Property Names

Property names are XML elements, so there are strict rules about what characters can appear in property names. The first character can only be:

- A letter (any Unicode letter, not just Latin, and including accented letters)
- Underscore (_)

Subsequent characters can be:

- Letter (any Unicode letter again)
- Digit (any Unicode number, not just 0–9)
- Hyphen (-)
- Underscore (_)

That means that XML element names may not include, in any location, punctuation, spacing, or any nonalphanumeric characters other than hyphen and underscore. The W3C Recommendation for XML lists every legal character range exhaustively.

Here's a list of sample legal property names. Note that case is important, so none of these property names is equivalent to other names:

```
getcontentlanguage
getContentLanguage
GETCONTENTLANGUAGE
get-content-language
get_content_language
_getcontentlanguage
W-2_Income
catégorie
```

The following are **illegal** property names:

```
W-2 Income      contains a space
--issue--       begins with a hyphen
1099_Income     begins with a number
X.509-Name      contains a period
```

These rules are stricter than most property name rules in pre-existing software packages which sometimes cause implementation problems. For example, Microsoft Exchange exposes a number of existing mail and calendar objects over WebDAV, but these objects already had property names, which did not always fit the XML element name restrictions. Some of the illegal property names were simply changed, but others were transformed into legal XML element names in a reversible manner.

Typically, clients display their own names for well-known properties. Windows Explorer (when configured to use English) displays directory listings with a "Size" column and displays information about each file including the "Type of File." The values come from the WebDAV properties getcontentlength and getcontenttype. In a French localized WebDAV client, those well-known properties might be displayed instead as "Taille" and "Type de contenu." These localized strings derive from the client's ability to display these well-known properties and localize all strings, not from the server.

A reversible transformation could allow users to type in any property name when creating a new property. It's easier for users if they don't have to learn the odd XML element name rules. However, neither the XML or WebDAV standards provide a standard transformation. The URL-encoding mechanism defined in the URL standard [RFC1738] is a familiar mechanism (see Section 3.1.3), but it uses the percent symbol (%), which is illegal in XML element names.

Microsoft implemented transformations using an algorithm very similar to URL-encoding. Each illegal character is replaced with a sequence of seven characters. The first and last characters are underscores, the second character is an x, and the middle of the sandwich is the Unicode hex code for the character (preceded by enough zeros to make up four characters). Thus, "first name" is transformed to the property name first_x0020_name. Microsoft clients automatically detect the pattern and reverse the transform. There is no completely reliable way to detect whether a property name is escaped, but errors should be rare.

4.4.5 Property Namespaces

Property names must be unique, even if the property name is intended to be used only by a single software package. For example, a WebDAV client implementation might want to put some custom information in a property called lock-semantics. How is that client supposed to guarantee that the property isn't already being used by some other client or by the server? Interoperability would be quite difficult if custom properties could easily overlap. With overlapping property names, clients might expect to write a property that the server has protected, or clients might fail to parse a property with a new value in a different format.

To solve this problem, WebDAV requires the use of namespaces. A **namespace** is simply a qualifier that disambiguates names. In XML documents, namespaces are abbreviated with prefixes, and the prefixes are put in front of property names, but we'll see later how that's done. The namespace for all the required WebDAV properties is the DAV: namespace.

Namespaces are defined in a W3C Recommendation that extends XML [Bray99]. A namespace must be a valid URI, so it can be any well-formed URL. A URL used as a namespace doesn't need to refer to a real resource, it just has to be in the correct URL syntax.

There are three basic approaches to choosing namespaces:

- Construct a URI including a string already assigned for use by you or your organization. This can be an IP address, a network card address, an *Object Identifier* (OID, [RFC3061]) or a DNS address. Many Microsoft namespaces are URLs containing a Microsoft DNS address, although the URL doesn't actually refer to a real resource.

  ```
  http://schemas.microsoft.com/office2000/
  ```

- Include a sufficiently random number or a *Universally Unique Identifier* (UUID, [Leach98]), and use that consistently. A couple of W3C proposals used UUID namespaces.

  ```
  urn:uuid:c2f41010-65b3-11d1-a29f-00aa00c14882/
  ```

- Reserve a meaningful and human-readable name using a process such as the IETF standards process. The DAV: namespace was reserved in this way [RFC2518]. New names as short as DAV: are discouraged, and most new names begin with urn:. Xml.org submitted an RFC [RFC3120] to reserve all namespaces beginning with:

  ```
  urn:xmlorg:
  ```

Table 4–2 contains actual examples of properties and namespaces used by a few shipping WebDAV implementations. Note how different the namespace names are.

Table 4–2   Examples of Properties and Namespaces

Namespace	Properties	Used By
DAV:	getcontentlength displayname	All WebDAV clients and servers
urn:schemas-microsoft-com:office:office	Author Words	Microsoft Office 2000
urn:schemas:httpmail	subject To	Microsoft Exchange 2000
http://www.xythos.com/namespaces/ StorageServer	quota size	Xythos WebFile Server

In ordinary text, namespaces are often placed in front of names: The property creationdate in the namespace DAV: is referred to as DAV:creationdate. However, this is only used as a convenience in human documents and is not actually part of any specification.

4.4.6 Property Values

All WebDAV properties are expressed in XML; that is, all property values are transmitted as strings within an XML envelope. However, some property values have additional syntax guidelines or value transformations.

- Some string values contain XML control characters (<, >, and & characters). The control characters must be carefully escaped or the entire value must be encapsulated. Section 7.1.4 of Chapter 7 contains details on both escaping and encapsulation.
- Some string values are valid XML fragments (e.g., the lockdiscovery property is defined to be valid XML) and thus can safely be embedded in XML without escaping.
- Date and time values are usually expressed in a subset of the ISO8601 format, although the getlastmodified property is a special case. Section 7.1.9 of Chapter 7 defines date/time values.

Data typing is done only through specification writing in WebDAV. That is, a property is known to be a particular type only by reading the design specification. There's no standard way of signaling the data type of an unknown property. There have been some W3C proposals and recommendations involving data typing of XML elements [Biron01]. A proposal has been made to the WebDAV Working Group for data typing WebDAV properties [Reschke03a], but no standard has emerged.

4.4.7 Internationalization

Since property values may be in different languages in WebDAV, it must be possible also to store and retrieve language information for each property. WebDAV is designed to comply with the standard IETF internationalization practices [RFC2277].

Some text must be accompanied with a language identifier for the client to display, render, or otherwise handle the text correctly [Dürst02]. Some examples:

- A text-to-audio engine must know whether the word *location* is a French or an English word to know how to pronounce it.
- A semantic language parser or translation tool must know the language to guess the meaning of *location*, because the word means "hiring" or "rental" in French.
- Many assume that any Unicode character is always displayed consistently, but this isn't true—some characters are displayed differently in the context of different languages.
- Sorting depends on language. English dictionaries sort *ll* as two separate letters, with *llama* appearing before *location*. However, Spanish dictionaries sort *ll* as a single letter following *l*, with *localidad* appearing before *llamar*.

XML has explicit provisions for tagging property values with a language code in an attribute called *lang* in the xml namespace. These languages are identified with standard codes

[RFC3066]. WebDAV reuses the standard XML mechanism. If the client sends a PROPPATCH request with a language specified for a property value, the server must store that information and return it whenever the property value is retrieved with PROPFIND.

The WebDAV specification doesn't say whether multiple variants of a property could exist in multiple languages. For example, if one client sets an employee title property to Engineer with a language value of en, and another client sets the same property to Ingénieur with a language value of fr, are both values stored, or does one replace the other? Most servers overwrite the property. These servers store a single language code (or nothing if the language is unknown) along with a single value for the property. On these servers and the clients that use these servers, the language identifier is still useful for display and rendering.

4.5 Locks

In WebDAV, locks are used to prevent users from overwriting each other's changes accidentally. Locks augment HTTP ETags in this sense, although support for ETags is still necessary for clients and servers to behave well when creating or changing resources. ETags can be used to reliably see whether a document has changed since it was downloaded; locks reserve a document so that it can't be changed between the time it was downloaded and the time the changes are uploaded.

Locking is an optional feature for WebDAV servers. A server may not support locks and would not advertise support for locks. WebDAV clients aren't required to use locks, but a client that is used to make changes to WebDAV resources must be prepared to receive errors when a resource is locked.

WebDAV defines only **write locks.** Write locks affect write operations, such as PUT, PROPPATCH, MOVE, and COPY. Write locks do not affect read-only requests like GET, thus ordinary Web browsers are unaffected by locks on Web pages. While a resource is locked, any other user (subject to normal permissions) may still download the latest version of the resource.

In Figure 4–6, the lock is represented with a box to show what it encompasses: a resource and the resource properties. Read operations are allowed "through" the lock, and write operations are blocked by the lock, as shown by the prohibited symbols.

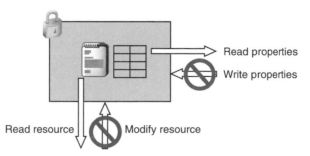

Figure 4–6 Locks prevent write operations on that resource only.

Two kinds of write locks may be supported. The common type is an **exclusive lock**, or one that prevents any other locks on the resource. Servers may also implement **shared locks**, which can exist together with other shared locks on the same resource (see Section 4.5.10).

Locks have expiration periods, which may be infinite. The user who created the lock may request that it be refreshed. The lock may expire and be removed automatically by the server, or the lock may be removed with an UNLOCK request.

Every lock has a **lock token** that uniquely identifies the lock. This token is required along with every write request, every lock refresh request, and unlock requests.

4.5.1   Locks and the Lost Update Problem

Locks solve the lost update problem with a minimum of user frustration, as illustrated in Figure 4–7. First, Client A opens the file for editing, issuing a LOCK request to reserve the file. While the file is reserved, Client B tries to open the file for editing as well. When the LOCK request fails immediately, the user can decide to wait until the lock is released before editing the file. The result is that the two users are forced to wait for each other, but their file remains consistent and incorporates both sets of changes.

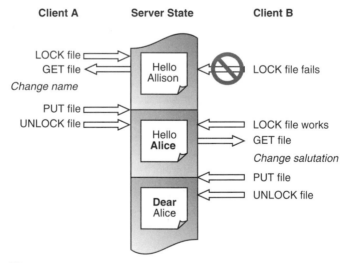

Figure 4–7   Locks solve the lost update problem by reserving the file.

Some authoring applications give the user an option to open the document "read-only" if a LOCK request fails. In Figure 4–7, Client B could have opened the document to read it initially and later reopened the document to change the salutation. When Word opens a document as read-only, it makes it very difficult for the user to then change the document and overwrite the original resource (Word tries to force the user to save in a different location). This is responsible client behavior in protecting the user from lost updates.

4.5.2   Lock Permissions

Most servers require users to have permission to change a file in order to be allowed to lock it. Otherwise, users who do not have write permission might inadvertently or maliciously lock a file. Even though a write lock is nearly useless to the user without write permission, the lock would still obstruct users who are permitted to make changes.

Windows client behavior provides one example of the reason servers do this. Windows Explorer launches Office whenever possible to read files in the Office file formats. Office 2000 always attempts to lock the files it opens—rather than ask the user every time, it makes the assumption that the file must be locked for editing. This is reasonable behavior because Office cannot tell in advance if the user has write permission, so it has no way of knowing if the lock is truly needed. Thus, any time a user navigates to an Office file to view it, the server is asked for a lock. If the server refuses to grant the lock based on lack of write permissions, Office will instead open the file as read-only and everybody gets what they want—the user who can read the file gets to read it, and users who can write the file aren't blocked by accidental locks.

4.5.3   Locks and Read Operations

Locks only block write operations (changes to content or properties); locks do not directly affect read operations. This decision allowed locks to be defined simply enough to solve the lost update problem alone, without attempting to solve other access control issues.

When a resource is locked, any user who normally has permission to read the resource can still do so. When a resource is changed, a subsequent read operation returns the latest changes, whether or not the resource is locked.

Ranged read requests are an interesting case. HTTP allows clients to request part of a resource by specifying a range of bytes for the server to return. Since the resource can change (invalidating the older ranges) between one ranged request and the next, HTTP clients always check to make sure the resource hasn't changed (using ETags; see Section 3.4 of Chapter 3). WebDAV seems to offer the ability to lock the file so that the byte ranges can be downloaded without any chance of the resource changing. However, in practice this trick isn't used. Most servers require the user to have write permission before allowing a lock, and it's not worthwhile to the client to try to lock the file (and probably fail due to permissions) just to do ranged read requests.

4.5.4   Locks vs. Access Control

A WebDAV extension [Clemm02] standardizes access control functionality, which includes write permission. Both locks and access control can prevent write operations, but they're used in different ways.

Since locks only cover write operations, a user who has permission to read a resource may read it even when it is locked by another user. Access control changes are needed to grant or remove permission to read a file.

One might imagine replacing locking with a way to revoke write permission; however, in practice this isn't workable. A single lock prevents all other users from writing the resource. In contrast, to prevent writes with access control changes, the client might have to modify several access control entries granting various permissions to several different users or groups. Even if the server had special functions to make revoking and granting write access more automatic, many users don't have permission to change access control settings on the same resources they can author.

Locking was relatively easy to define as a feature of WebDAV, whereas access control is much harder and is taking much longer to standardize. Locking and unlocking a file is much easier than trying to read or write permissions. It's also much easier to define how locks must behave than to define how permissions must behave.

A lock prevents any other user from changing permissions on the locked resource, just like any other change (although this was not formalized until the Access Control specification was published). However, the permission to change access control settings must be governed separately from the permission to write a resource. Many collaboration scenarios involve file administrators (who can change permissions) and file editors (who can change properties and bodies but not permissions). Access control usually provides greater granularity than locks do.

Access control lists are used for persistent control, whereas locks are used for transient control. A file may be locked for only a couple of minutes, and as soon as it's unlocked it's available to be updated by the same users who had write permission before the lock was created. Locks expire, so the server can easily keep the number of locks manageable by keeping timeouts short.

Chapter 13, *Access Control*, describes WebDAV access control in more detail, including the challenges in defining standard permissions and the granularity of access control entries.

4.5.5 Lock Owners

Locks are used to temporarily prevent write operations by any client that does not provide the lock token. However, as we'll see in Chapter 8, the lock token is a public piece of information, not a secret like a password. Any client can obtain the lock token; lock tokens are discoverable in order to handle clients that lose their lock tokens. However, an unauthorized client could obtain a lock token and attempt to use it. How does the server deal with these attempts?

Only the user that created the lock should be allowed to do write operations, refresh the lock, or remove it. Specifically:

- When a lock is created, the server must store the identity of the user who created the lock.
- When an update (or lock refresh or unlock) request is sent, the server should check both the lock token and the identity of the user.
- If either the lock token or the user identity is missing or different, the server should respond with an error. In the rare cases where a file is publicly writable, the identity of the original lock creator could be unknown, but only in this case should the server accept lock tokens from unknown users.

Note that both the token and the lock owner identity must be known. This double check is required because the lock owner may have more than one piece of WebDAV client software running with the same user identification. For example, the user may be running Office 2000 to edit the documents and at the same time use the sitecopy tool to organize files and collections. By requiring the lock token with any write request, WebDAV ensures that when Office 2000 has a lock on the resource, sitecopy can't move the resource until Office 2000 releases the lock. That's why locks include both lock tokens and owners: It's not enough to know that the authorized principal is accessing the resource, it must also be the right software.

One needn't worry about a loss of security just because lock tokens can be read by anybody. Since lock usage depends on the identity of the lock owner as well as the lock token provided, the lock token itself doesn't need to be a secret. User authentication to check the lock owner identity can be done with carefully designed and time-tested security systems.

4.5.6   Lock Timeout and Lock Refresh

Locks may expire after a designated lifetime, or they may last infinitely long. The ability to expire locks was made part of the standard because client software can leave locks around unwittingly, especially if the client faults or crashes in some manner. These forgotten locks could unnecessarily prevent authorized users from gaining access to change the locked resource, so eventually they are expired. As long as the client software is still active and the user is still updating the file, the client software should be able to continue refreshing the lock.

When creating a lock, the client can request a specific timeout duration, but the server makes the final decision. The server can grant a lock with a timeout either longer or shorter than that requested. When the lock timeout is reached and no refresh request has been received from the lock owner, then the server may remove the lock (and the lock token will be invalid).

The lock owner can refresh the lock any time before the timeout is reached by sending another authenticated LOCK request with the lock token. Client software should do this automatically, based on the timeout granted by the server. Most servers will successfully renew the lock an infinite number of times.

4.5.7   Locks Are Not Transactions

Locks are not transactions, even though they share some similarity. Transactions frequently include rollback and sandboxing functionality, but locks do not.

- **Rollback** is the ability to undo modifications by canceling the transaction. With WebDAV locks, modifications made while the lock existed remain after the lock expires or is removed.
- A **sandbox** is a way to work on data "out of sight" of other users so that other users do not see any changes until the transaction is committed. With WebDAV locks, any changes to the locked resource are visible to other clients.

The versioning extensions to WebDAV include rollback (uncheckout) and sandbox functionality (workspace or working resource), covered in Chapter 11, *Versioning*.

4.5.8 Removing Locks

The lock owner can remove the lock at any time. This request requires the lock token on an authenticated UNLOCK request. Ideally, client software would reliably unlock all resources when finished with them, but sometimes crashes occur or the network simply becomes unavailable to either the client or the server. Thus, the end of the timeout period also results in the removal of the lock (see Figure 4–8).

Locks can also be removed by a specially privileged user such as the administrator or resource owner. The administrator might have to use special software, perhaps a special administrative tool, but the server policy may also allow UNLOCK requests with sufficiently privileged user identification. Thus, all WebDAV clients must be able to deal with locks that disappear before the expected timeout.

No matter how a lock is removed, changes made to the resource while it was locked are permanent changes.

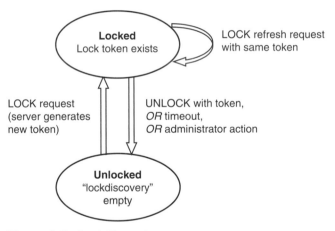

Figure 4–8   Lock life cycle.

4.5.9 Depth Locks: Locking Collections

To be completely WebDAV compliant, a server must support locks on collections if it advertises lock support at all. Microsoft IIS 5.0 is not completely compliant with WebDAV locking because it does not support locks on collections. The underlying file system does not support locks on folders, and IIS 5.0 stores all resources natively in the file system (and may allow them to be modified through local access, network file system protocols, or FTP).

What does it mean to lock a collection, since a collection doesn't have a body that can be changed? There are several ways in which a collection lock may prevent various operations.

1. Protect metadata: Only the lock holder may edit the collection's metadata.
2. Protect collection name and location in the hierarchy: Only the lock holder may move or rename the collection or any parent collection.
3. Protect the list of resources directly within the collection: Only the lock holder may add, delete, or rename any of the collection's children.
4. Protect the content of all the direct children: Only the lock holder may modify any of those children (as if each child were locked individually).
5. Protect the content of all of the collection's descendants: Only the lock holder may make any changes anywhere under the collection.

In WebDAV, any lock on a collection provides all of the protection described in items 1, 2, and 3. A full "tree" or infinite depth lock covers the last two items as well.

4.5.10   Shared Locks

Shared locks allow multiple users or processes to lock a file. Each holder of a shared lock can then supply the unique lock token for that lock to change the file. Each lock can be independently refreshed, timed out, or unlocked.

Shared locks do not show up very often, because shared locks require additional client coordination work. However, they do exist, and client software should not behave poorly when accessing a resource that happens to have multiple locks. If a client notices that a resource already has shared locks, the client should not take out another shared lock unless it has some way to know how the other lock holders are handling change control.

A frequent question is why WebDAV has shared locks in the first place, when exclusive locks offer stronger protection. The reason is that existing CM systems frequently had shared locks. The WebDAV designers wanted those systems to be able to implement WebDAV without major loss of functionality.

4.6   Summary

The WebDAV data model enforces consistent addressing, storage, and access for all the information in a repository. A well-defined data model means that clients and servers can be clear about the expected results of various interactions.

WebDAV URLs are HTTP URLs. These URLs include the scheme or protocol name, the server address with optional port, and a relative or path part. The path part of a WebDAV URL is additionally constrained so that the directory hierarchy is reflected in the path, just like file system paths. Directory URLs end in slashes.

Some WebDAV operations act on multiple files. This is done by sending a request to a collection URL and specifying the depth at which the operation will be executed. Depth operations always affect the resource being addressed as well as its child collections and resources.

Resource metadata can be stored as a set of properties with values. Every WebDAV resource has an extensible set of properties. Properties can be numbers, dates, times, or any other data that can be represented as a string. A set of standard properties is required on every resource, including resource type, creation date, and file size.

Locks solve the lost update problem in WebDAV. Any resource can be locked. A collection resource can be locked individually, or all its contained resources can be locked as well (depth infinity). Only the owner of the lock can use the lock token to make changes to a locked resource. Locks can expire so that server resources aren't reserved indefinitely.

CHAPTER 5

WebDAV Modifications to HTTP

WebDAV reuses HTTP methods in authoring scenarios. The most frequently used methods are OPTIONS, GET, PUT, and DELETE. WebDAV doesn't do very much to change the behavior of these methods, because a WebDAV server ought to work well with an HTTP client that uses these methods. However, it's worthwhile reconsidering several HTTP requests in the context of the WebDAV data model and authoring scenarios. Here are the major issues considered:

- WebDAV URLs have more defined semantics.
- WebDAV has a couple of new ways to see what functionality is supported by the server or by individual resources.
- WebDAV adds new status and error bodies in responses to HTTP methods.
- Authoring scenarios require more careful use of ETags and similar mechanisms to see when resources change.
- Authoring scenarios introduce new performance concerns when using the HTTP methods.

This chapter and the three that follow cover all of the elements of RFC2518. This chapter introduces WebDAV URLs, feature discovery, and some new requirements that WebDAV imposes on HTTP methods. Chapter 6, *WebDAV Hierarchy Operations*, covers the operations used to manage WebDAV resources: MOVE, COPY, and MKCOL. Chapter 7, *Property Operations*, covers properties names, values, and how properties are changed and retrieved with PROPPATCH and PROPFIND. Chapter 8, *Lock Operations*, describes locking, LOCK, and UNLOCK.

The requirements in RFC2518 are generally clear, but interoperability testing has found some ambiguity or tricky parts. Deployed implementations like Web Folders have implemented the standard fairly well, but with some bugs or certain expectations. Thus, these four chapters include a number of recommendations that go beyond the standard, based on the experience of WebDAV implementors and participants in standards discussions in the last five years.

5.1   WebDAV URLs and Feature Discovery

WebDAV uses HTTP URLs, but there are some differences in what the URLs mean to the client. This topic is intimately tied to feature discovery, so I've combined these two considerations, including how WebDAV extends the OPTIONS request and response.

5.1.1   Discovering WebDAV Support

Usually, the client software starts out with a URL typed in by a user, sent in email, or linked from another Web page. Starting with just a URL:

```
http://example.com:8080/hr/ergonomics/posture.doc
```

This is obviously an HTTP URL and a HTTP resource, but how can the client know if it's also a WebDAV URL and a WebDAV resource? The client needs to be able to find out in order to know if the server will accept methods like MOVE, COPY, PROPFIND, and PROPPATCH on that URL. The client can discover this through the OPTIONS request and response, as shown in Listing 5–1.

Listing 5–1   OPTIONS on a WebDAV resource.

Request:
```
OPTIONS /hr/ergonomics/posture.doc HTTP/1.1
Host: www.example.com
⏎
```

Response:
```
HTTP/1.1 200 OK
Date: Mon, 30 Jul 2001 00:30:15 GMT
Server: Apache/1.3.14 (Unix) DAV/1.0.2
DAV: 1,2
MS-Author-Via: DAV
Allow: OPTIONS, GET, HEAD, DELETE, TRACE, PROPFIND,
       PROPPATCH, COPY, MOVE, PUT, LOCK, UNLOCK
Accept-Ranges: bytes
⏎
```

The DAV header indicates that this resource supports WebDAV. It shows whether the server supports WebDAV Class 1 features alone or both WebDAV Class 1 and 2 features. The

`DAV` header contains comma-separated values, where the value 1 indicates Class 1 support, and the value 2 indicates Class 2 support. All WebDAV servers are required to support Class 1, which covers everything in RFC2518 other than locking. Class 2 includes locking as well.

We have already looked at a couple of these headers. The `Allow` header shows all the methods supported by the resource (Section 3.7.2), and the `Accept-Ranges` header shows that the server can accept byte-range requests (Section 3.7.12).

MS-Author-Via Header

Microsoft defined the `MS-Author-Via` header in order to indicate which protocol the client should use to author a Web page. Some Microsoft client software won't use WebDAV unless this header is present with the value DAV.

This header is not specified or defined in any standard; however, it is also used by some non-Microsoft WebDAV servers in order to interoperate with Microsoft Web authoring client software.

5.1.2 URLs to Collections

All WebDAV collections have URLs as well, very much like ordinary resources. WebDAV specifies that collection URLs end with a slash character (/). Although servers generally accept incoming collection URLs that do not end in a slash, servers should always generate collection URLs that do end in a slash.

```
http://example.com:8080/hr/ergonomics/
```

Collection URLs and Trailing Slash

The WebDAV RFC recommends that when a client requests a collection without including the trailing slash, the server should respond with a success message and a `Content-Location` header containing the correct URL. Theoretically, the client will use the full URL from then on. However, IE 5.0 and Netscape 4.7 ignore the `Content-Location` header and continue to use the URL without the trailing slash. This is more problematic than it sounds, because browsers handle relative URLs by appending the relative URL to the requested URL. With the trailing slash missing, the browser could construct URLs poorly. For example, the client could create:

```
http://example.com:8080/hr/ergonomicsindex.html
```

rather than

```
http://example.com:8080/hr/ergonomics/index.html
```

A server could use the **301 Moved Permanently** response to force the client to accept the proper URL (at the cost of an extra roundtrip).

Just as with a regular resource, a WebDAV client must use an OPTIONS request to find out if a URL ending in a trailing slash points to a WebDAV resource, as shown in Listing 5–2.

Listing 5–2 OPTIONS response for a WebDAV collection.

```
HTTP/1.1 200 OK
Date: Sat, 27 Oct 2001 19:16:54 GMT
Server: Apache/1.3.19 (Unix) DAV/1.0.2
MS-Author-Via: DAV
Allow: OPTIONS, PUT, LOCK, PROPFIND, PROPPATCH, UNLOCK,
       DELETE, MOVE, COPY
DAV: 1,2
↵
```

Based on this response, the client can be sure that the resource exists and is a WebDAV resource, but there's nothing reliable to prove that the resource is a collection.

The client should not rely on the format of the URL or on the OPTIONS response to determine if the resource is a collection. WebDAV allows servers to omit the trailing slash, so the URL is not a reliable indicator. The `Allow` header value might be a more reliable tool, but servers differ slightly in the methods they advertise in this header for a collection. The official way to tell if a resource is a collection is to use the resourcetype property (see Section 7.5.8).

5.1.3 Deconstructing WebDAV URLs

Since the path part of a WebDAV URL follows some well-defined rules (unlike the path part of an HTTP URL), clients can use those rules in reverse to figure out other valid URLs that may also be WebDAV resources. The only reliable way for a client to discover the parent of a given resource is by parsing its URL.

Imagine that the user clicks on the following link in email or on a Web page, and the WebDAV client has no prior knowledge of the resources on this server:

> `http://example.com:8080/hr/ergonomics/posture.doc`

The client can discover that `/hr/` is a WebDAV-compliant collection by querying its properties. Once it knows that, the client can deduce further facts:

- Because `/hr/` is a collection, `/hr/ergonomics/` is also a collection.
- `ergonomics` is a child of the "hr" collection.
- `posture.doc` is a child of the "ergonomics" collection

Now the client knows about three different resources on the WebDAV repository and can make behavioral predictions. For example, a list of the children of `/hr/ergonomics/` will include `posture.doc`. If `posture.doc` is then deleted or moved to another collection, then `/hr/ergonomics/` will no longer contain `posture.doc`.

One result of the WebDAV URL rules is that every operation that affects the name or parent collection of a resource also changes its URL. We'll see shortly how the MOVE method can be used either to rename a resource or move it to another directory, both of which will alter the URL of the resource.

5.1.4   Limits to HTTP URL Decomposition

It's important to remember that some elements in the path of a WebDAV URL may not be Web-DAV collections. Some of the early parts of the path might have another meaning to the server.

For example, a WebDAV server can be implemented using the Java servlet engine. Servlets are often configured to use addresses of the form:

```
http://example.com/servlet/servlet-name
```

The path fragment `servlet` is an instruction to the Web software to invoke the servlet engine, and the fragment `servlet-name` is an instruction to the servlet engine to run a particular servlet. Let's say a WebDAV servlet is configured as:

```
http://example.com/servlet/dav
```

If that URL points to a regular Java servlet, then the client can query a number of different URLs to see if they are WebDAV collections. Table 5–1 lists what the client finds.

Sometimes administrators want to use the same server or hostname to host multiple applications. For example, a server called `multi.example.com` may host several HTTP hierarchies with different functionality:

```
http://multi.example.com/mail    hosts a Web-based mail GUI
http://multi.example.com/dav     hosts a WebDAV repository
http://multi.example.com/cal     hosts a Web-based calendar
```

 Because these three addresses all refer to Web-based applications, each URL will respond successfully to an HTTP OPTIONS request. However, the three responses will be different. For the mail and calendar services, an OPTIONS response would look something like

Table 5–1   Sample URLs and Possible OPTIONS Responses

URL	What an OPTIONS Response Indicates
`http://example.com/`	An OPTIONS response without a DAV: header indicates that this is a normal Web server URL.
`http://example.com/servlet/`	An OPTIONS response without a DAV: header indicates that this is a normal Web server URL. The URL happens to point to a Java servlet engine.

Table 5–1   Sample URLs and Possible OPTIONS Responses *(Continued)*

URL	What an OPTIONS Response Indicates
`http://example.com/servlet/dav/`	An OPTIONS response with a DAV: header indicating Class 1 and Class 2 support. The URL happens to point to a Java servlet engine that implements the WebDAV specification.
	If the server allows clients to browse the repository but not lock the entire repository, the `Allow` header might show support for PROPFIND but not LOCK.
`http://example.com/servlet/dav/accounting/`	An OPTIONS response with a DAV: header indicating Class 1 and Class 2 support. The `Allow` header shows all the methods appearing in Listing 5–2. Thus, the resource is a full WebDAV resource that happens to be hosted by a Java servlet.

the regular HTTP OPTIONS response shown in Section 3.3.7. Only the second URL, where a WebDAV repository is hosted, will show WebDAV support through the DAV response header. The client now knows that only certain parts of the namespace support WebDAV functionality.

Unfortunately, early releases of Windows XP had a serious problem decomposing Web-DAV URLs. When a WebDAV repository is mapped to a drive letter using the Windows XP WebDAV drivers, the repository root must respond as a WebDAV resource. Given a URL such as `http://example.com/servlet/dav/accounting/`, the XP software immediately does an OPTIONS request to `http://example.com/`. If that URL does not appear to support WebDAV, then Windows XP fails the mapping request, even though the URL it was originally given would show WebDAV support if it were queried. The next section explains how a client like Windows XP should behave.

5.1.5   Finding the Repository Root with OPTIONS

Client software sometimes attempts to find out the root of a repository. This could be desirable in order to cache server feature support information, cookies, or authentication information or to be able to mount the root of the repository once rather than have to mount separately a number of collections deep in the repository.

A naive approach to this problem would be to assume that the root of the repository is the root path element, or /. However, as we've just shown, that can fail. If a client must find the topmost directory that supports WebDAV, it may have to try every element in the path.

Given the following URL:

```
http://example.com/servlet/dav/accounting/index.html
```

then the recommended approach to determining the root of the repository is to work up the collection chain and use OPTIONS requests to find out which elements are WebDAV collections. Each time, the client should check the OPTIONS response to make sure that the resource responds and that it supports WebDAV. (Although PROPFIND could theoretically retrieve the same information and more, it's not as reliable, because PROPFIND may be subject to more permissions restrictions than OPTIONS requests.)

In this case:

1. Send the first OPTIONS request to `/servlet/dav/accounting/`. Server shows WebDAV support, so we continue.
2. Send the next OPTIONS request to `/servlet/dav/`. Server shows WebDAV support again, so we continue.
3. Send the next OPTIONS request to `/servlet/`. Server may respond with a successful status code, but the `DAV` header is not in the response. Stop ascending now, because it's unlikely that `http://example.com/` will support WebDAV.
4. Mount or cache `/servlet/dav/` as the root of the repository.

5.2   New Response Status Codes

WebDAV employs most of the status codes defined in HTTP/1.1. In addition, WebDAV defines a few new status codes for WebDAV-specific situations. These are the new status codes:

- 102 Processing was introduced in order to be able to deal with time-consuming requests. The server may be able to respond to let the client know it's working on the response even though it's not done.
- 207 Multi-Status is a special response used when there may be multiple operation status reports that need to be combined into one response. 207 Multi-Status may have both success and failure codes, inside a text/xml body. The client must parse the body in order to pinpoint errors or successes (see Section 5.5.1).
- 422 Unprocessable Entity The server cannot successfully process request body. Usually, this crops up when a request like PROPFIND has an XML body. The XML body may be missing a required field or have some problem rendering it semantically incorrect. If the XML body is syntactically incorrect (not well-formed), 400 Bad Request should be returned instead. If the server does not support the body's content type, then 415 Unsupported Media Type should be returned instead.
- 423 Locked indicates that the resource is locked and cannot be altered without the correct lock token (and authorization).
- 424 Failed Dependency indicates that an action depended on another action that could not be completed. For example, in a single PROPPATCH request, some set operations might fail with specific error codes, and the remaining set operations must therefore fail

due to the atomic nature of PROPPATCH. This status code is used for the resources where the operation might otherwise have succeeded.

- 507 Insufficient Storage indicates that not enough space (memory, disk, quota) can be allocated to successfully complete this request.

 Not many WebDAV servers seem to use 102 Processing code; however, clients *must* be prepared to receive it and perhaps wait for the final response, rather than fail gracelessly. Some client developers claim that their software does support 102 Processing.

5.3   GET

One of the important design goals of WebDAV was that a Web page should be accessible in the same way via GET, with or without WebDAV functionality. The GET method does just what it always did: It downloads the Web page, image, or document. Even locks do not affect GET, because locks only affect write operations. Thus, ordinary Web browsers can browse a WebDAV site as easily as a Web site—and in fact, they do not know the difference.

Like Web servers, WebDAV servers frequently support GET requests to collections. The response is usually the same: a dynamically generated HTML page with links to all the members of the collection. This is generally not attempted by WebDAV clients because the PROPFIND response can contain a much more flexible set of information and is much better suited for machine parsing.

5.3.1   Getting Collections

GET behaves the same way with WebDAV collections as it did with directories in HTTP; that is, the behavior is undefined and may vary from server to server (Section 3.1.4). This may continue to be useful for HTTP client support, but it is not likely to be useful for WebDAV clients. Instead, WebDAV clients use PROPFIND (Section 7.2.1) to get properties for a collection and to list its contents in a machine-parsable format.

5.3.2   Resource Integrity

Because a WebDAV server is likely to be used for authoring, WebDAV clients and servers must be careful to download a complete resource body—more so than normal HTTP clients and servers. An incomplete or corrupted file body might be detected as soon as the file is opened. However, applications might not be capable of detecting corruption in all file types (e.g., plain text files). In authoring scenarios, an undetected corruption may not be noticed by the user either, and when the user saves his or her changes back to the server, the corrupted version is preserved.

There are a few simple ways to achieve more consistent resource integrity:

- A WebDAV server should always indicate the expected body length and never close the TCP connection uncleanly. These practices give the client extra information to check resource integrity.

- A WebDAV client should check the expected content length against the number of bytes received. If there is a mismatch or if the body length is not specified in any way, then the client might warn the user or indicate an error.

- The `Content-MD5` response header [RFC1864] can contain a digest value calculated from the resource body being transmitted. If a client receives this header in response to a GET request, the client can calculate its own body digest value and compare it to ensure that the resource was correctly transmitted. If both the server and client calculate the same digest value, it's extremely likely they have the same body content. Similarly, if a server receives this header in a PUT request, it should perform the same calculation and fail the PUT request if the digest does not match.

5.3.3 How to Retrieve Source Code

Web site software usually includes support for dynamically generated pages. Sometimes these are stored in the same directories as static pages. In Microsoft IIS, for example, Active Server Pages (ASP) files are stored with internal bits of script that are executed (usually, transformed into HTML fragments) whenever the file is retrieved. Java Servlet engines supporting the Java Server Pages (JSP) specification also store dynamic pages alongside static pages.

Authoring sites with dynamic pages presents a problem: When the Web page is retrieved with a HTTP GET request, the server automatically executes the script in the page and sends the result as the response. How can the author retrieve the full source code to modify the page? HTTP presents no solution to this problem.

WebDAV solves this problem by assigning the source code one or more new URLs, each different from the regular URL for the dynamically generated page. Clients can find out the source code URLs for a given Web page by querying the WebDAV source property (described in detail in Section 7.5.9) and then request the source code using those URLs.

Changing the source code of dynamic pages is even more complicated, and the WebDAV specification doesn't resolve all issues. For example:

- WebDAV does not specify whether the resource named by the URL in the source property must be a WebDAV resource, capable of being locked and having metadata.
- There's no defined way to create a new source code file and indicate that the server should process it rather than handle it as a static page.
- It's unclear how to represent the roles of multiple source files and how they relate to or depend on each other.

5.4 PUT

The PUT method is much more useful combined with WebDAV functionality than with HTTP alone. Now the client can figure out which resources are collections and what resources already exist in those collections. Then the client can either create new resources in a collection or modify

---

The Translate Header

Microsoft IIS 5.0 and Exchange 2000 implemented an alternative approach to retrieving source code. The custom-defined `Translate` header takes a value of T for true or F for false. When the value is F, the server returns the source code file for the resource, unprocessed. With a value of T, the resource is returned as it is for normal browsers. When the header is not present, it's assumed to be T, because that's the way normal browsers would send requests.

When Microsoft WebDAV clients are in authoring mode, as opposed to browsing, they send "`Translate: F`" with each request. For example, Office 2000 is an authoring tool and therefore sends this header.

The WebDAV Working Group rejected this approach because source code can involve more than one file per resource.

---

existing resources. The format in which the resource is sent is typically the format in which it is stored and returned in response to future GET requests.

Normally, PUT requests must include the `Content-Type` and `Content-Length` headers (in addition to the `Host` header required on every request). The `Content-Type` header is necessary so that the server knows what MIME type to store for the document, because file extensions are an unreliable way of determining the type of document. The client must send the `Content-Length` header unless it chooses another way to indicate the end of the body, such as chunked transfer encoding (Section 3.2.8). This is the only encoding that a client can assume the server will support. Thus, a file sent in a zipped format will remain a zipped file when stored on the server, and other clients will download the same zipped file.

When a resource already exists with the address used in the Request-URI of the PUT request, the server will normally overwrite the previous resource. If the client doesn't expect an existing resource to be overwritten, it must use the `If-None-Match` header (Section 3.7.6).

Normally, the body sent in a PUT request is stored exactly the way it was received after the transfer encodings are undone. However, some servers (e.g., the Tamino XML server) are known to modify the file so that the results of a subsequent GET return a slightly different body. The `Content-Length` of the stored file is immediately different from the length the client sent.

Normally, a file body doesn't change from one PUT to another, but some servers modify the file body in other situations. For example, Exchange 2000 modifies the bodies of some resources such as appointments when the properties of the appointment are changed. A client holding a lock on the resource may be surprised to see the body change when it hasn't issued a PUT request, but clearly with Exchange 2000 this can happen.

WebDAV defines a few new status codes that can be returned in response to a PUT request. These include 423 Locked, 424 Failed Dependency, and 507 Insufficient Storage. These errors are used to report PUT operation failures in distributed authoring situations: when the

> ## PUT and Dynamic Resources
>
> Only a few WebDAV servers (such as IIS 5.0) support authoring dynamic resources. When PUT can be used to create or overwrite dynamic resources, it behaves in much the same way as with static resources. These servers only support dynamic resources like JSP and ASP files where the source code is stored in a single file on the file system along with static resources. Thus, the Request-URI for the source code is the same as for the dynamically generated response.
>
> No WebDAV servers are known to allow the PUT method to overwrite auxiliary files such as class files or library files that may be used in generating dynamic pages.

resource is locked, when the parent collection hasn't been created yet, and when quota or disk storage has been used up.

PUT requests are frequently forbidden due to permission restrictions. As with other methods, if permission is denied, the server should use the status response 401 Unauthorized.

5.4.1 Partial PUT

Since WebDAV clients use PUT much more frequently, several have suggested using the HTTP Range header (Section 3.7.12) on the PUT request to enable the client to upload only part of a file. This doesn't work, because HTTP defines the Range header (including how to handle it and what errors to return) only for the GET method.

Even if a server added custom support for the Range header on PUT requests, the feature would be problematic:

- The Range header has no way to change the length of the file. It only expresses ranges of bytes within the known length of the body.
- Many file formats require internal consistency. A Word document might become invalid if only some of its bytes were changed. The client might intend to do multiple partial PUT requests to finish changing the file to a new valid document, but in the meantime, other clients could download a corrupted document.

This is still a useful feature in theory, but more protocol design is required to make it work.

5.4.2 Avoiding Lost Updates

Recall the lost update problem described in Section 2.4.2; a client can never know if a file has changed since it was last downloaded unless it uses ETags (Section 3.4) to tell the server what state the resource ought to be in.

WebDAV clients use PUT much more often, so now I'll show exactly how to avoid the lost update problem, whether or not the server supports locks (see Listing 5–3). The client includes the If-Match header (Section 3.7.6) with the ETag that corresponds to the state of the entity when it was downloaded. If all the ETags in the header match, then the request should go ahead. Otherwise, the server must fail the request.

 All WebDAV clients should use If-Match to avoid the lost update problem whenever possible. (Section 8.6.3 explains why this is needed even if the resource is locked.)

Listing 5–3   PUT using the If header.

```
PUT /hr/ergonomics/posture.doc HTTP/1.1
Host: www.example.com
If-Match: "etag1101"
Content-Length: xxx
Content-Type: application/ms-word
⏎
[body omitted]
```

If-Match may also be used with any other request method to ensure that the state of the resource on the server is what the client expects. If the state does not match, the request fails.

5.4.3   Creating New Resources Safely

PUT can also be used to create new resources on the server. The hierarchical namespace and data model allow the client to construct a new URL. The client takes the URL of the collection where it wants to create a resource, adds the name of the resource (separated by slash), and the result is the new resource's URL. For example, to create index.html in the collection /hr/, the client constructs the absolute path /hr/index.html.

It's very important for the client to ensure that it is indeed creating a new resource, because otherwise the client may overwrite an existing resource unwittingly and the content that was stored there will be lost. It's not enough to simply check to see if the resource exists by getting a directory listing before the PUT, because in the meantime, a resource with the same name can be created by another client. There are only a few special circumstances where it really doesn't matter if a resource of the same name already exists (e.g., when a backup process uploads all the resources in a directory, it may create or overwrite resources without checking).

To create a new resource without any risk of overwriting an existing resource, clients use the If-None-Match header. With the special * value indicating "any ETag," this header allows the client to assert that there must be no entity stored at this URL.

```
If-None-Match: *
```

If the resource does not exist—that is, if the requested URI does not refer to any entity at all—the request will be allowed.

A Poor Solution to Safe Resource Creation
IE 5.5 uses a poor approach when attempting to create a new resource; it sends a HEAD request to the resource it's planning to create. If the HEAD response returns with results, IE prompts the user whether to overwrite the existing resource. If the resource is 404 Not Found, IE 5.5 creates the file without prompting. The problem with this approach is that there's a period after the HEAD response during which a file with that name can be created by another client. The PUT request from IE 5.5 will overwrite that resource if it is created in the meantime.   It's not clear why IE 5.5 uses HEAD instead of locking; perhaps it was designed to function with Web servers as well as WebDAV servers.

5.4.4   Generating Unique URLs

Sometimes clients need to add a resource with a unique name to a collection. The client doesn't care what name the resource is given, it only wants to make sure to add a new resource rather than overwrite a resource already there. Section 5.4.3 described how to use conditional headers to avoid overwriting a resource if the name does conflict, but it would be nice to have a unique URL that won't conflict with one already there.

To do this, first the client should generate a relatively unique ID—it could include the user's ID or machine name plus a random number. The client can use HEAD as described earlier to see if the file already exists. If it does, choose another name. When the file is actually being created, the client should be sure to use the `If-None-Match: *` header on the PUT request.

Microsoft has a nonstandard solution for this little problem. With some Microsoft Web-DAV servers, the client may use the POST request with the parent collection as the target of the request. The server saves the body of the request as a new resource (just like PUT), but it generates a unique URL for the new file. Exchange 2000 is known to support this feature. However, this behavior is not required, nor is it advertised as supported; therefore, the client can't rely on the server behaving in this manner.

5.4.5   Pipelining

To modify or create a number of documents, an equal number of PUT requests must be generated. If the server supports pipelining (and most do), all the PUT requests can be shoved into a connection as fast as they can be streamed onto the network. This has the advantage of incurring the cost of the connection latency only once, instead of once per request. Keeping latency costs down is key to good performance over the Internet and is usually more important than keeping messages brief.

Pipelining PUT requests is only possible when each PUT request will be made independently of the success of previous pipelined requests.

5.4.6   PUT and Collections

PUT is not defined for a collection. It's not forbidden, so in theory a server could accept a PUT request on a collection and do something with the entity in the request body. No clients or servers are known to support this.

The WebDAV specification doesn't say exactly which error to use if a server receives a PUT request for a collection URL. The 409 Conflict error is a reasonable choice, but it is already defined for PUT, to be used when the parent collection doesn't exist yet. It might be more helpful to use 403 Forbidden.

Servers that don't allow PUT to a collection may still show PUT as an allowed method in the OPTIONS response for a collection (see Listing 5–2). One line of reasoning assumes that PUT is allowed to create a new resource inside a collection, so PUT should appear in the `Allow` header. Another line of reasoning is that PUT is not allowed on the collection URL itself; therefore, it shouldn't appear in the `Allow` header. Clients must be prepared for either behavior.

5.5   DELETE

WebDAV clients use DELETE much more often than HTTP clients. DELETE is used to clean up temporary resources and remove resources that are no longer wanted. Since DELETE was defined in HTTP for any kind of resource, DELETE can be used to delete collections as well as ordinary resources (see Listing 5–4).

Listing 5–4   Successful DELETE collection.

Request:
```
DELETE /users/alice/temp/ HTTP/1.1
Host: example.com
↵
```

Response:
```
HTTP/1.0 204 No Content
Date: Tue, 15 Nov 1994 08:12:31 GMT
Content-Length: 0
↵
```

When resources are locked, the DELETE request must include the correct lock tokens to successfully delete the resources. If the DELETE request is successful, then all locks on deleted resources are removed. All properties are removed as well.

WebDAV introduces some new status codes that may be returned in response to a DELETE request: 102 Processing, 207 Multi-Status, 423 Locked, and 507 Insufficient Storage.

5.5.1 Multi-Status Response

A DELETE request to a WebDAV collection is automatically assumed to have a depth of infinity, even if a `Depth` header was not sent by the client. In fact, the depth must be infinity because if a collection is deleted, all its children must be deleted.

When multiple resources are addressed in a single DELETE request and there are internal failures, it becomes more difficult to report errors. The request to delete a number of resources could fail for a number of reasons—the resources are locked or the user doesn't have permission and so on. WebDAV defines a special **Multi-Status** response body to hold as many error codes as necessary and a URL to associate with each error code so that the client can figure out which resources caused the request to fail. The client cannot assume that a 207 Multi-Status response is a success response. It is more frequently an error response, even though the response code is in the 200 block of codes.

Listing 5–5 is a failed attempt to delete a collection. The collection contained one locked child and one child that couldn't be deleted due to a permissions check failure.

Listing 5–5 DELETE collection with partial failure: Multi-Status response.

Request:
```
DELETE /users/alice/temp/ HTTP/1.1
Host: www.example.com
⏎
```

Response:
```
HTTP/1.1 207 Multi-Status
Content-Type: text/xml; charset=UTF-8
Content-Length: 230
Date: Wed, 12 Mar 2003 20:54:02 GMT

<?xml version="1.0" encoding="utf-8" ?>
<D:multistatus xmlns:D="DAV:">
   <D:response>
      <D:href>http://www.example.com/users/alice/temp/ ↵
         japan-trip-log.txt</D:href>
      <D:status>HTTP/1.1 423 Locked</D:status>
   </D:response>
   <D:response>
      <D:href>http://www.example.com/users/alice/temp/ ↵
         meeting-notes.txt</D:href>
      <D:status>HTTP/1.1 403 Forbidden</D:status>
   </D:response>
</D:multistatus>
```

The 207 Multi-Status response body always begins with the top-level `multistatus` element. This element always contains one or more `response` elements. Each `response` element corresponds to a different resource for which status information is being provided. Each `response` element always contains an `href` element to identify the resource and a `status` element to explain what happened to it. The `href` element contains a URI with the address to the resource, and the `status` element contains an HTTP/1.1 status code and text, formatted together as a string.

URLs in Multi-Status   The response in Listing 5–5 includes the full URL for the resource to which the error applies. Although this may not be sufficiently clear in the original RFC2518 document, it is necessary to include the full URL for each errored resource inside a 207 Multi-Status response.

 Successes in Multi-Status   The WebDAV specification says that success messages should not appear in the 207 Multi-Status response, on the theory that only errors need to be pointed out. In an atomic operation (such as PROPPATCH), there aren't supposed to be any successes if there are any failures. However, some server implementations include successes anyway, so the client must be prepared to ignore these. Some servers are known to return successes in 207 Multi-Status responses to MOVE requests. In fact, implementors increasingly recognize that success status codes are useful in Multi-Status responses, and the standard may change to reflect that.

Permissions Failures in Multi-Status   Permissions failures in 207 Multi-Status responses are a little peculiar because normally when a client receives a 401 Authorization Required response, the client prompts the user for authorization and repeats the entire request. However, when multiple operations are attempted, there may not be a single authorization (set of user permissions or credentials) that allows all operations to be accomplished. Therefore, the wisest thing for the client to do may be to retry the operations on the resources one by one, providing authorization as needed.

5.5.2   Handling XML Bodies

This is the first time I've shown an XML body as a request or response body. WebDAV uses XML to marshal large amounts of information in requests or responses. There are a couple tricky things to note.

Formatting of href Elements   The `href` element appears in many WebDAV XML bodies, but the Multi-Status response is the most common location. This element contains a text value that is a full URL. There are a couple of tricks to remember to handle this element correctly, because the set of valid URL characters is different from the set of valid XML characters, and invalid character escaping is different as well.

- URIs can legally contain the reserved character &, which must be escaped in XML. This character appears in HTTP URLs with parameters. If the & symbol appears in a

URI within XML it must be escaped as & when marshaled in an XML element. WebDAV resource URLs don't often contain &, so this usually isn't an issue.

- URIs can't contain the characters < or >. Thus, there's no need to escape these characters so that the XML is valid. If by chance a WebDAV processor receives an href element with the characters > or <, then the URI in the element is not legal and this can be rejected as a bad request (or response).

- URIs can contain characters that are valid in XML but must be escaped for the URI itself to be legal. For example, a space frequently appears in file names, but it must be escaped as %20 in a URI. A sender must not put the unescaped space character in a href element, because space is illegal in URI. However, a WebDAV recipient seeing a href value with a space could choose to accept the value and escape it.

- Leading and trailing spaces should not appear. They can be stripped if received in an href element.

Formatting of status Elements   The status element also contains text, but it's much easier to handle because none of the status numbers or text used in HTTP or WebDAV contain <, >, or &. The only trick to remember is that servers might include extra spaces or line returns in this value, even though they shouldn't. A client can easily handle this by trimming beginning or trailing white space from the value before handling the value.

Don't Forget Prefixes   Listing 5–5 showed the D: prefix used to represent the DAV namespace. It's rather traditional to use a mnemonic to help the reader when XML is shown in books or specifications, so WebDAV examples frequently show D: or d:. However, the sender can declare any prefix. The sender could declare the DAV namespace to be the default namespace and have no prefix, or the sender could assign prefixes more randomly so that the DAV namespace is indicated with a prefix like b32:. Prefixes are case-sensitive.

Handling Extensions   WebDAV requires that clients and servers be able to handle unknown elements by ignoring them. For example, the Multi-Status response could be extended with a custom element, so that this fragment appears in a response like Listing 5–5:

```
<D:response>
    <D:href>http://www.example.com/users/alice/temp/ ↲
        meeting-notes.txt</D:href>
    <D:status>HTTP/1.1 403 Forbidden</D:status>
    <e:status-explanation
        xmlns:e="http://www.example.com/namespaces/">
        You do not have permission to delete this resource.
    </e:status-explanation>
</D:response>
```

WebDAV requires that this custom element be ignored if it is not understood by the client. This rule applies to all WebDAV XML body marshaling. "Ignored" means that the body is processed as if the unrecognized element were not there. It does not mean that the recipient ignores the body or throws an error.

5.5.3 Atomicity

WebDAV does not require the DELETE operation to be atomic. If errors occur during the deletion of a WebDAV collection, the server may behave in a number of ways.

A server could roll back the operation when errors occur, as Xythos WebFile Server does. This is guaranteed to leave the collection with a consistent set of resources in containers that still exist. When the failed DELETE is done, no resources have actually been removed. To remove resources, the client must either issue more granular DELETE requests or fix what when wrong and issue the collection DELETE request again.

A server could also offer best-effort DELETE, as IIS 5.0 does. Typically, in this case, the server starts trying to delete individual resources one by one. If a collection within the DELETE scope is empty, then the server attempts to delete the collection. Whenever the server encounters a failure, it continues deleting other resources, but it does not delete collections that still contain children. If a server does best-effort deleting, the WebDAV specification requires that it keep around parents of undeleted resources, so that clients can still address these resources and perhaps fix what went wrong. The client may then be able to finish the incomplete DELETE by issuing more DELETE requests.

A server could also quit working when it reaches the first failure, but this doesn't seem to be as useful to clients as either the atomic or the best-effort implementations. For one thing, that gives the client information about only one error, when there could be several undeletable resources. In any case, if a resource cannot be deleted, its parent must not be deleted. Therefore, if the resource `/test/index.html` cannot be deleted, then `/test` must not be deleted either.

With any of these variations, the server must still inform the client which resources could not be deleted by returning error codes in the Multi-Status response. However, it's still hard for the client to tell if the server did an atomic DELETE or a partial DELETE. That's because the RFC2518 specifically says that the DELETE Multi-Status response should not contain the 424 Failed Dependency status code. Thus, a server like Xythos WFS cannot report all the resources that could have been deleted but were not because the whole operation was rolled back. The response from IIS 5.0 is likely to be much the same—it does not report all the resources that were successfully deleted. Both responses (atomic and partial failure) would look like Listing 5–5.

 The client must issue a PROPFIND request following a failed collection DELETE request in order to see which resources remain.

5.5.4 Destroy Data or Move to Trash?

A successful DELETE can behave in a couple of different ways:

• It can remove the data that is referred to by the Request-URI.

- It can remove the mapping between the Request-URI and the data that is referred to. The data may still be somewhere on the repository—for example, in a server-maintained "trash" or "recycling bin" collection.

The difference between these two behaviors depends on whether WebDAV methods operate on addresses (URLs) or on data (resources). This philosophical but sometimes practical debate has come up so many times, we'll explain the basic issues in the next section.

5.5.5 Operations on Addresses or Resources

There are a number of ways to think about operations when addresses are used as references for objects.

The first model is that operations apply to addresses. Under this model, when the client issues the DELETE request in Listing 5–4, the server unbinds or unmaps the address http://www.example.com/users/alice/temp/ from any resource it is pointing to. After a successful DELETE, subsequent responses to that URL return 404 Not Found.

The other model is that operations apply to resources. When the client issues the DELETE request in Listing 5–4, the server locates the resource addressed by http://www.example.com/users/alice/temp/ and erases, removes, destroys, or deallocates the resource. After a successful DELETE, subsequent responses to that URL return 404 Not Found.

 The client can't tell the difference between these cases, and WebDAV doesn't unambiguously require either behavior. The definition for DELETE on a noncollection in RFC2518 implies that the operation manipulates the address:

```
If the DELETE method is issued to a non-collection resource
whose URIs are an internal member of one or more collections,
then during DELETE processing a server MUST remove any URI for
the resource identified by the Request-URI from collections
which contain it as a member.
```

However, the definition for DELETE on a collection resource implies that the operation acts on the underlying resource itself, rather than the address:

```
DELETE instructs that the collection specified in the Request-
URI and all resources identified by its internal member URIs
are to be deleted.
```

Most of the time, it doesn't matter to the client. Either way, the client sends a DELETE request to a URL, and subsequent requests to that URL return 404 Not Found. However, it matters greatly when writing a server implementation, because a clean addressing model helps a server implementor design clean interfaces and classes. It also matters to protocol designers considering extending WebDAV (see the sidebar, *Addresses, Resources, and Bindings*).

Since HTTP and WebDAV don't ever state firmly whether operations apply to addresses or data, various WebDAV extension designers and server implementors have made different unconscious or conscious assumptions. The lack of a firm model means that it's easier for servers

---

Addresses, Resources, and Bindings

The decision as to whether operations apply to addresses or resources is especially relevant to proposals to extend WebDAV to support **bindings** [Clemm03]. A server may have two addresses for the same collection of resources, or in other words, two bindings to the same collection resource. If a DELETE request is applied to one of those two bindings, one can imagine two results:

- The server applies the operation to the URL such that only that binding is destroyed, and the other binding continues to point to the same collection.
- The server applies the operation to the underlying collection such that the collection and its descendants are erased from storage. Either both bindings disappear or one disappears and the other breaks.

The bindings proposals will have to have a consistent approach and explain how it applies in many cases or define on a case-by-case basis what happens when multiple bindings exist.

---

to behave in whatever manner best suits their designs and purposes. On the other hand, it also means that clients and users can't know as much about what a server will really do. Just because a DELETE operation was successful, the user can't assume that the server has destroyed the data.

5.6 Summary

WebDAV reuses the HTTP methods, particularly OPTIONS, GET, PUT, and DELETE, to fully support remote authoring. A few new status codes are defined for WebDAV-specific errors in response to these existing methods.

WebDAV URLs are HTTP URLs but with a few more restrictions in how they're constructed. The directories that contain a resource must be included in the path part of that resource's URL, just like file paths in local file systems. Collection URLs are more defined in WebDAV and must end in a slash (/).

Support for WebDAV on a Web server can be discovered with the OPTIONS method. The OPTIONS method can be sent to either the server as a whole or to specific URLs, because specific resources might have different features. The OPTIONS response shows which WebDAV features are supported.

The GET method works as it does in HTTP. Authoring clients only have a few extra considerations when using GET, such as the need to make sure that the entire resource was retrieved.

The PUT method works as it does in HTTP. Authoring clients also need to consider how to create new resources without overwriting existing resources and how PUT performs with large files or a large number of files.

The DELETE method works as it does in HTTP. In addition, the DELETE method may be used to delete multiple resources by addressing a collection. Because DELETE can address multiple resources, WebDAV defines a new response body for DELETE to show multiple errors.

Although WebDAV can theoretically allow GET and PUT to author source code, in practice this doesn't work. The specification doesn't provide enough information to know how to author the source files that generate dynamic Web resources, particularly when multiple source files are involved.

CHAPTER 6

WebDAV Hierarchy Operations

This chapter and the following two chapters cover the new WebDAV methods one by one, starting with those that affect the organization of files on the repository. The hierarchy manipulation methods are:

```
MKCOL
MOVE
COPY
```

Chapter 7, *Property Operations*, covers the metadata manipulation methods:

```
PROPFIND
PROPPATCH
```

Chapter 8, *Lock Operations*, finishes with the lock manipulation methods:

```
LOCK
UNLOCK
```

6.1 Why WebDAV Defines New Methods

WebDAV request operations are HTTP/1.1 requests with the same structure and protocol/version field but new method strings. The WebDAV designers could have gone with an approach like that taken by SOAP [Box00], which also extends HTTP, but where all requests are made using the same method (POST). There are advantages and disadvantages to each approach, and the advantages depend on the application.

The advantages to defining new methods for WebDAV:

- It's easy to filter for WebDAV requests by looking for the method name. This puts security more firmly in the hands of network administrators.
- HTTP access controls may be based on the method; for example, a user may have permission to do a GET but not a PUT. WebDAV works nicely with access control by defining new methods for operations that may have different permissions.
- It's easier to define body types, headers, and errors for new methods, rather than specify how new body types and new headers interact with old methods and old headers.

The primary disadvantage to defining new methods is that firewalls and proxies may block methods other than those defined in HTTP/1.1. WebDAV implementors have also found that some legacy Web application servers don't support new methods, making it difficult to implement a WebDAV server using those application servers as a platform. However, recent firewall, proxy, and application server releases tend to do a better job of handling new methods.

If you find yourself in a situation where the WebDAV methods are blocked or not supported by existing software, it's possible to tunnel the requests. Two basic approaches have been shown to work:

- If a firewall is blocking the WebDAV methods, try tunneling through the CONNECT request [RFC2817]. The CONNECT request allows Web browsers to make SSL and TLS connections to Web servers outside the firewall, even if the firewall only supports port 80 [Rescorla01]. This mechanism only tunnels through the firewall on the client's site when the client initiates the request. CONNECT allows clients to tunnel out, not in.
- If an application server does not support WebDAV requests from clients, put a trivial filter program in place before the request reaches the application server. This filter can replace the WebDAV request method with POST and insert a custom header specifying the original request method. After the application server passes the POST request to the WebDAV software, the original method can be recovered from the custom header.

These workarounds are less and less necessary as WebDAV becomes more widespread and better supported.

6.2 MKCOL: Create Collection

A collection on a WebDAV server acts as a container for resources. The name of the collection always appears in the URLs for resources inside it, determining part of the path to the resource. MKCOL is used to create new collections inside existing collections.

To create a collection, the client first builds the URL for the new collection by appending the new collection's name onto the parent collection's URL. It then sends a MKCOL request to the constructed URL (see Listing 6–1).

┌───┐
│ **Why MKCOL Is Not PUT**   │
├───┤
│ The PUT method is already used to create new resources. Why not reuse PUT to create │
│ a collection? One reason is that PUT might conceivably have its own meaning and │
│ behavior for a collection, different from the behavior for MKCOL. Collections may │
│ have members, but there's no technical reason that collections may not also have docu- │
│ ment bodies, just like regular resources. PUT could then be used to create or modify │
│ the collection's document content. This is not part of the standard, because many file │
│ systems have nowhere to store this document yet, but the possibility was envisioned by │
│ the WebDAV designers.   │
└───┘

Listing 6–1   MKCOL request and response.

Request:
```
MKCOL /hr/recruiting HTTP/1.1
Host: www.example.com
↵
```

Response:
```
HTTP/1.0 201 Created
Date: Sun, 29 Jul 2001 15:24:17 GMT
Content-Length: 0
↵
```

The server created a collection named `recruiting` inside the existing collection `hr`.
The parent collection `hr` must already exist, but `recruiting` must not. If a resource named
`recruiting` already exists, whether it's a collection or not, the request will fail.

The MKCOL request does not need a body, because there's no need for additional information to create a collection. However, extensions to WebDAV may use a body, so WebDAV
servers must be able to handle request bodies gracefully. If the server does not expect to see a
request body, it may not look for one, and can treat the request as if it does not have a body. If
the server does expect a request body but not one of the kind the client sent, it may return a 415
Unsupported Media Type status.

6.2.1   MKCOL and the Allow Header

The OPTIONS response for a collection typically does not show the MKCOL method in the
`Allow` header (as shown in Listing 5–2). The HTTP specification is unclear what `Allow`
means semantically. The WebDAV specification doesn't clarify either—it doesn't mention how
to treat the MKCOL method in the `Allow` header.

A MKCOL request to a URL for a collection that does exist must fail because MKCOL is not allowed to overwrite existing collections. Some implementors reason that MKCOL is forbidden on existing collections, thus it should not appear in the `Allow` header. Other implementors reason that since MKCOL is allowed to create a new collection within a parent collection, MKCOL *should* appear.

Following the same lines of reasoning, it's also unclear whether PUT should appear in the `Allow` header for a collection. Although a server may forbid PUT directly on a collection URL, it may allow PUT to create new resources within the collection.

Clients must be prepared for either behavior and not assume that MKCOL isn't allowed just because it doesn't show up. An OPTIONS request to the magic * URL should of course show MKCOL as an allowed method, because in that case, all methods supported anywhere on the server are shown. Server implementations do seem to handle the `Allow` header correctly in responses to OPTIONS *—that is, if the server supports OPTIONS * at all.

6.2.2   Status Codes for MKCOL

The successful response to a MKCOL request is always 201 Created.

The server may refuse a MKCOL request for the usual reasons: locks are involved, permission is denied, the server couldn't match conditions provided by client, and so forth. There are also a number of special reasons that a MKCOL request can be a failure:

- 403 Forbidden: The server does not allow the creation of a collection at this location. For example, some implementations might forbid creation of subcollections inside a "trash" folder or other special-purpose collection.
- 405 Method Not Allowed: The MKCOL method is not allowed on this resource. This would be the case for any resource that already existed, because MKCOL is only allowed on null resources or unmapped URLs.
- 409 Conflict: The parent collection does not exist, or a resource exists with the parent's name but it is not a collection.
- 415 Unsupported Media Type: The server does not support a body on the MKCOL request, or it does not support a body of the type sent by the client. Most server implementations either ignore a MKCOL request body or use this error, as WebDAV does not define a body for MKCOL requests. Server implementors *should* use the error because it's not safe to ignore request bodies that aren't recognized.

6.3   MOVE

The MOVE method is a way to rename resources within the parent collection, as well as move them from one collection to another, along with all dead properties. The client must specify the target location and name using a `Destination` header with a fully qualified URL that must include the host name (see Listing 6–2).

Listing 6–2   MOVE request and response for a regular resource.

Request:
```
MOVE /hr/drafts/application.doc HTTP/1.1
Host: www.example.com
Destination: http://www.example.com/hr/recruiting/application.doc
↵
```

Response:
```
HTTP/1.1 201 Created
Date: Sun, 29 Jul 2001 15:24:17 GMT
↵
```

This operation moves the resource `application.doc` to the destination directory without changing its base name (the last segment of the URL). After this operation, a request to the original URL in the `drafts/` collection will return 404 Not Found, whereas a request to the new URL in the `recruiting/` collection will return the resource.

6.3.1 Destination Header

The `Destination` header always specifies a single URL, which is the full destination URL, not just the destination parent URL. The URL must be a full legal URL (any illegal characters must be escaped).

The `Destination` header shown in Listing 6–2 shows how to move a resource to a new location without changing its name. Since the `Destination` header includes the full URL for the new resource including the base name, it's possible to rename the resource at the same time. If the request in Listing 6–2 contained this header instead, then the resource's base name would change as well as its parent collection.

```
Destination: http://www.example.com/hr/recruiting/job-app.doc
```

6.3.2 Depth Header

We introduced the semantics of applying operations over an entire tree, or to a specified depth, in Chapter 3, *HTTP Mechanics* (Section 3.3). MOVE is the first method to be introduced that allows the `Depth` header, although it doesn't require it because it's always possible to apply a reasonable default value. The defined values for the `Depth` header are 0, 1, and `infinity`. Note that the server should ignore case when parsing the value of the `Depth` header, but the client should use the exact case shown in the standard. The default value for the `Depth` header is `infinity`.

The example of moving a file `application.doc` didn't need the `Depth` header because the resource being moved is not a collection. Thus, the only conceivable value for the depth is 0. The server automatically handled the request as if a `Depth 0` header was present.

Since the MOVE method is legal on a collection, we must also consider what happens when the client sends the MOVE request to a collection. Can you move a collection without moving all of its descendants? What would happen to any members of the collection that can't be moved—where would they exist? Most file systems don't allow this to happen. Although it may be conceivable to apply a MOVE request with a depth of 0 or 1 to a collection, it's hard to define a consistent and interoperable behavior that could be supported on all server implementations. Thus, WebDAV doesn't allow a MOVE of a collection unless the collection and all its descendants are moved.

Since WebDAV only allows a value of infinity for the Depth header when moving a collection, the Depth header is not actually required when moving collections, either. The collection must always be moved along with all of its descendants. However, the client can still include the Depth header (see Listing 6–3).

Listing 6–3   MOVE request and response for a collection.

Request:
```
MOVE /hr/resumes/ HTTP/1.1
Host: www.example.com
Depth: infinity
Destination: http://www.example.com/hr/recruiting/resumes/
⏎
```

Response:
```
HTTP/1.1 201 Created
Date: Sun, 29 Jul 2001 15:24:17 GMT
⏎
```

If the client includes a Depth header with an illegal value, the server should return 400 Bad Request.

6.3.3   Depth noroot Extension

Microsoft has extended the Depth header syntax in several of its products in a way that isn't legal and may cause interoperability problems. The client sends a header with multiple comma-separated values:

```
Depth: infinity,noroot
Depth: 1,noroot
```

The meaning of the noroot value is to exclude the target URL itself (the root) from the operation. It's useful in a number of situations that would otherwise require multiple requests:

- To copy the contents of one directory to another existing directory without overwriting the existing destination directory

- To set a property on all the files in a directory but not the directory
- To get directory listings that don't include the directory itself

This was first seen in Hotmail traffic from Outlook Express. Exchange Server 2000 is known to support the extensions. Support on other servers has not been verified.

This practice is not legal, because the Depth header isn't defined to have multiple values. Worse, it is bad for interoperability. Sending this header value to a server that is not known to support the feature would most likely result in an 400 Bad Request, but it could also result in the server interpreting the depth incorrectly and performing the wrong operation.

6.3.4 The Overwrite Header

The MOVE method can also contain the Overwrite header. WebDAV defines the Overwrite header so that the client can specify what should happen if a resource already exists at the Destination URI. This header has two legal values, either T or F (true or false). Any other value should result in a 400 Bad Request response from the server.

A value of "T" on the Overwrite header indicates that the destination resource should be replaced if it existed at the time of the MOVE request. A value of F means that the client prefers the request to fail if the destination resource already exists.

The Overwrite header is considered to be a "precondition" header. Thus, any time the Overwrite header has a value of F and the destination already exists, the request should fail with a response of 412 Precondition Failed (see Listing 6–4).

Listing 6–4 MOVE request and response with Overwrite header.

Request:
```
MOVE /hr/drafts/candidate-application.doc HTTP/1.1
Host: www.example.com
Destination: http://www.example.com/hr/recruiting/candidate-⏎
application.doc
Overwrite: F
⏎
```

Response:
```
HTTP/1.0 412 Precondition Failed
Date: Sun, 29 Jul 2001 15:24:17 GMT
⏎
```

The default value for the Overwrite header is T (true), so a request without the Overwrite header will never fail in this manner—it will simply overwrite the destination if there is one. A client should explicitly include Overwrite: F when it doesn't expect to do an overwrite, because this allows the server to fail the request if the state of the world doesn't match what the client expects.

The `Overwrite` header is only defined for COPY and MOVE requests. Although it might be nice to be able to use it for PUT, MKCOL, or other write operations, it is not defined for those methods. Here's why:

- PUT doesn't need the `Overwrite` header because it can use the `If-Match` and `If-None-Match` headers, which are much more powerful.
- MKCOL doesn't need the `Overwrite` header because it can't be used to overwrite an existing resource.
- COPY and MOVE need the `Overwrite` header because `If-Match` and `If-None-Match` apply to the source resource (the Request-URI), not the destination.

6.3.5 Status Codes for MOVE

The MOVE response should never use 200 OK unless it has a body, which it normally will not. The 201 Created status code must be used if the destination resource did not previously exist and was created as a result of this operation. The 204 No Content status code must be used if the destination resource already exists. This allows the client to distinguish between the two cases.

It's important for the client to be able to distinguish between an overwrite and the creation of a new resource, because when resources are freshly created, the client may want to initialize some metadata. For example, the client might create a Title property or initialize access control settings on every resource when it is first created. The server might also initialize some property values that the client could be interested in seeing.

Some other special failure status codes for MOVE:

- 102 Processing: This status response indicates that the server is working on the answer (more detail in the next section).
- 207 Multi-Status: See the body of the response for individual success and failure codes.
- 403 Forbidden: The source and destination resource are the same, or the destination is a subdirectory of the source. Alternatively, this response could be used if the MOVE request would overwrite a parent of the source resource. For example, a request to move the collection `/a/b/b` to the collection `/a` would overwrite the parent of `/a/b/b` because it happens to have the same name.
- 409 Conflict: The parent collection does not exist.
- 412 Precondition Failed: Some precondition, such as the `Overwrite` header or the `propertybehavior` condition, could not be met.
- 502 Bad Gateway: The server cannot copy to the destination URL location, perhaps because it's on another server.

6.3.6 102 Processing Response

When the MOVE method is used with a collection, the server may take a long time to process the request. Clients must be prepared to wait a little while the response is generated before timing out and dropping the TCP connection. Clients can also give the user the choice of when to give up.

WebDAV introduces the 102 Processing response for servers to let the client know that the request will take a while. The server can send one of these responses immediately or after processing a while, or it can send multiple 102 Processing responses at intervals. The client must wait until the final response (see Listing 6–5). Servers do not frequently use this response.

 According to the standard, all clients must support the 102 Processing response; however, it's not clear whether they do in practice.

Listing 6–5   102 Continue example over single TCP connection.

Request:
```
MOVE /hr/resumes/ HTTP/1.1
Host: www.example.com
Depth: infinity
Destination: http://www.example.com/hr/recruiting/resumes
↵
```

Response:
```
HTTP/1.1 102 Processing
Date: Sun, 29 Jul 2001 15:24:17 GMT
↵

[time passes]

HTTP/1.1 102 Processing
Date: Sun, 29 Jul 2001 15:27:17 GMT
↵

[time passes]

HTTP/1.1 201 Created
Date: Sun, 29 Jul 2001 15:29:02 GMT
↵
```

The 102 Processing response interacts somewhat poorly with pipelining. Because there's no way to correlate pipelined requests with pipelined responses except by sequence, the 102 Processing response must be entirely completed before being able to respond to the next pipelined request.

6.3.7   The Multi-Status Response

The MOVE operation can act on several resources. Therefore, MOVE responses sometimes need to have more information than can be presented using a single status code. As with DELETE on multiple resources (Section 5.5.1), multiple errors are marshaled using the 207

Multi-Status response. Within the 207 Multi-Status message, each resource can be listed with the status code indicating why it couldn't be moved.

As with DELETE, the MOVE method is not atomic, which means that some resources may be moved and some remain. Success status codes do not appear in the response. Resources that could not be moved do appear with a status code.

Figure 6–1 shows a scenario in which a MOVE operation fails. The client asked to rename a collection from /hr/recruiting/positions/ to /hr/recruiting/openings/, but the source collection contains one resource locked by somebody else.

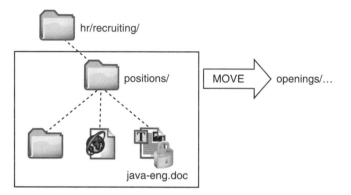

Figure 6–1   Directory to be renamed (moved) has a locked resource.

The client was unaware of this locked child and sent the MOVE request. The server began to handle the operation, creating the destination collection and moving some children. Then the server discovered the locked resource and stopped, failing to complete the operation. At this point, the server must respond with a 207 Multi-Status response (see Listing 6–6).

Listing 6–6   Partially failed MOVE request requiring Multi-Status response.

Request:
```
MOVE /hr/recruiting/positions/ HTTP/1.1
Host: www.example.com
Depth: infinity
Destination: http://www.example.com/hr/recruiting/openings/
↵
```

Response:
```
HTTP/1.1 207 Multi-Status
Content-Type: text/xml
Content-Length: xxx
Date: Sun, 29 Jul 2001 15:24:17 GMT
↵
```

Listing 6–6 Partially failed MOVE request requiring Multi-Status response. *(Continued)*

```
<?xml version="1.0" encoding="utf-8" ?>
<d:multistatus xmlns:d="DAV:">
    <d:response>
        <d:href>http://www.example.com/hr/recruiting/positions/↲
            java-eng.doc</d:href>
        <d:status>HTTP/1.1 423 Locked</d:status>
    </d:response>
</d:multistatus>
```

The response shows that `java-eng.doc` could not be moved and thus remained where it originally was. In fact, although it's not listed in the response, the `/hr/recruiting/positions/` directory must still exist in its original location: If its child couldn't be moved, the parent must remain to contain the child. Figure 6–2 shows the result of the partially successful MOVE operation.

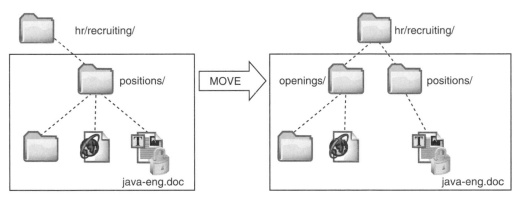

Figure 6–2 Results of partial MOVE operation: old directory still exists.

A server can handle a failed MOVE operation in several ways. It could fail the entire operation and not change any resources. A server could do "best effort" and move as many resources as possible, or it could quit as soon as it encounters an error.

 WebDAV introduced the status code 424 Failed Dependency for multistatus responses (Section 5.5.1) where an operation failed on one resource because of a failure on one resource. On the face of it, it seems that when a collection can't be moved because of a failed child move, this status code should be used. However, WebDAV specifies that 424 Failed Dependency shouldn't appear in a 207 Multi-Status response to a MOVE request, because the MOVE operation is not an atomic operation. The client can theoretically deduce which resources failed to be moved by starting with the explicit failures and then adding the parent collections of those failed resources.

6.3.8   Specifying Property Value Behavior

The WebDAV designers thought that clients needed a way to tell the server when property values
and behavior are important to preserve during a MOVE operation. In theory, the client may prefer not to do the MOVE at all, unless the server can guarantee that property values and important
semantics can be preserved. For example, it does the client little good to have the value of a live
property such as quota preserved after a MOVE if the server then fails to enforce the quota as it
did in the original location.

 This was a very reasonable idea at the time, but it turns out that servers have more information than clients do about how property values are preserved. Clients can't tell which
properties are live—the quota property is live on some servers, but it could be a dead property on another server. Servers where the quota property is live already have to know how
to preserve it. In practice, clients do not request special property value preservation behavior. Some servers do support the feature.

To attempt to specify property value preservation in a MOVE operation, the client adds a
body to the MOVE request (see Listing 6–7).

Listing 6–7   MOVE request specifying property value behavior.

```
MOVE /hr/drafts/chairs.doc HTTP/1.1
Host: www.example.com
Destination: http://www.example.com/hr/ergonomics/chairs.doc
Overwrite: F
Content-Type: text/xml
Content-Length: xxx
↵

<?xml version="1.0" encoding="utf-8" ?>
<d:propertybehavior xmlns:d='DAV:'>
<d:keepalive>*</d:keepalive>
</d:propertybehavior>
```

In this example, the asterisk (*) in the keepalive field indicates that all live properties must
be maintained for all resources being copied. If the server cannot guarantee the desired live
property behavior, it must fail.

The asterisk can theoretically be replaced by a list of property names in href elements;
however, this feature is not implemented at all. The WebDAV specification does not provide
enough detail to reliably put property names in href elements, because it does not specify how
a namespace and name of a property combine to form a legal URI.

The only other legal value for the propertybehavior element is:

```
<d:propertybehavior xmlns:d='DAV:'>
    <d:omit/>
</d:propertybehavior>
```

The omit body simply means that the server should attempt to copy properties and keep the live properties live, but it must not fail the overall request even if it has difficulty copying properties. It is the same as a request without the propertybehavior body.

The WebDAV Working Group plans to simplify or even deprecate the property keepalive feature if the WebDAV specification is reissued as a Draft Standard. No significant client/server interoperability has been demonstrated with the keepalive feature containing property names. The IETF process requires that each specification feature must either be proven interoperable or removed in order to publish a Draft Standard, and this feature is definitely a candidate for removal.

However, the server has to implement the logic to move and copy live properties one way or another, and WebDAV doesn't provide much guidance in defining desired behavior for the MOVE and COPY methods overall. A better approach is to define behavior individually for each property, since each property has different semantics. The DeltaV specification started this new practice, requiring certain properties to be moved or copied live.

6.4 COPY

The COPY request format is very similar to MOVE, so we'll cover it quickly. Like the MOVE method, it:

- Requires a Destination header
- Interprets the Overwrite header the same way
- Can use the Depth header
- Accepts the propertybehavior element in the body of the request

A successful COPY request results in two resources (or two collections of resources) with identical content and dead properties. The original resource or collection exists untouched, and a copy exists at the destination URL (see Listing 6–8).

Listing 6–8 COPY request and response for a regular resource.

Request:
```
COPY /hr/recruiting/opening-template.doc HTTP/1.1
Host: www.example.com
Destination: http://www.example.com/hr/recruiting/positions/web-↲
ui-designer.doc
↵
```

Response:
```
HTTP/1.1 201 Created
Date: Mon, 02 Sep 2002 03:20:57 GMT
↵
```

The resource created by the COPY operation should always have the same contents as the original. That is, if the original is a noncollection resource, the copy must have the same body. If the original is a collection, the copy must have all the same members as the original, and those members must have all the same contents as the original members. However, the copy may not have the same property values. To start with, the value of getcreationdate will almost certainly be different in the copy than in the original. Other property values may change or remain the same, depending on the definition of the property. Custom or "dead" properties must be copied intact.

6.4.1   MOVE = COPY + DELETE?

Now that we've defined COPY, do we really need MOVE? It seems reasonable to do a MOVE as a COPY of a resource to a new location, followed by deleting the old resource. The WebDAV specification compares a MOVE operation to a COPY followed by a DELETE of the source.

 However, that text has been taken too literally to mean that the server must behave exactly as if it had done a COPY + DELETE. Although a MOVE operation is similar to a COPY + DELETE, it is not identical.

Clients are unable to reliably use COPY and DELETE to achieve the same thing as MOVE:

- The user may be granted privileges to rename resources but not create or delete resources.
- The user may be approaching a quota limit, preventing creation of new resources, but renaming or moving would not be prevented.

It's also problematic for the server to implement MOVE internally as a COPY and DELETE operation. A moved resource ought to be the same resource it was before the move; it merely has a new name and location. In contrast, a COPY operation creates a new resource. Thus, MOVE should not change the creation date or the name of the resource creator, but COPY may reset those values. In general, metadata that is initialized only on creation of a new resource should be initialized when a resource is created with COPY but not when a resource is moved or renamed with MOVE.

MOVE, COPY, and Versioning

The debate on whether MOVE must behave identically to COPY + DELETE peaked during the design of versioning features. The designers realized that a MOVE and a COPY behaved very differently when old versions of the source resource existed. A MOVE operation must preserve older versions, whereas a COPY only copies the content of the latest version. Thus, the versioning specification clarifies the behavior that most servers followed already.

6.4.2 Depth and COPY

If a COPY request does not have a `Depth` header, the depth is assumed to be `infinity`. An infinite-depth copy operation was described in Section 4.3: It copies every resource in the collection recursively, including the collection itself.

A `Depth` header may be explicitly on a COPY request, with a value of either `infinity` or 0. The only data that is copied in a depth 0 COPY request is the metadata directly attached to a collection (this was also illustrated in Section 4.3). Thus, a COPY with depth 0 is a way of copying only the properties of a collection. It might also include metadata that isn't exposed as a property—for example, access control settings on a server that doesn't yet support the access control extensions to WebDAV.

A client may not send a COPY request to a collection with a `Depth` header of 1. This should result in 400 Bad Request.

6.4.3 Status Codes for COPY

Like MOVE, COPY results in a 201 Created status code if the destination resource did not previously exist, and 204 No Content if the destination resource already existed.

Some special failure status codes for COPY:

- 207 Multi-Status: See the body of the response for individual success and failure status and URLs.
- 403 Forbidden: The source and destination resource are the same, or the operation would overwrite a parent of the source (e.g., copy the collection `/a/b/b` to the collection `/a` would overwrite the parent of `/a/b/b` because it happens to have the same name).
- 409 Conflict: The parent collection does not exist.
- 412 Precondition Failed: Some precondition, such as the `Overwrite` header or the property behavior specification, could not be met.
- 502 Bad Gateway: The server cannot copy to the destination URL location, perhaps because it's on another server.

6.5 Summary

WebDAV extends HTTP with seven more methods, including MKCOL, MOVE, and COPY. These are used to organize Web resources in collections and change locations and names of resources. WebDAV also uses the HTTP methods, particularly GET, PUT, and DELETE, to fully support remote authoring. PUT must be used carefully with conditional headers to avoid accidentally overwriting changes from other users.

MKCOL is defined by WebDAV to create a collection. The Request-URI identifies the name and location of the collection to be created. MKCOL cannot overwrite an existing collection, only create a new one.

WebDAV also provides MOVE and COPY. The Request-URI identifies the source resource for the move or copy operation, and the `Destination` header identifies the destination. Both operations act on properties as well as resource bodies; however. some live properties may behave slightly differently.

MOVE and COPY support the `Overwrite` *and* `Depth` *headers.* The `Overwrite` header allows the client to specify whether the destination resources should be overwritten if any already exist. The `Depth` header can be `0` or `infinity` on a COPY request, but it must be `infinity` on a collection MOVE request.

CHAPTER 7

Property Operations

Now we see exactly how a client is supposed to find out what is inside
a collection. Typically, users want to see directory listings in order to
manage files.

A directory listing can simply be a fixed, standard format—or it can be flexible. Even local
file systems now show the need for flexibility—for example, in collections of photos where
users like to see thumbnails and pixel sizes in directory listings. WebDAV was designed with
this flexibility from the ground up, so it can handle not just directory listings, but also:

- Discovering which resources are locked and the kinds of locks each resource supports
- Handling custom collections like directories intended to hold and manage digital
  photos
- Retrieving the metadata for a single resource as well as a directory of resources
- Selecting which property values to retrieve so that listings aren't unreasonably large
- Handling the various features already in place in proprietary Web authoring systems so
  that they can add support for WebDAV

Thus, WebDAV defines a consistent semantic model for properties: Every resource has an
extensible set of properties, including a handful of standard properties. Properties can be downloaded for just one resource or for a collection, including all the resources in a collection.

The WebDAV methods for manipulating properties are PROPFIND and PROPPATCH. To
achieve the flexibility and easy parsability required, both PROPFIND and PROPPATCH make
heavy use of XML. XML is easy to parse, transform, and display. The XML results returned in a
PROPFIND response can be used to quickly generate rich directory contents listings, in any

visual format selected by the client. XML schemas are easy to extend, particularly when XML namespaces are used, which makes XML particularly attractive when custom metadata must be transmitted.

In this chapter, we'll see how PROPFIND and PROPPATCH work and what their XML formats look like.

7.0.1   HTML and HTTP Metadata

Even before WebDAV, Web servers already had a couple of ways to provide metadata. Some metadata appears in headers when a file is downloaded. For example, every GET response has a `Content-Type` header:

```
Content-type: text/html; charset=UTF-8
```

The HEAD method can even be used to download headers without downloading the entire resource body. However, there is no way for the client to ask for the header information for all the files in a directory, or for the client to explicitly create or change metadata.

The other place metadata already shows up in the Web is within HTML pages or other documents. For example, the following text may appear inside the header of an HTML file to tell browsers the content-type and character set to use:

```
<META HTTP-EQUIV="content-type" CONTENT="text/html; charset=UTF-8">
```

Other types of documents include metadata within the file body as well. Portable Network Graphics (PNG) files are images, but they include XML metadata as well as image information inside the file body. PNG metadata includes color and display information but also text information like description, keywords, and the date and time the image was last modified.

Unfortunately, metadata inside file bodies is hard to get at. The entire file must be downloaded, and the client must support the file type. Since just about every file type contains a different set of metadata in a different format, it's impossible to use this information to construct a directory listing. Moreover, as with HTTP header metadata, it's hard for users to annotate documents with their own metadata values. WebDAV's approach is to store properties outside the file body, which means that the metadata can be queried without getting the entire body and updated without changing the body.

7.1   Property Representation

WebDAV properties are expressed in XML in PROPFIND and PROPPATCH requests and responses. The first piece to put in place is how those properties are named and expressed in XML. This section attempts to build property representation from the ground up, combining rules about how to represent property names and property values. Then when I show complete PROPFIND and PROPPATCH request and response bodies in XML in Sections 7.2 and 7.3, all the pieces will be in place to understand those examples.

7.1.1 Basic Property Value Example

A property value is represented in WebDAV messages as the text contents of an XML element. The element name is the property name. The element namespace is the property namespace (see Listing 7–1).

Listing 7–1 Basic property name/value example.

```
<D:getlastmodified
    xmlns:D="DAV:">Thu, 16 Aug 2001 23:24:33 GMT ↲
</D:getlastmodified>
```

In this example, getlastmodified is the property name, DAV: is the property namespace, and the value is a string formatted as a date.

7.1.2 Property Name Only

Sometimes only the property name will appear (PROPFIND requests, Section 7.2.1). When this is required, the property name element is shown the same way but without a value. For example, the getlastmodified property is named like this:

```
<D:prop xmlns:D="DAV:">
    <D:getlastmodified/>
</D:prop>
```

XML marshals empty elements two ways, so it's also possible to see:

```
<D:getlastmodified></D:getlastmodified>
```

An XML parser will treat these two as equivalent, so the WebDAV implementation doesn't have to worry about both.

7.1.3 Empty Property Values

An empty property value is different from a property that does not exist. When a property exists on a resource but has no value, it can appear empty. The formatting of empty property values appears identical to showing property names, but the context is different (this is used in PROPFIND responses, Section 7.2.2). The following example is excerpted from a larger

---

Listing 7–2 Empty property value.

```
<D:prop>
    <D:resourcetype/>
</D:prop>
<D:status>HTTP/1.1 200 OK</D:status>
```

---

response. The status is showing that the property value was returned successfully; therefore, the value must be empty (see Listing 7–2).

Again, the equivalent XML syntax may be used to compress an empty value representation to:

```
<D:resourcetype></D:resourcetype>
```

7.1.4 Making Property Values Safe

XML needs a way to hold any kind of text without changing the XML parsing or making the XML document invalid. This is done by making the text "safe." In XML documents, < and > are the only control characters, and & is used as an escape character, so these three characters are the only ones that must be treated specially. Any property containing these characters must be made safe to keep the XML document parsable and valid. Otherwise, the XML document may be unparsable or the recipient may misinterpret what characters comprise the property values.

There are two ways to make text safe for XML. One is to wrap the text in a special begin and end string, unlikely to occur naturally in text. This is called *encapsulation*. The other method, called *escaping*, replaces each illegal character with a string that can be used to restore the original character when the text is removed from the XML.

Encapsulation   XML defines a way of encapsulating text that may contain illegal characters: The text is preceded by <![CDATA[and followed by]]>. CDATA sections cannot nest and may not include]]>. A property named transit has its value kelowna-->penticton encapsulated as:

```
<x:transit><![CDATA[kelowna-->penticton]]></x:transit>
```

Character Escaping   Text can also be made safe for XML by escaping each illegal character individually. Characters are escaped with the same mechanism used in HTML. Angle brackets (< and >) are replaced with < and >, respectively. Natural occurrences of the ampersand character (&) must be replaced with the string &.

A property named transit with a value of kelowna-->penticton is escaped as:

```
<x:transit>kelowna--&gt;penticton</x:transit>
```

 The XML 1.0 specification states that character escaping must not be used inside the CDATA encapsulation (one character-safety operation inside another). That means that escaping and encapsulation aren't supposed to be done in the same step. However, you'll often see double transformations in the real world because one software process will escape characters, and then another process will encapsulate, or vice versa. For example, when the client uses HTML-style escaping for a piece of text, the server may later encapsulate the value in CDATA, even if it's already legal. If the text begins with <![CDATA[, unencapsulate it; otherwise, unescape it. The recipient should only undo

> ### Decimal and Hexadecimal Character References
>
> In XML 1.0, it's legal although rare to escape characters using the decimal or hexadecimal (hex) representations defined in the ISO/IEC 10646 character set. The decimal code for a character is prefixed by &# and ends in ;, and the hex code for a character is prefixed by &#x and ends in ;. Thus, there are three valid escapings for the single character >:
>
> ```
> &gt;
> &#26;
> &#x1a;
> ```

one layer of character-safety transformations at a time; otherwise, the value may actually be changed to a different string than it was originally.

When property values are set by the client, the client may choose to encapsulate or encode the value when sending it to the server. The server may or may not use the same method for making the value safe when it returns the property value, so the client must be prepared to accept a different encoding than the one used when the property value was set.

7.1.5 Storing Property Value Text

Servers must store property names, namespaces, and values and the language of the property if it was provided by the client. There are several approaches to storing properties, and countless variations exist.

- The server may store the property value as sent by the client (whether unadorned, escaped, or encapsulated). It may then return the property in exactly the format it was sent and stored. (This is probably easiest for a WebDAV-only system, where property values will always be in XML. Systems that present property values to non-WebDAV clients will probably prefer to store property values in their "real" format instead.)
- The server may unescape or unencapsulate the property value when it is received, before storing the value. When sending the property value out in XML, the server may check to see if it needs to be made safe. If it does, the server could use either mechanism to make the data safe.
- The server may unescape or unencapsulate the property value when it is received, before storing the value. When sending the property value out in XML, the server may always perform a transformation to make the data safe, whether it needs to be made safe or not.
- The server may keep track of the data type of known properties in order to decide whether to escape, encapsulate, or leave alone. For example, if the property is known to be an integer, it doesn't have to be transformed to be safe text for XML.

Since servers may choose any variation on any of these options, and since clients may also submit property values that have been transformed (made safe) multiple times, clients should be prepared to encounter strings like any of the following examples. The third and fourth examples are technically illegal because they contain both kinds of escaping, but they might occur anyway.

```
<![CDATA[<P> This value was made safe through encapsulation. </P>]]>
```

```
&lt;P&gt; This value was made safe through escaping. &lt;/P&gt;
```

```
<![CDATA[&lt;P&gt; This value was already made safe through escaping,
but the server encapsulated it anyway. &lt;/P&gt;]]>
```

```
&lt;![CDATA[&lt;P&gt;This value was already safe through encapsulation,
but the server escaped it anyway.&lt;/P&gt;]]&gt;
```

7.1.6 Whitespace

Between XML elements, it doesn't matter how many whitespace characters (tabs, carriage returns, new lines, or spaces) are included. However, whitespace does matter inside XML text element values. Thus, a string property could have a value of a single space, two spaces, or no spaces—and these are all different, valid values. This sometimes causes confusion when whitespace characters are added for readability in testing or debugging. For example, if a test application put spaces before or after a date, inside the element tag, the recipient could find this to be an invalid date value, since date values are not supposed to have spaces. For the date property named getlastmodified, the following representation would be **invalid** unless the spaces were removed:

```
<D:getlastmodified>2001-05-11T17:33:11Z       </D:getlastmodified>
```

For empty property values in particular, this can cause confusion. The following example is not an empty value for the resourcetype property; it is an illegal value consisting of whitespace:

```
        <D:resourcetype>  </D:resourcetype>
```

Implementors should think carefully before adding or stripping leading or trailing whitespace. That's why in this book I've been very careful, adding whitespace to improve readability, but only where it doesn't change the meaning of the example. The ϟ character is used when a new line couldn't be avoided, even though it shouldn't be considered part of the example.

7.1.7 Internationalization

Property names and property values must both be internationalizable. They may contain characters such as accented characters, Arabic or Hebrew script, Chinese characters, and so on. The

XML body of a WebDAV message may use one of several character sets, including the required character sets UTF-8 and UTF-16. Thus, any Unicode character may be represented in an XML document and included in a WebDAV property name or property value.

XML supports Unicode via the UTF-8 and UTF-16 encoding. The recipient may have to convert string properties from the XML encoding character set to an internal representation, but in some languages this is automatic. Properties must be stored in a format compatible with their character set.

 All WebDAV implementations *must* support both UTF-8 and UTF-16 because either set can be used in requests and responses. Other character sets must be negotiated.

Careless handling of character sets may lead to problems:

- One client may set a property using a PROPPATCH method with a XML body in UTF-8 format. Another client may set a property using UTF-16. The server must be able to return both properties in an XML document in which all properties are expressed in a consistent character set. Thus, the server must be able to do transformations between character sets.
- Property names may be expressed with UTF-8 or UTF-16 characters. The server must be able to compare two property names to see if they are the same property.
- If the server supports DAV Search and Location (DASL) or some other mechanism for comparing property values, the character set must be taken into account. Sort order is particularly difficult.

7.1.8   XML-Valued Properties

Some WebDAV property values are strings intended to be parsed as XML. These values contain one or more self-contained XML elements. If the value is not well-formed XML or is incomplete, then the sender has no choice but to encapsulate or escape the value. If the value is well-formed and complete, then the sender might choose to put the value directly into the XML stream. Let's take the example of an XML-formatted value:

```
<home>555-1234</home><work>555-4321</work>
```

We'll put this inside a property named phone in the http://example.com/contacts namespace:

```
<x:phone xmlns:x="http://example.com/contacts">
   <home>555-1234</home><work>555-4321</work></x:phone>
```

That was easy, but only because the inner value does not use namespaces, and there's no need to handle prefixes. When namespaces are used, namespace prefixes must be chosen so that they are unique within a **scope**. The scope of a namespace declaration includes the element where the declaration is placed and every element in the hierarchy underneath, but not any part of the document outside that XML element. If the namespace is defined on the root element, it applies to all elements inside the document.

If the property value uses a new namespace not already declared within the scope, a new prefix must be chosen. For example, we'll modify the preceding example so that the home and work elements are defined in the http://example.com/contacts/phonetypes namespace.

```
<x:phone xmlns:x="http://example.com/contacts"
  xmlns:y="http://example.com/contacts/phonetypes">
  <y:home>555-1234</y:home><y:work>555-4321</y:work>
</x:phone>
```

A sender might be tempted to apply a simple rule: "Always declare a new prefix for every namespace appearing in the value." However, XML scoping rules prevent this if the same namespace is already declared in the same scope. For example, when the resourcetype property, in the DAV: namespace, takes a value that includes the DAV: namespace, the same prefix must be reused:

```
<D:resourcetype xmlns:D="DAV:"><D:collection/>
  </D:resourcetype>
```

It would be incorrect for a sender to attempt simply to encapsulate an XML value:

```
<D:resourcetype xmlns:D="DAV:"><![CDATA[<D:collection/>]]> ↲
  </D:resourcetype>
```

The problem with the preceding example is that it gives the resourcetype property a value, which is a string equaling <D:collection/>. That's not the same as a value that is an empty XML element named collection in the DAV: namespace. In the former case, an XML parser will return a string-typed variable. In the latter case, an XML parser will return an XML element or node variable, with its namespace.

WebDAV implementations have to go to some trouble to put XML-formatted properties into legal XML documents. Servers can have trouble storing XML-formatted property values such that the property is reconstructed together with its namespaces without any prefix collisions. A WebDAV server needs to detect whether the client has sent an XML-formatted value for a custom property so that later the server knows whether to do prefix correction when it marshals the value in XML. Luckily, XML parsers can do that easily.

7.1.9 Date and Time Properties

Date and time properties, such as creationdate, are represented as strings in an ISO8601 format subset recommended by the IETF [RFC3339]. The format allows dates alone, times alone, or dates and times together and can include time zone information.

Some examples of values for a timestamp property such as creationdate are:

```
1997-12-01T17:42:21-08:00
2001-05-11T17:33:11Z
```

The part up to the "T" is the date. The part after the "T" and before the hyphen or "Z" is the time. The last piece is the time zone, either the GMT ("Zulu") time zone or a number of hours offset from GMT. In this case, the time zone is eight hours before GMT; a plus sign would appear if the time zone were after GMT.

Although the ISO 8601 format can be parsed by humans, it's typically transformed into more readable format for actual display; for example, "7:33 a.m., Saturday May 5, 2001." When the date is formatted for display, some accuracy may be omitted.

Note that although ISO 8601 allows date and time formats that are incomplete (e.g., the date without a time specified, or the time without a date specified), WebDAV makes further restrictions on timestamps; the date must be fully specified and the time must be fully specified, including time zone.

The getlastmodified property is a little different from regular date/time representations. Since it's defined by its relationship to the `Last-Modified` header in HTTP/1.1, it uses the same format, even though this format has interoperability and internationalization problems and is no longer recommended for IETF protocols. The format for the `Last-Modified` header and thus the getlastmodified property is defined in RFC2616. An example of the format is `Tue, 15 Nov 1994 12:45:26 GMT`.

 Timestamp Interoperability Challenges Dates and times are difficult to do interoperably, particularly when the precision can vary. Some sample problems:

- Precision: Does the time 7:42:21 match the time 7:42:21.00? Does it match 7:42:21.01? How are these two times sorted?
- Is 15:00 before or after 16:00 if they are in different zones?
- Is 24 a legal hour value? Is 60 a legal second value?
- Should two-digit year representations (from legacy software) be translated to a four-digit year, or should the uncertainty be preserved?

7.2 PROPFIND

This section covers retrieval of properties or property names through the PROPFIND method defined in WebDAV.

7.2.1 PROPFIND Request

When querying metadata, clients need to be able to specify which resources to query and which properties to return. The first is achieved with the target URI and the `Depth` header. The second is achieved by listing the properties desired in an XML request body. The body is in a simple format (see Listing 7–3).

Listing 7–3 PROPFIND request for getlastmodified property.

```
PROPFIND /hr/ergonomics/ HTTP/1.1
Host: www.example.com
Depth: 1
```

Listing 7–3   PROPFIND request for getlastmodified property. *(Continued)*

```
Content-type: text/xml; charset="utf-8"
Content-Length: xxxx
⏎
<?xml version="1.0" encoding="utf-8" ?>
<D:propfind xmlns:D="DAV:">
   <D:prop>
      <D:getlastmodified/>
   </D:prop>
</D:propfind>
```

A PROPFIND request body always has a `propfind` element as the top-level document element. Within the `propfind` element, a number of elements can appear, depending on the purpose of the request. If the client is asking for a specific list of properties, then the `prop` element appears inside the `propfind` element. Finally, the `prop` element contains any number of empty property name elements in any order.

7.2.2 PROPFIND Response

The PROPFIND response is another Multi-Status response, just like those used in response to `depth infinity` MOVE, COPY, or DELETE requests (Section 5.5.1). The `multistatus` element is the root of the response body, followed by one `response` element for each resource listed. These `response` elements can be in any order because PROPFIND has no way of specifying order. The client must sort the results in order to be able to list the contents of the collection in a reliable order.

The PROPFIND response extends the Multi-Status response. Recall that for MOVE, COPY, and DELETE of collections, the Multi-Status response can include one status element inside up to N response elements, where N is the number of resources affected. PROPFIND must contain N response elements, and each of those contains M property status elements, where M is the number of properties requested. Therefore, a PROPFIND Multi-Status response can contain much more information, even though it shares the same response framework.

Inside the `response` element for each resource, the server must include the resource's URL, any requested property values that it can return, or error codes for the property values it can't return. When the property value is included, it's formatted as shown in Figure 7–1, with the property value inside an XML element that has the same name and namespace as the property. Listing 7–4 is a complete PROPFIND response.

Each `response` element in Listing 7–4 has at least one `propstat` element to hold the property identification, status code, and possibly value. Each `propstat` element has one `status` element, plus a number of property names that belong with that status element. In Listing 7–4, only the HTTP/1.1 200 OK status code is used, because there were no errors.

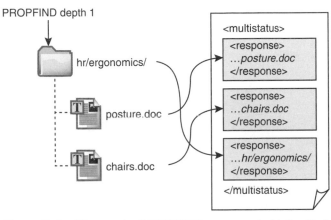

Figure 7–1   Diagram for PROPFIND response in Listing 7–4:
Response elements are unsorted.

Listing 7–4   PROPFIND response with getlastmodified property.

```
HTTP/1.1 207 Multi-Status
Date: Sun, 29 Jul 2001 15:24:17 GMT
Content-Type: text/xml; charset="utf-8"
Content-Length: xxxx
↵
<?xml version="1.0" encoding="utf-8" ?>
<D:multistatus xmlns:D="DAV:">

<D:response>
   <D:href>http://www.example.com/hr/ergonomics/posture.doc ↲
</D:href>
   <D:propstat>
      <D:prop>
         <D:getlastmodified>Thu, 16 Aug 2001 23:24:33
            GMT</D:getlastmodified>
         </D:prop>
      <D:status>HTTP/1.1 200 OK</D:status>
   </D:propstat>
</D:response>

<D:response>
   <D:href>http://www.example.com/hr/ergonomics/chairs.doc ↲
</D:href>
   <D:propstat>
      <D:prop>
         <D:getlastmodified>Sun, 26 Aug 2001 00:08:21
            GMT</D:getlastmodified>
```

Listing 7–4   PROPFIND response with getlastmodified property. *(Continued)*

```
        </D:prop>
      <D:status>HTTP/1.1 200 OK</D:status>
   </D:propstat>
</D:response>

<D:response>
   <D:href>http://www.example.com/hr/ergonomics/</D:href>
   <D:propstat>
      <D:prop>
         <D:getlastmodified>Sun, 26 Aug 2001 00:06:01
            GMT</D:getlastmodified>
      </D:prop>
      <D:status>HTTP/1.1 200 OK</D:status>
   </D:propstat>
</D:response>

</D:multistatus>
```

7.2.3   Reporting Errors in PROPFIND Responses

Listing 7–5 shows a possible PROPFIND error. In the example, a client asks for a property on a resource that doesn't normally support that property. The getetag property does not exist on collections, because collections do not have ETags. The client also requests getlastmodified, which does exist on a collection. This shows how the failure and the success are reported in the same response.

Listing 7–5   PROPFIND request and response showing errors and successes.

Request:
```
PROPFIND /hr/ergonomics/ HTTP/1.1
Host: www.example.com
Depth: 0
Content-type: text/xml; charset="utf-8"
Content-Length: xxxx
↵
<?xml version="1.0" encoding="utf-8" ?>
<D:propfind xmlns:D="DAV:">
<D:prop>
   <D:getetag/>
   <D:getlastmodified/>
</D:prop>
</D:propfind>
```

Listing 7–5   PROPFIND request and response showing errors and successes. *(Continued)*

Response:
```
HTTP/1.1 207 Multi-Status
Date: Sun, 29 Jul 2001 15:24:17 GMT
Content-Type: text/xml; charset="utf-8"
Content-Length: xxxx
⌐
<?xml version="1.0" encoding="utf-8" ?>
<multistatus xmlns="DAV:">
<response>
   <href>http://www.example.com/hr/ergonomics/</href>
   <propstat>
      <prop>
         <getlastmodified>Sun, 26 Aug 2001 00:06:01
            GMT</getlastmodified>
      </prop>
      <status>HTTP/1.1 200 OK</status>
   </propstat>
   <propstat>
      <prop><getetag/></prop>
      <status>HTTP/1.1 404 Not Found</status>
   </propstat>
</response>
</multistatus>
```

The getlastmodified property is returned successfully, but getetag is not. The name of the errored property is returned associated with a status of 404 Not Found. Other status codes are also possible in other situations: 403 Forbidden, 401 Not Authorized, and so forth.

The `response` element must contain a separate `propstat` element for every different status code. In this case, only two status codes are used, so only two `propstat` elements appear.

7.2.4   Finding the Names of Properties

WebDAV also defines a way for the client to find the names of all properties that exist on a resource. This is great for the server because it may be significantly faster to send property names than to calculate some values (as for lockdiscovery). It can also help the client because not only is the response shorter (thus faster), it also is the only way that is guaranteed to include all the properties that exist on the resource.

To find out what properties exist on a resource, the client should ask for the property names only, using the `propname` element inside a PROPFIND request body (see Listing 7–6).

This request means "tell me the names of properties that exist on the resource." The `propname` element is always empty.

Listing 7–6   PROPFIND to discover what properties exist.

```
PROPFIND /hr/ergonomics/ HTTP/1.1
Host: www.example.com
Depth: 0
Content-Type: text/xml; charset="utf-8"
Content-Length: xxxx
↵
<?xml version="1.0" encoding="utf-8" ?>
<propfind xmlns="DAV:">
   <propname/>
</propfind>
```

The response is a slight variation on the regular PROPFIND response format. The property elements do not contain the values of the properties (see Listing 7–7).

Listing 7–7   PROPFIND response showing what properties exist.

```
HTTP/1.1 207 Multi-Status
Date: Sun, 29 Jul 2001 15:24:17 GMT
Content-Type: text/xml; charset="utf-8"
Content-Length: xxxx
↵
<?xml version="1.0" encoding="utf-8" ?>
<multistatus xmlns="DAV:">
<response>
   <href>http://www.example.com/hr/ergonomics/</href>
   <propstat>
      <prop xmlns:ns1="http://www.xythos.com/namespaces/StorageServer">
         <creationdate/><displayname/><getlastmodified/>
         <lockdiscovery/><resourcetype/><supportedlock/>
         <ns1:quota><ns1:size>
      </prop>
      <status>HTTP/1.1 200 OK</status>
   </propstat>
</response>
</multistatus>
```

This response shows that all the WebDAV properties that might be expected on a collection do exist on this collection, along with two custom properties (quota and size). The definitions and meanings of the `multistatus`, `response`, `propstat`, `prop`, and `status` elements are unchanged.

7.2.5 AllProp Is Not What It Seems

 Can a WebDAV client ask the server to send it the values of all the properties that exist on a resource? In theory, yes, but in practice, the answer is no. WebDAV defines an `allprop` element that means "send me all the properties that exist on the resources in the scope of the request." However, many servers do not return all the properties that exist on a resource. Some server administrators or implementors don't return all properties because some live properties and large properties are expensive to calculate, consume a noticeable amount of bandwidth (particularly in depth 1 or depth infinity requests), and are probably not needed.

These servers are all theoretically noncompliant, but when noncompliance is this widespread and intentional, the real problem is with the standard. The versioning standard extending WebDAV already specifically requires that live versioning properties must not be returned in response to `allprop` requests. The WebDAV standard may be revised so that reasonable server implementations will be compliant.

 The client shares part of the responsibility for conserving bandwidth, particularly in PROPFIND. A client should never ask for all properties on all resources in a large collection. A depth infinity allprop request may simply be forbidden on some servers, and even if not, the client should not attempt that request.

However, a depth 0 or depth 1 allprop request may still be appropriate and useful. The client may want to retrieve the values of the dead properties (dead properties were defined in Section 4.4.3), along with the properties defined in RFC2518. As long as this request targets a reasonably small number of resources, it can be used responsibly (see Listing 7–8).

Listing 7–8 PROPFIND request for all RFC2518 properties and dead properties.

```
PROPFIND /hr/ergonomics/posture.doc HTTP/1.1
Host: www.example.com
Depth: 0
↵
<?xml version="1.0" encoding="utf-8" ?>
<D:propfind xmlns:D="DAV:">
   <D:allprop/>
</D:propfind>
```

As usual, the `propfind` is the top-level element in a PROPFIND request body. Instead of `propname` or `prop` with a list of property names, it now contains the `allprop` element, which is empty.

There's also a short form of this request. If a PROPFIND request does not contain a body, the server interprets it as an `allprop` request (see Listing 7–9).

Listing 7–9 PROPFIND request with no body.

```
PROPFIND /hr/ergonomics/posture.doc HTTP/1.1
Host: www.example.com
Depth: 0
⌐
```

In general, however, the client should only ask for the properties it actually plans to use. If the client needs to discover the names of unknown properties, use `propname` instead of `allprop`.

7.2.6 Large Response Bodies

Some PROPFIND responses, even when the depth of the request is only 1, can be quite large. Collections are not limited in the number of resources they can contain, and some newer Web-DAV features may lead to very large collections. The WebDAV ACLs proposal uses a collection of "principal" resources to allow client software to list the users that may be granted access to a file. The ACL proposal also defines a couple of very large properties.

 Even a limited PROPFIND request to a collection with many resources can result in a very large answer.

Large responses pose a scaling problem to servers. Normally, the response headers show the length of the entire response. Since the headers must be sent before the body, the natural way to achieve this is to buffer the response in memory as it's created. The server finds the length of the buffered body before sending the `Content-Length` header and then sends the body. This can use large amounts of system resources when multiple large responses are being handled simultaneously.

The brute-force approach to this problem is to omit the `Content-Length` header and send the body as it is being generated. This requires the connection to be closed when the body is finished, so that the client will know what the end of the response is. This approach is not recommended in HTTP/1.1 communication. However, this brute approach is the only approach available for HTTP/1.0 compliant clients [Krishnamurthy99]. At least with a PROPFIND response, it is always possible to detect a truncated message (if the connection closes accidentally)—the XML body must end with </multistatus>.

A more sophisticated approach is to use chunked transfer-encoding (Chapter 3, Section 3.2.8). This encoding is defined for HTTP/1.1 specifically in order to deal with long bodies of unknown length.

Clients must be able to handle both chunked transfer encoding and responses with unknown content length where the end of the body is signaled by closing the connection.

7.3 PROPPATCH

PROPPATCH requires a new kind of request syntax to change properties and property values. Clients need to be able to set values and remove a number of properties in the same request.

However, only one resource can be addressed in a PROPPATCH request (the `Depth` header is not supported).

7.3.1 PROPPATCH Request

WebDAV marshals the PROPPATCH request information in an XML body with `set` and `remove` elements to change or create properties and remove them. Multiple `prop` elements can appear inside the `set` and `remove` elements, but Listing 7–10 just shows one of each.

Listing 7–10 PROPPATCH request.

```
PROPPATCH /hr/ergonomics/chairs.doc HTTP/1.1
Host: www.example.com
Content-Type: text/xml
Content-Length: xxx
↵
<?xml version="1.0" encoding="utf-8" ?>
<propertyupdate xmlns='DAV:'
   xmlns:X="http://www.example.com">
   <set><prop><X:publish>true</X:publish></prop></set>
   <remove><prop><X:temp-property/></prop></remove>
</propertyupdate>
```

In Listing 7–10, the client is asking the server to set the value of the publish property in the `http://www.example.com` namespace to `true`. If the property didn't exist already, it should be created. The client also wants temp-property in the same namespace to be removed. Note that it's necessary to have a syntax to remove elements, because an empty property is not the same as a property that's not there. Thus, it wouldn't be sufficient for the client to set the value of the property to an empty string.

The `remove` element contains only property names, not property values; the property name element must be empty. Note that if the property to be removed does not exist, the server must not return an error.

7.3.2 Implementing Atomic Requests

WebDAV defines the PROPPATCH operation to be atomic; all the property changes must be made together or not at all. Not all servers support atomic PROPPATCH, unfortunately. Instead, IIS 5.0 does best-effort PROPPATCH, where some properties may be changed and others unaltered. Servers are not normally supposed to use success responses within Multi-Status response bodies, but IIS does, since it may successfully change some properties but not others and the client needs to know which.

Despite recurring discussion about this requirement of WebDAV, there is no clear and satisfactory solution. The original intent of defining PROPPATCH as atomic was that it was assumed that resources would have multiple dependent properties. For example, the client might want to set publish to `true` only if draft can be set to `false`.

Some argued to abolish the atomicity requirement with the assumption that clients more frequently want to have best-effort property changes applied. However, that's not a good reason to change the atomicity requirement, because clients have another way to do best-effort property changes without incurring multiple roundtrips: by pipelining multiple PROPPATCH requests, each with one property set request.

 A somewhat stronger argument against atomicity might be derived from a pragmatic look at implementation experience. It can be a little difficult for servers to implement atomic PROPPATCH. Atomic operations can require transaction capability, so that the server can roll back property changes that have already been made when a later part of the request fails. However, mod_dav supports atomicity even though it's based on a nontransacted file system. Servers that are based on transacted database storage, like Zope and Xythos Web-File Server, do, of course, implement atomic PROPPATCH.

Given that most servers do support atomic PROPPATCH, modern WebDAV clients that respect the standard will probably have an expectation that a failure means no changes were made. If some properties were changed and others were not, the client might experience a number of caching and resource integrity problems based on mismatched expectations.

7.3.3 PROPPATCH Response

A successful PROPPATCH response must have all properties changed successfully, but normally a Multi-Status is used anyway. This could allow properties that already existed and are being modified to report back a 200 OK, while properties that are being newly created could report back a 201 Created. It seems, however, that most servers simply report 200 OK for every property that was changed (removed or set), regardless of whether the property existed before.

A PROPPATCH response is a slight simplification of the PROPFIND response because it can only contain one `response` element. That may contain a number of `propstat` elements, depending on how many properties were manipulated. The values are never included, just the property names and namespaces.

Listing 7–11 is what a successful response to the request in Listing 7–10 might look like.

Listing 7–11 PROPPATCH response.

```
HTTP/1.0 207 MultiPart Response
Date: Sun, 29 Jul 2001 15:24:17 GMT
Content-Type: text/xml; charset=UTF-8
Content-Length: xxx
⏎
<?xml version="1.0" encoding="utf-8" ?>
<D:multistatus xmlns:D="DAV:"
   xmlns:ns1="http://www.example.com">
```

Listing 7–11   PROPPATCH response. *(Continued)*

```
<D:response>
   <D:href>http://www.example.com/hr/drafts/chairs.doc</D:href>
   <D:propstat>
      <D:prop><ns1:publish/></D:prop>
      <D:status>HTTP/1.1 200 OK</D:status>
   </D:propstat>
   <D:propstat>
      <D:prop><ns1:temp-property/></D:prop>
      <D:status>HTTP/1.1 200 OK</D:status>
   </D:propstat>
</D:response>
</D:multistatus>
```

7.3.4   PROPPATCH Response with Failures

When the PROPPATCH request fails, any property that could not be set is returned in the body with an appropriate error code such as 403 Forbidden. Any property that could have been set but was not because the request must be done atomically is returned with a status of 424 Failed Dependency.

Recall that the request in Section 7.3.1 attempted to set the value of the publish property and to remove the temp-property property. Since PROPPATCH is atomic, if either of those operations fail, both must fail. To illustrate this, imagine that the set request for publish fails because the property value was rejected by the server. There's no reason to fail to remove the temp-property property other than the failure to set publish, so the appropriate status code for temp-property is 424 Failed Dependency (see Listing 7–12).

Listing 7–12   PROPPATCH response body with failed dependencies.

```
<?xml version="1.0" encoding="utf-8" ?>
<D:multistatus xmlns:D="DAV:"
   xmlns:ns1="http://www.example.com">
<D:response>
   <D:href>http://www.example.com/hr/drafts/chairs.doc
   </D:href>
   <D:propstat>
      <D:prop><ns1:publish/></D:prop>
      <D:status>HTTP/1.1 409 Conflict</D:status>
   </D:propstat>
   <D:propstat>
      <D:prop><ns1:temp-property/></D:prop>
      <D:status>HTTP/1.1 424 Failed Dependency</D:status>
```

Listing 7–12   PROPPATCH response body with failed dependencies. *(Continued)*

```
   </D:propstat>
</D:response>
</D:multistatus>
```

7.3.5   PROPPATCH to Nonexistent Resource

The WebDAV specification doesn't explicitly state what to do with a PROPPATCH request when the resource doesn't exist. We can imagine two possibilities: either the server returns 404 Not Found, or it creates a new resource and returns 201 Created. Most servers do the former. The specification writers intended PROPPATCH to fail when the resource doesn't exist, because all the methods that are intended to create new resources are carefully documented to explain that behavior and how it must work, but PROPPATCH does not include this kind of documentation.

Microsoft Exchange 2000 will allow PROPPATCH of a null resource to create a regular resource that cannot be made a collection. This is nonstandard behavior, although it doesn't seem to be particularly harmful.

7.4   How Properties Are Stored

WebDAV does *not* restrict the number of properties on a resource or in the repository, the maximum size for a property name or a property value, or the total amount of metadata that exists on a resource.

However, a few WebDAV server implementations may have such restrictions. For example, the default mod_dav configuration restricts the maximum size of a property to 8kb (although this can be increased by plugging in a different back end). This might make it infeasible for clients to store an image as a property (so usually images are stored as a resource body). Server designers should ensure that any property size limits are set appropriately high, because there isn't a good way in WebDAV to communicate the server's limits to the client. Instead, the server simply rejects the client's request with 507 Insufficient Storage, which might mean that the property is too big, the file is too big, the disk is full, or the user's quota is full.

Some WebDAV servers store property values in a database; others store them in special property value files in the file system, separately from the resource bodies. Some file systems are capable of storing streams of data alongside file body streams, in which case the properties can be stored in the data stream. Properties must be moved and copied with the resource entity no matter how they are stored. The choice of storage should not affect property values, character sets, or size.

7.5   Required Properties

The required WebDAV properties are displayname, getlastmodifed, creationdate, getcontentlength, getcontentlanguage, getcontenttype, resourcetype, and source. Conveniently, this list includes all the values you might expect to see in a directory listing in typical file explorer software: the resource name, the kind of resource it is, when it was last changed, and how big it is. This means that WebDAV properties can easily be used to integrate remote repository navigation into existing user interfaces, as was done with Web Folders on Windows, WebDAV-FS on Mac OS X, and Nautilus on Linux.

In addition to the required properties, three live properties are optional: getetag, supportedlock, and lockdiscovery. The first can't be supported if the server doesn't support ETags, although support for both the getetag property and other ETag functionality is strongly recommended. The two lock-related properties are required if locking support is advertised.

All the properties defined in WebDAV are live properties by definition. That means any behavior required for live properties (such as how properties are moved and copied) applies to all of these.

7.5.1 creationdate

The creationdate property is straightforward; it holds the date and time when the resource was created. The resource may have been created with a PUT request, an MKCOL request, a COPY, or some other operation.

Although WebDAV is silent on these matters, normally a file moved from one location to another or simply renamed does not have its creationdate value reset. However, a COPY operation necessarily creates a new resource, so in that case, creationdate is given a new value on the target resource.

Some WebDAV servers protect the creationdate property, but others do not. If a client wants to change the creationdate property, it can try. However, it may be better for the client to use a custom property. For example, if the client is backing up local files and wants the backup to include the file system creation timestamp, the client should create a new dead property for that value.

The creationdate format is the standard IETF recommended date/time format described in Section 7.1.9:

```
<D:creationdate>2003-03-03T20:59:00Z</D:creationdate>
```

7.5.2 displayname

The **display name** of a resource is the string that should be shown to the user. Often, it's a different string than the file name. Many systems restrict file names to limited sets of characters, but display names for resources ought to be able to handle international character sets. When WebDAV was defined, there were few reasonable options for displaying non-ASCII characters in URLs, so displayname was defined in part for better internationalization characteristics.

Some examples of valid displayname property values:

```
readme.htm
Marketing Plan
Les Misérables
```

Many WebDAV servers (Exchange 2000, IIS 5.0, Xythos WFS 4.0) tie the value of displayname to the URL so that if the final element in the URL path is `readme.htm`, the
value of displayname must also be `readme.htm`. This doesn't contravene any normative
statements in the WebDAV RFC, but it doesn't match what the WebDAV designers had in
mind. It means the displayname value must be unique within a collection, and it can't
change without making links break. On these implementations, the displayname property
is protected so that clients cannot change the value directly. If a resource is renamed with a
MOVE request, the value of displayname automatically changes.

Exchange 2000 defines another way to assign friendly, non-unique names to files. The user
may change the value of a subject property, which is initially given the same value as displayname but may be changed. The subject value does not have to be unique within a collection,
so a user may see many emails in an Exchange 2000 folder with the same subject but different
URLs and displayname values.

The mod_dav implementation treats displayname almost as if it were a dead property.
When a new resource is created on a mod_dav server, displayname is left blank. It is writable, so
the user can give it a value later. The disadvantage to this approach is that the property will be
left blank most of the time, so it ends up being ignored by clients.

The different implementations seem to have left the displayname property at an impasse,
unusable. Since clients can't rely on the property being writable, clients don't use it as a display
name. The working group could update the standard to declare it to be a writable property, but
this would make some deployed clients and servers uninteroperable or noncompliant. Some discussions have involved defining a new property that is clearly required to be writable, but the
question is still wide open.

7.5.3   getcontentlanguage

Getcontentlanguage must exist on every resource and must be returned whenever the client
asks for all the properties on a resource. Its value is obtained from the HTTP `Content-
Language` header the client sends when the resource body is updated, and it can be returned by
the server in the same header when the body is retrieved. Getcontentlanguage only applies to the
body, not the properties, of a resource. The property value can contain multiple language codes
separated by a comma if the document is expressed in multiple languages.

A value of this property is a "language tag" as defined for HTTP/1.1. HTTP/1.1 uses the exact
same language tags in the responses to GET requests. A language tag includes both a language code
such as EN for English and a country code such as US for United States. Some examples:

```
en          Any variant of English
en-ca       English as spoken in Canada
en, fr      English or French
```

The server usually resets the value of this property based on each request that updates
the body of the resource. If a PUT request includes the HTTP `Content-Language` header,
then the value can be set directly from this header. (The syntax and allowed values are the

same.) When handling COPY and MOVE, the server should apply the source resource's language value.

Unfortunately, language information isn't often provided or used by clients. There are two disadvantages to this failing:

- The obvious drawback to missing language information is that users don't have this information. Users might want to download a document only if it is in a specific language, but they can't tell until the document has been downloaded.
- The less obvious drawback is that some text display choices such as font and layout depend on the language. Some languages share Unicode characters, but these same characters are displayed differently depending on the language selected. Language information helps clients display the document the way it was intended to be viewed.

 I recommend that clients send this information when creating resources (or set the value later) if they have a reasonable idea what the value should be. As of 2002, only the Microsoft SharePoint WebDAV client is known to send the `Content-Language` header.

Server implementations of WebDAV vary in their behavior with respect to the `Content-Language` header and getcontentlanguage property, even though the feature is a requirement of RFC2518. Xythos WebFile Server (WFS) saves the property if it is provided in the header but returns an empty property value if no language information is available. In contrast, mod_dav always returns a value derived from the system settings and ignores the value of the `Content-Language` header sent by the client. In any case, servers should *not* return 404 Not Found for this (or any) required property.

7.5.4   getcontentlength

The getcontentlength property value is an integer. It can be most accurately interpreted as "the value of the `Content-Length` header if the contents were to be retrieved using a GET request." In most cases for static resources, this is also the size of the resource body in storage.

 The property value may not be accurate, depending on the server implementation and its tradeoffs in arriving at an accurate number. In some server implementations, the file storage size may be greater or less than the number of bytes in the response to GET—for example, if the stored file includes metadata that is stripped out before sending or if the file is stored zipped or on tape. In this case, it may be too time-consuming for the server to calculate the exact length, and instead the stored size is used as an approximation, even though this is does not comply with the specification.

Dynamic Web pages can, of course, vary in length with each GET request. If a WebDAV server supports dynamic resources, it must deal with this problem in some manner. Since authoring clients that support WebDAV are typically more interested in the source code for a dynamically generated resource than in the result, a server may reasonably provide the length of the source code when clients request the getcontentlength property.

7.5.5 getcontenttype

The getcontenttype property is quite useful because clients can use it to display an informative icon in directory listings. Before downloading a file called README, the client can see whether it will be in text format or not. WebDAV, like HTTP and email [RFC2045], uses MIME types to express the content format.

The server originally gets the value of this property from the `Content-Type` header on the PUT request that creates the resource. If the resource was created with COPY or MOVE, the server gets the content type from the source resource.

Examples of values for the getcontenttype property include:

`text/plain`	*Ordinary unformatted text*
`text/html`	*Text formatted using HTML*
`image/jpeg`	*An image represented in the JPEG format*

7.5.6 getetag

The ETag of a document is a token or tag used to identify a particular content instance. It's used throughout the World Wide Web for clients and proxies to find out if a document has changed or not (see Section 3.4). The client or proxy can then decide whether to load it from a cache instead, potentially saving bandwidth and returning results faster. The concept is simple: Merely change the ETag of the document every time its contents change.

WebDAV provides the ETag as a property, which gives clients an important benefit: They can find out all the current ETags in one request. The client can then quickly choose which files to update if several files are stored locally in a cache or a synchronized local copy.

W h y   U s e   E T a g ?

Although it's theoretically possible to use a sufficiently accurate value of getlast-modified to see if a resource needs to be updated or synchronized, it's not easy or reliable. Servers and clients both may have clock skew, time zones make it complicated, and the timestamp has to be accurate.

ETags were defined in HTTP to reliably figure out when to update or synchronize a resource. WebDAV makes this even easier, by providing a way (PROPFIND) to retrieve the ETag values for all the resources in a collection.

The value of an ETag and the value of the getetag property are the same: an opaque blob as far as the client is concerned. No attempt should be made to learn anything from the structure or contents of the ETag, because it's only required to be unique, not meaningful.

The ETag value must change when the body changes but not when only property values change. There are a couple of problems with tracking property changes with ETags:

- HTTP clients aren't aware of properties, yet they use ETags in caching. An HTTP client will unnecessarily download an entity that hasn't changed if its ETag changes. This is only a performance issue.
- WebDAV clients that use GET and then PUT to author files must use the ETag to verify that the file hasn't changed between the GET and the PUT. Even if the client locked the file, the lock may have expired accidentally. If the ETag indicates that the file has changed, users may be prompted to overwrite nonexistent changes or throw away their own changes unnecessarily. It's best to cause this kind of user confusion as seldom as possible.

7.5.7 getlastmodified

Many file systems display the time a file was last modified in detailed directory listings. WebDAV provides this property for that functionality. This property should not be used for caching if ETags are available, because dates are less reliable than ETags, but it's still quite useful for displaying to the user.

The issue of whether property changes result in an updated getlastmodified value has been discussed quite a bit because it's underspecified in RFC2518. I recommend tracking modifications to the body only, not properties, for a number of reasons:

- The basic language in the RFC implies that since the property is linked to the `Last-Modified` header on a GET request, it should take the same value. That is, it contains the date that the content returned by a GET request was last modified.
- Implementations that store resources directly in the file system need to use the file system semantics for the property. Usually in this case the modified date only changes when the body or content is updated.
- Clients may depend on the value of the property to refresh a cache of the resource or decide whether to overwrite it. A value that changes when properties change would involve unnecessary work and possible confusion.

Some WebDAV Working Group members argued that properties were an important part of the context of a resource, and clients needed to know when properties changed as well (perhaps to synchronize property values, too). However, clients can't rely on this unless all servers behave the same way, which they don't. The Apache module mod_dav and Microsoft's implementations of WebDAV update the getlastmodified timestamp only when bodies or contents change. At least one Oracle implementation updates it for every property change. A new property could easily be defined for the last time properties were updated.

7.5.8 resourcetype

The resourcetype property is used to distinguish between an ordinary resource (represented by an empty property value) and a special kind of resource, a collection. It's also intended to be easily extensible so that a resource can advertise that it is a new type, even a custom type defined in a custom namespace. Thus, the value of this property is expressed in XML.

Microsoft Web Folders doesn't do a good job of handling the resourcetype property. It assumes that if the property is not empty, then the resource must be a collection. Of course, it might not be a collection—it might be a custom or new resource type that does not have any children to query. This quirk makes it difficult for protocol extension designers to add new kinds of resources that aren't collections (such as versions, added by DeltaV, which we'll see in Chapter 10, *WebDAV Products and Tools*) without making life hard for Web Folders users.

When a client sees a resourcetype it doesn't recognize, it should assume it's a regular non-collection resource. That probably means it can be locked, moved, or copied.

7.5.9 source

The source property is intended to contain the URLs to the source files that are used to build a dynamic resource. The property is empty on static resources. On a dynamic resource, the property may contain one or several URLs because some dynamic Web pages are compiled from multiple source files. In theory, this should allow clients to author dynamic pages on Web sites.

A source URL might be a regular URL, but it might also be a parameterized URL. Any of these could be source URLs:

```
http://www.example.com/stockticker.jsp?getsource=true
http://www.example.com/__src/hr/emp-view.jsp
http://www.example.com/cgi-bin/emp-view.c
```

The source property is another complex XML-valued property. Listing 7–13 is taken straight from RFC2518.

Listing 7–13 Sample value for source property.

```
<?xml version="1.0" encoding="utf-8" ?>
<D:prop xmlns:D="DAV:" xmlns:F="http://www.foocorp.com/ Project/">
   <D:source>
      <D:link>
         <F:projfiles>Source</F:projfiles>
         <D:src>http://foo.bar/program</D:SRC>
         <D:dst>http://foo.bar/src/main.c</D:DST>
      </D:link>
      <D:link>
         <F:projfiles>Library</F:projfiles>
         <D:src>http://foo.bar/program</D:SRC>
         <D:dst>http://foo.bar/src/main.lib</D:DST>
      </D:link>
      <D:link>
         <F:projfiles>Makefile</F:projfiles>
         <D:src>http://foo.bar/program</D:SRC>
```

Listing 7–13 Sample value for source property. *(Continued)*

```
        <D:dst>http://foo.bar/src/makefile</D:DST>
      </D:link>
    </D:source>
</D:prop>
```

In theory, the client can simply GET each of the destination (dst) URLs in the property to view the source code. In practice, it's not so simple. Do destination URLs in the property point to WebDAV resources, HTTP resources, or others? Do all the source (src) URLs have to be the same URL? Does the source URL have to be the URL of the resource this property appears on? Is this property interoperable with or without the `projfiles` extension in the custom namespace?

The whole issue of authoring source code is seriously underspecified. In addition to the questions arising from the format of the source property, there are even more unanswered questions:

- To edit source code, should the client PUT to the original resource URL or the new one?
- How does a client add a new source file?
- What happens if more than one resource points to (uses) the same source code?
- When a dynamic resource is the source of a MOVE or a COPY operation, is the new resource created at the destination a dynamic resource or a static snapshot?
- Can any collection contain dynamic resources or only some?
- What kind of dynamic resources are supported on this server—JSP, ASP, CGI?

Not surprisingly, no known WebDAV server or client fully supports the source property, and certainly no interoperability has been shown. Some WebDAV servers (e.g., Microsoft Exchange 2000, Xythos WebFile Server) do not handle dynamic content at all. Other servers do support dynamic content, but they may not have a way of knowing what the URL is to get the unevaluated source code for the page (e.g., mod_dav).

IIS 5.0 does support dynamic content and does know where the source code is for some kinds of pages, including Active Server Pages. However, IIS 5.0 does not use the source property. The IIS 5.0 mechanism is the `Translate` header, which is described in Section 9.2.1.

The WebDAV specification is not clear on how to return properties that are required but do not have values, such as the source property on a static resource. The server may return an empty value for this property or return 404 Not Found.

7.6 Summary

The WebDAV property model gives every WebDAV resource a number of required properties and unlimited custom properties. Every property has a name, a namespace, and a value. The standard properties are in the `DAV:` namespace, whereas custom properties are in a namespace defined by the creator of the custom property. Property values can be strings, dates, numbers, or XML.

PROPFIND is used to discover property values. This method uses the `Depth` header to define how many resources the server must include in the results. `Depth 1` PROPFIND requests are very common as the standard way to get a listing of a directory's contents. The PROPFIND method can be used to ask for all properties defined in RFC2518 plus all custom properties, or it can be used to specify exactly which property values to return.

PROPPATCH is used to set or change property values or remove properties. Unlike PROPFIND, the PROPPATCH method only acts on a single resource, but PROPPATCH can change several properties in one request. The method is atomic: All property changes defined in the request are made, or none is made.

WebDAV requires seven live properties. These are creationdate, displayname, getcontentlanguage, getcontentlength, getcontenttype, getlastmodified, and resourcetype.

Three more live properties may be supported. The lockdiscovery and supportedlocks properties are required if the server supports locks. The getetag property is required if the server supports ETags.

Lock Operations

So far, all the methods and headers defined must be supported by all WebDAV servers. This chapter introduces the optional locking functionality. Locking is part of Class 2 WebDAV support, so if the server's response to an OPTIONS request only has DAV: 1 (Class 1 support), none of the requests in this chapter can be used (Class 1 and Class 2 support were defined in Chapter 5, Section 5.1.1). If the server supports WebDAV Class 2, all the operations in this chapter are supported as well as all the operations listed in Chapters 6 and 7.

A lock is a way of temporarily restricting access to modify a resource. The lock affects all users or principals, including the user who created the lock if the lock token is omitted in modification requests. Only the lock creator may use the lock token to modify the locked resource.

This chapter covers:

- How to create locks with the LOCK method
- How locks are removed by either server (with timeouts) or client (with the UNLOCK method)
- How to modify locked resources with the If: header providing lock tokens
- How other operations affect and are affected by locks

8.1   Lock Tokens

Every lock is identified with a token that must be universally unique. The lock token must be used in subsequent requests to change the locked resource or to unlock it.

Each lock token is a URI. Most servers use the `opaquelocktoken:` URI scheme defined by WebDAV for this purpose. The `opaquelocktoken:` scheme is used to construct valid URIs containing only a UUID followed by optional custom characters.

```
opaquelocktoken:f81d4fae-7dec-11d0-00a0c91e6bf6#myserver1234
```

It is also legal to use any syntactically correct URI, including a URL. For example:

```
http://example.com/locktokenURLspace/1234-5678-9012.lock
```

Since the lock token is opaque to the client, the uniqueness and the server's performance concerns (in generating lock tokens or looking up locks) are more important than how it looks or what kind of URI it is.

Clients must store the lock token in order to use it later to modify the resource or to refresh or remove the lock.

8.2   LOCK Method

The LOCK request is used in WebDAV both to get new locks and to refresh existing locks.

8.2.1   Creating a Lock

The server needs a number of pieces of information to create a lock. Listing 8–1 is an example of a LOCK request that locks a single file for exclusive use, followed by a run-through of each piece of information that appears in the request.

Listing 8–1   LOCK request.

```
LOCK /hr/ergonomics/posture.doc HTTP/1.1
Host: www.example.com
Timeout: Infinite
If-Match: *
Content-Type: text/xml; charset="utf-8"
Content-Length: xxxx
↵
<?xml version="1.0" encoding="utf-8" ?>
<D:lockinfo xmlns:D='DAV:'>
   <D:lockscope><D:exclusive/></D:lockscope>
   <D:locktype><D:write/></D:locktype>
   <D:owner xmlns:x="http://www.customapp.com/ns/">
      <x:lock-user>alice@example.com</x:lock-user>
      <x:created-by>Text Editor v1.2.5</x:created-by>
   </D:owner>
</D:lockinfo>
```

Table 8–1 takes each relevant piece of information in the request—the request URI, the new header, and the request body—to show what each piece means.

Table 8–1   Information Provided in a LOCK Request

Where	Information
Request-URI	The URL of the resource to be locked.
`Timeout` header (optional)	The desired lifetime of the lock. This header is optional. Values for the header may be either `Infinite` or an integer specifying a number of seconds. If the value is an integer, it is prefixed with `Second-`. `Timeout: Second-360` Multiple values may be included in a comma-separated list, starting with most preferred: `Timeout: Infinite, Second-604800` The server may ignore the suggested timeout completely.
`lockscope` element in body	Whether the lock is to be exclusive or shared. This element may contain either the `exclusive` or the `shared` element only: `<lockscope><exclusive/><lockscope>` or: `<lockscope><shared/><lockscope>`
`owner` element in body	A client-provided identifier for the lock owner (string or XML). The server must save this identifier and return it in the lockdiscovery property so that other users and other client software can see some information about the lock creator. In Listing 8–1, the client responsibly identified the user as well as the application software that created the lock. See Section 8.2.6 for more considerations relating to this field.
`locktype` element in body	The type of lock. Even though the only legal value is the `write` element, this element must appear anyway. Future protocol extensions may identify new types of locks. `<locktype><write/><locktype>`

Assuming the LOCK request is successful, most of the same information (plus the lock token) is returned in the response, as shown in Listing 8–2. The lock information is also preserved in the lockdiscovery property as long as the lock exists. The format of the response body is the same as the format of the lockdiscovery property, which we cover in more detail in Section 8.5.1. The client should pay particular attention to the lock token and the timeout, in case the server chooses a different timeout value. Since there are no restrictions on how the server chooses a timeout value, the value could be shorter or longer than the timeout requested by the client.

Listing 8–2   Response to LOCK successfully locked the resource.

```
HTTP/1.1 200 OK
Date: Sun, 29 Jul 2001 15:24:17 GMT
Lock-Token:opaquelocktoken:e71d4fae-5dec-22d6-fea5-00a0c91e6
Content-Type: text/xml; charset="utf-8"
Content-Length: xxxx
⏎
<?xml version="1.0" encoding="utf-8" ?>
<D:prop xmlns:D="DAV:">
<D:lockdiscovery>
   <D:activelock>
      <D:locktype><D:write/></D:locktype>
      <D:lockscope><D:exclusive/></D:lockscope>
      <D:depth>0</D:depth>
      <D:owner xmlns:a="http://www.customapp.com/ns/">
         <a:lock-user>alice@example.com</a:lock-user>
         <a:created-by>Text Editor v1.2.5</a:created-by>
      </D:owner>
      <D:timeout>Second-604800</D:timeout>
      <D:locktoken>
         <D:href>opaquelocktoken:e71d4fae-5dec ↴
            -22d6-fea5-00a0c91e6</D:href>
      </D:locktoken>
   </D:activelock>
</D:lockdiscovery>
</D:prop>
```

The status code for a successful LOCK response on an existing resource must be 200 OK. The body must contain the value of the lockdiscovery property at the point of time right after the lock is created (that means that if multiple shared locks existed, the response would show all of them). As the user requested, an exclusive write lock was granted. The server did not grant an infinite lifetime but instead chose a timeout of one week. The server also realized that since the request was made on a noncollection, the depth must be 0.

Note that the lock token is shown both in the body and in the Lock-Token header. This is required by RFC2518 in response to the creation of a new lock.

Clients should pay attention to the LOCK response return code. The return code is 201 Created, not 200 OK, if a new resource was created. The client may have expected there to be an existing resource to lock, but there's a chance the existing resource was just deleted by another user. Clients should use the If-Match or If-None-Match header on a LOCK request to make sure that the correct resource is being locked. The request in Listing 8–1 shows how to use the If-Match header to assert that the resource must exist; otherwise, the server should fail the request rather than create a new resource.

8.2.2 Locking a Collection

When the Request-URI identifies a collection, the LOCK request may include a `Depth` header. If the `Depth` header is omitted, the server must choose a default depth of `infinity`. The values `0` and `infinity` are supported when locking collections, but a depth of `1` is never supported with a LOCK request (thus, servers should respond with 400 Bad Request to a LOCK request with a depth of `1`).

Depth Infinity A lock depth `infinity` on a collection is easy to interpret: Lock the collection and every descendant of the collection, as illustrated in Figure 8–1. No write operation, whether PUT, PROPPATCH, COPY, MOVE, or DELETE, can be applied to the collection or any descendant of the collection without providing the correct lock token. It also means that if this is an exclusive lock, then none of the descendants of the collection can be locked with a different lock until the infinite-depth lock is removed.

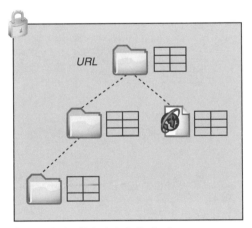

Figure 8–1 Depth infinity lock.

Despite the apparent simplicity, there are some difficult issues to deal with when infinite-depth collection locks are used. These issues are more related to the `If` header syntax than to the application of the lock itself, so we'll discuss that in a bit (Section 8.4.3). In the meantime, it's enough to point out that some servers (including IIS 5.0) don't support this type of lock, and most clients don't use it.

Authoring applications may never need infinite-depth locks, because typically the user opens files one at a time to edit them, and the application locks each file as it is opened. Multiple resources may be opened for simultaneous editing, but there's no need to lock the parent collection (which would prevent other users from creating new resources).

File management clients may sometimes need to lock collections, but even for these clients, operations on many files at once are rare. When the user does want to operate on entire collections, it's often possible to use a single infinite-depth COPY or MOVE request, in which case a lock may not be required.

Clients do not use collection locks much. Perhaps it's because IIS 5.0 doesn't support collection locks, and it's easier for clients to rely on features that are supported by all popular WebDAV servers. Perhaps clients do not use infinite-depth locks much because the If header is quite complicated to use with multiple resources (see Section 8.4.13).

When a collection descendent is included in the scope of a depth infinity collection lock, even though the descendent is not directly locked, the value of its lockdiscovery property must include all the lock information.

Depth 0   A depth 0 lock on a collection means that the collection's contents and metadata, but not the contents or metadata of its children or other descendents, are protected from changes. The contents of a collection are usually interpreted as the list of children, so if the list changes, that's governed by the lock. Changes that take place that don't affect the list of children are allowed, however. Figure 8–2 shows how the lock encompasses changes to the collection itself, its membership list, and its properties but not the content of its descendents.

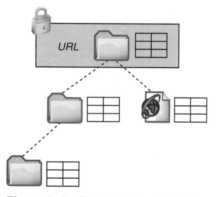

Figure 8–2   Depth 0 collection lock.

Here are a few examples to illustrate this concept. If the collection /hr is locked with a depth 0 lock, some write operations are always affected, and some are affected only under certain circumstances. These requests *are* affected by a depth 0 lock on /hr:

- PROPPATCH the locked collection.
- DELETE a child of the locked collection because that would alter the contents of the collection.
- MKCOL or PUT when these result in a new child being created in the locked collection.
- MOVE a child to or from the locked collection.
- MOVE the locked collection somewhere else, or MOVE to a destination that overwrites the locked collection.
- COPY to a destination that overwrites the locked collection, or COPY, which creates a new child inside the locked collection.

These requests are *not* affected by the same depth 0 lock:

- PROPPATCH any resource inside the collection.
- DELETE or MOVE requests that result in the removal of a resource within the locked collection but not a direct child of the locked collection.
- PUT, MKCOL, COPY, or MOVE requests that result in the creation of a resource within children of the locked collection (inside subfolders).

There are a couple of interesting use cases for the depth 0 collection lock. The most useful case is simply to change properties. If the repository supports access control, depth 0 collection locks would be quite useful so that the client can get the access control information, modify it, and resubmit the changed access control information to the server.

Another use case is to be able to create a resource without risk of overwriting an existing one (a problem first discussed in Section 5.4.3). When a resource is locked depth 0, only the holder of the lock can create new resources in the collection, but the lock doesn't prevent other users from modifying the body or properties of existing child resources. To ensure that a file creation is not overwriting an existing resource, the client can issue a LOCK (depth 0) on the collection, a PROPFIND on the collection to see if the resource exists, and then the PUT or MKCOL request to create the new resource. Of course, an infinite-depth lock would serve the same purpose, but that would be overkill, unnecessarily preventing other users' actions.

8.2.3 Creating Lock-Null Resources

If a LOCK request is sent to an unmapped URL, rather than return 404 Not Found, the server must create a lock-null resource (and return a status of 201 Created).

 Lock-null resources are a special kind of resource invented to prevent the lost update problem for new resources. They are unnecessary, not broadly implemented, and may be obsolete in future drafts of the standard.

Lock-null resources were invented to help prevent two clients sending a PUT request for a new resource at nearly the same time. The client with the second PUT will unintentionally overwrite the content first put there. It's not sufficient to just check to see if the resource already exists, because with the latency of requests over the Internet, there's no guarantee that the resource will be in the same state when the actual PUT request is made.

A lock-null resource behaves in the following manner:

- It is protected by the lock in the same way it would be if the resource existed—the lock token must be in the If header for changes to be allowed.
- It does not show up in the parent collection as a child member.
- It does not support methods other than PUT, MKCOL, OPTIONS, PROPFIND, LOCK, and UNLOCK. (Other methods must result in an error.)

- It supports the lock-related properties, lockdiscovery and supportedlocks, but not the get* properties (e.g., getcreationdate, getcontenttype).
- It can be converted from a lock-null resource to a collection *or* a noncollection resource.
- If the lock is removed before the lock-null resource is converted to a regular resource, the lock-null resource is removed as well.

After the lock-null resource is created, the next step is usually for the client to convert the lock-null resource into a regular resource or collection, using the lock token, of course. Now the resource is no longer a lock-null resource, so it behaves as a regular resource or collection, and property changes can be made. When all the write operations are complete, the client will probably unlock the resource.

Preventing Overwrite on Create with Collection Locks

Clients can also ensure that their new resource won't overwrite another new resource by locking the entire collection. However, users may not have permission to lock the whole collection, and this prevents other users from modifying other resources that aren't even affected by the new resource creation.

The best way to solve this problem is to put a conditional header on the creation request, as described in Section 3.7.6:

```
If-None-Match: *
```

8.2.4 Refreshing a Lock

Another use of the LOCK method is to refresh an existing lock on a resource (see Listing 8–3). An existing lock can be renewed or refreshed any time before it expires.

Listing 8–3   LOCK request to refresh a lock.

```
LOCK /hr/ergonomics/posture.doc HTTP/1.1
Host: www.example.com
Timeout: Second-300
If: (<opaquelocktoken:e71d4fae-5dec-22d6-fea5-00a0c91e6>)
↵
```

The Timeout header is optional on a lock refresh request, but the If header is required. The syntax and meaning of the Timeout header are unchanged. The If header is required in order to supply the correct lock token, because there may be more than one shared lock on a given resource. Although the If header syntax has not been described yet, there will be a lot to say about it shortly (see Section 8.4.2).

8.2.5   Lock Timeout

The server controls lock timeout. It has a great deal of flexibility:

- It can grant a shorter timeout than the client requested.
- It can grant a longer timeout than the client requested.
- It can remove timed-out locks aggressively as soon as the timeout is reached or allow a grace period.

Servers grant shorter lock timeouts than requested to keep unused locks to a minimum in a system where there are many authors collaborating or to reduce the system resources required to track and maintain locks. Many servers refuse to grant infinite length locks, but there's no reason that the client can't request those anyway. Typically, the server responds with the maximum lifetime it allows.

It's a little less obvious why servers grant a longer lock timeout than the client requests, but this practice arises from real implementation experience. The MS Web Folders implementation Office 2000 uses requests lock timeouts as short as two minutes. That requires the client software to refresh the lock at least that often, as long as the user still has the document open for editing. A server receiving lock refresh requests every two minutes from thousands of clients may see a noticeable performance degradation from this practice. Thus, the server grants the client a longer lock timeout. Happily, Web Folders does not refresh every two minutes if the lock lifetime granted by the server is longer.

Grace periods are also found in existing lock timeout implementations because Web Folders doesn't give itself much leeway when refreshing locks. See Section 8.6.2 for client lock refresh guidelines and an explanation of why the Web Folders practice causes many user errors.

Although the server has final power to choose a timeout, the client should try to give an opinion if the client has useful extra information about what the user intends. When a user opens a document in Word and makes changes, Word automatically locks the file for a short time. That's reasonable, because Word will be editing the document only as long as the software is still active and connected to the network.

In contrast, a client application that allows the user to "check out" or synchronize files for editing offline may choose to lock certain files for a longer period, say from 12 to 72 hours. In this case, the client application has some indication that the author wants to reserve the file and prevent changes from other users. The lock will then last even while the author's editing software is inactive or not connected to the network.

8.2.6   Use of the Lock Owner Element

When a user wants to modify a resource but a lock already exists, often the only recourse is to wait until the lock expires or is removed. However, if information about the lock owner is provided, it's possible the user may be able to ask the lock owner to remove the lock. Thus, the `owner` tag is included in the lockdiscovery property so that one human user can contact another.

The value of the lock `owner` tag may be XML or a string. The client defines the value when the lock is created. The client should provide useful identification information about the user who created the lock. This could be an email address and a client software identification string, as shown in the examples here. It could also include a full name, a URL to a Web page, a Principal URL as defined by the Access control extensions to WebDAV, or some other construct related to user or client identity. Although it's not specified, the `owner` tag can contain an `href` tag if the information identifying the lock creator is formatted as a URI (this is shown by the examples in RFC2518, although it's not required). Clients and servers must be prepared to handle a regular string, one or more `href` tags, or any other XML construct.

 WebDAV interoperability events have supplied a great deal of information about how to use and how not to use the `owner` element, since it wasn't unambiguously defined in RFC2518 yet it's extremely useful. Some clients (most notably those from Adobe) use the lock-owner field to contain custom machine-parsable information about the lock and the software that created the lock. The information is not intended for the user to view, but instead for communication between client software.

Servers should not enforce any particular syntax in the owner value, or some clients will fail to interoperate. Some clients send nothing in this element. A server could use authentication information to replace a blank or missing owner value with some information identifying the user, but the server should not alter a nonblank owner value, or some clients will fail to interoperate.

8.2.7 Special Status Codes for LOCK

If the resource is already locked with an exclusive lock, the server returns 423 Locked. Moreover, if the resource is already locked with a shared lock and the client requests an exclusive lock, the server responds with a 423 Locked.

Both 200 OK and 201 Created indicate that locks were created. The latter shows that a lock-null resource (or in the case of IIS 5.0, a locked empty resource) was created.

Many server implementations can return a 401 Unauthorized or 403 Forbidden response if the user asking for the lock does not have permission to perform write methods on a resource. Although it might be useful for a client to be able to lock a resource while reading it, to make sure that the resource doesn't change during the read, most clients don't do this.

8.3 UNLOCK Method

The UNLOCK request is used to release a lock so that the resources locked may be modified or locked by other users. The syntax is simple (see Listing 8–4).

 Note that the lock token must be provided for the server to know which lock to remove, because there may be more than one on a resource. Also note that the user sends his or her authorization. The server should only allow the lock creator to remove a lock, even though

---

Listing 8–4 UNLOCK request and response.

```
UNLOCK /hr/ergonomics/posture.doc HTTP/1.1
Host: www.example.com
Lock-Token:
   <opaquelocktoken:a515cfa4-5da4-22e1-f5b5-00a0451e6>
Authorization: Basic dGVzdHVzZXI6dGVzdHVzZXI=
```
↵

Response:
```
HTTP/1.1 204 No Content
Date: Sun, 29 Jul 2001 15:24:17 GMT
```
↵

---

the lock token was provided. Typically, only the user for whom the lock was created can remove the lock, but some servers allow specially privileged users, such as the resource owner, to remove any lock.

Clients should release locks when they're no longer being used. Otherwise, stale locks prevent other authorized users from making their own edits.

8.3.1 Removing Another User's Lock

Under certain circumstances, client software may find it desirable to use the lockdiscovery property to discover the lock token and try to remove the lock, even if the lock was originally taken out by some other client process on the same machine or another user. Provided the server supports this, it can be done in a responsible manner by the client:

- Client may choose not to offer or allow this operation unless the lock was created by the same user who is currently logged in.
- Client should warn the user. "Are you sure you want to remove this lock ... "
- Client must only use the discovered lock token to do an UNLOCK, even if the server allows the lock token to be used with any method. Then, if necessary, the client can create a new lock for its own write operations. If this is done properly, then when the holder of the original locktoken tries to update the file, that client will be informed that the original lock disappeared and so knows that changes may have been made.
- An automated client should not remove locks that it didn't create. A consistent string in the lock owner string could help the automated client determine which locks it created.

DAV Explorer and Goliath are two WebDAV clients that are known to allow the user to grab the lock token and do away with the lock, even if the lock was created by another user or process.

 The server also has an important role in allowing locks to be used and removed in a responsible manner. The server should only allow the lock token to be used by the same authorized user who created the lock, except potentially when a user with a high level of permissions needs to destroy the lock. Still, even users with high levels of permissions should not be allowed to alter a resource using a lock taken out by a different authorized user, because the client software that took out the lock originally will have no way of detecting that its lock has been used to make modifications. Instead, if the lock is deleted, the client that originally took out the lock will know as soon as it tries to use the lock (perform a write operation, renew, or unlock) that it is no longer valid and it must begin again.

8.3.2 Special Response Codes for UNLOCK

A successful response to UNLOCK is 204 No Content because the response message has no body. The most common failure status codes are:

- 401 Unauthorized: If the client isn't authorized to unlock the resource (it's somebody else's lock).
- 400 Bad Request: If the client does not provide a lock token.
- 412 Precondition Failed: If the client provides a lock token to unlock a resource that isn't locked or provides an incorrect lock token.

8.4 Using Locked Resources

Whenever a locked resource is updated, the lock token must be provided in the request. This is done by including the lock token in the If header along with the request.

The If header is a conditional header, like the HTTP headers If-Match, If-None-Match, and If-Modified-Since. Its role as a conditional header is combined with an additional role: It's used by the client to provide the lock token when updating locked resource. Since a WebDAV server must receive the lock token to allow any change to a locked resource, the client must both provide the lock token and make sure that the condition in the If header is true.

The dual purpose of the If header was intended to ensure that clients don't overwrite a resource in a mistaken belief that it is locked and protected from lost updates. If a client issues a LOCK request and then a PUT request with the lock token, it's possible that the lock was lost in between those two requests through a server failure, a client failure, or a connection failure. If the lock was lost, then it's possible that the resource changed, and the PUT request is overwriting an important change. It would be good client design to provide the lock token as well as provide a conditional on the request, saying to the server, "Do this PUT operation, using this lock token, if the lock is still there." The design of the If header combines the provision of the lock token and the conditional together to enforce this good client design. As we'll see later, clients don't always want this to be enforced (Section 8.4.13).

When a change request fails because the correct lock tokens are missing, the response code is 423 Locked. When the request fails because the If header conditional checks fail, then the status code is 412 Precondition Failed (as with the HTTP/1.1 conditional headers). If both problems occur on a single request, the server must choose one of the two status codes.

Although the `If` header is only necessary with write operations on locked resources (PUT, MOVE, COPY, etc.), it can also be used with read operations or on unlocked resources. In those situations, the `If` header behaves solely as a conditional on the request operation.

8.4.1   Overwriting a Single Locked Resource

I've shown a simple and common example of the `If` header in refreshing a lock (Section 8.2.4). The next most common use of the `If` header is in a request that updates a single locked resource. This kind of request uses the `If` header in the same way, providing a single lock token that corresponds to the resource identified in the Request URI (see Listing 8–5).

Listing 8–5   Request using PUT with lock token.

```
PUT /hr/ergonomics/posture.doc HTTP/1.1
Host: www.example.com
If: (<opaquelocktoken:e71d4fae-5dec-22d6-fea5-00a0c91e6>)
Content-Type: application/ms-word
Content-Length: xxx
↵
[Word file goes here...]
```

If the lock token in this `If` header matches the target resource (i.e., if there is a valid lock on `posture.doc` with this lock token), then this request will succeed.

This is a simple example of the **untagged list** syntax, one of two syntaxes supported by the `If` header.

8.4.2   If Header Features

The `If` header supports a number of features by supporting two different syntaxes and two kinds of tokens:

- Lock tokens can appear in the `If` header, enclosed in angle brackets (already shown previously).
- ETags can appear in the `If` header, enclosed in square brackets. Section 8.4.3 shows an example and explains what this accomplishes.
- Multiple tokens are ANDed together as shown in Section 8.4.3.
- Any token can be checked for *not* matching by including a NOT keyword, as shown in Section 8.4.7.
- An untagged list is one in which each token must apply to every resource affected by the current operation. These are described in Section 8.4.3 as applied to a single resource and in Section 8.4.5 as applied to multiple resources.

- Tagged lists offer a slightly more complicated but more powerful syntax, where each token is tagged with a full URL to specify what resource to compare the token to. The full syntax for tagged lists is in Section 8.4.6.
- Parentheses can group together multiple tokens in either tagged lists or untagged lists. Multiple groups are ORed together, as shown in Sections 8.4.3 and 8.4.5.

Tagged lists can do almost everything untagged lists can do except apply a single token to multiple resources. The best syntax for the job depends on the job—sometimes one syntax is easier to get right than the other. It seems to require a fair amount of experience and experimentation for client implementors to choose the right If header syntax and apply it to an operation on locked resources. The examples here should give some idea.

8.4.3   Untagged Token Lists

The simpler of the two syntaxes defined for the If header is the untagged syntax. An untagged token list contains tokens without any URL "tags." Each token must be compared to all the resources affected by the operation.

One header can have multiple token lists. Each list is grouped with outer parentheses. Within one list, all tokens must match for the request to succeed: In Boolean terms, the token matches are combined with AND logic. Between lists, the server must apply Boolean OR logic. Therefore, for a request with the If header containing untagged token lists to succeed, all tokens in at least one list must match the request-URI resource.

Preventing Caching

RFC2518 recommends that whenever a client uses the If header, the server should take steps to prevent non-WebDAV proxies from returning cached results. HTTP/1.0 and HTTP/1.1 defined different headers for this purpose, so the client may include both headers in any GET request with the If header.

```
HTTP/1.1: Cache-control: no-cache
HTTP/1.0: Pragma: no-cache
```

The client will delete the locked resource shown in Figure 8–3. To delete this file only if it's unchanged, the client needs to provide both an ETag (to ensure that it's unchanged) and a lock token (for the delete to be permitted). The request in Listing 8–6 will succeed only if the ETag is correct AND if the resource is still locked with the lock token given.

8.4.4   Untagged Token List and OR

Imagine a backup client has archived copies of an old resource. Over time, the client has made several backed-up copies. Now it wants to delete the old resource from the main repository, but

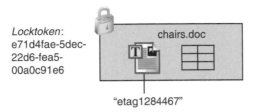

Locktoken:
e71d4fae-5dec-
22d6-fea5-
00a0c91e6

chairs.doc

"etag1284467"

Figure 8–3 ETag and lock token for resource.

Listing 8–6 Use of If header with lock token and ETag.

```
DELETE /hr/ergonomics/chairs.doc HTTP/1.1
Host: www.example.com
Cache-control: no-cache
Pragma: no-cache
If: (<opaquelocktoken:e71d4fae-5dec-22d6-fea5-00a0c91e6>
    [etag1284467])
⏎
```

only if the archive contains the correct backed-up copies. There are two copies in backup for which source ETags were recorded when the resource was retrieved. Figure 8–4 shows the backup client, its table of archived resources and ETags, and the state of the server.

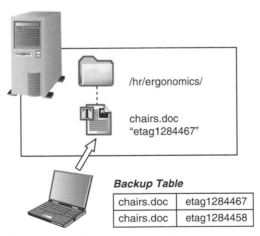

/hr/ergonomics/

chairs.doc
"etag1284467"

Backup Table

| chairs.doc | etag1284467 |
| chairs.doc | etag1284458 |

Figure 8–4 Comparing two ETags to one resource to see if it is already backed up.

To construct a single efficient DELETE request that confirms that a backup exists, the backup client must provide both ETags and tell the server to compare them with a logical OR operation. This is accomplished with the request shown in Listing 8–7. The `If` header contains two lists, each enclosed in parentheses, and the conditions from the two lists are compared using OR logic. Each list contains one ETag. Thus, either ETag can match the resource being deleted, and the request will succeed.

Listing 8–7   If header example matching either of two ETags.

```
DELETE /hr/ergonomics/chairs.doc HTTP/1.1
Host: www.example.com
Cache-control: no-cache
Pragma: no-cache
If: ([etag1284458]) ([etag1284467])
↵
```

8.4.5   Untagged Lists on Requests Covering Multiple Resources

Requests can apply to multiple resources when the depth of the operation is 1 or `infinity`, and when the request has a destination as well as a source. When multiple resources are addressed with untagged tokens in the `If` header, each token must be compared to every addressed resource.

For this example, the client will attempt to move an entire collection to an archive location, which is merely another collection within the top-level collection (see Figure 8–5). The whole top-level collection is locked in order to achieve this goal. (There may be other top-level collections like `finance/` that are not locked.)

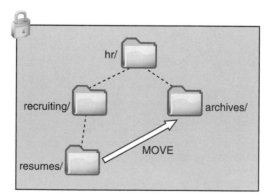

Figure 8–5   Moving a resource to another location within a collection lock.

To be allowed to perform this action, since `hr/` is locked, the client must provide the lock token somehow (see Listing 8–8).

Listing 8–8 If header with one lock token applying to multiple resources.

```
MOVE /hr/recruiting/resumes/ HTTP/1.1
Host: www.example.com
Destination: http://www.example.com/hr/archives/resumes/
Depth: infinity
Overwrite: T
Cache-control: no-cache
Pragma: no-cache
If: (<locktoken:e71d4fae-5dec-22d6-fea5-00a0c91e6>)
↵
```

This request will only succeed if all the resources involved are locked with the same lock, because only one lock token is provided and it isn't tagged with a specific resource's URL.

What if the two collections (source and destination) aren't covered by the same lock (see Figure 8–6)?

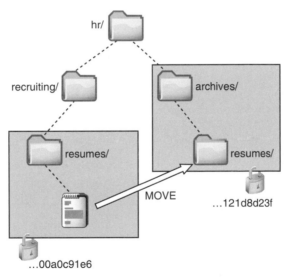

Figure 8–6 Moving a locked resource into a locked collection.

To make this MOVE request succeed, the client must include both lock tokens in the `If` header. One way of providing both lock tokens and still having the condition check pass is to allow each resource to match one lock token, using the OR syntax (see Listing 8–9).

Since the source matches one lock token and the destination matches the other (it doesn't matter which), this request will succeed. The server must make sure that both lock tokens are provided, and they are. The condition evaluates to `true` because one of the tests succeeds for each resource.

Listing 8–9   If header matching two lock tokens against two resources.

```
MOVE /hr/recruiting/resumes/gburlow.txt HTTP/1.1
Host: http://www.example.com
Destination:
   http://www.example.com/hr/archives/resumes/gburlow.txt
Depth: 0
Overwrite: T
Cache-control: no-cache
Pragma: no-cache
If: (<opaquelocktoken:e71d4fae-5dec-22d6-fea5-00a0c91e6>)
   (<opaquelocktoken:e71d4fae-5dec-22d6-cc76-121d8d23f>)
↵
```

 Each of the two lock tokens must appear in separate parentheses (instructing the server to compare with an OR, not an AND) because otherwise the server will attempt to match both lock tokens against both resources.

8.4.6   Tagged Token Lists

The previous MOVE example (Listing 8–9) could have succeeded in a number of cases, not just with a lock on `resumes/` and a lock on `archives/`. The request would also succeed if the `resumes/` collection were locked with one token, and the other token did not refer to any lock. Sometimes, the client may want to construct loose conditions as in Listing 8–9. However, it's also possible to construct much more specific conditions, which explicitly state what resource is locked and with exactly which lock token.

Tagged token lists are the mechanism used to apply multiple lock tokens to specific resources. "Tagged" means that each token list is associated with a complete URL for the resource to which the token applies. The tokens associated with a URL are only compared to that resource, not to all resources.

A client addressing the scenario in Figure 8–6 can also issue the request in Listing 8–10, to be very explicit about the state of resources. For the request to succeed, the two URLs in the `If` header must each be locked with a specific lock token.

Listing 8–10   Tagged If header matching tokens against specific URLs.

```
MOVE /hr/recruiting/resumes/gburlow.txt HTTP/1.1
Host: http://www.example.com
Destination:
   http://www.example.com/hr/archives/resumes/gburlow.txt
Depth: 0
Overwrite: T
Cache-control: no-cache
```

Listing 8–10   Tagged If header matching tokens against specific URLs. *(Continued)*

```
Pragma: no-cache
If: <http://www.example.com/hr/recruiting/resumes/gburlow.txt>
   (<opaquelocktoken:e71d4fae-5dec-22d6-fea5-00a0c91e6>)
   <http://www.example.com/hr/archives/resumes/>
   (<opaquelocktoken:e71d4fae-5dec-22d6-cc76-121d8d23f>)
⌐
```

 The URLs in tagged token lists must be absolute URLs and they must be encapsulated in angle brackets. Otherwise, the syntax is the same as that of an untagged list, and the logic for combining tokens inside and outside of parentheses remains the same:

When multiple tagged lists are present, a successful match must be reported from every tagged list. In other words, tagged list conditional results are combined with the Boolean AND operation. For example, if the If header contains two resources and four tokens as follows:

> <resource1> (token1) (token2) <resource2> (token3) <resource2> (token4)

The server must then translate to Boolean logic:

> ((resource1 matches token1) OR (resource1 matches token2))
> AND (resource2 matches token3) AND (resource2 matches token4)

Note that tagged lists are not compatible with untagged lists. Thus, there is no way to set up a condition asking if "all resources addressed match token A, AND one resource matches token B." In addition, since each set of tokens is associated with only one URL, there is no way to compare a group of resources with a token, except by specifying each resource individually.

Tagged lists are also useful for the case when only a few locked resources are affected in an operation addressing many resources. Let's take a scenario where the client wants to DELETE a collection in which there were many resources but only one is locked, as shown in Figure 8–7.

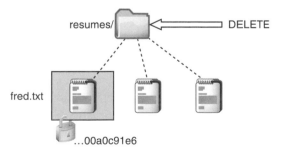

Figure 8–7   DELETE collection with one locked child.

To make this operation succeed, the client could issue the request shown in Listing 8–11.

Listing 8–11 Tagged If header matching one token against only one resource.

```
DELETE /hr/archives/resumes/ HTTP/1.1
Host: http://www.example.com
Cache-control: no-cache
Pragma: no-cache
If: <http://www.example.com/hr/archives/resumes/fred.txt>
   (<opaquelocktoken:e71d4fae-5dec-22d6-fea5-00a0c91e6>)
⏎
```

There may be other ways to delete a collection containing a locked resource using the Not syntax (Section 8.4.8), but this is a common approach to providing the lock token required in that scenario.

8.4.7 If and Not

Finally, the If header also supports negation when checking for matches. A token match may be negated by preceding the token with the word Not. Each negation applies to only one token and may not apply to a clause.

```
If: <http://www.example.com/hr/index.html>
   (Not <locktoken1> [Etag])
```

Here the Not refers only to the first token following it, <locktoken1>. Thus, the request will succeed if locktoken1 *does not match* a lock on index.html *and* if the ETag *does match* the content ETag of index.html. That's a contrived example but a legal one.

The only case I've seen for the Not syntax being particularly useful is to allow the client to construct a condition that always evaluates to true and use that condition in an OR clause so the entire header evaluates to true.

This header cannot possibly fail the precondition check, because the client used an obviously false lock token with the Not syntax, in the context of several lists compared with OR. The request could still fail with 423 Locked if the client did not provide enough lock tokens, but it can't possibly fail from having too many lock tokens or having the right lock tokens associated with the wrong URLs.

The <no-lock> token is not part of the WebDAV specification and is unlikely to be what the server expects to see in a lock token. A server might respond to a request with the If header in Listing 8–12 with the status 400 Bad Request or 500 Server Error, but this would not help the client. We recommend that WebDAV servers make sure that they handle this or similar tokens as semantically correct tokens.

Listing 8–12 If header with clause guaranteed to succeed.

```
If: (<opaquelocktoken:example.com:2907>)
    (<opaquelocktoken:example.com:2908>)
    (Not <no-lock>)
```

8.4.8 No-tag-list Productions

Table 8–2 provides a number of examples of valid "no-tag-list" If header syntaxes with a brief explanation of what they mean.

Table 8–2 If Header no-tag list Examples

Example	Explanation
If: (["7618-7118"])	The resources affected by the request must have this ETag.
If: (<opaquelocktoken:example.com:2907>)	The resources affected by the request must all be locked with this lock token.
If: (<opaquelocktoken:example.com:2907> ["7618-7118"])	The resources affected by the request must all be locked with this lock token AND have this ETag.
If: (<opaquelocktoken:example.com:2907>) (["7618-7118"])	The resources affected by the request must be locked with this token OR have this ETag.
If: (<opaquelocktoken:example.com:2907>) (<opaquelocktoken:example.com:2908>) (Not <no-lock>)	The resources affected by the request must be locked with one of the real lock tokens OR not locked with the made-up token.

8.4.9 Tagged List Productions

Table 8–3 provides a number of examples of valid tagged list If header syntaxes with a brief explanation what they mean.

8.4.10 Matching Tokens to Indirectly Locked Resources

The WebDAV specification states that "If the state of the resource to which the header is applied does not match any of the specified state lists, then the request *MUST* fail." It also says that "Every state token or ETag is either current, and hence describes the state of a resource, or is not current, and does not describe the state of a resource." Clearly, when a resource is directly locked, the lock's token must "match" that resource for as long as the lock is valid.

Table 8–3 If Header Tagged List Examples

Example	Explanation
If: \<http://www.example.com/file1\> (\<opaquelocktoken:example.com:2907\>)	File1 must be locked with the given lock token.
If: \<http://www.example.com/file1\> (\<opaquelocktoken:example.com:2907\>) \<http://www.example.com/file2\> (\<opaquelocktoken:example.com:2908\>)	File1 must be locked with the lock token "...2907" AND File2 must be locked with the lock token "...2908."
If: \<http://www.example.com/file1\> (\<opaquelocktoken:example.com:2907\>) \<http://www.example.com/file2\> (\<opaquelocktoken:example.com:2908\>) (["1234-5678"])	The clause for File1 says that File1 must be locked with the lock token "...2907." The clause for File2 has two lists. Multiple lists are combined with an OR, so File2 must be locked with the lock token "...2908" OR have the ETag "1234-5678." Finally, the two clauses are combined with AND.
If: \<http://www.example.com/file1\> (\<opaquelocktoken:example.com:2907\>) \<http://www.example.com/file2\> (\<opaquelocktoken:example.com:2908\> ["1234-5678"])	The clause for File1 says that File1 must be locked with the lock token "...2907," as above. The clause for File2 contains only one list with two tokens. Two tokens in the same list are combined with AND. File2 must match its lock token, AND File2 must match the ETag. Thus, all three conditions are ANDed together.

When a resource is included within a collection lock (depth infinity), the lock token must also match child resources. In 2002, some WebDAV implementors argued that a lock token would only match the exact URL of the resource where the lock was created (the collection URL). Meanwhile, some client software had already been deployed assuming that the URL of any resource indirectly included in the lock ought to match the lock token—a more liberal policy that is easier for the client to get right. That implies that servers should apply the more liberal policy in order to interoperate widely with client software. The current consensus on the Web-DAV mailing list is that the liberal policy is beneficial and has no drawbacks.

8.4.11 Matching Tokens to Unmapped URLs

If a collection is locked with depth infinity, the client must provide the lock token to create a new resource anywhere within the collection or any subcollection. In the first example in Section 8.4.5, the collection /hr/ contained both the source and the destination resources, and /hr/ was locked with depth infinity. The destination resource does not exist until it is created, yet it is being created within a locked collection. The example used an untagged lock token in the If header:

```
If: (<locktoken:e71d4fae-5dec-22d6-fea5-00a0c91e6>)
```

WebDAV requires that any token in the `If` header match every resource affected, and clearly both the destination collection and the new resource are affected by the request. One could split hairs about whether the not-yet-created resource's URL can possibly match any token when the resource doesn't exist yet, but it's simpler if servers allow this to work. The intent is clear and the correct lock token is present to allow modifications. In this case as in the previous, a liberal policy is preferred because otherwise clients have too much trouble making their requests succeed.

If the collection is locked with a depth 0 lock, a new resource added to the collection does not become indirectly locked. However, the collection's lock token is still required in order to add the new resource to the collection's member list. In this case, the client would have to issue a more carefully constructed `If` header to make the request succeed. The next section gives some suggestions.

8.4.12 Adding a Resource to a Locked Collection

There is another way for clients to create resources inside locked collections, in which the `If` header can be parsed unambiguously. The client can tag the lock token with the URL of the root of the lock. If the collection `/hr/recruiting/resumes/` is locked with the lock token `opaquelocktoken:f81d4fae-7dec-11d0-a765-00a0c91e6bf6`, a resource may be added to the locked collection as shown in Listing 8–13.

Listing 8–13 Adding a resource to a locked collection.

```
PUT /hr/recruiting/resumes/ldusseault.txt HTTP/1.1
Host: www.example.com
Content-Type: text/plain
Cache-control: no-cache
Pragma: no-cache
If: <http://www.example.com/hr/recruiting/resumes/>
   (<opaquelocktoken:f81d4fae-7dec-11d0-a765-00a0c91e6bf6>)
If-None-Match: *
Content-Length: xxxx
↵
Resume of Lisa Dusseault [...]
```

The client uses the `If-None-Match:*` header when it is using PUT and intending to create a new resource. The server will fail the request if the resource already exists.

After this request is handled, if the collection is still locked with depth `infinity`, then the new resource must also now be affected by the existing infinite-depth lock, and the new resource can only be altered by providing the same lock token. If the collection is locked with depth 0, the new resource can now be altered without providing the collection's lock token.

8.4.13 Comments on the If Header

The If header has a number of drawbacks and issues. Implementation and interoperability testing experience have addressed most of these issues.

 Confuses Two Purposes The If header confuses two purposes. First, there's the "conditional" purpose: Expressions provided by the client must evaluate to true before the server is allowed to process a request. Second, it's the only way the client can provide the correct lock token in a request to write a locked resource. Since these two purposes were combined into one header, it's impossible to separate the concerns. For example, the client can't easily send a lock token for a lock that may be expired and have the request succeed whether it is expired or not.

This approach forces certain choices on the client. It presumes that the client prefers to have the request fail if the lock has disappeared. However, in some situations, client implementors would like to make other choices.

The client can attempt to circumvent the enforcement of the If header by causing the conditional statement to evaluate to true under all circumstances. The client could put all its lock tokens in parentheses and append (Not <no-lock>) at the end of an untagged list production, as shown in Table 8–2. Since that clause evaluates to true, and since the server combines groups of untagged lists with OR, the entire If header must evaluate to true. This approach requires careful use of ETags to avoid overwrite, because now it's possible for the client to shoot itself in the foot and overwrite a resource where the lock expired and the resource already changed. This approach hasn't been tried much in practice, so it may expose server bugs.

Complete Boolean Logic Not Possible Despite the complexity of the If header, it doesn't allow complete Boolean logic in matching state tokens. The tagged list syntax allows an AND clause to appear within an OR clause, but not the inverse. A NOT production can apply to a single token but can't be applied to a clause. The same URL may not appear more than once in the same IF header, so there's no way that two conditions on the same resource can be compared with OR. It's impossible to express the statement *resource A matches lock1 or lock2 or resource B matches lock3 or lock4* because the If header syntax does not allow nested tagged lists.

A clever client implementor can translate many kinds of complex conditions into the format required by applying transformations. For example, the statement *NOT (resource A matches lock1 or resource B matches lock2)* can't be directly expressed because the negation here applies to the whole statement, whereas the If header syntax applies the NOT keyword only to one list. However, the statement can be transformed into *(NOT resource A matches lock1) AND (NOT resource B matches lock2)*, which can be expressed in the If header syntax.

Ignored Clauses RFC2518 specifies that the server determines which resources the current operation applies to. When it parses the If header, the specification requires that the server only evaluate the clauses tagged by those resources. The rest of the clauses are ignored. That makes it too hard for clients to know what clauses will be evaluated and which will be ignored. The WebDAV Working Group has discussed this issue and decided to recommend instead that servers should go ahead and process all clauses anyway. The next revision of the WebDAV specification will redefine this requirement.

Advanced Syntax Is Not Used Much   Not many clients create multiclause conditionals for the `If` header. The full syntax is complex, and there's some evidence that servers do not support the `If` header in the same way. A vicious circle could ensue because features that clients don't use aren't reliably implemented by servers. When a server feature hasn't been tested, it almost certainly doesn't work. Interoperability testing events and shared test suites are helping to fix this situation.

Header May Be Too Long to Be Transmitted Correctly   Tagged token lists can get pretty long, and Web infrastructure may not support that well. Proxy servers in particular have proved incapable of handling very long header values. Thus, the client may have all the lock tokens for a big MOVE operation and be able to correctly marshal them with the right URL tags into a big `If` header, but the request may be rejected by a proxy before reaching the server. Alternatively, the proxy could unknowingly truncate or split the header value, most probably transforming it into a malformed header that the server rejects.

It's really hard to say what header length is safe or unsafe. Some products designed to secure [Alliance01] or boost the performance of [Servertec03] Web servers and proxies can be configured by the administrator to reject requests with headers of certain lengths or with a specified total header length. Since the administrator can choose the length, an overzealous administrator could cause real interoperability problems.

8.5   Lock-Related Properties

The properties described here are available on a resource only if locking is supported.

8.5.1   lockdiscovery

Clients need some way of discovering what locks exist on a resource, if any, and the lockdiscovery property serves that purpose. Since a resource may have several locks, the lockdiscovery value may have several components. The information about a single lock includes several more pieces of information, including the client-provided `owner` value that might be expressed in XML. Thus, lockdiscovery is a multivalued XML-formatted property.

Every lock on the resource shows up as an additional `activelock` XML element in the value of the lockdiscovery property. Each `activelock` element contains a set of XML tags with information about the lock:

- `locktype`: Describes the type of lock (write lock being the only standard type).
- `lockscope`: Describes whether the lock is exclusive or shared.
- `depth`: Does the lock apply only to this resource (0) or to its descendants as well (`Infinity`)?

- owner: A client-provided string or XML fragment intended to contain information to help users get in touch with the lock's creator (e.g., to ask them to unlock it), possibly as well as information about the client software that created the lock.
- timeout: The time remaining on the lock (or Infinite).
- locktoken: This must be provided in case the client software loses the token.

This example builds on the first LOCK response in this chapter, Listing 8–2. Some time has passed since that response, so the timeout shows the countdown or time remaining on the lock lifetime. This property value would normally appear inside a PROPFIND response (see Listing 8–14).

Listing 8–14   Example lockdiscovery property value.

```
<lockdiscovery xmlns="DAV:">
   <activelock>
      <locktype><D:write/></locktype>
      <lockscope><D:exclusive/></lockscope>
      <depth>infinity</depth>
      <owner xmlns:x="http://www.customapp.com/ns/">
         <x:lock-user>alice@example.com</x:lock-user>
         <x:created-by>Text Editor v1.2.5</x:created-by>
      </owner>
      <timeout>Second-604625</timeout>
      <locktoken><href>opaquelocktoken:e71d4fae-5dec-22d6 ↲
            -fea5-00a0c91e6be4</href></locktoken>
   </activelock>
</lockdiscovery>
```

8.5.2 supportedlock

The supportedlock property returns an XML-formatted listing of the kinds of locks that may be created on this resource. Sometimes this information applies to the whole server, and the value returned by this property is always the same. An implementation could allow different kinds of locks depending on the kind of resource. For example, collections might only support exclusive locks, while ordinary resources support both exclusive and shared locks. Most WebDAV servers will return a consistent value much like the example in Listing 8–15, indicating that both exclusive and shared write locks are supported on all resources, as required by WebDAV.

Listing 8–15   Example supportedlock property value.

```
<D:supportedlock>
   <D:lockentry>
      <D:lockscope><D:exclusive/></D:lockscope>
```

Listing 8–15 Example supportedlock property value. *(Continued)*

```
        <D:locktype><D:write/></D:locktype>
    </D:lockentry>
    <D:lockentry>
        <D:lockscope><D:shared/></D:lockscope>
        <D:locktype><D:write/></D:locktype>
    </D:lockentry>
</D:supportedlock>
```

Bug in supportedlock

An early version of the WebDAV RFC omitted the `lockscope` and `locktype` elements in its example value for the supportedlock property.

```
<D:supportedlock>
<D:lockentry><D:exclusive/><D:write/></D:lockentry>
<D:lockentry><D:shared/><D:write/></D:lockentry>
</D:supportedlock>
```

Microsoft IIS 5.0 implemented the property based on the example, not on the defining text, so the implementation perpetuated the specification's error for several years. The property value is still useful if special client code detects this case.

8.6   Client Responsibilities

Locks can be used in ways that frustrate users and subvert the purpose of locking. Clients have several responsibilities to improve interoperability.

8.6.1   Why Client Software Must Store Lock Tokens

If the client loses track of a lock token, the token may be rediscovered by querying the lockdiscovery property. Rediscovery of lock tokens allows clients to gracefully handle crashes, data losses, or simply lost messages from the server. Typically, the software presents the user with information about the lock, and asks if the user would like to remove the lock.

 Some early WebDAV client implementations did not store the lock token. Instead, the client software relied on the server to provide the lock token in the lockdiscovery property whenever needed. This is a bad idea. Clients must store lock tokens for as long as the locks exist. It's not enough for the client to simply cache lock tokens in memory while the client is running; when the client exits, those locks must be unlocked or the lock tokens must be stored for use next time.

Storing lock tokens is a burden for the client, so why is it required? On first examination, the WebDAV server seems to enforce proper use of lock tokens. After all, the server only allows the client to use the lock token successfully if it's authenticated as the lock creator. Most of the time, the authorization check prevents inappropriate use of the lock token, but there are two cases in which the server cannot prevent misuse:

- In the case in which unauthenticated users are allowed to take out locks, the server can't identify who is allowed to use the lock token. The server must allow any request to use a lock token when the lock creator didn't authenticate.
- When two authoring clients are run by the same user to edit the same file, the authorization check can't tell the difference. For example, you might open a file on your work computer, make changes and go home, and then open the file on your home computer. Two authoring clients can accidentally overwrite each other's changes, just as two authors can.

A WebDAV server may have no way to avoid these corner cases of the lost update problem. Unless all client software stores the lock token for the duration of the lock, users may suffer the lost update problem despite locking the resource.

A server's access control policies may allow users other than the lock creator to access the lock token and "hijack" the lock. Some servers allow administrators or resource owners to remove locks. This can be a desirable feature because it allows the server to keep lock timeouts high and still gives resource owners control over their resources. However, client software should only hijack a lock at the explicit request of the user, because it's very disruptive to the user who made the original LOCK request. Clients should only allow hijacking when doing an UNLOCK (and the server may limit hijacking in the same way). If the hijacking user wants to make changes, a new lock can be obtained.

8.6.2   Renew Often, Renew Early, Unlock Promptly

For many reasons, a client can lose a lock; it can be pretty confusing to the user when this happens, because the user doesn't know whether it's safe to overwrite the file anyway. To prevent this, it's tempting for the client to ask for long timeouts. However, long timeouts prevent other users from making changes in the case of orphaned locks. A timeout of an hour to a day seems like a reasonable compromise, but the decision would change depending on the type of client. A client that automatically creates locks, like Office 2000, probably shouldn't reserve locks for more than a day or so. However, a client that does offline synchronization and locks files at the user's request might reasonably lock a file for a week.

If lock timeouts are around an hour or a day, there are plenty of chances for the client to fail to renew the lock.

- The laptop the client was running on went to sleep.
- The network connection was lost during the time the lock needed to be renewed.
- The user's authentication information timed out and the user wasn't around to enter his or her password again.
- A bug exists in client or server software.

To keep these renewal failures to a minimum, client software should attempt to renew the lock well before the expiration so that there's a grace period for the client to try again before really losing the lock. The client could renew hour-long locks every half hour or day-long locks every few hours.

Finally, the client should unlock the file when the lock is no longer needed, rather than let the server time out and clean up the lock. This practice lets other users get on with their changes.

8.6.3 Verifying Lock Persistence

Section 3.7.6 explained how to avoid overwriting somebody else's changes by using the `If-Match` header: If the ETag is still the same, then the resource hasn't been changed. You'd think that when a resource is locked, this step isn't necessary any more—but it still is. There are several (hopefully rare) cases where the file can change even though it was originally locked:

- The lock was accidentally not renewed (some possible causes were listed in the previous section).
- An administrator removed the lock before its expiration. Some servers allow administrators to remove locks through a non-WebDAV interface in order to be able to clean up inappropriate or inconvenient locks.
- Another client chose to get the lock token using lockdiscovery and then used the lock token to destroy the lock and change the resource. Since WebDAV does not consider the lock token to be a secret, this may be possible, depending on how the server treats lock and unlock permissions. It's up to the server implementation whether to limit UNLOCK to the lock creator. The choice depends on how much control the server gives to the user and the resource owner, as well as how often the server requires administrator intervention for unusual cases like destroying locks. Thus, servers for different purposes (Web site authoring, file sharing, document management) might legitimately make different choices here.

 The inclusion of the lock token in the `If` header provides some protection from situations where the client wasn't up to date on the lock state. The `If` header is a conditional test as well as a way to provide lock tokens, so the request must be failed by the server if the condition fails. That means that the client's information on the lock state must be correct (or the condition must be loosely constraining) before the operation is allowed. That safeguard may prevent lost updates in cases where the original user's lock disappears and another change is made to the file before the original user's change is uploaded.

In any case, it's safest to use ETags as well as lock tokens whenever possible, to verify that the resource is still in the expected state.

8.6.4 Managing Deadlocks

Clients may have to take out multiple exclusive locks on multiple resources in order to complete some operations safely. For example, both Alice and Bob might want to move résumés around between `/hr/recruiting/resumes/` and `/hr/archives/resumes/`. If they pick different collections to lock first and hold onto the first lock waiting to get a second lock, they could both wait a long time (see Figure 8–8).

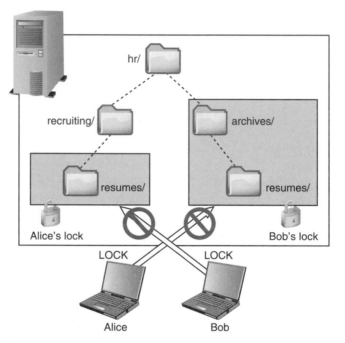

Figure 8–8   Deadlock: Two clients each waiting to get a second lock.

Servers can do nothing to prevent these kinds of deadlocks. Therefore, it's up to the client to be aware of the problem and act responsibly to avoid remaining deadlocked. The only workable approach is for every client to back off and give other clients a chance to complete their operations. This means that clients should never hold onto a lock while waiting to get another lock. Instead, release the successful lock and try to get both locks later. Random short waits, with exponentially increasing backoff, is a common technique in such scenarios.

It's sometimes possible to lock a parent collection such that only one lock is needed. (In this case, either Alice or Bob could have locked `/hr/` if they had sufficient permissions.) However, since this approach may block more operations than is necessary, it's not always appreciated by other users, because a collection can't be locked if one of its descendants is already exclusively locked, and vice versa.

8.6.5 Handling Lock-Null Resources

Not all servers support the full specification for lock-null resources. The specification itself may be changed since there are so many problems with lock-null resources. Therefore, client implementers must tread carefully. A responsible client should behave as follows:

- Use the `If` header and an ETag whenever locking existing resources in case the server will not clean out the lock-null resource when the lock goes away. In fact, use ETags whenever working with resources that are believed to exist and not to have changed.
- Do not rely on being able to use MKCOL on a lock-null resource. Instead, follow a MKCOL request quickly with a LOCK request (perhaps in a pipelined request, even though it's not normally recommended to have one pipelined request rely on another succeeding). This practice introduces a possible race condition, but the only pragmatic way to avoid problems is simply to do the two requests quickly.
- Do not create lock-null resources and leave them in that state. Either quickly convert them to regular resources with PUT or attempt to clean them out using UNLOCK so that other clients can either see the new resource or not have to worry about it.
- If unlocking a lock-null resource, check to see if the server actually removed it. If it did not, attempt a DELETE to clean up.

8.6.6   Using Shared Locks

Shared locks require more client effort to use correctly and responsibly. In addition to all the considerations for exclusive locks, a client with a shared lock must also consider how to coordinate changes to the resource locked with a shared lock. How this is done depends on why the client is using shared locks. There are at least four possible cases involving different coordination.

Advisory Locks   Sometimes locks can serve a purpose that is closer to "advisory" than "preventative." All the lock owner wants to do is put up a flag saying "I'm modifying this file, change it at your own risk." This doesn't prevent others from modifying the same file, but it's likely to make the other clients aware that the resource is in use. If a CM system uses advisory locks already, shared locks may be supported for backward compatibility. To make advisory locks work well, client software must communicate frequently with the user, letting the user know how the resource is locked and whether changes will be overwritten.

Read Locks   Client software may request a shared lock in order to prevent the resource from being changed while the client reads the resource. Normally, this isn't a concern in WebDAV, but some large resources may be downloaded using byte ranges (see Section 3.7.12), and it's easier to download a file in multiple ranges if it doesn't change between requests. A shared read lock is much more useful than an exclusive read lock because other users reading the same resource can take out their own shared read lock. The resource can't be changed until the last client has finished downloading the resource and releases the last shared lock.

Sharing Locks Among Processes   Sophisticated client applications involving multiple processes may have an out-of-band mechanism for coordinating changes to the same WebDAV resource. These processes may all be acting in concert on behalf of the same user. The processes could be running on the same computer or on different computers. Shared locks may be helpful for these processes to reserve the resource for changes without blocking other processes out. Each process must mark the shared lock so that the other processes know that the locks can indeed be used in this manner.

Custom Locking   Some systems may require a different lock model than the one Web-DAV provides. It may be possible for these systems to use shared locks, then to use some non-standard mechanism (such as custom dead properties) to communicate information about who may modify the file at what point. For example, a custom workflow process might use shared locks to transfer lock protection from one user to another at a certain phase of the process. The client applications involved in this process must mark the shared locks so that other applications can be sure this is how the lock is being used.

8.7   Lock Interactions

It's not always obvious how locks interact with the various operations we've already covered, so now we'll review those operations with a focus on how they must behave in various situations involving locks.

Recall that WebDAV does not clearly apply the DELETE method either to the address or to the resource (Section 1.3.2). WebDAV locks apply more consistently to addresses than to resources. Thus, when a collection is locked with depth infinity, it's easier to understand how things work if you assume that the address of the collection is what's really locked, along with all "sub-addresses" or all URLs within the collection's namespace. When a single resource is locked, it's best to assume that it's actually the address that is locked, not the data. Based on this model, most lock behavior makes sense.

- A COPY operation copies data to a new URL. If the source URL was locked, that remains locked, and no new lock is created on the destination URL.
- When a new resource is created within a locked collection (depth infinity), the new resource URL is locked just like the rest of the locked namespace. The body of the new resource cannot be changed without the lock token.

However, the model isn't entirely self-consistent. Another important part of the model is that when the data is disassociated from an address, the lock associated with that address disappears:

- A DELETE operation on a locked URL also makes the lock disappear. (However, a DELETE operation on a resource inside a locked collection only deletes the child resource, not the lock on the collection.)

- A MOVE operation associates a new URL with existing data. If the moved resource was directly locked, its lock is destroyed, and neither the unmapped source URL or the new destination URL are locked. RFC2518 specifically requires this behavior even though it makes rename operations behave unexpectedly for users. Client software could attempt to get a new lock immediately if this makes most sense to their users, or it could even go to more work to lock the destination and then MOVE the source over it, preserving the destination lock.

The final wrinkle in the model is that even though DELETE and MOVE behave as if a lock can't exist on an unmapped URL, RFC2518 defines lock-null resources that are locks on unmapped URLs. The model confusion is likely to be reduced somewhat when WebDAV goes to Draft Standard if lock-null resources are removed from the standard; however, most behavior will generally remain the same.

8.7.1 Adding Resources

The methods PUT, MKCOL, COPY, and MOVE all create one or more new resources that didn't exist previously. MOVE is more complicated, so it's addressed in Section 8.7.4.

There are only three cases in which a lock can affect the creation of a new resource, and they are mutually exclusive. All cases require the lock token to be used in the request:

- The parent collection (where the new resource will be created) is locked with depth 0. In the case of COPY and MOVE, this is the parent of the "destination" URL. With PUT and MKCOL, this is the parent of the Request-URI. When the new resource is created, it is unlocked, but the parent remains locked. The new resource may now be modified without providing any lock token.
- The parent collection is locked with depth infinity. When the new resource is created, it becomes part of the depth infinity lock and may not be modified without providing the lock token.
- There is a lock-null resource where the new resource is to be created. This case only applies to PUT and MKCOL. The resulting resource is still locked, with the same lock token.

In the case of COPY, the source resource could be locked, could be within a locked collection, or could be a collection that contains locked resources. None of these source locks affects the COPY operation whatsoever. Because locks apply to URLs, a source lock is not duplicated when the resource is copied and is not removed during the operation. The source lock token is not required in order to be able to complete a COPY operation, because the source resource is not being modified.

WebDAV doesn't allow a lock-null resource to be the destination of a COPY (or MOVE) request. If the client needs to lock a location before copying to it, and no file exists, the client must first LOCK the URL, then apply PUT or MKCOL to the URL to turn the lock-null resource into a regular resource as appropriate, then use the URL as the value of the Destination header in a COPY request to finally put the correct content in place. The PUT method might contain an empty body, in which case the server should create a zero-length resource (see Listing 8–16).

Listing 8–16 Example creating a placeholder resource.

Create placeholder:
```
PUT /hr/resources/ergonomics/placeholder.txt HTTP/1.1
Host: www.example.com
Content-Type: text/plain
If-None-Match: *
Content-Length: 0
⏎
```

Response:
```
HTTP/1.0 204 No Content
Date: Sun, 29 Jul 2001 15:24:17 GMT
ETag: "870be-8f0-39ee6a4e"
Content-Length: 0
⏎
```

The placeholder resource could also be locked after it is created. Either way, it helps other clients to see what type and name are given to the placeholder, so this might be a good practice in other situations, too.

8.7.2   Modifying Locked Resources

PUT and PROPPATCH can both be used to modify existing resources. COPY and MOVE can also be used to modify a pre-existing destination resource. Modifying a resource does not affect whether it is locked or unlocked, no matter whether the resource is locked itself, contains a locked resource, or is contained within a locked resource. Of course, the lock tokens must be provided, but the locks themselves are unchanged.

8.7.3   Deleting

When a resource that is directly locked is deleted, its lock disappears. When an indirectly locked resource (within a collection locked with a depth infinity lock) is deleted, it is simply removed from the lock, but the lock remains in place unchanged. These two cases are mutually exclusive.

Since lock-null resources do not support DELETE, there's no interaction to worry about there. Instead, a lock-null resource will disappear when its lock is removed, so UNLOCK will achieve the effect of a DELETE. On servers that do not remove the lock-null resource when it is unlocked, the client must check after the UNLOCK to see if it must be followed by a DELETE to actually get rid of the resource.

8.7.4   MOVE and Locks

Moving resource can be complicated because there can be locks at the source and at the destination. The WebDAV designers had to pick one model: keep the source lock, keep the destination lock, or keep neither. They chose to keep the destination lock. COPY also effectively keeps the destination lock, so the two methods are consistent. There are a number of cases to consider for the source lock (the destination lock behaves as it did with COPY):

- A directly locked resource is moved. The source lock disappears because it is not transferred with the MOVE operation, and it has nothing to lock any more.
- An unlocked collection contains one or more locked resources. When the collection is moved, all the internal locks disappear. If some of the internal resources were lock-null resources, they must be removed entirely.
- A resource is moved out from inside a locked collection. The collection lock remains unchanged. The resource that is moved out from inside a locked collection is no longer affected by the original collection lock.
- A resource is moved within a locked collection. As long as it remains inside the locked collection, it remains covered by the same lock.

In all of these cases, all of the lock tokens are required for the MOVE request to succeed.

8.8 Problems with Lock-Null Resources

Lock-null resources are created when a client sends a LOCK request to a resource that does not exist. Lock-null resources behave differently from locked resources in a few specified ways. These special resources bring a number of complications and problems.

8.8.1 Poor Implementation Support

The WebDAV Interop event in the summer of 2001 made it clear that very few servers fully implement the specification for lock-null resources. Only Xythos WebFile Server supported all required lock-null behaviors. Most servers, like WebSite Director and Microsoft IIS 5, supported locking null resources, but they created an empty normal resource, which cannot be turned into a collection and which does not disappear when unlocked.

What are the reasons for this poor support? Sometimes it's due to existing architecture limitations. Microsoft IIS 5.0 could not easily support lock-null resources, because it was built to use the file system to store resources, and that architecture was extended only minimally and carefully to support WebDAV. NTFS supports regular file locks, so individual file locking via WebDAV could be supported consistently. However, NTFS has neither collection locks nor null locks, so it was impossible to safely and quickly implement these features. Any NTFS-based client working on the same files would either override the lock or see incompatible server behavior. The first choice would mean collection and null locks would be insecure, and the second choice would mean that NTFS clients would no longer interoperate reliably with an NTFS server. Neither of those choices was acceptable, so Microsoft chose not to support collection locks or lock-null resources as specified and to leave IIS 5.0 noncompliant.

Some clients (such as the Adobe clients) require the ability to LOCK a nonexistent resource and then PUT to it. IIS 5.0 interoperates with these clients because IIS 5.0 handles a LOCK to an unmapped URL by creating a regular empty resource and locking it. It's an empty locked resource, not a special lock-null resource, but it works for PUT (just not for MKCOL). Unlike lock-null resources, the empty locked resources show up in PROPFIND responses, and they do not disappear when moved. Other server implementors can currently get away with the same shortcut and still interoperate successfully with known clients, and it may even become the standard behavior when WebDAV is updated.

8.8.2   Lock-Null Resources Behave Poorly in Name Collisions

A lock-null resource could be created with a given name and still be a lock-null resource at the time when another client attempts to create a resource with the same name. The second client to attempt to create the resource might try to do this a number of ways.

First, some simplistic clients (MS IE is one example) attempt to see a collection's contents or do a HEAD request to see if a resource exists before attempting to create it. These clients won't see the lock-null resource, yet the PUT request will fail because the client wouldn't provide a lock token.

Second, HTTP or WebDAV clients could send a PUT request with the If-None-Match: * header to make sure that no entity tag matches the requested resource—that is to say, it doesn't exist. WebDAV doesn't specify how a lock-null resource matches an ETag or the * syntax. One could imagine this conditional header either failing or succeeding. One way or another, the PUT will not succeed, because the client sending the PUT was unaware of the lock-null resource and of course won't provide a lock token. Still, the client might be confused to see a 423 Locked response and be unable to find any locked resources or confused to see a 412 Preconditions Failed response and not be able to tell why.

Third, WebDAV clients could attempt to LOCK an unmapped URL to create a lock-null resource, not knowing it already is a lock-null resource. Again, the LOCK request wouldn't have the correct lock token, so even though the server will treat it as a renew request, it will fail.

8.8.3   Detecting Lock-Null Resource Creation

A client must be able to tell the difference between the creation of a lock-null resource and the creation of a lock on an existing resource. The distinction is important because the client might be under the impression that it is locking a normal resource when it issues the LOCK. If the resource previously existed but was simply deleted by another client, the LOCK request would succeed anyway, creating a lock-null resource. The next likely step for the client is to try to GET the body of the resource, but this will fail on a lock-null resource, as required by RFC2518.

The status code in the response to the LOCK request differentiates the results of the request. If the response code is 200 OK, an existing resource was locked. If the response code is 201 Created, a new lock-null resource was created. RFC2518 does not cover this explicitly in the listing of response codes for the LOCK request, so existing servers are probably not very reliable in using the 201 Created code. I recommend using this code whenever a null-resource is created in order to give clients more information in the response. Clients should watch out for an unexpected response of 201 Created and undo the operation if creation of a lock-null resource wasn't expected.

A more reliable technique is for the client to use the `If-Match` header on every LOCK request. Then the request will only succeed if the resource is still in the state the client expected.

8.8.4   Lock-Null Resources Disappear in Collection Moves

When a collection containing lock-null resources is moved or renamed with the MOVE request, those lock-null resources become unlocked and thus disappear. This is a consequence of the decision that a lock must not be moved from the URL where it was created and that it must disappear when that URL is no longer mapped to a resource. When the locks are removed, the server must clean up the lock-null resources.

8.8.5   Lock-Null Resources May Not Be Destination of a COPY

There doesn't seem to be a reason for this restriction in WebDAV, but it's there in the standard. Clients should therefore not attempt to COPY to a lock-null resource. However, should a server accept this operation anyway, there shouldn't be any real problems.

8.8.6   Solving Too Many Problems

The main purpose of lock-null resources was to avoid the overwrite problem that can occur if two users try to create two resources with the same name, at or near the same time. On top of this basic problem were three concerns the working group tried to address. We'll take each concern separately, explain how the concern affected the design of lock-null resources, and examine the consequences and alternatives.

Overwriting Collections   If the overwrite problem must be considered when creating normal resources, surely it must be considered when creating collection resources as well. This consideration led to the design of lock-null resources such that they can become regular collections with a MKCOL operation.

This concern sounds reasonable, but it is useless. Unlike PUT, MKCOL is only used to create collections, not to change them. MKCOL is only allowed on a resource that did not previously exist. There is no overwrite problem or race condition. If two clients send MKCOL to the same URL at around the same time, the second client always gets an error.

The consequence of trying to solve this nonexistent problem was that a resource created as a result of a LOCK could not be a regular resource. The designers foresaw implementation difficulties transforming a regular resource into a collection and decided that a resource created as a result of a LOCK must be a special kind of resource, neither a collection nor a file-like resource. This motivated the requirements that the special kind of resource not respond to a GET, PROPPATCH, MOVE, and COPY. Unfortunately, this special kind of resource is unnecessarily complex and has been poorly implemented.

Reserving New Collection for Property Updates   Another issue that lock-null resources might successfully address is the need for a new collection to be reserved to the process that created it until the new collection is correctly configured. For example, between the MKCOL and the subsequent LOCK request from Alice, Bob may discover the new collection and change properties, add content, or lock it himself.

If Alice could lock the collection on or before the time it is created, then Alice could configure the collection properly before allowing other changes. For example, Alice could set access control such that Bob's changes won't be allowed.

This is one of the few issues that only lock-null resources successfully address.

Cleaning Up Lock-Null Resources May Be Difficult   Here the concern is that a client that mistakenly or intentionally creates a lock-null resource may not have permission to delete the lock-null resource. The concern is real because some servers may grant write permission without granting delete permission. To deal with this concern, WebDAV requires the server to remove lock-null resources when they become unlocked (if the resource hasn't already been turned into a normal resource through PUT or MKCOL).

The consequence of this requirement is that lock-null resources must be handled differently during an UNLOCK operation, during the expiration of a lock, and when a locked parent collection is moved and that lock disappears. Such special-case code is prone to errors.

There are two reasons that this concern, although real, need not be addressed:

- The cleanup problem isn't addressed in other situations. If a client creates a new resource with PUT or creates a new collection with MKCOL, there is just as much potential the client won't have permission to delete those resources. It seems inconsistent and insufficient to address cleanup in only certain odd cases.
- Clients can easily avoid common causes of the need for cleanup. Most of the cleanup concern seems to be for cases when the client did not intend to create a new resource but did so accidentally. The client can avoid this kind of accident simply by using a conditional header on the LOCK request (as with every method that can create a resource), as shown in Listing 8–17. With a correct conditional header, the request will only work if the resource is still in the state the client believes it is in.

Given that there is a workaround that doesn't involve any special-case code, and given that the cleanup problem is a general problem but not too severe a problem, it doesn't seem reasonable to solve the general problem only in one instance when the solution adds such complication.

Listing 8–17 Using If-Match to avoid accidental resource creation on LOCK.

```
LOCK /hr/ergonomics/chairs.doc HTTP/1.1
Host: www.example.com
Cache-control: no-cache
```

Listing 8–17   Using If-Match to avoid accidental resource creation on LOCK. *(Continued)*

```
Pragma: no-cache
If: ([valid_etag_here])
Timeout: Infinite
Content-Type: text/xml; charset="utf-8"
Content-Length: xxxx
↵
<?xml version="1.0" encoding="utf-8" ?>
<D:lockinfo xmlns:D='DAV:'>
   <D:lockscope><D:exclusive/></D:lockscope>
   <D:locktype><D:write/></D:locktype>
   <D:owner>username@host.org</D:owner>
</D:lockinfo>
```

8.8.7   A Simpler Approach: Locked Empty Resources

So, will a simpler approach be better overall? Recall that Microsoft IIS 5.0 simply creates an empty locked regular resource and needs no further special logic. Is this approach sufficient? Many participants in the WebDAV Working Group think so. When RFC2518 is changed to become a Draft Standard, the behavior of lock-null resources will probably be simplified.

In the MS IIS 5.0 approach, when a LOCK request is addressed to a nonexistent resource, the server will create a zero-length document of some predefined type (likely application/octet-stream or text/plain). Then all methods can work as they do on regular resources, without special-case logic, and the client can PUT the real content, potentially changing the content type, at leisure.

Although this solution doesn't solve the problem of creating a locked collection, the benefits seem to outweigh the costs, given how poorly and inconsistently null resources have been implemented.

8.9   Summary

Locks are the mechanism WebDAV provides to solve the lost update problem. A lock on a resource reserves it so that it can only be changed by the lock creator, and even then only when the client software provides the correct lock token.

LOCK is used to create and refresh locks, and UNLOCK is used to remove locks. Locks can be created on individual resources or on collections. Locks can be created on collections such that the lock covers all the collections internal resources or none of them (protecting only the collection's metadata).

Locks may have a limited lifetime. A WebDAV server may limit lock lifetime so that when a lock is accidentally left around, it eventually expires and gets cleaned up. Locks can also disappear once in a while before timeout, if administrators or resource owners have permission to remove unwanted locks.

The If *header is used to provide the lock token when locked resources are updated.* The If header is complicated, but a little care should allow clients to use it successfully. Clients should also use If-Match and If-None-Match headers to fully protect resources from lost updates.

Lock-null resources are special resources, created by LOCK, which reserve a URL so that it can be turned into a collection (MKCOL) or ordinary resource (PUT). Although many servers do not fully support lock-null resources, a client should be able to reserve a URL with LOCK and then use PUT.

CHAPTER 9

Putting the Pieces Together

So far, we have mostly seen WebDAV requirements for individual requests and responses. A few more issues are involved in using multiple requests in an ongoing communication with real clients or servers. In this chapter we address this topic with a user scenario illustrating how real WebDAV clients and servers use WebDAV methods to accomplish tasks.

Although we introduce no new methods in this chapter, some new headers appear, typically for content negotiation, authentication, and connection control. Some are from HTTP and others are proprietary. Most can be ignored, but a WebDAV server must support some of the nonstandard headers that Microsoft Web Folders use if it needs to interoperate with Web Folders.

We cleaned up the headers and XML bodies in the traces by adding spacing and line returns to improve readability. The formatting does not change the validity or meaning of the messages, except for the introduction of some line returns that are indicated with the same special symbol used previously.

9.1 Scenario Walk-Through

The scenario used in this chapter to generate examples continues with the same fictional people and situations we've used throughout this book. Alice, a manager in the Human Resources (HR) department of a medium-sized company, creates a new document in a WebDAV repository. After editing the document to her satisfaction in her own WebDAV home directory, she places the document in a publicly readable collection where it can be reviewed. When the document has been reviewed, Alice sets a publish property so that the file will be picked up by the nightly process that copies files to a regular Web server, where employees look up this kind of information.

Alice uses widely available tools to accomplish this task: Microsoft Web Folders, Microsoft Word, and an open-source command-line tool called cadaver (*www.webdav.org/cadaver*). The server hosting the repository is running Xythos WebFile Server (WFS, *www.xythos.com*). More detail on each of these tools can be found in the next chapter.

The WebDAV repository Alice uses has two top-level collections:

- The /hr/ collection holds HR information published internally for employee access. It's a publicly readable internal Web site, so employees can use their Web browsers to access files.
- The /users/ collection is a restricted area where employees of the HR department have their own private collections for storing and working on documents. The /users/ directory has private directories for Alice and other users (see Figure 9–1).

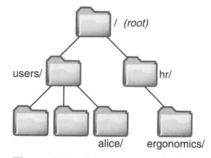

Figure 9–1 Structure of collections on repository.

To create and publish a file from scratch, here are the steps Alice performs:

1. Open a Web Folder (in Windows Explorer) and navigate to her alice/ directory.
2. Create a new collection and name it.
3. Create a new file using Word 2000 (includes locking the file).
4. Edit the file using Word 2000.
5. Close Word 2000 (includes unlocking the file).
6. Copy the file to the publishing location.
7. Publish the resource by setting a custom property.

The entire trace would be too long to include in this chapter (it contains many similar and lengthy PROPFIND requests and responses), so we have not repeated redundant requests. The traces sometimes include only the interesting parts of a request or response. Areas that are discussed in the text are shown in bold text.

9.2   Open Web Folder

Alice has previously configured a Web Folder, which in Windows serves as a mount point to a WebDAV repository. This Web Folder allows Alice to quickly navigate to the root of the repository at `http://www.example.com/`.

A Web Folder allows Windows Explorer and Office software to work with files stored on a remote WebDAV repository. It's similar to mounting the DAV repository as a drive, but it doesn't use a drive letter. Other applications cannot use the Web Folder, because it only works with Explorer and Office.

Windows Explorer can be used to view the contents of a Web Folder and do common file management operations (move, copy, rename, delete). In addition, Office software can be used to open files from and save them to the repository: The Open and Save dialogs in Office applications show My Network Places, where the user can select a Web Folder and then select files or directories inside the WebDAV repository. This chapter includes both Explorer and Office operations using Web Folders.

The process of opening a Web Folder and navigating through a few directories takes five PROPFIND requests (see Figure 9–2).

Not all of these requests are necessary for a client that caches a little more information. For example, the client could cache the Basic authorization challenge information from a previous connection, skip the `Depth 0` request entirely, and shave two roundtrips off this process.

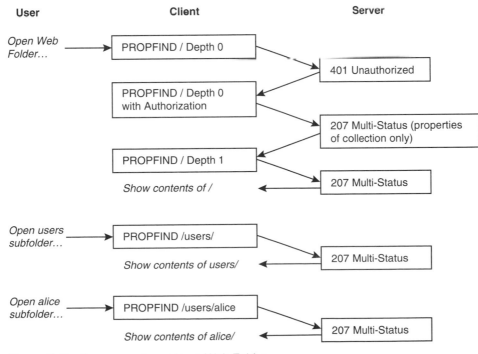

Figure 9–2   Summary of opening a Web Folder.

Web Folders does not use OPTIONS to find out what features the server supports. Perhaps Web Folders instead uses the PROPFIND response to see whether the server supports the supportedlock and lockdiscovery properties to confirm that the server supports locking.

9.2.1 Unauthenticated Request

Alice first opens the Windows Explorer tool and then opens the Web Folder that points to the WebDAV repository on `www.example.com`. This action triggers Web Folders to send a PROPFIND request to the server to get the properties of the repository's root collection. However, Web Folders doesn't immediately attempt to log Alice in. Since Alice's folder is not publicly readable, the server returns a 401 Unauthorized response.

The PROPFIND request from Web Folders is a `depth` `0` request because initially Web Folders is only interested in the collection properties. The request has no body, which makes it equivalent to an `allprop` request. The request has a `Content-Type` header even though there is no body—this is a client software bug. The request contains a nonstandard Microsoft header, the `Translate` header, to indicate that Web Folders is an authoring client, as opposed to a read-only browser. These quirks are explained in more detail after the request listing (see Listing 9–1).

Listing 9–1   PROPFIND request from Web Folders.

```
PROPFIND / HTTP/1.1
Content-Language: en-us
Accept-Language: en-us
Content-Type: text/xml
Translate: f
Depth: 0
Content-Length: 0
User-Agent: Microsoft Data Access Internet Publishing Provider DAV 1.1
Host: www.example.com
Connection: Keep-Alive
↵
```

Notice that this request does not include a body. A PROPFIND request without a body is equivalent to an `allprop` request, a request for all the properties on the resource.

Interesting Standard Headers   In this example, the `Content-Type`, `Depth`, and `Connection` headers are worth discussing.

- The `Content-Type` header is meaningless because the request doesn't have a body. To work around the client software bug, the server can simply ignore the header if there is no `Content-Length` header and no body arrives immediately.

- The `Depth` header is 0, meaning that the client is only interested in the properties of the root collection.
- The `Connection` header (see Section 3.5.1) means that the client is able to keep the TCP connection open if the server is also willing.

Nonstandard Translate Header   This Web Folders request, like many from Web Folders, includes the `Translate` header with a value of false. This is a nonstandard header invented by Microsoft (briefly introduced in Section 5.3.3). It is not part of the WebDAV standard and may be safely ignored by WebDAV servers except when the client is attempting to GET a dynamically generated Web page.

Originally, the `Translate` header (with a value of false) meant that the server should not translate the Web page if the Web page is dynamically generated; instead, the server should return the unprocessed source code at that location. However, the header is included on all Web Folders requests, including requests like this one, where the Web page is not being requested. Thus, the header means that the client is advertising that it is an authoring client, not a regular Web browser.

The server may make a number of different choices based on the presence of `Translate: f`. For example, it could calculate the size of the resource differently, depending on whether the client is an authoring client or a browsing client. The header may also be safely ignored in most cases.

9.2.2   Authentication Challenge

The response to the PROPFIND request is an error, indicating that authorization is required and that the client is unauthenticated (see Listing 9–2). The 401 Unauthorized response must contain the `WWW-Authenticate` header to show the client the authentication methods that are available. The response has a body, although bodies on error responses are optional.

Listing 9–2   401 Unauthorized response.

```
HTTP/1.0 401 Unauthorized
WWW-Authenticate: BASIC realm="www.example.com"
WWW-Authenticate: Digest realm="www.example.com",
   stale=false, nonce="ec2cc00f21f71acd35ab9be057970609",
   qop="auth", algorithm="MD5"
Cache-Control: no-cache
Pragma: no-cache
Date: Sat, Sun, 18 Nov 2001 22:23:32 GMT
Content-Type: text/html; charset=UTF-8
Content-Length: 187
Server: Tomcat Web Server/3.3 Final ( JSP 1.1; Servlet 2.2 )
↵
```

Listing 9–2   401 Unauthorized response. *(Continued)*

```
<html><title>Error 401</title><body>
Error: 401
<BR><H1>Forbidden</H1><BR>That action is not authorized. Please ensure
that you are authenticated.<BR>
<p><p></p></p>
</body></html>
```

Authentication Challenge   The WWW-Authenticate header values are the most important part of this response. These, along with the status code, indicate that the client must provide authentication information and how it may do so. WFS supports both standard authentication mechanisms, Basic and Digest [RFC2617]. This Digest authentication challenge was explained in Section 3.6.2.

Error Response Body   This response does have a body, even though error responses aren't required to have a body. The body includes HTML text in case the client is interested in displaying the body—some Web browsers do. However, in this case, Web Folders does not display the body. Instead, Web Folders understands the 401 Unauthorized response status code and prompts Alice for her username and password. When these are entered, the PROPFIND request is repeated, with the Authorization header.

9.2.3   Authenticated PROPFIND

The next PROPFIND request authenticates the client as Alice on the given realm. It's identical to the previous PROPFIND request, with the addition of the Authorization header (see Listing 9–3).

Listing 9–3   PROPFIND request with authorization.

```
PROPFIND / HTTP/1.1
[same headers as previous PROPFIND request]
Authorization: Basic dGVzdHVzZXI6dGVzdHVzZXI=
⏎
```

Web Folders chose to use Basic authentication, even though the server offered Digest, which is more secure. Clients ought to choose the more secure authentication scheme. It's possible that the Web Folders designers believed that the order in which the server returned the schemes indicated a preference for the first one, the Basic authentication scheme. However, that belief is not supported by the standard on HTTP authentication schemes.

9.2.4   Collection Properties Response

Now that the client is authenticated, the server can respond successfully. WFS keeps authenticated users logged in with session cookies, so it sends session cookies in the `Set-Cookie` header. A successful PROPFIND response is a 207 Multi-Status response, as described in Section 7.2.2. This particular response body contains some nonstandard data-typing attributes, which WebDAV does not require but that are necessary to interoperate with Web Folders (see Listing 9–4).

Listing 9–4   Successful response to PROPFIND.

```
HTTP/1.0 207 Multi-Status
Set-Cookie: XythosSessionID=2600-2141502937;
   Expires=Tue, 31-May-2005 09:33:57 GMT; Path=/
Set-Cookie: XythosUser=alice@1;
   Expires=Tue, 31-May-2005 09:33:57 GMT; Path=/
Content-Type: text/xml; charset=UTF-8
Date: Sun, 18 Nov 2001 22:23:32 GMT
Content-Length: 928
Server: Tomcat Web Server/3.3 Final ( JSP 1.1; Servlet 2.2 )
↵
<?xml version="1.0" encoding="utf-8" ?>
<D:multistatus xmlns:D="DAV:"
   xmlns:b="urn:uuid:c2f41010-65b3-11d1-a29f-00aa00c14882/">
   <D:response>
      <D:href>http://www.example.com/</D:href>
      <D:propstat>
        <D:prop>
           <D:resourcetype><D:collection/></D:resourcetype>
           <D:displayname><![CDATA[]]></D:displayname>
           <D:creationdate b:dt="dateTime.tz"> ↲
              1970-01-01T00:00:00Z</D:creationdate>
           <D:lockdiscovery></D:lockdiscovery>
           <D:supportedlock>
              <D:lockentry>
                 <D:lockscope><D:exclusive/></D:lockscope>
                 <D:locktype><D:write/></D:locktype>
              </D:lockentry>
              <D:lockentry>
                 <D:lockscope><D:shared/></D:lockscope>
                 <D:locktype><D:write/></D:locktype>
              </D:lockentry>
           </D:supportedlock>
           <D:getlastmodified b:dt="dateTime.rfc1123"> ↲
              Sat, 17 Nov 2001 22:23:32 GMT</D:getlastmodified>
        </D:prop>
```

Listing 9–4 Successful response to PROPFIND. *(Continued)*

```
        <D:status>HTTP/1.1 200 OK</D:status>
      </D:propstat>
    </D:response>
</D:multistatus>
```

Allprop Response   This is the server's response to a request for all properties on the resource. However, it only includes dead properties and those defined in RFC2518, as many servers do (as discussed in Section 7.2.5). In this specific case, the collection does have additional live properties that aren't shown, such as those required to support access-control and versioning features. These are expensive to calculate and are unlikely to be useful to Web Folders.

Datatype Attribute and Namespace   The response includes an odd-looking namespace with an attribute named dt. The namespace was given the arbitrary prefix b:, just as the D: prefix is arbitrary for the DAV namespace.

The dt attribute indicates the datatype of the XML element, showing that the creationdate value is in the W3C and IETF recommended date and time format (dateTime.tz) [RFC3339]. The getlastmodified value is in a less portable date format (dateTime.rfc1123) defined in a much older specification [RFC1123].

An obsolete W3C working document defines the UUID namespace, the dt attribute name in that namespace, and two values for that attribute. Although that specification did not become a standard and is not a WebDAV requirement, Web Folders uses the datatype mechanism anyway. The server implementation includes the nonstandard datatype information in order to interoperate fully with Web Folders. Web Folders will not display dates in directory listings unless the datatype attributes are present.

Other clients must ignore attributes they don't understand, like the dt attribute, and in practice they do this perfectly well.

Cookies   Two cookies are given to the client in the response headers. Cookies are a common and standardized HTTP feature [RFC2965]. However, cookies are not required for WebDAV support, so servers that use cookies can't count on WebDAV clients to return them.

```
    Set-Cookie: XythosSessionID=2600-2141502937;
        Expires=Tue, 31-May-2005 09:33:57 GMT; Path=/
    Set-Cookie: XythosUser=alice@1;
        Expires=Tue, 31-May-2005 09:33:57 GMT; Path=/
```

These cookies identify a session that the server uses to keep Alice logged in without having to authenticate Alice on every request. The server offers both Basic and Digest authentication to identify the user, but it switches to session cookies once the user is identified, because:

- Session cookies are more secure than Basic authentication. When the client chooses to use Basic in every request, the chances of the user's ID and password getting discovered multiply. The password is valid until the user changes it, on every system that has the same password. If a hacker obtains a session cookie instead of a password, that cookie expires eventually, and the only compromised server is the one that gave out the cookie.

- Session cookies are less secure than Digest but perform better. Digest provides some protection against replay attacks with nonces (Section 3.6.2), whereas session cookies are subject to replay attacks. However, Digest requires that the user's password be verified on receipt every time. If the user's password is stored on a directory server or password server rather than on the WebDAV server, the process of verifying that every time can be very slow. The session cookie allows the WebDAV server to verify the password once, and then it caches the session ID to be checked against future requests.

If a server decides to use session IDs, these should not be easily guessable and they should time out periodically to require a new Digest authentication.

Some WebDAV clients do not use cookies, instead sending the `Authorization` header on all requests. Support for cookies is entirely optional for both clients and servers.

9.2.5 Directory Contents Listing

In the next step, still in the process of opening the Web Folder, the Microsoft client sends another PROPFIND request. This is the third request shown in Figure 9–2, still part of opening the Web Folder. The Web Folders client still doesn't know the contents of the root folder, so it can't display the folder yet. This time, the client requests specific property names in the PROPFIND request (see Listing 9–5).

Listing 9–5 PROPFIND to get directory contents.

```
PROPFIND / HTTP/1.1
Content-Language: en-us
Accept-Language: en-us
Content-Type: text/xml
Translate: f
Depth: 1
Content-Length: 489
User-Agent: Microsoft Data Access Internet Publishing
   Provider DAV 1.1
Host: www.example.com
Connection: Keep-Alive
Cookie: XythosSessionID=2600-2141502937; XythosUser=alice@1
Authorization: Basic YWxpY2U6Ym9yaXNhbmRrb3Jpcw==
↵
```

Listing 9–5   PROPFIND to get directory contents. *(Continued)*

```
<?xml version="1.0" encoding="UTF-8" ?>
<a:propfind xmlns:a="DAV:" xmlns:b="urn:schemas-microsoft-
com:datatypes">
   <a:prop>
      <a:name/> <a:parentname/> <a:href/> <a:ishidden/>
      <a:isreadonly/> <a:getcontenttype/> <a:contentclass/>
      <a:getcontentlanguage/> <a:creationdate/>
      <a:lastaccessed/> <a:getlastmodified/>
      <a:getcontentlength/> <a:iscollection/>
      <a:isstructureddocument/> <a:defaultdocument/>
      <a:displayname/> <a:isroot/>
      <a:resourcetype/>
   </a:prop>
</a:propfind>
```

Depth   In this request the `Depth` header has a value of 1. The client is now asking for the specified properties for all child resources of the root collection, as well as the root collection itself. It's unclear why Web Folders didn't just begin with this request and skip the `Depth: 0` request entirely.

Cookie   The new request includes the cookies that the server provided. It also includes the `Authorization` header because Web Folders needs to stay logged in and has no way of knowing that the cookies provide a session ID that will keep the user logged in. The server could use either the session ID or the `Authorization` header to figure out who the user is, but WFS uses the session ID to improve performance. WFS continues to use the session ID and ignore the `Authorization` header until the session ID is missing or timed out.

Nonstandard Properties   Note that Web Folders is requesting a number of nonstandard properties. These are highlighted in Listing 9–5. Web Folders works even if it doesn't receive values for these properties, so the server can omit them and still interoperate with Web Folders.

The custom properties are in the `DAV:` namespace, even though they were defined by Microsoft and never standardized. Using the `DAV:` namespace for custom properties is strongly discouraged. The `DAV:` namespace is a URI scheme registered with the IANA (*www.iana.org*) for use by the IETF and the WebDAV Working Group. Use of the `DAV:` namespace without following the standards process can lead to real interoperability problems because clients and servers rely on particular semantics for properties. All custom properties should use a custom namespace, not the one reserved for the WebDAV standards.

9.2.6   Directory Contents Response

The response body is again a Multi-Status document, but this time it lists the direct children of the collection. The body includes one `response` element for each resource inside the root collection, plus a `response` element for the root collection itself. The framework is shown first because the entire body is quite long, and then we show the `response` element contents for just one item (see Listing 9–6).

Listing 9–6   Response to PROPFIND Depth: 1.

```
HTTP/1.0 207 Multi-Status
Content-Type: text/xml; charset=UTF-8
Date: Sun, 18 Nov 2001 22:23:32 GMT
Content-Length: 3444
Server: Tomcat Web Server/3.3 Final ( JSP 1.1; Servlet 2.2 )
⏎
<?xml version="1.0" encoding="utf-8" ?>
<D:multistatus xmlns:D="DAV:"
   xmlns:b="urn:uuid:c2f41010-65b3-11d1-a29f-00aa00c14882/" >
   <D:response>
      <D:href>http://www.example.com/</D:href>
      [omitted]
   </D:response>
   <D:response>
      <D:href>http://www.example.com/hr/</D:href>
      [omitted]
   </D:response>
   <D:response>
      <D:href>http://www.example.com/users/</D:href>
      [omitted]
   </D:response>
</D:multistatus>
```

This is just the response framework; the property information for each resource has been omitted to keep the example brief. Note that the server no longer needs to send the client the `Set-Cookie` header; the client already has the cookies.

With this information, the client is able to show that the root collection of `www.example .com` contains two resources. It needs the property information for each of those resources to know how to display them. Listing 9–7 shows what one of the `response` elements looks like in detail with all the property information provided by the server.

Listing 9–7   Excerpt from PROPFIND response: Property values for /hr/ collection.

```
<D:response>
   <D:href>http://www.example.com/hr/</D:href>
   <D:propstat>
      <D:prop>
```

Listing 9–7 Excerpt from PROPFIND response: Property values for /hr/ collection. *(Continued)*

```
            <D:creationdate b:dt="dateTime.tz"> ↲
               2001-11-17T00:26:07Z</D:creationdate>
            <D:getlastmodified b:dt="dateTime.rfc1123"> ↲
               Sat, 17 Nov 2001 00:26:08 GMT</D:getlastmodified>
            <D:displayname><![CDATA[hr]]></D:displayname>
            <D:resourcetype><D:collection/></D:resourcetype>
         </D:prop>
         <D:status>HTTP/1.1 200 OK</D:status>
      </D:propstat>
      <D:propstat>
         <D:prop>
            <D:name/><D:parentname/><D:href/><D:ishidden/>
            <D:isreadonly/><D:getcontenttype/><D:contentclass/>
            <D:getcontentlanguage/><D:lastaccessed/>
            <D:getcontentlength/><D:iscollection/>
            <D:isstructureddocument/><D:defaultdocument/>
            <D:isroot/>
         </D:prop>
         <D:status>HTTP/1.1 404 Not Found</D:status>
      </D:propstat>
   </D:response>
```

This response shows when the collection was created and last modified as well as its display name and type. Successful property values are returned with the 200 OK status code. All the other properties that Web Folders requested do not exist for that resource, so the server returns those property names associated with the 404 Not Found status code.

9.2.7 Navigation

After the last response, the client can finally display the contents of the Web folder, showing two collections. Alice opens the `users` collection and then opens the `alice` collection within that. Web Folders sends one more PROPFIND request for each folder that is opened (shown in Figure 9–2). These PROPFIND requests are identical to the example just shown, other than the Request-URI.

9.3 Create a Folder

Now that Alice is viewing her personal collection, she chooses New... from the File menu, and then selects Folder. Microsoft Explorer always creates new folders with the name New Folder, and then allows users to rename the folder. This behavior is exactly how Explorer works with a local folder.

Web Folders uses MKCOL to create a new WebDAV collection called New Folder and uses PROPFIND to check the new folder's properties. Then Web Folders prompts the user for a real name and uses MOVE to rename the collection (see Figure 9–3).

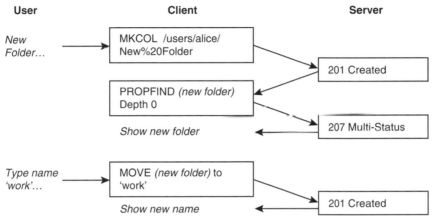

Figure 9–3   Summary of creating new collection.

Although Web Folders required three requests to create a new folder, a client with a greater concern for performance could arrange to have a different UI that only required one request (MKCOL).

The MKCOL and MOVE request and response details are interesting, as is the response to the PROPFIND. These interactions are covered in the next few sections.

9.3.1   MKCOL

Web Folders uses MKCOL to create New Folder (see Listing 9–8). The space in the name is escaped so that it is a legal URL (Section 3.1.3).

Listing 9–8   MKCOL request and response.

```
MKCOL /users/alice/New%20Folder HTTP/1.1
Accept-Language: en-us
Translate: f
User-Agent: Microsoft Data Access Internet Publishing
   Provider DAV 1.1
Host: www.example.com
Content-Length: 0
Connection: Keep-Alive
Cookie: XythosSessionID=2600-2141502937; XythosUser=alice@1
↵
```

Listing 9–8 MKCOL request and response. *(Continued)*

```
HTTP/1.0 201 Created
Content-Length: 0
Cache-Control: no-cache
Pragma: no-cache
Date: Sun, 18 Nov 2001 22:25:38 GMT
Server: Tomcat Web Server/3.3 Final ( JSP 1.1; Servlet 2.2 )
↵
```

The client continues to send the `Accept-Language`, `Translate`, `User-Agent`, `Host`, `Content-Length`, `Connection`, and `Cookie` headers with each request. The client continues to send every one of these headers in every request, and that's boring, so from here on I'll omit them in order to draw attention to what matters or is new. Most of these headers are not useful or required in an MKCOL request. Only the `Host` header is required with the MKCOL request.

9.3.2   New Folder Properties

Web Folders now sends a PROPFIND request because it needs some property values (probably the creation date) to know how to correctly display the new folder in Explorer. This request also verifies that the new folder exists, has the expected name, and is not locked but may be locked. Since the PROPFIND request is no different from that shown in Listing 9–3, I'll show only the response body to show the properties of a newly created collection (see Listing 9–9).

Listing 9–9   PROPFIND response fragment for new collection.

```
<D:response>
   <D:href>http://www.example.com/users/alice/New%20Folder/</D:href>
   <D:propstat>
      <D:prop>
         <D:resourcetype><D:collection/></D:resourcetype>
         <D:displayname><![CDATA[New Folder]]></D:displayname>
         <D:creationdate b:dt="dateTime.tz"> ↲
            2001-11-18T22:25:38Z</D:creationdate>
         <D:lockdiscovery></D:lockdiscovery>
         <D:supportedlock>[omitted]</D:supportedlock>
         <D:getlastmodified b:dt="dateTime.rfc1123"> ↲
            Sun, 18 Nov 2001 22:25:38 GMT</D:getlastmodified>
      </D:prop>
      <D:status>HTTP/1.1 200 OK</D:status>
   </D:propstat>
</D:response>
```

The response shows that the new folder was created and is not locked (lockdiscovery is empty) but may be locked (the value of the supportedlock property was omitted from the example because it's the same for every resource). It shows that the name of the collection is New Folder. That means that the Xythos server chose to undo the HTTP character escaping and store the resource name without escape sequences.

String Escaping   Clients must be prepared to deal with servers that unescape escaped strings and servers that store escaped strings as is, because RFC2518 doesn't require either behavior. The RFC also does not specify what the displayname property value should be, but most servers set the value of that property to the last part of the path to the resource and do not allow that value to be modified.

9.3.3   Collection Name Change

After creating the new collection, Web Folders allows the user to change the name of the new collection from New Folder to something else. The name change causes Web Folders to send another PROPFIND depth-0 request to the *parent* of the new folder (not to the new folder) and then a MOVE method on the new folder itself.

It's not clear what purpose this new PROPFIND request serves, because it's a depth-0 request. It doesn't retrieve the contents of the parent collection, so it can't be used to see if the new collection still exists or if another collection already exists with the new name chosen by the user. It may be used to determine if the parent collection is locked or to see if the parent collection supports some nonstandard WebDAV feature. We won't show this request or response because it's so similar to the last PROPFIND example, but instead we skip straight to the MOVE request and response that actually perform the rename (see Listing 9–10).

Listing 9–10   MOVE method to rename a collection.

```
MOVE /users/alice/New%20Folder HTTP/1.1
Destination: http://www.example.com/users/alice/work
Content-Length: 0
Overwrite: F
[typical headers omitted]
↵

HTTP/1.0 201 Created
Content-Length: 0
Cache-Control: no-cache
Pragma: no-cache
Date: Sun, 18 Nov 2001 22:26:40 GMT
Server: Tomcat Web Server/3.3 Final ( JSP 1.1; Servlet 2.2 )
↵
```

The request simply names the new location. The response is a 201 Created message, which makes it clear that the client did not overwrite a collection that already existed with the name `work` but instead created a new resource at that URL. An existing collection would not have been overwritten in any case, because the client request includes the directive not to overwrite existing resources in the `Overwrite` header.

9.4 Create a New File

Now that Alice has created a new collection, she wants to create a new Word file and save it in that collection. Since a Web Folder already exists pointing to the WebDAV repository, Word is capable of saving a file right to the repository.

Many requests are involved in creating a new file. Web Folders confirms that the Web Folder location is still reachable, and then the user navigates to the correct location, before the file can actually be saved. Most of the methods involved in this process are requests we've already seen in detail, so we'll simply list the first line for each request. New methods not yet seen in this chapter are more interesting and are shown in full.

From Word, Alice chooses File:Save As..., then chooses Network Places and selects the Web Folder for this repository. Now the GUI needs to display the contents of the directory and confirm the functionality the server supports. This is done with two requests:

```
OPTIONS / HTTP/1.1
PROPFIND / HTTP/1.1
```

The GUI displays the results of the PROPFIND, the two folders `/hr/` and `/users/`, so that Alice can either decide to save here or drill down into a subdirectory. Alice wants to save the file in her new collection, so she navigates to its location. Each time Alice opens a folder, Word needs to display its contents, so another PROPFIND request is generated for each level.

```
PROPFIND /users HTTP/1.1
PROPFIND /users/alice HTTP/1.1
PROPFIND /users/alice/work HTTP/1.1
```

Once inside the right directory, Alice types in the name for the new document and presses Save. Word generates three requests to lock the file, save it, and confirm the results:

```
LOCK /users/alice/work/ergo-accessories.doc HTTP/1.1
PUT /users/alice/work/ergo-accessories.doc HTTP/1.1
HEAD /users/alice/work/ergo-accessories.doc HTTP/1.1
```

In summary, eight requests are made by the client to navigate and open a new file. Most of the requests are necessary, given Word's user interface and the directory structure in the scenario. The OPTIONS response could have been cached on the client machine for a short while, but it's a good idea to refresh that information if it's not recent (see Figure 9–4).

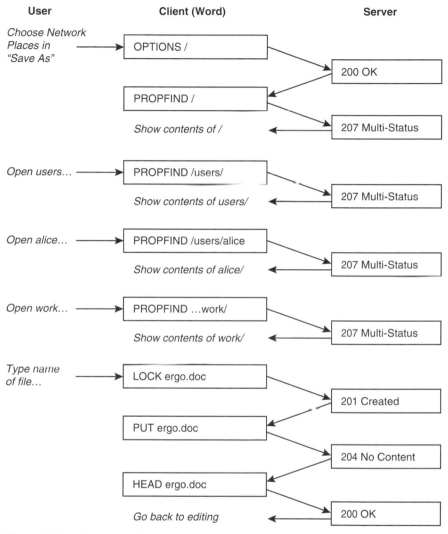

Figure 9–4 Summary of saving new file.

9.4.1 LOCK Creates New Resource

Web Folders uses LOCK to create the new resource that Word hasn't even begun to edit yet. Web Folders requests a very short-duration exclusive write lock (see Listing 9–11).

Listing 9–11 LOCK request to create new resource.

```
LOCK /users/alice/work/ergo-accessories.doc HTTP/1.1
Accept-Language: en-ca, en-us;q=0.5
```

Listing 9–11   LOCK request to create new resource. *(Continued)*

```
Content-Length: 159
Timeout: Second-120
Translate: f
User-Agent: Microsoft Data Access Internet Publishing
   Provider DAV 1.1
Host: www.example.com
Connection: Keep-Alive
Cookie: XythosSessionID=2600-2141502937; XythosUser=alice@1
⌐
<?xml version="1.0" ?>
<lockinfo xmlns="DAV:">
   <locktype><write/></locktype>
   <lockscope><exclusive/></lockscope>
   <owner>alice</owner>
</lockinfo>
```

Owner   The owner field Web Folders provides isn't very informative—alice is a Windows user ID, *not* the user ID provided to log in to the WebDAV server. If the user is logged in to a home computer, the Windows user ID might be meaningless to all other users. (Many users log in to their home computer as "administrator" or do not log in at all.) If the user is logged in to an intranet with a Windows user ID, then other users on the same network can figure out what user alice is, but users on other intranets or home users can't get anything meaningful out of the value. Client software should attempt to do a better job of providing useful lock owner information, including a full user name, the userid that was provided to log in to the WebDAV server, and the client software identification.

Missing Content-Type Header   This request shows that Microsoft clients do not always send the Content-Type header, even when the request has a body. A LOCK request is supposed to have a XML body, and the server can examine the first five non-whitespace characters of the body to confirm that it is XML.

Servers seem to support requests like this without the Content-Type header. There is a Content-Length header, so at least the server has some indication that it should expect a request body (as opposed to a new request). Still, this example is noncompliant and should not be emulated by other clients.

User-Agent   The User-Agent value is the same one used when requests are triggered by actions in Windows Explorer. That's because Office 2000 and Windows 2000 Explorer use the same underlying software to handle WebDAV requests. Office 2000 is closely linked into the Web Folders software—it can only use Web Folders that have already been configured, and it can't directly access a new URL even if the URL, points to a WebDAV server.

Two-Minute Lock   Two minutes is a rather short lock duration. It requires the client software to send another LOCK request every two minutes, as long as the user is editing the file, to keep the lock alive. If a server does not want to handle LOCK requests this frequently, it can grant a longer duration. The longer duration will be honored by Web Folders—it will not send a refresh LOCK request until the exact second the server's chosen time period expires.

9.4.2   Creation of Lock-Null Resource

The LOCK request was sent to a URL that was not previously associated with a resource, so WFS creates a lock-null resource and responds with a 201 Created status and the lock token (see Listing 9–12).

Listing 9–12   Response to creation of lock-null resource.

```
HTTP/1.0 201 Created
Lock-Token: <locktoken:vserver1-LockTokendocstore1:9100>
Content-Type: text/xml; charset=UTF-8
Date: Sun, 18 Nov 2001 22:29:14 GMT
Content-Length: 385
Server: Tomcat Web Server/3.3 Final ( JSP 1.1; Servlet 2.2 )
⏎
<?xml version="1.0" encoding="utf-8" ?>
<D:prop xmlns:D="DAV:">
<D:lockdiscovery>
   <D:activelock>
   <D:locktype><D:write/></D:locktype>
   <D:lockscope><D:exclusive/></D:lockscope>
   <D:depth>0</D:depth>
   <D:owner>alice</D:owner>
   <D:timeout>Second-119</D:timeout>
   <D:locktoken>
   <D:href>locktoken:vserver1-LockTokendocstore1:9100</D:href>
   </D:locktoken>
   </D:activelock>
</D:lockdiscovery>
</D:prop>
```

201 Created   The 201 Created status shows that not only was the lock request successful, but a new resource was created. If the server hadn't created a new resource, it would have used the status 200 OK.

Lock Token Twice   The lock token, which the client must use in subsequent requests, is provided in two locations, as the WebDAV specification requires. Some clients depend on the lock token being in the header; other clients depend on the lock token being in the body.

Timeout   The timeout is a little less than the client requested, because the lock response was generated a fraction of a second after the lock was created. The client must always check the timeout anyway in case the server granted either a shorter or longer timeout than was requested. Since the lock creation response may be delayed on the network, the client should include a grace period anyway.

9.4.3   First Upload Request

As soon as the resource is locked, Word sends a copy of the new file. There may not be anything in the file, but it's a good idea to upload a blank but valid Word document immediately anyway. Other clients may be able to browse Alice's collection and download the file as soon as it's created. Since the file has a Word .doc file name extension, some clients will attempt to open the document in Word. It's better for those clients to see an empty Word document than a Word error message saying that the document is null. Note that even an empty Word document is almost 20,000 bytes long (see Listing 9–13).

Listing 9–13   PUT request to create file over lock-null resource.

```
PUT /users/alice/work/ergo-accessories.doc HTTP/1.1
Accept-Language: en-ca, en-us;q=0.5
If: (<locktoken:vserver1-LockTokendocstore1:9100>)
Translate: f
Content-Length: 19456
Host: www.example.com
Connection: Keep-Alive
Cookie: XythosSessionID=2600-2141502937; XythosUser=alice@1
⏎
[body omitted]
```

The PUT request saves the initial content of the file to the server. It includes the lock token, as it must, because the resource is locked.

Missing Content-Type   An important header is missing in this request. Web Folders does not tell the WebDAV server the MIME type of the request body (it should be `application/msword`). The server has no way of telling what MIME type to use for the getcontenttype property, so it must use the default MIME type (`application/octet-stream`).

9.4.4   Server Saves File

The server saves the exact request body as the resource body. It generates a unique ETag for the new resource body (see Listing 9–14).

Listing 9–14   Response to PUT request.

```
HTTP/1.0 204 No Content
Content-Length: 0
Cache-Control: no-cache
Pragma: no-cache
Date: Sun, 18 Nov 2001 22:29:15 GMT
ETag: "9300-9800"
Server: Tomcat Web Server/3.3 Final ( JSP 1.1; Servlet 2.2 )
↵
```

The 204 No Content status code shows that the resource was not created (it was created when it was locked), but its body was updated successfully. It also shows that the resource was given the ETag 9300-9800. The client should save the value of the ETag and use it in future requests, to make sure that the resource never changes unexpectedly. However, Web Folders is not as careful about using ETags as it could be.

9.4.5 Confirm File Upload

The last client step in creating the file is to confirm the file was saved, using the HEAD request. This request may confirm that the name is identical to what the client expected and that the length is correct, or it may serve to get the exact last modified datestamp. It may be important to check the name, because although Web Folders does caseless comparison on resource names, WebDAV servers must treat URLs as case sensitive. This is yet another Web Folders bug (see Listing 9–15).

Listing 9–15   HEAD request to verify new resource.

```
HEAD /users/alice/work/ergo-accessories.doc HTTP/1.1
If: (<locktoken:vserver1-LockTokendocstore1:9100>)
[typical headers omitted]
↵
```

Note that it's not necessary to include the lock token in the HEAD request. The lock token is only required on requests that modify the resource. It doesn't hurt to include it in every request to the locked resource, and it may even be useful because it lets the client confirm the lock is still there (see Listing 9–16).

Listing 9–16   HEAD response.

```
HTTP/1.0 200 OK
Content-Type: application/octet-stream
Content-Length: 19456
```

Listing 9–16   HEAD response. *(Continued)*

```
Accept-Ranges: bytes
Last-Modified: Sun, 18 Nov 2001 22:29:15 GMT
ETag: "9300-9800"
Cache-Control: private
Date: Sun, 18 Nov 2001 22:29:16 GMT
Server: Tomcat Web Server/3.3 Final ( JSP 1.1; Servlet 2.2 )
↵
```

The HEAD response shows the resource type, content length, ETag (showing the resource hasn't been changed), and date last modified. It's just like the response to a GET request, except it doesn't contain the body.

9.5 • Editing a File

Word normally saves files automatically while a user edits. However, when you use a Web Folder, auto-saves happen in a local temporary file cache. New content isn't sent to the server until the user chooses to save the file.

While the file is opened in Word, Web Folders automatically keeps the lock alive by refreshing it just as it is supposed to expire (see Figure 9–5).

Web Folders issues a PUT operation every time the user chooses to save the file. Some WebDAV clients, like Xythos WebFile Client, do not save as frequently as Web Folders does. Instead, the Xythos client conserves bandwidth by caching changes on disk for a time and uploading changes to the server asynchronously. This allows the client to respond very quickly to a user save request, and the user can go on editing the document, even if the upload is slow. However, once in a while the user might attempt to view a document with some other tool and could be confused to see a document that doesn't yet contain the user's latest changes.

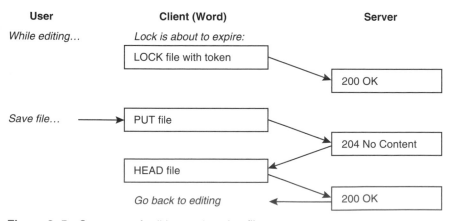

Figure 9–5   Summary of editing and saving file.

9.5.1   Automatic Lock Refresh

Roughly every two minutes as Alice is working on the file, Web Folders automatically
refreshes the lock. Web Folders chooses 119 seconds as the refresh lifetime of the lock, possibly because that's the value the server chose when the lock was created. If the client or the
server chooses a different lifetime for the lock, the refresh requests would occur at a different
rate (see Listing 9–17).

Listing 9–17   LOCK request to refresh a lock.

```
LOCK /users/alice/work/ergo-accessories.doc HTTP/1.1
If: (<locktoken:vserver1-LockTokendocstore1:9100>)
Timeout: Second-119
[typical headers omitted]
↲
```

The LOCK request no longer needs a body, because it's just used to refresh the lock identified using the request URI and the lock token (see Listing 9–18).

Listing 9–18   Response to LOCK request to refresh a lock.

```
HTTP/1.0 200 OK
Content-Type: text/xml; charset=UTF-8
Date: Sun, 18 Nov 2001 22:32:53 GMT
Content-Length: 385
Server: Tomcat Web Server/3.3 Final ( JSP 1.1; Servlet 2.2 )
↲
<?xml version="1.0" encoding="utf-8" ?>
<D:prop xmlns:D="DAV:">
<D:lockdiscovery>
   <D:activelock>
      <D:locktype><D:write/></D:locktype>
      <D:lockscope><D:exclusive/></D:lockscope>
      <D:depth>0</D:depth>
      <D:owner>alice</D:owner>
      <D:timeout>Second-119</D:timeout>
      <D:locktoken><D:href> ↲
         locktoken:vserver1-LockTokendocstore1:9100</D:href>
      </D:locktoken>
   </D:activelock>
</D:lockdiscovery>
</D:prop>
```

The server responds successfully. This time, the status code is 200 OK, not 201 Created, because no new resource was created as a result of this LOCK request.

The server includes the complete lock information every time the lock is refreshed. The lock type, depth, owner, and timeout are identical. None of this information can be changed in a lock refresh action except timeout. The lock token must also be included again.

9.5.2   User Action to Save File

When the user chooses to save, Word does nothing if the file hasn't been changed since the last save. If the document has changed, Word pops up a dialog that says "Transferring http://www.example.com/hr/alice/work/ergo-accessories.doc." The entire new body of the file is sent to the server synchronously—the user must wait until the entire request is sent and the response received before being allowed to continue editing. There is no way in HTTP or WebDAV to upload partial files (Section 5.4.1).

The file is saved with a PUT request, identical to the one used to save the content initially, except of course with new body content and content length value. Web Folders even continues to erroneously omit the `Content-Type` header.

Every time Word saves the file, the Web Folders code also performs a new HEAD request to confirm the document status. Again, it's not certain exactly why Web Folders does this; it could be to confirm the server's file size, date last modified, or URL.

These two requests and responses are not shown in full because they do not differ substantially from the PUT and HEAD examples in Listings 9–13 through 9–16.

9.6   Close the File

When Alice finishes editing the document, after saving her last changes, she exits Word. Since Alice is no longer editing the file, the lock can be released. Before doing this, however, Web Folders does another PROPFIND request to the document itself. The reason for this isn't apparent—Web Folders already knows the lock token and has used it in previous requests (see Figure 9–6).

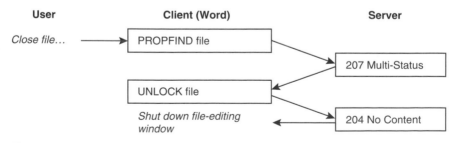

Figure 9–6   Summary of closing a file in Word.

9.6.1 UNLOCK

To release the lock, Web Folders sends a straightforward UNLOCK request. The request must include the correct lock token (see Listing 9–19).

Listing 9–19 UNLOCK request and response.

```
UNLOCK /users/alice/work/ergo-accessories.doc HTTP/1.1
Lock-Token: <locktoken:vserver1-LockTokendocstore1:9100>
[typical headers omitted]
⏎

HTTP/1.0 204 No Content
Content-Length: 0
Cache-Control: no-cache
Pragma: no-cache
Date: Sun, 18 Nov 2001 22:33:47 GMT
Server: Tomcat Web Server/3.3 Final ( JSP 1.1; Servlet 2.2 )
⏎
```

The user has permission to unlock the resource, so the lock is discarded successfully. Now other users or other client software can edit the resource, as long as authentication succeeds.

9.7 Copy to Publishing Directory

When Alice is finished editing the file in her own working directory, she decides to publish the file. First, she has to get a copy of the file to the place where she wants to publish it, /hr/ergonomics/. Alice accomplishes this task using the Explorer and Web Folders to copy the file and paste it to the destination. She checks to make sure the file is successfully copied and that it is viewable in its new location, and then she deletes the original copy in her work folder. Alice could also have used a Web Folders move (which would issue a WebDAV MOVE request), but sometimes users explicitly copy files instead of moving them.

Web Folders issues many OPTIONS and PROPFIND requests while Alice navigates to select a source directory, select a destination directory for the copy, and return to the source directory to delete the original file. The copy and delete operations are of course performed with the COPY and DELETE methods.

9.7.1 COPY File to Publish Location

The COPY request simply names the source and destination URLs, much like the MOVE request. The response is 201 Created, which means that the COPY request caused a new resource to be created at the destination (see Listing 9–20).

Listing 9–20   COPY request and response.

```
COPY /users/alice/work/ergo-accessories.doc HTTP/1.1
Destination:
   http://www.example.com/hr/ergonomics/ergo-accessories.doc
Overwrite: F
[typical headers omitted]
⏎

HTTP/1.0 201 Created
Content-Length: 0
Cache-Control: no-cache
Pragma: no-cache
Date: Fri, 30 Nov 2001 22:53:58 GMT
Server: Tomcat Web Server/3.3 Final ( JSP 1.1; Servlet 2.2 )
⏎
```

The Overwrite header value of false means that the client doesn't expect there to be a resource at the destination URL to be overwritten.

It's a good idea to include the Overwrite header, even though it's not required. If the Overwrite header is not present, it defaults to a value of true. That would overwrite the resource at the destination, even if the client didn't believe that a resource existed there.

9.7.2   Delete Working Copy

The DELETE request shows yet another nonstandard Microsoft syntax, the Destroy header, along with all the typical headers. The response is a simple success (see Listing 9–21).

Listing 9–21   Web Folders DELETE request and response.

```
DELETE /users/alice/work/ergo-accessories.doc HTTP/1.1
Destroy: NoUndelete
Content-Length: 0
[typical headers omitted]
⏎

HTTP/1.0 204 No Content
Content-Length: 0
Cache-Control: no-cache
Pragma: no-cache
Date: Fri, 30 Nov 2001 22:54:09 GMT
Server: Tomcat Web Server/3.3 Final ( JSP 1.1; Servlet 2.2 )
⏎
```

Destroy Header   The "noundelete" value of the `Destroy` header specifies that the file should be destroyed when it is deleted. It may seem obvious that deleting a file should destroy it, but there are other options: It could be marked for deletion, hidden, or moved to a Recycle Bin or trash folder.

When WFS gets DELETE requests for ordinary resources, it automatically moves them to a trash folder to allow users to recover from mistakes. In this case, it moves the file to a directory called `/users/alice/trash/`. Alice can view this directory using Web Folders or any other WebDAV client. She can empty it by deleting the files in the trash folder. When files are deleted from trash folders in WFS, they are destroyed completely.

Since the `Destroy` header is not standardized anywhere and WFS doesn't recognize this header, WFS moves the file to the trash folder rather than follow the client instructions. The `Destroy` header shows how easy it is for nonstandard protocol extensions to make a protocol less interoperable. The client was asking for specific action, but the server could not know that because the client used a nonstandard header.

9.8   Publish Document

Alice's department has a very simple publishing workflow process. Documents are saved somewhere within the `/hr/` collection, where the content can be verified and links can be tested. Every night, a process copies files from the `/hr/` collection to the regular corporate Web server. However, this process only copies files that have a special property set. This property is named publish, and its value can be either `true` or `false`. It's in the namespace `http://www.example.com/namespace/`, a well-chosen namespace name because it includes the domain name of the company that defined the custom property.

This simple process allows files to be reviewed and tested in place before they are published. When a document is finally "ready for prime time," the publish property is created and set to `true`.

Alice asks Bob to double-check the new document. To review the document, Bob makes sure he can download the file and view it properly using IE 5.0. When Bob approves the document, Alice will use PROPPATCH to set the publish property so that all employees can view the new file.

9.8.1   Browser Request for WebDAV Resource

Bob uses IE 5.0 to open the link from Alice. IE 5.0 is fairly concise in GET requests. The request needs no authentication, because the file was placed in a publicly readable directory (see Listing 9–22).

Listing 9–22   GET from Internet Explorer 5.0.

```
GET /hr/ergonomics/ergo-accessories.doc HTTP/1.1
Accept: image/gif, image/x-xbitmap, image/jpeg, image/pjpeg,
   application/vnd.ms-powerpoint, application/vnd.ms-excel,
```

Listing 9–22   GET from Internet Explorer 5.0. *(Continued)*

```
    application/msword, */*
Accept-Language: en-us
Accept-Encoding: gzip, deflate
User-Agent: Mozilla/4.0 (compatible; MSIE 5.01; Windows NT 5.0)
Host: www.example.com
Connection: Keep-Alive
↵

HTTP/1.0 200 OK
Content-Type: application/msword
Accept-Ranges: bytes
Last-Modified: Sun, 18 Nov 2001 22:29:16 GMT
ETag: "9300-9801"
Cache-Control: private
Content-Length: 21504
Date: Fri, 30 Nov 2001 22:46:09 GMT
Server: Tomcat Web Server/3.3 Final ( JSP 1.1; Servlet 2.2 )
↵
[document body not shown]
```

The Anonymous request contains no authorization header and no session cookie, so the request is anonymous. It succeeds because the file is publicly readable. The file was copied to a publicly readable collection, and according to this server's policy, the file was made publicly readable, too. That's not a standard requirement; it's how this particular server was configured to handle permissions.

9.8.2   Setting Publish Property

The new document is in place and readable, and Bob finds no errors, so it's ready to publish. Bob emails Alice to let her know it's ready. Alice must now edit the value of that property on the resource so that the nightly site copy process will pick it up.

Alice can't use Web Folders to set the value, because Web Folders doesn't offer any functionality to view or change custom properties. Therefore, Alice uses a simple command-line tool called cadaver to set the property. There is more information on what cadaver can do in the next chapter.

There are other options besides using cadaver to set properties. For example, the Xythos WebFile Client allows the user to set a custom property name and value (but does not allow the user to choose a namespace).

Listing 9–23 shows the complete cadaver version 0.17.0 user interface interaction, as Alice sets one property value. The characters Alice typed are shown in bold, and the rest of the characters are generated by cadaver or the operating system.

Listing 9–23   Command-line user interface for cadaver.

```
$ cadaver
dav:!> open http://www.example.com/hr/ergonomics/
Looking up hostname... Connecting to server... connected.
Authentication required for www.example.com on server
'www.example.com':
Username: alice
Password: ????????
Connecting to server... connected.
Connecting to server... connected.
dav:/hr/ergonomics/> set namespace http://www.example.com/namespace/
dav:/hr/ergonomics/> propset ergo-accessories.doc publish true
Setting property on 'ergo-accessories.doc': (reconnecting...done)
succeeded.
dav:/hr/ergonomics/> quit
Connection to 'www.example.com' closed.

$
```

This listing shows what the user does to set the property value, but what is cadaver doing "under the covers"? To open the connection, cadaver does an OPTIONS request, then a PROPFIND request to make sure that the resource opened is a collection. Then, when the user sets the property, cadaver sends a single PROPPATCH request.

Unlike Web Folders, it matters to cadaver what features the server supports, and it makes no assumptions. That's why it issues the OPTIONS request (see Figure 9–7).

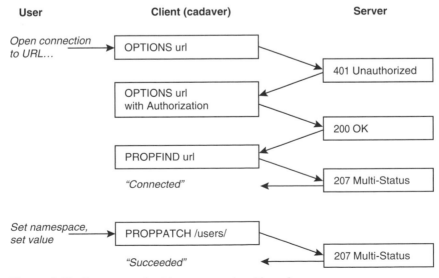

Figure 9–7   Summary of setting a property with cadaver.

9.8.3 OPTIONS

The OPTIONS request is sent first without authentication. The server responds with a `401 Unauthorized`, just like Listing 9–2. The response includes the following headers:

```
WWW-Authenticate: BASIC realm="www.example.com"
WWW-Authenticate: Digest realm="www.example.com",stale=false,
    nonce="79820df5e55635e3df79581c4f01e8f7", qop="auth",
    algorithm="MD5"
```

Unlike Web Folders, cadaver chooses the more secure authentication algorithm, Digest authentication, and resends its OPTIONS request with the `Authorization` header (see Listing 9–24).

Listing 9–24 OPTIONS request from cadaver.

```
OPTIONS /hr/ergonomics/ HTTP/1.1
User-Agent: cadaver/0.17.0 neon/0.12.0-dev
Keep-Alive:
Connection: TE, Keep-Alive
TE: trailers
Content-Length: 0
Host: www.example.com
Authorization: Digest username="alice",
    realm="www.example.com", uri="/hr/ergonomics/",
    nonce="79820df5e55635e3df79581c4f01e8f7",
    response="fa3c7169539554a6571613b87512c0f4",
    cnonce="RnJpLCAzMCBOb3YgMjAwMSAyMjowMzoyOCBHTVQ=",
    algorithm="MD5", nc=00000001, qop="auth"
⌐
```

In the request cadaver sent, three headers and header values appear that we haven't seen before.

Keep-Alive The `Keep-Alive` header is now obsolete. It was defined in RFC2068 (HTTP/1.1 specification dated January 1997, replaced by RFC2616 in June 1999), but RFC2068 did not specify any values. That RFC says "The Keep-Alive header itself is optional, and is used only if a parameter is being sent. HTTP/1.1 does not define any parameters." Thus, cadaver should not have included the header at all. However, it does no harm in this case.

Connection: TE, Keep-Alive The string `TE` in the `Connection` header means that the cadaver client supports chunked transfer encodings. The string `TE` must appear in the `Connection` header whenever the `TE` header is present. `Keep-Alive` indicates that the server can keep the connection open. The `Connection` header is defined in HTTP/1.1 [RFC2616].

TE: Trailers   The string TE means Transfer-Encoding again, but now it's a header of its own. The value trailers means that the client can accept trailer fields with a chunked transfer-encoding response. Trailer fields allow the server to put the headers at the end of the response rather than the beginning. It can help server performance in some cases, but WFS ignores the header and sends a regular un-encoded response. The TE header is defined in HTTP/1.1 [RFC2616].

9.8.4   OPTIONS Response

The server responds with its standard OPTIONS response for a collection. This response includes the basic WebDAV support header (DAV), as well as a nonstandard header that Microsoft clients look for (MS Author-Via) and a header from the Internet Draft for WebDAV Searching (DASL) (see Listing 9–25).

Listing 9–25   OPTIONS response for a collection.

```
HTTP/1.0 200 OK
Set-Cookie: [omitted]
Content-Type: text/html
DAV: 1,2, access-control, ticket
MS-Author-Via: DAV
Allow: OPTIONS, PROPFIND, PROPPATCH, LOCK, UNLOCK, DELETE
DASL: <DAV:basicsearch>
Accept-Ranges: bytes
Xythos-WFS-Version: Xythos WebFile Server 3.2.0.0
Date: Fri, 30 Nov 2001 22:03:27 GMT
Server: Tomcat Web Server/3.3 Final ( JSP 1.1; Servlet 2.2 )
⏎
```

DAV Header   The DAV header shows that WFS ("Xythos WebFile Server 3.2.0.0") supports WebDAV level 1, level 2 (locking) as well as access-control and ticket. The access-control feature is nearly standardized by the WebDAV Working Group and discussed in Chapter 12, *Multifile Versioning*. The ticket string advertises a feature that was proposed in an expired Internet Draft.

It's not a good idea to use a simple short string like ticket to advertise a feature, unless that short string is standardized through the IETF. Two servers could advertise support for a feature named ticket but not mean the same thing by that name, unless it's standardized. Although the ticket feature was proposed in an Internet Draft, drafts expire and later implementors may be ignorant of the proposal. WebDAV does not make any recommendations as to what to do in this situation, but common sense suggests using something more unique than a simple string, such as a string including a domain name.

Defining a complete new header isn't typically recommended, since doing so has an even greater risk of colliding with other headers of the same name.

DASL Header   The DASL header shows that Xythos WFS supports the Distributed Authoring Search and Location (DASL) syntax, which is the WebDAV search proposal currently going through the standards process. Cadaver can ignore all of this.

MS-Author-Via Header   WebDAV requires the MS-Author-Via header to understand that the server supports WebDAV [q304133]. The server puts this header in all OPTIONS responses rather than try to guess if the client is Web Folders or not.

9.8.5 Setting a Property

When the user asks to set a property value on a resource, cadaver sends a single PROPPATCH request (see Listing 9–26).

Listing 9–26   PROPPATCH request from cadaver.

```
PROPPATCH /hr/ergonomics/ergo-accessories.doc HTTP/1.1
User-Agent: cadaver/0.17.0 neon/0.12.0-dev
Keep-Alive:
Connection: TE, Keep-Alive
TE: trailers
Content-Type: text/xml
Content-Length: 191
Host: www.example.com
Authorization: Digest username="alice",
   realm="www.example.com",
   uri="/hr/ergonomics/ergo-accessories.doc",
   nonce="79820df5e55635e3df79581c4f01e8f7",
   response="fa076245916613bb64d5b4c1dbaa2a6c",
   cnonce="RnJpLCAzMCBOb3YgMjAwMSAyMjowMzoyOCBHTVQ=",
   algorithm="MD5", nc=00000002, qop="auth"
⏎
<?xml version="1.0" encoding="utf-8" ?>
<propertyupdate xmlns="DAV:">
   <set>
      <prop>
         <publish xmlns="http://www.example.com/namespace/">
            true
         </publish>
      </prop>
   </set>
</propertyupdate>
```

No Cookies   Note that cadaver ignores the cookies sent in the OPTIONS response and instead sends the Digest `Authorization` header again. This is an excellent choice; Digest is much more secure than using cookies or Basic authentication, and it protects the user's password and identity more effectively.

No Prefixes   Cadaver does an interesting trick with the namespaces in this request. The root element of the XML body contains a declaration of the `DAV:` namespace as default namespace. That means that all elements in the body without a prefix are in the `DAV:` namespace—except for the `publish` element, where the default namespace is redefined as `http://www.example.com/namespace/`. Recall that namespace declarations apply to an XML scope, which includes anything contained within the element where the declaration is made. Since the `publish` element contains the `www.example.com` namespace declaration, that scope ends when the `publish` element ends. The default namespace reverts to being the `DAV:` namespace. Any compliant XML parser should handle this properly without intervention.

Digest Details   This time, the `Authorization` header has a different value for the `response` and `nc` (nonce-count). Digest authentication is designed so that replay attacks aren't possible. Contrast that with Basic authentication, where replay attacks are done simply by copying the entire header value and using it over and over again to reauthenticate. The `response` value contains a digest of the request body, which means that it provides some protection from modification or corruption of the request body in transit.

9.8.6 PROPPATCH Response

The PROPPATCH response is a success, confirming that the property in the given namespace on the requested resource successfully had its value changed. The headers for this response are very similar to other responses, so only the body is shown in Listing 9–27.

Listing 9–27   PROPPATCH response: 207 Multi-Status response body.

```
<?xml version="1.0" encoding="utf-8" ?>
<D:multistatus xmlns:D="DAV:"
   xmlns:ns1200="http://www.example.com/namespace/">
<D:response>
   <D:href>http://www.example.com/hr/ergonomics/ergo- ↲
      accessories.doc</D:href>
   <D:propstat>
      <D:prop><ns1200:publish/></D:prop>
      <D:status>HTTP/1.1 200 OK</D:status>
   </D:propstat>
</D:response>
</D:multistatus>
```

The server refers to the same example namespace but assigns it a prefix ns1200. The DAV: namespace is also given a prefix D:. Although the prefixes differ, the namespaces are completely consistent with the PROPPATCH request.

9.9 Summary

The interactions in this chapter illustrate all the WebDAV methods plus a couple from HTTP used commonly in distributed authoring scenarios. The requests all come from real deployed WebDAV clients—Microsoft Web Folders and a free Unix client called cadaver. The responses all come from Xythos WebFile Server.

Web Folders uses nonstandard protocol mechanisms and has a couple of obvious bugs. Most of these can be ignored, such as the nonstandard Translate and Destroy headers. However, a server wanting to interoperate with Web Folders must support the nonstandard datatype attribute in PROPFIND responses that tells Web Folders the format in which date properties are expressed.

Web Folders could be designed to be faster. Word and Web Folders make a bunch of requests with no discernable purpose, such as the PROPFIND request just before an UNLOCK request. This wastes a considerable amount of time and bandwidth and can make even a reasonably fast server seem slow to a user.

A user might use more than one WebDAV client in an authoring scenario. For example, Web Folders allows users to directly edit resources on a repository with the Office suite, whereas cadaver allows users to directly manipulate properties. Both clients provide file management features over WebDAV.

An ordinary WebDAV server can be used to enact a simple workflow process. In our example that process is managed via properties and values that are created by client software or the user, without any special logic on the server.

CHAPTER 10

WebDAV Products and Tools

There are so many WebDAV products and tools that it's only barely possible to write a single chapter about them. The important tools are covered here in some detail, but some of the more obscure or emerging products are only mentioned briefly. The *www.webdav.org* site hosts a more up-to-date list of products supporting WebDAV.

This chapter is a survey of the kind of WebDAV products and tools that exist, with the goal of making administrators and planners aware of the range of options. It does not serve as a user, programmer, or administrator guide for any of these tools. Please consult product documentation for those purposes.

10.1 Client Software

The number of approaches to writing WebDAV client software is surprisingly high. Each approach involves different models for whether the files are stored only on the server or are cached locally or even primarily stored locally. Each approach involves a different way of presenting the user interface.

Stand-Alone WebDAV Explorer A few WebDAV clients are designed primarily as WebDAV clients, but they are in the minority because most users don't want yet another client application unless it's a really important one. The standard approach seems to be to implement a graphical user interface to mimic the way an existing file system explorer tool works, such as Windows Explorer. Typically, users browse through folders by clicking to open them. Cadaver, although not a graphical tool, is similar to these Explorer tools because it exists only to send WebDAV commands.

Mounted Drive Client   A client that acts a mounted drive makes a remote repository appear as if it is a locally mounted hard drive or other storage device. On Windows, a mounted drive client typically allows the client to enter a WebDAV URL to a collection and then assigns a local drive letter to that remote repository. Then any application that opens or saves files can theoretically use the remote repository. This works even for applications that do not support WebDAV.

A mounted drive client may also keep a local cache of remote files and directory structure, synchronizing these with the server. When the user is online, local caching can allow a file and folders to be reopened more quickly. The files may even be available offline. However, it's quite difficult to keep property values synchronized offline, because WebDAV provides no reliable way to tell when properties change.

The user interface for a mounted drive client may be quite minimal, like those for Web Folders, Windows XP WebDAV Redirector, and Xythos WebFile Client. All that is needed is a way for the user to mount a new repository, because there can be much reuse of the existing navigation user interface on the client operating system.

Authoring Applications Using WebDAV for Primary Storage   This is the largest category of WebDAV client software. Most Microsoft and Adobe authoring applications now have the ability to store documents on a WebDAV. The approach can be very straightforward, simply allowing the file to be saved to a remote location identified by an HTTP URL rather than a local folder. However, in practice it may be a little more complicated. For example, MS Office requires the user to set up a Web Folder first and does not allow the user to save directly to a named URL.

Authoring Applications Using WebDAV to Publish   The Adobe authoring applications typically allow the user to publish documents directly to a WebDAV location. The user is expected to publish the document to the repository only when it is complete, and so the application does not save the file to the repository periodically while it is being edited (unlike Office). This is because the Adobe usage scenarios are different from the Office usage scenarios:

- Users are not expected to be connected to the Internet or a local area network at all times. Thus, they must always be able to easily save the document locally. The connection, when it exists, may be as slow as a home telephone line.
- Documents may be very large. Saving the document multiple times to the WebDAV server while it is being edited may be prohibitively slow.

Given these different assumptions, Adobe chose a slightly different user model. Rather than incorporate WebDAV support directly into the File Open and Save dialogs (which are still only used to save locally or to a locally networked file system), these applications present a publishing "workflow" interface to users.

Applications Using WebDAV to Store Custom Shared Data   A few applications are capable of storing not their primary document data but secondary, shared data, on a WebDAV repository. Adobe Acrobat does this with annotations to Acrobat documents.

Site Management Tools   Some Web site management tools are now capable of using WebDAV to manage the site. The simple but powerful command-line tool "sitecopy" is an example.

10.1.1   Microsoft Web Folders and Office

Microsoft added WebDAV client functionality to Office and Windows by extending Internet Explorer (and thus, the regular Windows Explorer) to allow it to mount WebDAV repositories. Office cannot use WebDAV without one of these mount points, called a Web Folder.

Stand-Alone Web Folders   Web Folders is an extension to Microsoft Explorer, the file and folder navigation user interface that comes with Microsoft Windows. A Web Folder makes a WebDAV repository appear like a local file folder. Users can open and create subfolders and move and copy files as though the files were local. Files can be moved and copied within the repository, between the repository and a local drive, or between two repositories.

Web Folders supports SSL, and it can use either Basic or Digest authentication. When given the choice between Basic and Digest, however, it chooses the first one it sees, rather than the most secure.

Web Folders does a little more than just WebDAV. It can also mount an FTP repository, a Windows network directory share, a Web server running Office Server Extensions, or a Web server running the FrontPage protocol. In the Microsoft literature, it's sometimes difficult to distinguish between features supported via WebDAV and features available only via FrontPage or Office Server Extensions using proprietary mechanisms. For example, the discussion and subscription features of Office Server Extensions are not available using WebDAV.

Office 2000   When Office 2000 (or later versions) is used along with Web Folders, more functionality becomes available. It's now possible to open and save to and from the repository directly within the authoring application. When files are opened and closed, they are automatically locked and unlocked, thus greatly improving the experience for multiple authors.

It's still not possible, however, to view or change properties. Even properties defined in RFC2518, such as creationdate, are not visible.

Other Applications   Most Windows applications do not really work with Web Folders. Web Folders appears to be a drive, so the user can double-click on a file within a Web Folder to open it in the appropriate application. However, most Windows applications are incapable of saving the file back to the Web Folder (the application would have to use a special library component to do so). Instead, the file is opened as if it were a regular Web resource, not a WebDAV-capable resource. There are two possible behaviors:

- If the Web browser can display the file, the file will be opened in the Web browser, like a regular Web page.
- If the Web browser can't display the file, the Web browser will prompt the user to download the file or open it. If the user chooses to open the file, it will be saved to the Web browser's cache and opened by the application that is configured to open that file type. However, if the user tries to save from that application, the file will be saved to the local cache, rather than to the WebDAV repository.

Still, Web Folders is a useful way to access files on a WebDAV server. Even without the ability to directly save files from these applications, the user can edit and save files locally and then use Web Folders to copy the content to the WebDAV server.

How to Get Web Folders   Web Folders is available with IE 5.0 and 5.5 as an optional Web authoring feature, available to select during installation. Thus, any Windows platform that can install IE 5.0 or later can use Web Folders.

Windows IE 6.0 does not include Web Folders as an install option, because Windows 98 Second Edition, Windows 2000, and WinME come with Web Folders already installed.

The user might find it a little difficult to find information about Web Folders because it's not a product; it's a feature that is available with several products. It's probably easiest to go to the Microsoft Web site (*www.microsoft.com*) and start searching. Microsoft Support articles explain how to install and use Web Folders in IE 5.0 [q195851] and how to get Web Folders [q298637].

Web Folders Limitations   In addition to working only with Office (so far), Web Folders has some limitations as a WebDAV client:

- It is not possible to manually lock or unlock WebDAV resources on the server. Office applications use locks automatically, not in response to user commands.
- The only properties that users may view are getcontentlength, getlastmodified, and getcontenttype. Further, users can see getlastmodified only if the WebDAV server supports a specific nonstandard data type attribute (Section 9.2.4).
- Custom properties cannot be created, changed, or viewed.
- Web Folders is slow to use over the Internet. Although it uses an Internet standard protocol, it was designed with intranet latency speeds in mind. It uses many more requests to achieve an operation than other clients tend to. On a fast connection or a local area network, this should not be a problem.

Server Support for Web Folders   Microsoft IIS 5.0, Apache mod_dav, and Xythos WebFile Server have all demonstrated support for Office Web Folders. However, it can't be assumed that a server supporting WebDAV can automatically support Web Folders. There are a number of tricks to making Web Folders work—most important, returning the MS-Author-Via header and using the custom data types discussed in Sections 9.2.4 and 9.8.4.

10.1.2   Windows XP WebDAV Redirector

Windows XP integrates WebDAV more directly into the file system. A user can create a mount point, or network drive mapping, to a WebDAV repository. Once this mapping is created, the WebDAV repository is assigned a drive letter and can be used just like any network drive. This includes opening and saving files directly from regular applications such as Notepad and Word-Pad, as well as creating files and folders and moving and copying files between drives, so the Redirector is more powerful than Web Folders.

The XP Redirector works from the command line as well as from the Explorer GUI. Users can enter commands to mount drives:

```
net use * http://www.webdav.org/ passwrd /user:username
```

Unfortunately, early versions of the redirector had a few problems:

- Windows XP assumes that any WebDAV repository begins at the root of the server path. If a user mounts `http://www.example.com/hr/ergonomics`, then the OPTIONS request to `http://www.example.com/` must show WebDAV support or the Redirector will fail.
- The XP Redirector does not handle default namespaces (at least for the `DAV:` namespace) as required by the Namespaces recommendation. To work with the XP Redirector anyway, WebDAV servers must use specific, non-null prefixes for namespaces rather than declare the namespace default.
- The Basic authentication headers include the NT domain name in the user name by default, rather than use the standard "realm" field provided by the server. The server can easily see this, so the server can allow the XP Redirector client to authenticate by stripping off the NT domain name.
- The Digest authentication header also includes the NT domain name in the user name. Here it's even harder for the server to make allowances, because the username isn't sent in the clear, it's irreversibly hashed. The server must apply the hash algorithm to the exact same string that the client used in order for the hashes to match. Another possible workaround is for the user to specifically select "log on as a different user" in the mount wizard.

Hopefully, these problems will be fixed in service packs or Windows XP updates.

10.1.3   Mac OS X WebDAV-FS

Mac OS X was the first operating system to ship with full built-in WebDAV client support that any application can use. The WebDAV-FS client acts as an explorer, displaying the remote repository much as if it were a local file folder. There are a few known problems:

- In early releases of Mac OS X, WebDAV-FS does not connect to servers running on ports other than port 80.
- WebDAV-FS does not support SSL/TLS.

10.1.4   Adobe Authoring, Graphics, and Web Design Products

An increasing number of Adobe products use WebDAV to share images, Web pages, and other files among a group of collaborators. In many of Adobe's authoring products, the WebDAV support may be a little hard to find because the protocol is part of its "workflow" support. For example, in Photoshop, the user must follow the "workflow" process in order to publish documents to a WebDAV server.

Some product highlights:

- GoLive 5.0 can upload and synchronize a locally edited Web site with a WebDAV server.
- Photoshop 6.0, ImageReady 3.0, InDesign 2.0, and Illustrator 10 use WebDAV in workflow support, to publish finished files to a WebDAV server or load files from that location. Work in progress is saved locally.
- Acrobat 5.0 not only shares Acrobat documents online, it allows colleagues to add comments to Acrobat documents (without changing the document itself) and view each other's comments by storing those documents on any WebDAV server.
- InScope adds workflow management and richer collaboration to InDesign 1.5, Photoshop 6.0, and InCopy 1.0 using the WebDAV protocol.

10.1.5   Xythos WebFile Client

Xythos WebFile Client is a drive-mounting client for Windows. It supports FTP as well as HTTP/WebDAV.

The Xythos client allows some offline capability as well. Even when the computer with the Xythos client software is no longer connected to the network, the user can modify cached resources. When the Xythos client regains access to the network, cached resources are synchronized.

The Intellittach feature makes it easier for users to share files via email. Rather than email the entire file and end up with multiple (perhaps inconsistent) stored versions, Intellittach encourages users to email each other links to WebDAV resources.

The Xythos client offers advanced WebDAV functionality: custom property manipulation, versioning, and access control management.

10.1.6   kStore Explorer

The kStore Explorer client from kCura is a remote repository explorer for Windows, or a tool for managing documents on a repository. It supports standard WebDAV repositories in general as well as Exchange and Sharepoint servers, including some of the nonstandard features of those servers.

kStore Explorer has powerful search and filtering functionality, making it an exceptional client for navigating large repositories with many files. It also has strong metadata support to make it particularly useful when the repository uses custom properties.

10.1.7   Goliath for Macintosh

Goliath is an open-source WebDAV browsing client for Macintosh. It was the first application to implement WebDAV on Macintosh.

10.1.8   Dreamweaver 4

Macromedia Dreamweaver is a popular Web site development application. Version 4 of Dream-weaver includes support for WebDAV in order to improve interactions between Dreamweaver and a content management system.

10.1.9   WebDrive

South River Technologies sells another drive-mounting client for Windows platforms. It supports FTP and FrontPage extensions as well as HTTP/DAV. WebDrive allows any file-based application to store and access files on a WebDAV repository.

10.1.10   XML Spy

XML Spy is an Integrated Development Environment (IDE) for applications based on XML. Like many modern IDE packages, XML Spy can store files directly on a shared code repository. WebDAV is one of the protocols supported for communication with the code repository.

10.1.11   DAV Explorer

DAV Explorer is a straightforward WebDAV browser, developed in Java at the University of California at Irvine (*www.ics.uci.edu/~webdav/*). It presents a tree view of a WebDAV repository and supports many advanced WebDAV features.

10.1.12   Davfs

Davfs is the WebDAV Linux File System (*http://dav.sourceforge.net/*). It allows the user to mount a WebDAV repository as a local disk drive. Davfs is part of the Mandrake Linux distribution (as of version 9.0).

10.1.13   Cadaver

Cadaver is a free Unix command-line tool written by Joe Orton. Cadaver acts much like a traditional FTP client by making a connection to a server and then accepting commands directly from the user. A cadaver example was part of the extended interactions covered in the last chapter.

10.1.14   DAVe

DAVe is another free Unix command-line tool. It is written in Perl, so it may be easily used on other platforms. It operates in much the same manner as cadaver or FTP: The user starts the tool and gets a special "dave" prompt. Then the user can type commands to download or upload files, lock, set properties, copy or move resources, or create collections.

10.2 Server Software

Several classes of WebDAV server also exist. Those presented here are classified the functionality that is the primary focus of the server implementation:

- Servers that are primarily Web servers but support WebDAV for Web page authoring, such as IIS 5.0 and Apache with mod_dav
- Servers that are primarily for file sharing or file management, supporting WebDAV as a file sharing protocol, such as Xythos WebFile Server and Oracle IFS
- Servers that focus on an more specific data-oriented application but use WebDAV to expose the application data, such as Exchange 2000

10.2.1 Microsoft Internet Information Server

Microsoft Internet Information Server (IIS) 5.0, which is part of Windows 2000, is primarily a Web server but includes built-in support for WebDAV.

In addition to the methods defined in RFC2518, IIS 5.0 supports the SEARCH method. This looks much like the WebDAV SEARCH proposal [Reschke03b]; however, the search syntax is SQL, rather than the XML structure defined so far by the WebDAV WG. A Microsoft Support article contains a very basic example [q293885] and points to additional resources for more information.

IIS 5.0 does not support a few WebDAV required features, however:

- Although it advertises support for locking, collections cannot be locked.
- PROPPATCH requests are not atomic. Some parts of the operation may succeed and others may fail. Successes and failures are fully reported in Multi-Status responses.

A Microsoft Support article [q221600] describes how to enable WebDAV support in IIS 5.0 and how to verify that WebDAV has been enabled.

10.2.2 Apache and mod_dav

The first fully compliant WebDAV server was the open-source Apache module *mod_dav*. It adds WebDAV support to any Apache-hosted Web site, either 1.0 or 2.0. Apache 2.0 ships with mod_dav already included, so many Web sites can support WebDAV just by turning it on. Nearly 400,000 Web hosts advertised mod_dav support as of April 2003 [SecuritySpace03]. Excellent information on the mod_dav architecture and features can be found at the site *www.webdav.org/mod_dav/*.

Mod_dav supports all the features in RFC2518, including locking and custom property support. It is viewed as an exemplary implementation of the WebDAV specification and referenced often for interoperability questions. With the addition of the Catacomb extension module, mod_dav can be configured to support searching as well [Kim02].

Mod_dav is also used as a basis or platform for other WebDAV servers or applications. Oracle, IBM, and Rational have all used mod_dav in development. It is highly extensible, supporting such customizations as a plug-in storage module or "repository layer." Graduate students at the University of California at Santa Cruz implemented the Catacomb database-backed storage module for mod_dav, which plugs in using this repository layer.

Several software companies have rebundled mod_dav with extensions. Apple based its Mac OS X WebDAV server on mod_dav and uses it as a basis for its iDisk service. The IBM HTTP Server product includes mod_dav. Oracle has plugged mod_dav into an Oracle database solution for file storage.

The Apache/mod_dav solution works on many platforms, including Mac OS X, Windows, Linux, and Unix operating systems.

10.2.3   Microsoft Exchange 2000

Exchange 2000 is a mail, calendaring, and newsgroup hosting server that supports WebDAV (with some extensions) for access to all its application information. The WebDAV support is part of what is called the Microsoft Web Storage System, supporting a consistent representation of resources and metadata accessible over several protocols (including HTTP, WebDAV, IMAP, and POP).

Because Exchange 2000 offers much more functionality than a regular WebDAV server, it has many custom extensions. Many of these features are somewhat specified in support articles, Software Development Kits (SDKs), documentation, and books [Martin00]

New Properties and Namespaces   Custom properties exist to represent email messages, contacts, tasks, appointments, and news messages as regular resources with extended metadata. Custom properties also exist for specialized collections, such as collections that contain appointments (calendars). For example, on an email resource, the sender and recipient properties contain email addresses. A few of the new properties were published as an Internet Draft [Hopmann98]. Others are published in Microsoft product documentation or support articles.[1]

PUT Can Send Email   To send an email, Microsoft Exchange supports the PUT method to create a new resource inside a special email submission collection. Support article q296713 has examples showing how to discover which collection to submit email to and how to send the PUT.

POST Can Create Resources   Posting a document body to a collection creates a new resource with that content. The server chooses a unique resource name. This frees the client

---

1.   Support article q296126 has an extended example showing how to create or modify a contact using PROP-PATCH, including names and namespaces for many contact properties. Article q308373 does the same for creating or modifying appointments.

from having to choose a unique resource name for actions like adding a new appointment, where the subject, location, and time are more important than the resource name.

PROPPATCH Can Create Resources PROPPATCH can be used to create a new resource, not just to change properties on an existing one. A support article [q308373] explains how to use PROPPATCH to create a new appointment, which the server will forward to meeting attendees.

Data Types Exchange 2000 makes extensive use of datatypes on its properties (using the same technique that Web Folders does for data-typing timestamps). Any datatype beginning with mv. is a multivalued property. For example, string datatype is obviously a string, but mv.string indicates a property that can contain multiple string values, each string encased in an XML element.

Subscription/Notification Support SUBSCRIBE, UNSUBSCRIBE, NOTIFY, and POLL are new HTTP methods described in the Exchange SDK documentation at *msdn.microsoft.com*, allowing subscriptions to event notifications (these also use some custom headers). Thus, an email client can be notified when mail arrives, rather than sending periodic, expensive PROPFIND requests.

Ranged Row Requests A new syntax for the HTTP/1.1 Range header, working with SEARCH and PROPFIND, allows clients to retrieve partial results for these kinds of requests. For example, an email client can choose to download information for exactly 20 email messages, no matter how many are in the mailbox, if screen space only allows 20 to appear at a time.

SQL Search Like IIS 5.0, Exchange supports the SEARCH method with custom SQL syntax [q293885], rather than the standard syntax defined by the WebDAV SEARCH proposal [Reschke03].

MKCOL Request Body The MKCOL method can take a couple of custom bodies. Article q289871 has an example of a MKCOL request body, similar to a PROPPATCH request body, to set certain property values on the directory as soon as it is created.

Another type of body is similar to the SEARCH request body. This creates a persistent search folder, with the contents of the folder continually updated to contain the current matches for the search criteria [Lee00].

Access Control Access control properties are exposed through WebDAV [q317891]. However, these properties are not compliant with the official WebDAV ACL proposal and are not even similar in syntax or names.

10.2.4 Xythos WebFile Server

Xythos WebFile Server (WFS) is a stand-alone WebDAV repository product. As a current employee of Xythos, I have led the development of WFS since 2001.

WFS is intended to replace existing repositories where users share files. WFS can be run as is to provide WebDAV file storage and sharing. WFS provides a Java API to extend or modify server capabilities.

WFS includes a Web UI for its WebDAV server. In cases where users may not have a fully featured WebDAV client available and installed on their local computers, they can connect to the Web UI with any browser and manage their documents on the repository or browse or search for other documents.

WFS supports the DeltaV standard, including core versioning and some of the optional DeltaV features. It supports the Access Control protocol (which is in the process of standardization). The Access Control protocol requires the WebDAV server to expose user and group information (so that permissions can be granted to either users or groups), so Xythos WFS offers a module to connect to an LDAP server in order to get that user and group information from a central user database.

WFS also supports several features documented in Internet Drafts, which may or may not be progressing to Proposed Standard:

- The WebDAV SEARCH proposal [Reschke03] uses a full XML syntax to express search queries. This is quite unlike the search syntax supported by Microsoft servers, which use SQL queries directly embedded in a minimal XML body.
- Tickets allow temporary access to a file to a user who may not be authenticated. A ticket is like a password to access a file [Ito01].
- Quotas on collections allow administrators to limit use of storage space. Two properties expose the quota limit and the amount of space used as it is counted against the quota [Korver03].

10.2.5 DAV4J

The DAV4J WebDAV servlet, running on a platform including the WebSphere AppServer and Apache, provides WebDAV server functionality. A neat feature of this combination is that the WebDAV support can be enabled on only part of the hosted site. For example, a production site and an authoring or testing site can be hosted on the same server, and only the authoring/test part of the site allows WebDAV requests.

10.2.6 Tamino WebDAV Server

SoftwareAG produces the Tamino WebDAV Server along with the Tamino XML Server. SoftwareAG and the Tamino developers site explain and illustrate how these two products can be used together to rapidly develop data-oriented client/server applications.

Tamino WebDAV Server supports the access control protocol extensions and the DeltaV standard as well as the base WebDAV protocol. The server also supports the Java Content Repository API for extending content management with custom business rules.

10.2.7   Microsoft SharePoint Portal Server

Microsoft SharePoint Portal Server 2001 advertises support for "Microsoft WebDAV." What this actually means is that it supports Web Folders access and uses some WebDAV methods. However, it isn't interoperable with most WebDAV clients for even the simplest functionality, because Sharepoint uses many proprietary methods, headers, and properties. It supports versioning but uses mechanisms very unlike those of the DeltaV standard for WebDAV versioning (discussed in Chapter 11, *Versioning*).

It may not be possible for a non-Microsoft-based client to interoperate completely with SharePoint Portal Server, because some of the server's properties include binary representations of properties meaningful only on the Microsoft platform.

10.2.8   Other Known Servers

WebDAV support has been reported for a number of other Web site and document management server products, server components, and server applications. This list includes CoVia, Intraspect, Virtuoso, the Opentext LiveLink gateway, MagiDAV, CyberTeams, and Microsoft BizTalk.

10.3   Services

A few WebDAV-enabled services are available on the Internet. Some charge a monthly fee for usage; however, some are free.

Internet-hosted storage service startups seem to be rather unstable. Several startups have already appeared and disappeared. If the services mentioned here no longer exist, it may still be possible to find newer replacements supporting much the same functionality.

10.3.1   Apple iDisk

Apple's iDisk service is a WebDAV-based service for Macintosh users only, supporting primarily the iTools software utilities. Now that iDisk supports WebDAV in addition to the Apple Filing Protocol, Goliath and other WebDAV clients can use the service. Apple also makes it possible to share and synchronize calendars with iCal using WebDAV.

As with so many other technologies, Apple seems to have done the best job of making online storage hosting user-friendly, judging from user reviews. Mac OS X makes it easier than any other client to encrypt files on the client before storing them on the server—thus ensuring user privacy.

User groups and Macintosh special-interest sites have some speculations about Apple's plans for iDisk. Some suggest support for network computers and network booting, where the user's personal information is stored on iDisk rather than on the local device. Others claim that an Apple-designed PDA called iWalk will access files on iDisk with built-in wireless support.

10.3.2   IBackup

Pro Softnet Corporation provides the IBackup service (www.ibackup.com) so that customers can back up important files easily to a remote location. IBackup advertises support for Microsoft Web Folders and other WebDAV client software. It uses SSL by default to provide privacy.

10.3.3 My Docs Online

My Docs Online (*www.mydocsonline.com*) offers a general-purpose WebDAV-enabled file storage service. The site specializes in wireless access to the repository. For example, a new feature allows a wireless device user to instruct the service to fax a given document to a specified fax number—printing it out without printer support.

10.4 Compliance Tests

A compliance test can be a useful resource to check the sanity of a WebDAV server implementation. No compliance tests exist for WebDAV clients; it would be extremely difficult to run tests against an arbitrary client, because clients initiate requests and do not respond to them.

10.4.1 Litmus

Currently, one compliance test suite exists for WebDAV servers. Litmus (available at *www.webdav.org/neon/litmus/*) tests the features required by RFC2518, including locking. It has been used with a couple servers so far, and the wrinkles are being ironed out, but it's already useful to test server implementations.

One limitation of the Litmus test is that it doesn't just check for expected successes, it also checks for specific errors. That involves a big assumption on the part of the Litmus suite—that it knows the situation well enough to know exactly which error is most appropriate. For example, the 0.5 release of Litmus assumes that an MKCOL request with a body must return a 415 Unsupported Media Type error. That error is only required if the server does not handle the body. In most cases, the server will not handle any MKCOL body type, and in almost all cases, the server will not handle the odd body type, Litmus uses in the request. However, there's a small chance that the server will handle the body somehow and Litmus will be wrong in flagging an error.

10.5 Summary

Many WebDAV products, both clients and servers, are already available and deployed. WebDAV client software typically falls into a few categories that solve different problems.

Some WebDAV clients are authoring applications. By far the biggest focus of these applications is on their authoring functionality, not on WebDAV support. However, these applications do support WebDAV in order to download a WebDAV resource to edit, lock it while it is being edited, and upload it back to the repository automatically. This category includes Microsoft Office and the Adobe authoring applications.

Some WebDAV clients are remote repository explorers. These clients focus on the WebDAV functionality and how the user can find and manage documents on the repository. This category includes kStore Explorer on Windows, cadaver on Linux, and Goliath on Mac OS X.

Some WebDAV clients allow a remote repository to be mounted as a local drive. These clients allow any local authoring application to author remote documents as if they were stored locally. These clients typically do not have as much ability as the explorer-type clients to expose the remote repository's advanced features to the user. This category includes Xythos WebFile Client on Windows, DAVFS on Linux, and WebDAV-FS on Mac OS X.

WebDAV servers come in a wide variety. Some WebDAV servers focus on collaborative authoring and file sharing in general. Others, like Exchange 2000 and the Tamino server, have more specific functionality exposed through WebDAV.

CHAPTER 11

Versioning

Versioning is the ability to access multiple historic instances of a file, even if an older instance was replaced with a newer instance. Versioning helps users collaborate more smoothly by allowing them to see a historical record, compare versions, and restore material that was removed. Versioning functionality was originally intended to be part of WebDAV, a legacy that survives in the protocol's name (Web-based Distributed Authoring and Versioning). After a couple years of development work on WebDAV, the working group agreed to postpone versioning in order to more quickly standardize the basic protocol on its own.

WebDAV was seen from the first as a protocol for Web site authoring. Web sites often consist of files of different kinds (source code, text, and images), which are modified by several participants (programmers, writers, designers, and artists). Managing such a Web site well requires sophisticated tools. One of the tools in the typical site management toolbox is **versioning**, which allows past versions of a resource to be viewed or restored if problems arise.

WebDAV is now used in several complex source management systems as the basis for communication between a source control client (which may be integrated with a software development environment) and a source management server. The source files under management may be the software code used to build any kind of software product, from an operating system to an open-source chat client. Alternatively, the source files may not be software code but a set of files from multiple authors and other content producers. These files could combine to produce a print or multimedia presentation, from a book to a movie. All these source management scenarios require versioning support.

In 1999, the DeltaV Working Group was split off from the WebDAV Working Group so that it could collect the right participants to standardize versioning functionality for WebDAV. Its goal was to produce an RFC specifying the WebDAV extension mechanisms to support versioning [RFC3253], which it did in 2002 when RFC3253 was published. Along the way, goals and scenarios documents were also produced. Even though these documents didn't become standards themselves, they helped guide the working group and document working group decisions of the time. The versioning goals draft [Amsden99] was last updated in 1999 and no attempt was made to standardize or finish it in any way, but still it contains some useful explanations of versioning concepts.

DeltaV became a standard in 2002 [RFC3253]. Systems supporting DeltaV are not yet widely available, which is to be expected at this time with such a substantial specification. The systems that do support or are planning support for DeltaV vary widely in functionality and features, even to the level of basic model characteristics, and there is not yet much interoperability. The richness of functionality and flexibility of its feature set are precisely the characteristics that make it difficult to implement a DeltaV client that can interoperate with more than one server. Instead, client/server pairs (often from the same software vendor) interoperate with each other only, not with clients or servers from other pairs.

Despite the current lack of proven interoperability, several software vendors find it important to support DeltaV. The hope is that with time, the vendors' systems will converge more than they already have and make it possible for generic clients to talk to multiple servers. I consider DeltaV to be a stake in the ground at this point, part standard and part experiment. DeltaV defines a number of features and many of the details of how those features work together. Time will tell which features are implemented together, which features clients use most often, and how these features are combined interoperably.

This chapter and the next cover versioning concepts required for DeltaV and provide an overview of how DeltaV implements those concepts. The DeltaV feature set is described in enough detail to explain what you might be able to expect from a system supporting DeltaV, and figures illustrate the relationships between resources. However, due to lack of time and space, this book does not serve as a complete guide to the DeltaV standard.

11.1   Introduction to Versioning

Versioning functionality solves a few common user problems. These problems are so universal that they can be experienced even by a single user working on a single file on a local machine. We approach versioning first from the point of view of solving these simple problems. Only in later sections do we need to address more complex issues introduced by multiple simultaneous authors or multiple related files.

Document and source versioning software has a long history. The industry has accumulated a raft of terminology, unfamiliar perhaps even to those who already use source control software (some of the most advanced versioning software that exists). There are large differences in how versioning problems are solved, so even a reader familiar with one source control system must pay attention to terminology in case it's used differently. This chapter introduces the DeltaV terminology, with a quick reference to other terminology that you might be familiar with.

11.1.1 Simple Problems

Nearly everyone who has ever worked on a document on a computer has saved the document only to realize that they have just deleted something important. Once the file has been saved, typically the change can't be undone. This type of mistake is frustrating and inconvenient, so vendors of software applications attempt to do something about it. How can software allow users to quickly fix a mistake that has been saved in the file? One way is to save a backup copy of the file. The first save creates a file; for example, `overview.doc`. The second save moves `overview.doc` to `overview.bak` and saves the new work as `overview.doc`.

With this approach, the user can recover at least one older copy of the document. The user had better hope that the missing material wasn't deleted in the next-to-last copy as well! The next obvious step is to keep more past copies around. Application software can automatically store and track a number of past versions of a file (either storing versions locally or on a network file server). Typically, versions are numbered, so the software can create in sequence `overview.doc-v1`, `overview.doc-v2`, and so on. Once the application creates the version, it should never be altered.

Having application software store versions as normal files is problematic: Only that application knows that the files are past versions and are not intended to be edited. The application software creates a mess of files, and the user doesn't know if those files can be deleted or edited. It would be a lot cleaner if the file system could handle the versions. A file system that supported versioning could display the main file, hide all the old versions, and only pull them out when they're needed. The application software probably needs to know a little bit about what's going on in order to help the user access older versions, but mostly the file system can take care of the versioning.

The file system can expose information about each version, such as the time it was created and who saved it, in order to make it a little easier to select the right older version. With this information available, you can see that recovering from mistakes isn't the only kind of problem versioning can solve. Version information can help a user find out:

- When did I introduce specific material into (or remove material from) the document?
- What did the document look like on a given date?
- Was this change made at the same time as some other change?

Although these aren't often pressing problems in document repositories, it can be useful to be able to figure out what happened in the past. In source code, however, bugs are sometimes introduced accidentally to code that worked before. It can be very important find out exactly what a source file contained in the past (when the code worked) to be able to quickly and properly fix the bug.

11.1.2   Versioning and Backup Functionality

For users who are familiar with powerful backup software, versioning may seem very similar to backup functionality, and it is. Versioning and backup solve many of the same problems in different ways, and neither feature is quite a substitute for the other. Many systems employ both if storage is rather cheap compared to the cost of loss of information. Some quick points of comparison between the two:

- Storing versions as local files won't help you if your hard disk crashes. The local file system should be backed up even if versioning is used.
- Storing versions on a server (such as a network share) may still involve a single point of failure if the server's hard disk crashes. The versioning server's file system should be backed up, too.
- Backups take snapshots at a fixed point in time. In a daily backup system, only one daily copy will exist, even for a file that has changed greatly in that one day. There may be redundant daily copies of a file that hasn't changed in months. In contrast, versioning takes a snapshot only when the file changes, so the versions more closely reflect the change history.
- Backup systems typically require an administrator to set up, manage, and restore lost files. In contrast, a local versioning system allows users to retrieve older versions without administrator assistance. Versioning systems may even be simple enough to be installed by any user (e.g., if your local file system kept version history from the day you installed the operating system).

11.1.3   Basic Versioning Components

The core components of any versioning system are pretty much the same:

- Versions are the past instances of a resource. These are historical only, not modifiable.
- Versioned files are those files for which the repository maintains a history of versions.
- Unversioned files may still exist in the same repository. The server may not maintain a history of all resources.
- Folders still exist and frequently hold both versioned and unversioned files, even in the same folders. However, ideally versions do not show up in the same folders as the versioned and unversioned files, because users tend to want to "clean them up" (see Figure 11–1).

11.1.4   DeltaV Data Model

DeltaV is the specification that extends WebDAV to introduce versioning. DeltaV is also the name of the working group where the DeltaV specification was developed.

   DeltaV was designed based on a consistent data model extending the WebDAV data model. The data model provides the framework for all the versioning functionality. The model

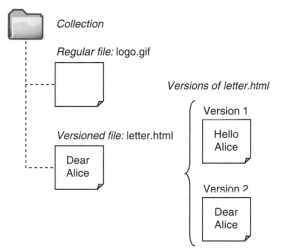

Figure 11–1   Common versioning components.

doesn't dictate how data is stored on the server, but it does identify the elements on which operations may be done and how they must be represented. The data model is similar to that of many existing versioning systems.

The DeltaV data model defines a few new resource types and many new live properties. Many of the live properties simply contain URLs to other resources, and these properties serve as links between resources. This gives the implementor a great deal of flexibility to put resources in custom locations on the repository. Rather than store two related resources in the same directory, the implementation can store them anywhere and use the live properties to expose the relationship.

Thus, clients must not make assumptions concerning the location of DeltaV resources. The server may well host special DeltaV resources in the same collections as non-DeltaV resources—the same collections that an ordinary Web browser or WebDAV client might browse. Some resources may not actually appear as static resources in static collections, instead being generated dynamically to appear at the URL the server designated.

11.2   Core Versioning

DeltaV has a core set of functionality that is required for implementation by any DeltaV compliant server. This section addresses the core versioning model, how to list and access versions, and how to turn on versioning for a resource.

There's a lot of conceptual material to cover in DeltaV, so I won't cover all the requirements or error messages. The DeltaV specification very clearly defines preconditions, or the state the resources must be in for the request to succeed, and the unique identifier that is returned for each failed precondition. It also defines postconditions, or the state the resources must be in after the request has succeeded, and the unique identifier that is returned for each failed postcondition. Thus, DeltaV uses precondition and postcondition identifiers not only for declaring requirements, but also as a way to provide extra information in the response to a failed request. See Section 11.10.2 for more information on how the precondition or postcondition identifiers are marshaled in a response body.

11.2.1   Version-Controlled Resources

When a regular WebDAV resource has versioning "turned on," it retains the same location and URL but is now a **version-controlled resource** (VCR). The VCR contents and properties change over time, like a regular WebDAV resource. WebDAV operations behave the same way they normally do a lot of the time. In fact, to ordinary WebDAV clients, the VCR appears to be an ordinary resource.

A VCR may be **checked out**, which means that it is being modified, or **checked in**. For now, assume that a VCR is checked in because a VCR begins in a checked in state when it is first created. These two states are defined more fully in Sections 11.3.2 and 11.3.4.

A VCR is related to a particular set of version **resources**. The set of versions constitutes the entire **version history** for the VCR. The **target version** is usually the most recently created version (the latest version), but it can be another version instead as shown in Section 11.6.1. The target version is identified by the checked-in[1] property if the VCR is checked in. A checked-in VCR will always appear to have the same content and dead properties as its target version.

The live properties of a VCR may be different from the live properties of the target version. For example, the WebDAV property lockdiscovery exists on a VCR but not on any version. (Versions can't be locked, because they can't be updated.)

The creationdate property exists on both versions and VCRs, but on the latter, the property should contain the date the resource was created, which may precede the creation date of the target version. The getlastmodified property on a checked-in VCR should be the same as the creationdate of the latest version.

VCRs and unversioned resources may coexist inside ordinary WebDAV collections, and they have the same resourcetype property value. The resourcetype property value stays the same so that existing non-DeltaV clients can interoperate with DeltaV resources as if both versionable and unversioned resources were simple RFC2518 resources. In order to see if a resource is versioned, a DeltaV client must check to see if the resource has DeltaV properties like checked-in or checked-out.

11.2.2   Versions

A resource can have a number of **versions** corresponding to instances of that resource. Those versions themselves are resources, too. However, typically versions do not appear in the same collection as the resource, because a directory listing containing versions mixed with versioned resources might confuse clients or users. A DeltaV client takes special steps to discover the existence and location of versions and typically shows the list of versions only when the user is interested in that information.

---

1.   This property, along with every other property in this chapter, is in the regular DAV: namespace.

A version has a body and properties and a URL, just like any regular WebDAV resource. The server automatically creates a new version when a VCR is changed, and the server decides where to put it and what URL to assign to it.

Versions are linked to other versions according to their derivation. When a new version is derived from an older version, the new version is called a **successor** of the older version, and the previous version is a **predecessor** of the new version. The predecessor of a given version isn't necessarily the most recent pre-existing version, although it often is. The first version is the **root version** and has no predecessor. The **latest version** is the one most recently created, and it has no successor.

The body and dead properties of a version must never change, whether it's an older version or the one just created.

Storing Versions

Versioning systems are frequently built on top of nonversioning file systems. The simplest approach to storing versions would be to store a full copy of the file every time a new version is created. However, it may be wasteful to store full copies when one version may differ from the next only slightly. Instead, many systems store a **delta** or a **diff** for each new version, where each delta is a precise description of the difference between the new version and the previous version.

Although versions may be stored as deltas, DeltaV requires full bodies to be sent. This choice does have costs for both network and software performance, but it would complicate the standard, and in this case optimization choices are best made at a lower level. General mechanisms for transferring deltas rather than full files have already been defined for HTTP [RFC3229].

Each version has its own live properties, which may have different values. For example, the creationdate property of each version should have the date the version was created (which is the same as the getlastmodifed property for the same version). Most live properties on versions won't change over time. However, some are designed to change, such as successor-set, which changes when a new successor version is created.

Some useful properties of versions:

- predecessor-set contains the list of versions from which this version was derived.
- successor-set contains the list of versions that were derived from this version.
- version-name is the name of the version, any value chosen by the server.
- creator-displayname is a server-calculated property with some user-readable description of who created the version.
- comment can be any text string, but it's usually some explanation of why the version was created or how it differs from the previous version (set by the version's creator).

11.2.3 Core Versioning Model

Figure 11–2 illustrates the basic components in a DeltaV-compliant repository. The client can look at the properties of each resource to find out the kind of resource it is.

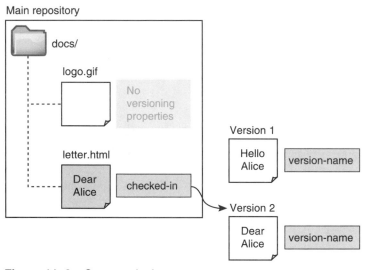

Figure 11–2   Core versioning.

We already know the resources without any versioning properties: docs/ is a regular collection, and logo.gif is a regular resource.

The file letter.html has the same resource type as logo.gif (an empty resource-type value), but it also has the checked-in property, so the client can tell that letter.html:

- Is a version-controlled resource.
- Is checked in, so may not be writable as is (shown shaded in Figure 11–2).
- Has a target version identified by the URL in the value of the checked-in property. (In figures in this chapter, properties with URL values like checked-in are shown with arrows pointing to the resource they refer to.)
- Has the same contents and dead properties as its target version.

If the client is handed a URL to a resource that it found to have the version-name property, the client can deduce that it is a version, that it is not writable, that it can't be checked out or checked in, and so on.

Note that a version must have the same resource type as the VCR it came from. A version is by definition not a new resource type but an existing regular resource that behaves differently. All of the resources represented in Figure 11–2 would have an empty resource type except one, and that's the docs/ collection.

11.2.4 Accessing Versions

Assume that a resource exists, and the user wants to find out if past versions exist and access one of them. How is this done? The first step is to find out if a resource is a VCR or not. If it is, it will have either the checked-out or the checked-in live property, depending on its current state. The checked-in property contains the URL to the target version, so the client can simply use that URL to find out more about the target version. The client could then query the target version's predecessor-set property to find the previous version's URL, and thus eventually discover every version in the version history.

Discovering version URLs one by one is slow. Thus, DeltaV requires every VCR to support the **version-tree** report to allow all versions to be discovered in one request. The version-tree report is a special kind of report available with the REPORT method defined in DeltaV, described in the next section.

To query the properties of a single version, the client issues a PROPFIND request directly to the version. Similarly, to download the body of a version, the client issues a GET request.

11.2.5 Viewing All Versions

DeltaV defines reports in order to streamline frequent but expensive information-finding processes. Usually, the information returned in a REPORT could be also found by querying live properties across a number of resources and collating the results. However, both client and server may find the processing and communication costs of that approach prohibitive.

In a REPORT request, the client asks for a specific report known to be supported by the server. The client may also provide some variables that affect the report output. For example, in the version-tree report, the client provides the names of the properties it wants to see for every version returned in the report results.

Functionally, the version-tree report is very similar to a depth 1 PROPFIND response. However, a depth 1 PROPFIND response could not be used to find all the versions in a version tree, because the versions may not be in the same collection and because there could be other resources in the same collections where versions appear. DeltaV makes no requirements about where versions must exist.

In Listing 11–1, only one property is requested (the version-name property), but any number of properties can be requested, as in a PROPFIND request. The response is a 207 Multi-Status response just like a PROPFIND response showing two versions.

Listing 11–1 REPORT request and response (version-tree report).

```
REPORT /docs/index.html HTTP/1.1
Host: www.example.com
Content-Type: text/xml; charset="utf-8"
Content-Length: xxxx
↵
```

Listing 11–1   REPORT request and response (version-tree report). *(Continued)*

```
<?xml version="1.0" encoding="utf-8" ?>
<D:version-tree xmlns:D="DAV:">
   <D:prop>
      <D:version-name/>
   </D:prop>
</D:version-tree>

HTTP/1.1 207 Multi-Status
Content-Type: text/xml; charset="utf-8"
Content-Length: xxxx
↵
<?xml version="1.0" encoding="utf-8" ?>
<multistatus xmlns="DAV:">
   <response>
      <href>http://www.example.com/vers/index.html.1</href>
      <propstat>
         <prop>
            <version-name>V1</version-name>
         </prop>
         <status>HTTP/1.1 200 OK</status>
      </propstat>
   </response>
   <response>
      <href>http://www.example.com/vers/index.html.2</href>
      <propstat>
         <prop>
            <version-name>V2</version-name>
         </prop>
         <status>HTTP/1.1 200 OK</status>
      </propstat>
   </response>
</multistatus>
```

11.2.6   Turning on Versioning

If a resource does not have the checked-out or checked-in property, it is not a version-controlled resource. The client can ask the server to turn it into a VCR with the VERSION-CONTROL method. The VERSION-CONTROL method does not need a body in this case (see Listing 11–2).

Listing 11–2   VERSION-CONTROL.

```
VERSION-CONTROL /docs/index.html HTTP/1.1
Host: www.example.com
↵
```

Some versioning servers require all files to be under version control. These servers automatically create VCRs whenever a new resource is created with PUT. Many source control systems have the policy that all noncollection resources must be version controlled. The client can tell if a new resource has been created as a VCR only by querying the resource after it has been created.

Note that DeltaV defines no way to undo a VERSION-CONTROL. In other words, there's no direct way to turn a VCR into a regular resource. A VCR's latest version can be copied to create a new nonversioned resource, but of course that's a new resource with new values for properties like creationdate.

11.3 Editing Version-Controlled Resources

Armed with information about the VCR and its versions and how they relate together, we can discuss how to modify them.

11.3.1 CHECKOUT and CHECKIN

In existing versioning systems, clients frequently check out files before they start editing them, and they check them in again when finished. DeltaV supports a checkin/checkout model because it's common and solves a number of subtle problems.

"Check out" and "check in" are widely used phrases that often have different meanings in different software systems. In some versioning systems, when a file is checked out by one user, it cannot be checked out by another user, but in other systems a file can be checked out twice. In some systems, checking out downloads the resource content to the client machine, but in other systems the content is downloaded in a separate operation. At least the order of operations is consistent across versioning systems using this terminology: The client checks out the file, edits it, and then checks it in again. Usually, the checkin operation creates the new version.

DeltaV introduces the CHECKOUT and CHECKIN methods. CHECKOUT sets the state of the VCR to checked out, and CHECKIN returns it to the checked-in state and creates a new version. A VCR can only be changed while it is checked out.

If the user checks out a resource and then decides not to make changes after all, there must be a way to make the resource checked-in again without creating a new version. This operation is called UNCHECKOUT. If any changes were made while the resource was checked out, these are thrown away as the UNCHECKOUT restores the VCR to the same contents and dead properties of the previous target version. The server returns the VCR to the checked-in state.

DeltaV is built on WebDAV, so DeltaV can use the GET, PUT, LOCK, and UNLOCK methods. There's no need to reinvent the functions those methods provide. Thus, CHECKOUT does not download the content of the resource, GET does. CHECKIN does not upload the content of the resource, PUT does. CHECKOUT does not prevent other users from changing a resource because locks already provide that functionality. So what do CHECKOUT and CHECKIN do on their own? There are several functions.

- There's no other way to edit a resource on the server and then back out changes. This provides a useful "rollback" functionality for versioned resources.
- It's often useful to combine a set of related changes into a single new version (e.g., new content and new property values). The client signals the beginning of a set of related changes with CHECKOUT and the end of the changes with CHECKIN. That's why no new version is created until CHECKIN. Multiple PUT and PROPPATCH operations can be done in between, and only one new version is created.
- Other users can see that a resource is being edited as long as it is checked out. CHECKOUT is often done long before the first PUT or PROPPATCH, so it corresponds to the intention to edit the resource. While the resource is checked out, other users see that the resource is being edited and may choose not to edit it.

CHECKOUT and CHECKIN are explicit methods that cause the server to perform the requested operation. There are also occasions when the server must perform the same operation automatically. Although we haven't yet discussed what causes an automatic CHECKOUT or CHECKIN operation, the behavior of the operation is identical.

Locks and Checkouts

Since locks have timeouts and checkouts do not, it may be difficult to tie locks and checkouts together. A client may prefer to lock a resource as long as it is checked out, but the server may not allow infinite length locks. If the lock expires while the checkout still exists, then other users may edit the resource while it remains checked out by the original user (and this may easily happen unintentionally, through non-DeltaV-aware clients).

Servers supporting CHECKOUT should support long-lived locks to minimize this problem.

The next sections fill in the details of checking out a resource, editing a checked-out resource, checking it in, and cancelling a checkout.

11.3.2   CHECKOUT and Checked-Out VCRs

A CHECKOUT operation changes the state of the VCR from checked-in to checked-out (see Listing 11–3). No new versions are created. When a resource is checked out, it is not locked or downloaded to the client. Those operations are already covered by LOCK and GET methods, and there's no need to overload checkout to include those operations. With this separation of concerns, the client has more flexibility to perform exactly the desired set of operations.

When a VCR is checked out, its target version gets a new live property: The checkout-set property of the target version must contain the URL of the VCR that was just checked out.

Listing 11–3 CHECKOUT example.

```
CHECKOUT /docs/index.html HTTP/1.1
Host: www.example.com
↵


HTTP/1.1 200 OK
↵
```

While a VCR is checked out, the resource may be edited. The contents of the VCR are now independent of any version already created. The changes made on a checked-out VCR do not create a new version; instead, changes are applied to the content and dead properties of the VCR as it currently appears. The VCR content and dead properties were initialized to those of the target version when it was checked out, but they diverge from that version as changes are made and saved. Compare Figure 11–3 with Figure 11–2; when the VCR is checked out, its body can be different from the body of any historical version.

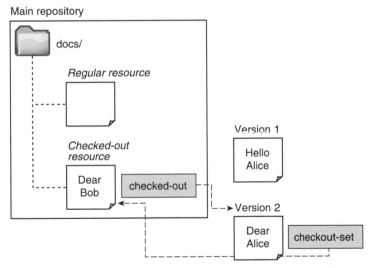

Figure 11–3 Checked-out VCR has independent contents from any version.

Note that all clients, including other users, can view and modify a checked-out resource normally.

- When any client issues a GET request to a VCR, the server must respond with the results of the latest PUT to the VCR, not with the body of the latest version.
- When any client issues a PROPFIND, the server must return the properties of the VCR, not the properties of the latest version.

- Any client can issue a PUT or PROPPATCH to a checked-out resource, too. These are subject to access control and locks as usual.
- Any client may attempt to CHECKIN the checked-out resource if it is not locked.

The client that does the CHECKOUT must separately issue a LOCK request to prevent other clients from using PUT, PROPPATCH, or CHECKIN.

In the checked-out state, the VCR has different values for some live properties. For example, the getlastmodified property value changes every time a write operation is used. The checked-out property only exists in this state. Its value is an `<href>` element containing a link to the target version.

> **Who Checked Out This Resource?**
>
> DeltaV does not specify a way to find out who checked out a resource. DeltaV defines the creator-displayname property for any resource, but it indicates who originally created the resource; thus, its value never changes. After the checkin is completed, the client can look at the creator-displayname property to find out who created the version.

11.3.3   Editing a Checked-Out Resource

After a successful CHECKOUT operation on a VCR, the client software may issue write requests like PUT and PROPPATCH. The client software may also COPY content from somewhere else, in which case the checked-out VCR's URL is the destination of the COPY method. Listing 11–4 is an example of using PUT to update a checked-out VCR. This request does not create a new version, because the resource isn't checked in yet, but it does modify the VCR's contents and live properties, as if the VCR were a regular resource.

Listing 11–4   PUT request to a checked-out VCR and success response.

```
PUT /docs/index.html HTTP/1.1
Host: www.example.com
Content-type: text/html
Content-length: 11
⏎
Hello world

HTTP/1.1 204 No Content
ETag: "12345-09876"
⏎
```

Soon after the CHECKOUT, the client software should set the comment property on the VCR. DeltaV defined the comment property to contain a human-language description of the reason the version was created and perhaps how it is different from the previous version. Since DeltaV does not define a way to find out who checked out a VCR, I recommend using the comment property to say who checked out the VCR (and why it was checked out, if that is known). The property may be changed again just before CHECKIN, because in many existing versioning systems, users are prompted for a text description when they decide to check in, and this is the place to put such information.

Client application software can save a temporary copy of the content on the local file system while it is being edited. Every time the user chooses to save the work, the local copy is changed. Only when the user decides to check in does the client issue one PUT request with all the new content, one PROPPATCH request to set the comment property and any other new property values, and finally CHECKIN.

In an alternative model, the client may issue a number of PUT operations throughout the editing session. This alternative model can be used in a number of situations:

- The user's latest save should not be lost if the client machine crashes. This benefit may be outweighed by the cost of the PUT operation, depending on the size of the file and the bandwidth of the connection.
- If the client machine has no local storage, every save must PUT the content to the server.
- Editing can begin on one client machine and proceed on a different client machine, continuing the work done so far, if each save is PUT to the server.
- The user may want to see the results of the work in progress on the server before checking in. For example, the user may be editing a Web page and can use a Web browser to view the page in its current state and make sure all the links work before checking in.
- Other users may see the work in progress and perhaps help edit the new version.

One way of looking at the DeltaV model is that CHECKOUT and CHECKIN reflect user decisions to start and finish editing the file, whereas GET and PUT are performed whenever the software needs to.

When the client sends the CHECKIN request, the server will respond with the URL of the newly created version.

11.3.4   CHECKIN and Checked-In VCRs

When a checked-out VCR gets a CHECKIN request, it is returned to the checked-in state, and one new version is created (even if no changes were made). The server assigns a new URL for the new version. The body and dead properties of the new version are copied from the VCR at the instant of the CHECKIN, as shown by the large arrows in Figure 11–4.

At CHECKIN, the server must remove the checked-out property of the VCR and restore the checked-in property. It must also set the value of the checked-in property on the VCR to point to the newly created version, which makes it the new target version.

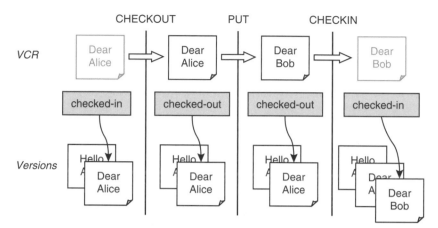

Figure 11–4 State of a resource through checkout, write operation, and checkin.

When the new version is created, the value of the predecessor-set property must be the URL of the version from which it was derived. With the functionality defined so far, the predecessor must be the previous target version. The successor-set property for a new version is empty (but the property should exist). The server assigns a value to the version-name property which is distinct from all other version names in the same version history.

CHECKIN also causes some changes to live properties on the previous target version. The URL of the VCR is removed from the checkout-set property, and the successor-set property has a new value added, which is the URL of the new version (Figure 11–5).

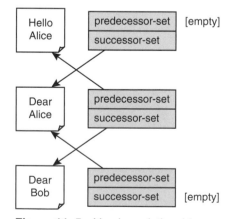

Figure 11–5 Version relationships.

In the response to a CHECKIN request, the server tells the client the location of the newly created version. A successful response status is 201 Created rather than 200 OK, because of the new version created (see Listing 11–5).

Listing 11–5 CHECKIN example.

```
CHECKIN /docs/index.html HTTP/1.1
Host: www.example.com
⏎

HTTP/1.1 201 Created
Location: http://www.example.com/his/vers1/32.html
⏎
```

Now that the VCR is checked in again, the server must not allow it to be altered. It has the same contents and dead properties as its target version.

11.3.5 UNCHECKOUT

UNCHECKOUT takes the VCR from checked-out to checked-in state without creating a new version. The checked-in property is restored to the value it had before, and the checked-out property is removed. Any live properties that were altered on any version (like checkout-set) are restored to the way they were before. The resource content and dead properties are restored to those of the target version.

The resource's URL is not affected by UNCHECKOUT. That means if a MOVE operation is applied to a resource while it is checked out, the MOVE operation is not undone when the UNCHECKOUT operation is applied. The UNCHECKOUT operation still restores the original content and dead properties in the new location.

11.4 Labels

The DeltaV label feature allows versions to be tagged with human-readable strings indicating their purpose, relevance, or identity. Consider the process of preparing documents for general publication. As the document is successively reviewed and edited, increasingly minor changes are made. The document authors might want to keep track of several important versions for each document: the latest version sent out for review, which version was approved, or which version was finally published. The labels "reviewed," "approved," and "published" will be applied to up to one version for each document.

11.4.1 Managing Many Versions with Labeling

Even though CHECKIN helps users create new versions only when needed, some documents will eventually have too many versions to keep track of without help. It's very useful to be able to **label** versions to keep track of them more effectively, and DeltaV does specify how to label versions. Although labels could simply be stored as a dead property of a version, a number of requirements led to the development of a special mechanism for labeling.

The label should be a property so that it can be retrieved with other metadata without requiring extra roundtrips. It's particularly useful to be able to retrieve the labels for every resource in a collection or for all versions in a version history. Both of these operations are automatically possible if the label is defined as a property. The client issues PROPFIND depth 1 to get labels for all resources in a collection and asks for the version-tree report to get labels for all versions in a version history.

The property has some extra syntactic and semantic rules that the server must enforce. The semantic rules help clients manage labels.

- Two versions in the same version history cannot have the same label. Only one version can be the "published" version. The server must check and enforce this restriction whenever label values are changed.
- A version may have more than one role or relevance, so it may have more than one label. If the label is a property, it must be capable of taking multiple values. There isn't a standard mechanism for multiple values, so DeltaV defines how to do that.

DeltaV defines the label-name-set property with these two rules. The property value can contain any number of (including zero) `label-name` elements, and each element contains a label string (see Listing 11–6).

Listing 11–6   Label-name-set property value.

```
<D:prop xmlns:D="DAV:">
   <D:label-name-set>
      <D:label-name>published</D:label-name>
      <D:label-name>reviewed</D:label-name>
   </D:label-name-set>
</D:prop>
```

11.4.2 Modifying Label Values

Although label-name-set is a property, it cannot be modified with PROPPATCH (it is a protected property). There are a few reasons for this choice.

- Most version properties cannot be modified after the version has been created, because the property values are part of the version history. Servers might forbid PROPPATCH on versions in order to enforce that. However, it's not always clear at first what label to apply to a version. (Imagine labeling a version "approved," only to find a mistake later.) Labels must be modifiable even after the version has been created.
- Multiple users may add and remove labels from versions. It must be possible to add a new label without accidentally removing a label just added by another user. However,

---

How to Select a Label String

DeltaV is silent on what label strings mean. The `published` and `reviewed` values used here are simply the kinds of strings that humans might apply to labels. In a software repository, the label strings might contain version and build numbers, like `3.3.0.10`.

Labels can be defined and used by rich client software as well as by humans. For example, a workflow software package may follow rules involving labels: Whenever a certain label is applied, the software automatically notifies the resource owner. When labels are defined and used by software, care should be taken to ensure that the label is unique, so that human-defined labels don't interfere. A simple way to accomplish this is to prefix a meaningful string with an XML namespace. For example, if the meaningful string is to be `workflow-publish`, then a unique label name would probably be `http://www.example.com/workflow-publish`.

---

we can't use locks to protect labels from this special-case lost update problem, because a server might not allow versions to be locked.

Instead of PROPPATCH, DeltaV defines a new method, LABEL, to change a label. The LABEL method allows a user to add a label to the label name set without knowing the entire set. The LABEL method also provides a way to remove a label or move it from one version to another. The LABEL method is complicated and it is a single-purpose solution, but it does solve the problem (see Listing 11–7).

Listing 11–7 LABEL request.

```
LABEL /his/vers1/32.html HTTP/1.1
Host: www.example.com
Content-Type: text/xml; charset="utf-8"
Content-Length: 1234
⏎
<?xml version="1.0" encoding="utf-8" ?>
<D:label xmlns:D="DAV:">
   <D:add><D:label-name>approved</D:label-name></D:add>
</D:label>
```

 The LABEL request takes an XML body. The root element must be the `label` element. Inside the `label` element, there may be at most an `add` element, a `set` element, or a `remove` element. Each of these three must contain one and only one `label-name` element. This means that only one label can be altered on a version per request.

The add element is used to add a label that didn't exist before. The set element is used to add the label to the version identified in the Request-URI and remove it from whatever version previously had that label. If no other version previously had that same label, then it is treated like an add request.

When handling the LABEL request, the server must enforce the rule that every label must be unique for all versions in the same version history. That's because the label is used to uniquely identify a version from that set. However, not every version must have a label—a version may have an empty label-name-set if that version isn't particularly notable or important.

11.4.3   The Label Header

To use labels, the client can retrieve all the label values for a set of versions (using the version-tree report), search for the appropriate label, and then do operations on the version that has that label. There's also a shortcut: DeltaV defines a header that requests the server to apply the operation to whatever version has the specified label. This header can cut out expensive queries and processing. For example, the user could download the "published" version of a resource in a single request to that resource. The Label header takes a single label as its value (see Listing 11–8).

Listing 11–8   LABEL header on a request.

```
GET /docs/index.html HTTP/1.1
Label: published
...
```

In this case, the server should select the version labelled published from index.html and return the body of that version. If the target resource is not version-controlled, the server must handle the method as if the Label header were not there and just return the resource's body.

Unfortunately, the Label header isn't very useful, because there is a serious problem in the way it is specified. The header can't be used on nonversioned collections, because the RFC says in Section 8.3 that if the requested resource (the collection) is not version-controlled, then the Label header must be ignored. In other words, it's useless to send a Label header on a request to a regular collection—the server will ignore it. That's a shame, because the designers of labeling originally intended to allow a client to select related versions from multiple files using labels. For example, the client might want to view the last modifed date of all the file versions labeled with the 3.3.0.10 release label. To do this, the client might want to send a PROPFIND request to the root collection with the Label header, but the server will ignore the header if the root collection isn't versioned. Instead, the client must make the PROPFIND request separately for each child of the collection.

There are more complicated problems with the Label header and version-controlled collections. Given the known problems, the authors of the DeltaV specification have discussed

> **Difficulties Comparing Natural-Language Strings**
>
> The mechanism for comparing the value of a label is clearly specified for a programmer to implement but may be unsatisfactory for users. This is a general unsolved problem, not unique to labels, but it happens to crop up here because the server is asked to compare strings that may be natural-language string values.
>
> Because the server compares case-sensitive URL-escaped UTF-8 strings, many labels that humans consider matches will not be considered matches by the server. For example, accented characters will never match unaccented characters. There are even characters that look the same to the human eye but have different UTF-8 encodings and thus fail in equality tests.

removing the `Label` header and possibly replacing it with a report, even though the `Label` header is already in the RFC. In the meantime, clients should not rely on the `Label` header, even if support for the LABEL method is present.

11.5 Using Existing WebDAV Methods with Versioning

Some WebDAV methods behave differently on servers supporting Delta V.

11.5.1 DELETE

DELETE operations are special in versioning systems. Many systems do not allow versions or VCRs to be deleted, because it must always be possible to recover past state.

It must be possible to remove a resource from a collection, even if this action doesn't destroy the resource content. Thus, DeltaV allows the DELETE method to delete a checked-in VCR, but this does not destroy all the saved versions that are related to the resource.

 Since DeltaV does not specify whether the client must check out the resource prior to deleting it, I recommend that servers accept DELETE both on checked-out and checked-in VCRs.

DeltaV needs a way to access versions of deleted resources. Recall that you can use the VCR URL to discover a set of versions by asking the server for a version-tree report. However, when the VCR is deleted, the versions still exist and there must be some way to be access them. A new kind of resource type was introduced to serve as a gateway: A **version-history resource** (VHR) is a permanent resource with a permanent link to a set of versions. The VHR is created as soon as a VCR is created, and it continues to exist after the VCR is deleted. VHRs exist in a special collection, with URLs chosen by the server. The server publishes the URLs to the VHR collections in the body of a special OPTIONS response (see Section 11.10.3), so the client can discover VHRs by using PROPFIND to browse those collections.

There are three ways to discover the URL of a VHR:

- While the VCR exists, its version-history property will give the URL of the VHR.
- If the URL of a version is known, the VHR that the version belongs to is named in the version's version-history property.

- If the VCR has already been deleted and no version URLs are known, the client can browse the collections that hold VHRs, looking for the right one.

VHRs don't quite allow a perfect historical reconstruction after a VCR has been deleted. There is no way to tell, for example, what version was the target version just before the resource was deleted. There is no way to tell what URL or URLs the VCR had before it was deleted. There is no standard way to recognize a VHR when browsing through the VHR collections, so presumably these collections can only contain VHRs. At least the content bodies and properties of versions are still available, so a human has a chance of recognizing a deleted resource by looking at that information. Human intervention is almost certainly necessary to restore a deleted resource based only on the functionality described in DeltaV.

VHR support is not mandatory. On systems that don't support VHRs, a DELETE (if permitted) is permanent and the versions are no longer available. Some systems may even allow individual versions to be deleted.

11.5.2   Version History Resources

VHRs were introduced in the previous section and are defined more completely here. VHRs have their own URLs, separate from all VCRs. These URLs all exist in VHR collections, and clients may be prevented from creating regular resources in those collections.

A VHR is created whenever an existing resource is put under version control. The server automatically assigns a URL to the new VHR. A VHR must exist for each VCR. The VHR is truly a new kind of resource—its resource type is `<DAV:version-history>`.

A VHR has no body, but it has a number of properties that link to versions. In fact, much of the specification of VHRs involves how to find the URL to one kind of resource given another kind of resource.

1. If you have the URL to a VHR, you can:
   a. Use the version-set property to get the URLs for all versions.
   b. Use the root-version property to get the URL to the original version.
   c. Use the REPORT request to get the `locate-by-history` report for a collection, returning all the VCRs that relate to your VHR. There can be many VCRs sharing the same version history.

2. If you have the URL to a VCR, you can:
   a. Use the version-history property to get the URL for the VHR.
   b. Use the checked-in property to get the URL for the target version, or use the checked-out property to get the URL for the version on which this VCR is based.
   c. Use the version-tree report to get a list or tree of all the version URLs.

3. If you have the URL to a version, you can use the version-history property to get the URL for the VHR.

Note that DeltaV defines no way to go straight from the version URL to the VCR URL. That's because the core DeltaV model must be compatible with the advanced DeltaV model, including features like workspaces (Section 12.2). Workspaces introduce a way for multiple VCRs to share the same versions and version history, so DeltaV does not require the server to link each version back to all those VCRs (see Figure 11–6).

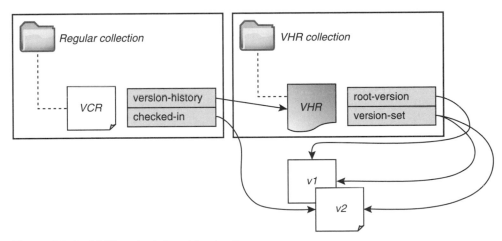

Figure 11–6   VHR and relationships to other resources.

11.5.3 COPY

The COPY method existed before DeltaV, but DeltaV adds some new concerns. First, we'll discuss what happens to the version history if the source or the destination is a VCR.

How should COPY work? The desired behavior for COPY is clearest when the source is a regular resource and the destination is a VCR with an associated version history. Clearly, the server should not overwrite the destination and its entire history with the single body of a regular resource. What if the source resource was just a template or a file in a contributions folder? The user probably intended the source content to overwrite only the latest version of the destination. Thus, the model for COPY behavior is that the result should be the same if the client did a GET and PROPFIND of dead properties, followed by PUT and PROPPATCH to the new location.

That model leads to the following behavior (see Table 11–1), with the caveat that if the Overwrite header on the request has the value F and the destination exists in any form, the request must be failed.

Because the destination is altered in a COPY operation, if the destination is a VCR it may have to be checked out first. A new version may be created immediately if the COPY destination is a VCR with auto-versioning (see Section 11.6.2). The new version may be created later if the destination is a checked-out VCR which is later checked in. The request will fail if the destination is checked in and auto-versioning is off.

Table 11-1   Use Cases for COPY

Scenario	COPY Behavior
Source is a VCR, destination does not exist.	Creates a *regular* resource at the destination URL, consisting only of the body and dead properties of the source.
Source is a VCR, destination is not versioned.	Overwrites the content at the destination but does not convert it to a VCR. The content copied is the target body and dead properties from the source.
Source and destination are both VCRs.	Copies the current body and dead properties from the source to the destination, which may create a new version. Leaves the destination version history in place.
Source is not versioned but destination is a VCR.	Copies the body and dead properties from the source to the destination, which may create a new version. Leaves the destination version history in place.

DeltaV doesn't specify what to do if the client sends the `Overwrite: F` header on a COPY request when the destination is a VCR. One could imagine two ways to interpret this:

- The destination is a VCR representing many versions, so it's not being overwritten, and the COPY should succeed.
- The client may not be a DeltaV client. As far as that client is concerned, the `Overwrite: F` header must consistently work such that if the destination exists, the request fails.

For the sake of the non-DeltaV client and for consistency with MOVE when the destination is a VCR, I recommend that servers use the second option and fail the request. However, since this isn't specified in the standard, there is no way for the client to rely on this behavior. Unfortunately, the client has no real workarounds here. There are no conditional headers that would allow the client to insist that if the destination exists already, the COPY must fail. Thus, the burden on the server to do the right thing is even heavier.

The source of a COPY request may be a version, but the destination may not be. A VHR may not be either the source or the destination of a COPY.

11.5.4   MOVE

MOVE is even more difficult than COPY because both the source and the destination are modified. The definition must include what happens to the version history at the source (if the source is a VCR) as well as the version history at the destination.

The rename scenario makes the desired behavior of MOVE most obvious. Clearly, if a client is using MOVE to rename a VCR (the source is a VCR and the destination does not exist), the result of the operation must be a VCR with the same version history, contents, and properties but a new URL. DeltaV specifies this by saying that a MOVE must be applied by doing a depth infinity DELETE operation on the destination first. To apply that definition to the case where the destination is a VCR as well, we can see that the destination is completely replaced by the source. The original destination version history may still be available (if the server supports VHRs), but the destination URL no longer links to it.

DeltaV does not require either the source or the destination to be checked out prior to a MOVE request, so the server should be able to handle each case. If the source of the MOVE is checked out prior to the MOVE, then it should remain in that state after the operation (see Table 11–2).

Table 11–2 Scenarios for MOVE

Scenario	MOVE Behavior
Source is a VCR, destination does not exist.	Moves the source resource and its version history. After the MOVE, the destination resource is a VCR with the same version history the source had before the MOVE. If it was checked out before the MOVE, it remains checked out.
Source is a VCR, destination is not versioned.	As above, but overwrites the destination with the source resource and the source's version history. After the MOVE, since the original destination resource wasn't a VCR, no record exists of its previous history.
Source and destination are both VCRs.	Overwrites the destination with the source resource and the source version history. After the MOVE, if VHRs are supported, the VHR previously associated with the destination must remain accessible in the version history collection. If the destination was checked out before the MOVE, changes made during the checkout would be completely lost, not having been checked into any permanent version.
Source is not versioned, but destination is a VCR.	Overwrites the destination VCR with an unversioned resource. Unless the server supports VHRs, all the versions that were at the destination are lost.

If the `Overwrite` header is false and any resource exists at the destination, the request is failed.

Because version histories at the destination can be lost if a destination VCR is overwritten, client implementors should be cautious in issuing MOVE operations of this kind. The client software could present a warning to the user or not allow the operation at all unless the user is willing to explicitly delete the destination first. The server could also reject MOVE requests when the destination has a version history, but there is no specific error code to use to indicate why the operation is forbidden.

Neither the source nor the destination of a MOVE request may be a version or a VHR.

11.6   Using Non-DeltaV Clients

It is possible to deploy a DeltaV repository in which only DeltaV-compatible clients are fully supported and plain WebDAV clients can browse but are unable to author resources on their own. That's the easy behavior: The repository simply has to forbid write operations to checked-in resources.

Although accepting this kind of limitation for DeltaV as a whole would have made its design simpler, it was always thought that DeltaV systems should be WebDAV compliant: A non-DeltaV client should be able to view and edit versioned resources. This section discusses how backward compatibility is ensured and managed.

In addition to allowing plain WebDAV clients to modify checked-out resources with PUT and PROPPATCH, DeltaV servers must consider how GET, LOCK, MOVE, and COPY are handled with non-DeltaV clients.

11.6.1   Read Operations and UPDATE

An HTTP client can use GET without knowing if the resource supports WebDAV. Similarly, a WebDAV client can use GET and PROPFIND without having to know if the resource is under version control. If the server supports UPDATE, this feature changes how all these read requests work. UPDATE does this by changing the target version of a VCR, which also changes the checked-in property value to point to the new target version. Section 11.2.1 explained that a target version is the version whose contents and dead properties are exposed by the checked-in VCR. Figure 11–7 shows a resource where the target version, and thus the content exposed in the checked in VCR, is not the latest version.

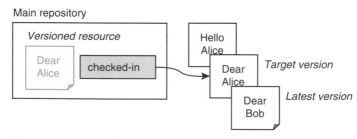

Figure 11–7   Versioned resource after UPDATE.

There are a number of reasons to use UPDATE:

- To allow other clients to see a version that isn't the latest version, if a previous version is more appropriate to display.

- So that when the resource is subsequently checked out, modifications to the checked-out resource can begin from the content in a previous version. This is an easy way to roll back to a previous version's contents: UPDATE to the previous version, CHECKOUT, and then CHECKIN.
- As we will see in Chapter 12, other features use UPDATE in interesting ways.

Here are some of the operations affected:

- A PROPFIND request to a checked-in VCR will return the dead properties of the target version, not necessarily the latest version. However, PROPFIND always returns the live properties of the VCR, which are often different from the live properties of the target version.
- If a VCR is used as the source of a COPY request, the body and properties that are copied depend entirely on the target version of the source VCR.
- A CHECKOUT request to a VCR checks out the target version, using that version's content as a starting point for the new version. When CHECKIN happens, it's the previous target version that gets a new successor added.

11.6.2   Auto-Version: Enabling Write Operations

Write operations are a little harder to handle, because a WebDAV-only client will not know to do CHECKOUT and CHECKIN operations. The server could forbid all write operations on VCRs that aren't checked out, but this would prevent existing WebDAV authoring applications being used with DeltaV servers. Therefore, the server must have a way to allow write operations and automatically create new versions.

DeltaV defines the auto-version property on a VCR to indicate or control how the server will handle write operations without an explicit CHECKOUT operation. The server must either manage or watch the property value and enforce behavior accordingly. Clients may be interested in the value of this property to predict what the server will do, or they may on some servers be allowed to give the property a new value to change auto-versioning behavior for that resource. Table 11–3 explains each of the possible values for this property.

If the auto-version property is not null, then write operations on that VCR can succeed even when it is checked in. The server must behave as if the client sent CHECKOUT and CHECKIN operations at certain points in time. Those points in time depend on the value of auto-version.

The auto-version property can be empty or contain one of four values: `checkout-checkin`, `checkout-unlocked-checkin`, `checkout`, or `locked-checkout`.

The `checkout-unlocked-checkin` value is particularly useful because it allows any WebDAV client to edit the resource, including both clients that don't understand DeltaV and clients that don't use locks. It has excellent characteristics when locks are used. Some nonversioning WebDAV clients, such as the Office 2000 client, always lock a resource while editing it online. While the resource is locked, the client may issue many PUT requests.

Table 11–3 Auto-version Values

checkout-checkin	The server will check out and check in the VCR along with every write operation. This can result in many versions but is guaranteed to capture changes. Although the operations are the same as the explicit CHECKOUT and CHECKIN methods, the resource is never left in the checked-out state by a non-DeltaV client.
checkout-unlocked-checkin	The server will automatically check out a VCR when it is changed. If the resource is not locked, the server will also automatically check it in (just like checkout-checkin). However, if the VCR is locked, then the server won't check in the resource until it is unlocked. The resource appears in checked-out state from the first write operation until the UNLOCK request.
checkout	The server automatically checks out the VCR when it is modified, but checkin is not done automatically. The resource remains checked out, preventing other clients from checking out the resource in place. Thus, a change by one non-DeltaV client leaves the VCR checked out indefinitely. Other non-DeltaV clients may make changes while the VCR remains checked out, but no new versions are created until a DeltaV-aware client sends a CHECKIN request.
locked-checkout	The server checks out the resource when it receives a write operation on a locked resource. However, the server does not allow write operations at all if the resource is not locked. When the lock goes away, the server checks in the resource. This option is slightly different from checkout-unlocked-checkin because it forces the client to lock or check out the resource before being allowed to edit it.

Saving the result of every one of these PUT requests would take a lot of storage space and may not be useful to others. Instead, the server can wait until the client unlocks the resource (in the case of Office 2000, this happens when the user closes the file) to check it in. In case the client connection is lost, the server should check the resource in when the lock expires rather than leave it indefinitely checked out. This is a good idea, although DeltaV does not require it.

The checkout value is not so useful because it requires versioning-aware clients to check the resource in eventually; otherwise, all changes will accumulate without creating new versions. However, it can be useful when a version-control client is used in conjunction with a regular WebDAV authoring tool: The version-control client can be used to check out and check in the resource, while the authoring tool can be used to edit the resource. Many source control versioning systems already operate in this manner.

Clients may be able to change the value of the auto-version property to tell the server exactly how to automatically create versions. Servers are not required to allow the property to be changed, however. Servers may support all four options, some, or none. The value of the property could change depending on the resource.

Whenever a VCR is checked in after being edited in place with auto-versioning, the server must automatically set the target version of the VCR to be the new version. Otherwise, nonversioning clients would never see the results of their work.

11.6.3 Locking

Locking deserves special consideration because if non-DeltaV clients can unknowingly check out or check in a resource, a DeltaV client could also accidentally check out or check in. Avoiding accidental checkouts is easy: Don't issue a write operation to a VCR unless it's already checked out. Avoiding accidental checkins is a little tricker because the resource may be checked in if it is locked and then unlocked. The client should not issue LOCK and then UNLOCK (without any CHECKOUT before or between) unless it knows the server's auto-versioning behavior.

Server implementors have a great responsibility here to think through locking and versioning to make sure all possible combinations of operations behave properly. Otherwise, it's too difficult to write a client that can interoperate with a variety of servers. These are guidelines I've developed for servers based on the requirements in the DeltaV specification as well as an analysis of how a client would attempt to perform various tasks:

- The server should allow a LOCK operation on a VCR (assuming the client has write privileges) even if it isn't checked out and even if there is no auto-versioning allowed, because the client may do the CHECKOUT next. It's important for clients to be able to do LOCK first to protect their checked-out resource from changes by other clients.
- The server must allow clients to issue CHECKOUT on a locked VCR, even if auto-versioning makes the CHECKOUT unnecessary. The client needs to be able to explicitly check out the locked resource to show to other clients that it is checked out. Otherwise, the resource would not appear as checked out until the first PUT request, as DeltaV requires.
- If the client does an explicit CHECKOUT before or after a LOCK request, then issues an UNLOCK request, the server *must not* check in until an explicit CHECKIN request is received (even if auto-versioning would normally cause the resource to be checked in on UNLOCK). The client may want to remove the lock in order to allow another client application to edit the resource before checking in later. This allows two clients to synchronize modifications to a checked-out resource to create one collaborative new version.

Locking before checkout is highly beneficial to avoid race conditions, too. A DeltaV client might issue a PROPPATCH request to a resource it believes to be checked in, to quickly change a property value. If another DeltaV client checked out the resource just before the PROPPATCH request without locking the resource, the property change would accidentally become part of the checkout, not an independent change. With checkout state, there's no parallel to the way the `If` header allows the client to verify lock state (Section 8.4.2), so the client can't make operations conditional on the checkout state of the resource.

11.6.4 "Safe Save" Problems with Existing Clients

It's not easy to support regular WebDAV clients editing VCRs. Some applications use "safe save" algorithms that can accidentally overwrite versioned resources with unversioned resources. Safe save algorithms were designed for local or remote unversioned file systems, but these applications sometimes use a layer that mimics the local file system, so the application is unaware it is even using a versioning repository.

When saving a file, the application needs to have a backup copy in case something goes wrong while making changes. File system write operations are often done piece by piece, so if the write is interrupted in the middle, the file could be left corrupted. To keep from corrupting an important file in this manner, the application may save to a temporary file. If all the partial writes work, then the application can move or copy the temporary file over the original file. Since the operating system is responsible for the move or copy operation working atomically, this process should help avoid file corruption. The temporary file may be deleted or left around as a backup.

For example, TextEdit on Mac OS X creates a backup file by appending a tilde character (~) to the file name and saving the file. TextEdit can be configured not to keep backup files, but unfortunately it still creates the backup files and then deletes them. When the Mac OS X WebDAV client receives these commands from TextEdit, the client requests a MOVE of `my.txt` to `my~.txt`, PUT to `my.txt`, then DELETE `my~.txt`. Let's walk through the confusion this causes:

1. The MOVE of `my.txt` to `my~.txt` is treated as a rename, so the version history that was linked to `my.txt` will instead be associated with `my~.txt`. The URL `my.txt` now has no resource and no version history.
2. PUT of `my.txt` will create a new resource, which may or may not be made version-controlled by the server. Imagine other users of the file discovering that the version-controlled file has become unversioned somehow and lost all its version history.
3. The DELETE of `my~.txt` either destroys the version history or at least deletes the reference to the version history.

One could imagine having special logic in the server to deal with this situation. The server could decide to forbid the DELETE of a VCR, but this would leave a clutter of backup files.

Alternatively, the server could watch for PUT operations to URLs that previously had a version history, and the server would restore (perhaps duplicate) the version history. However, there are legitimate MOVE/PUT combinations where the new file is supposed to have a new version history. The server could also look out for telltale file names such as those with a first part ending in ~, but in practice there are many such temporary file-naming systems, and some of them are stupidly similar to what a human might name a file.

Finally, it's difficult to watch for all safe save algorithms, because they differ greatly, not only in how they name files but also in what operations are used. Apple's default mail program does a PUT to a temp file and then a MOVE to the real URL. Some Macintosh OS X software using system APIs employs a four-step procedure to save new content to my.txt:

1. MOVE my.txt to my~.txt (move the original file out of the way).
2. PUT data1234.txt (create a completely new URL rather than upload to the official URL).
3. MOVE data1234.txt to my.txt (start using the official URL).
4. DELETE my~.txt (cleanup).

 It's unclear why these four steps are used. Perhaps two layers of software each performed a different safe save, and their operations combined in this way. Or, maybe the application designers wanted to confirm that both the save operation and the move operation worked before deleting the original. It doesn't matter, because with all the variations in potential safe save algorithms, servers can't deal with all of them.

Safe save algorithms are not recommended for use with any WebDAV server, and particularly not with DeltaV servers. If client software must use a safe save algorithm, there is one that will work adequately with versioning, although it is not ideal:

1. Choose an unlikely temporary file name, not one that users could easily stumble upon. PUT the new content to the temporarily file name first, creating a temporary resource. Check that the content was uploaded correctly. Note that the server may automatically create that resource as a VCR.
2. COPY the temporary file to the real file. In a versioning system, this will create a new version of my.txt with the content from the temporary file. (This only works if auto-versioning is allowed, but that's immaterial since a change would not have been allowed in the first place.) Do not use MOVE, because this will overwrite the destination version history.
3. DELETE the temporary file to clean up. Note that if it was created as a VCR, then the process may leave a new VHR in the version history collection, but it will not be visible to most operations.

11.7   Version Trees

In the simplest versioning systems, the set of versions is just an ordered list, representing a linear line of descent where each version has at most one predecessor and at most one successor. Many more advanced versioning systems allow more complicated relationships.

11.7.1 Forking

Normally, when two users edit a document and don't want to overwrite each other's changes, they use locks to serialize their changes. This way only one user can make changes at a time. When that user releases the lock, the other user can see all the changes made so far and begin from that point. However, that's not the only way to manage multiple users changing a file.

Imagine that Alice is officially working on a document, but Bob wants to create an unofficial draft of the document. Bob needs to make several versions before his unofficial draft is ready to be considered as an alternative to the official version. Bob wants to check in his versions without affecting Alice. Versioning lets both Alice and Bob make their changes independently and save changes from either user as separate versions.

The next step to make this simultaneous-change model really useful is to keep the versions created by Alice and Bob distinguishable. This process is called **forking**. Rather than mingle all versions together in a single listing, the versioning repository identifies two lines of versions. Each user can create subsequent versions on his or her own line. It's easy for Carl to view both lines and understand where the two sets of changes started and how each version fits into the picture. Carl can even contribute to Bob's unofficial draft and check in those changes for Bob to see, still without affecting Alice's work.

Forking is often represented spatially. A single user's changes to a document are pictured in the version history in one dimension, a linear series of versions created over time. When several users are working on the document independently, the version history is represented in two dimensions as a **version tree** containing at least one **fork**. Now a version has one predecessor but may have **multiple successors**.

The version tree in Figure 11–8 shows one fork. Each arrow between resources shows the successor at the head of the arrow and the predecessor at the tail. The root version (v1) has two successors, v2 and v3. Bob created this fork to work on his draft material in v3. Carl added to the fork in v4, rather than the main line of work. This doesn't prevent Alice from adding new versions to the main line of work at any time.

Some versioning systems encourage forking. Whenever two users make independent unmerged changes to the same resource, a fork is automatically created in the version tree. The fork makes it clear that the changes are not integrated with each other, rather than make it appear as if the second change was intended as a replacement for the first change. Other versioning systems discourage forking by making the client specifically request that a fork be created. The flexibility of DeltaV allows both kinds of systems with the fork-ok property.

Figure 11–8 shows two forks identified by the name of the user who edited the versions in each fork. It happens that Bob made changes on one fork and Alice on the other. It's also possible for Bob to want to make changes on the fork created by Alice, and vice versa. Therefore, although forks are often associated with multiple users working separately on their own forks, that's not always the case. In fact, it's possible for a single user to intentionally create a fork on a single-author document. A user might do this to keep track of two independent sets of changes. For example, when publishing a chapter of a book, an author might fork the version tree. Then

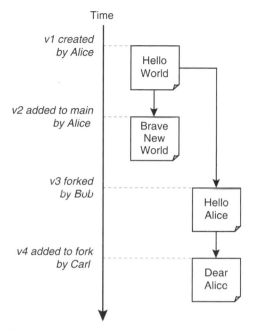

Figure 11–8   Version tree with fork.

the author can fix minor typos in the "published" fork of the version tree, and she can make major changes to the fork dedicated to a complete rewrite.

11.7.2 Creating Forks

In DeltaV, a fork is present whenever a version has more than one successor. The client causes this to happen by creating more than one new version that points to the same predecessor version, and when the server cleans up the relationships between versions, one version ends up with more than one successor. There are several ways to fork with the functionality defined so far and even more ways to fork when working resources and workspaces are thrown in.

Using UPDATE   A client can create a fork by checking out any version that already has a successor and checking it in again. This can be done by checking out a resource whose target version is a version that has a successor:

1. UPDATE the VCR to point to a version that already has a successor.
2. Make sure checkout-fork and checkin-fork are allowed on that version (see Section 11.7.5).
3. CHECKOUT the VCR. If checkout-fork was discouraged, include the `fork-ok` element in the CHECKOUT request body.
4. CHECKIN the VCR. If checkin-fork was discouraged, include the `fork-ok` element in the CHECKIN request body.

Editing Predecessor-Set   A client can also create a fork by using PROPPATCH to change the predecessor-set of a checked-out VCR such that the predecessor-set names a version that already has a successor. This is one way a user could decide after checking out that the resource ought to have a certain predecessor no matter which version was checked out.

1. CHECKOUT the VCR.
2. PROPPATCH the predecessor-set property on the VCR. To create a fork, give the property value the URL for a version that already has a successor.
3. CHECKIN the VCR. If checkin-fork is discouraged in the version identified in Step 2, include the `fork-ok` element in the CHECKIN request body.

11.7.3   Avoiding Forks

If checkout-fork is allowed but checkin-fork is forbidden, the client should be able to check out the resource whether or not the target version has a successor and may even be able to check in later as long as the checkin doesn't create a fork. The client can attempt to prevent the fork by fixing up the predecessor-set property of the checked-out resource so that the only predecessor is a version that has no successors (the latest version).

11.7.4   Simple Merge

Once forks exist, it's very likely that users will want to merge forks. Bob and Carl show their draft to Alice, and Alice decides it's got good ideas. Alice manually incorporates those changes into the official draft and creates v5. To show to all users that the content has been merged, it would be nice for the version tree to show that v5 was created with two predecessors, v2 and v4. A new user can then understand quickly that the latest content merges two lines of work (see Figure 11–9).

A client can merge two forks by causing a version to be created that has two predecessors. The two predecessor versions need not be on different forks before the merge, but that's the usual case. The client can do this by combining the content of the two predecessors in a checked-out resource, setting the predecessor-set of the checked-out resource to contain both predecessors, and checking it in. It may be necessary to ask the user to approve the merge of content or to choose which content to use in the merge result.

If the server allows a checkin where the predecessor-set has multiple values, it must change the successor-set of each predecessor so that all the relationships are consistent. The effective result of this operation is a merge in the version tree, or the combination of two or more forks into one.

 DeltaV was created with complex version trees in mind by default. A server can't advertise that it has only linear version trees; therefore, clients must assume forks and merges can exist in any version tree.

Note that DeltaV also has a method called MERGE, described in Section 12.4. The mechanism just shown does not use the MERGE method, yet it accomplishes a merge. The MERGE

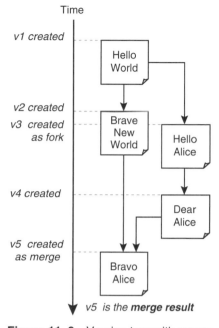

Figure 11–9   Version tree with merge.

method does the same thing simultaneously for multiple files, and this chapter does not cover multiple-file scenarios.

11.7.5   Are Forks Permitted?

Before seeing how to create a fork, the client may check the checkin-fork and checkout-fork properties to see if the server will permit the fork. These properties are required on every version and can be empty or contain the values forbidden or discouraged. If one of these properties is empty, it means the related action is allowed. If checkout-fork is allowed, then a client may check out a version that already has a successor or is already checked out. If checkin-fork is allowed, the client may do a checkin, which would create a fork.

The discouraged value means that the server will not allow forks to be created accidentally. The client must submit a CHECKIN request with an XML body. The body must contain the fork-ok element inside a root element named checkout. This request forces the server to accept the checkin and create a fork.

The properties are also required on every checked-out resource, but here they mean something slightly different: They determine the values of checkout-fork and checkin-fork to be set on the new version that will be created after checkin.

Many server implementation choices are possible with these two properties and three values because the values can vary from resource to resource. These are a few of the most obvious and most consistent scenarios:

- To prevent forks entirely, the server should make sure that the checkout-fork and checkin-fork properties both have a value of `forbidden` on all versions. Both properties are protected. Note that this also prevents multiple checkouts.
- To prevent forks but allow multiple checkouts (working resources, which we'll see in Section 11.8), the server can make checkout-fork allow any checkout but make checkin-fork always forbidden. The predecessor-set property should be writable on checked-out resources. The client must can edit predecessor-set to ensure that the version created on CHECKIN will have as predecessor a version that does not already have a successor.
- To support forks (and multiple checkouts) completely, the server should make sure that the value for both checkout-fork and checkin-fork is empty or `discouraged` on all versions.

The client may even be allowed to change the value on a checked-out resource, which should cause the server to enforce the user's chosen behavior. However, the client can't tell if checkin-fork and checkout-fork are writable on a resource without trying that specific resource. The server could make the properties writable on checked-out resources but not on an existing version. The DeltaV specification implies that these properties may be writable, but some existing servers do not support forks and have implemented these properties as unwritable everywhere.

11.8 Multiple Checkouts with Working Resources

The fork and merge features we've just seen allow multiple users to work on files, but they don't allow multiple users to check out files simultaneously. With all the features described up to this point, Bob can create a fork by checking out a version that already has a successor. However, Bob can't check out his version while Alice has her version already checked out—he has to wait for Alice to check in first. In multiuser versioning systems, this isn't always acceptable.

If Alice already has the document checked out and is editing it in place, Bob needs to be able to check out his file to a different location and edit the file there. DeltaV provides the **working resource** feature to allow this functionality. The working resource has its own URL, so Bob can PUT and PROPPATCH in that location, separate from Alice's changes to the VCR location.

11.8.1 Creating Working Resources

A working resource is created with a CHECKOUT request. To create a working resource based on the target version, the client can send a CHECKOUT request to the VCR with an XML request body. The XML contains the `apply-to-version` element inside a `checkout` root element. This request creates a working resource with the auto-update property pointing to the VCR. This means that when the working resource is checked in and a new version is created, the server will automatically update the VCR's checked-in property to point to the new version (see Listing 11–9).

Listing 11–9 CHECKOUT of a VCR to create a working resource.

```
CHECKOUT /docs/index.html HTTP/1.1
Host: www.example.com
Content-Type: text/xml; charset="utf-8"
Content-Length: 1234
↵
<?xml version="1.0" encoding="utf-8" ?>
<D:checkout xmlns:D="DAV:">
   <D:apply-to-version/>
</D:checkout>

HTTP/1.1 201 Created
Location: http://www.example.com/wr/docs/index1.html
↵
```

In response to the CHECKOUT request, the working resource is created with a URL chosen by the server. Working resources could theoretically appear in some regular collection in the repository, but they are more likely to appear in some reserved namespace. There is no way to browse for working resources.

Whenever a VCR is checked out with `apply-to-version`, the server must perform these steps:

1. If the target version has a successor, make sure it allows checkout-fork.
2. Create a working resource where the checked-out property points to the target version. Initialize the contents and dead properties of the working resource from the contents and dead properties of the version.
3. Set a live property called auto-update on the working resource. This property points to the VCR, which will be automatically updated when the working resource is checked in.
4. Mark the version checked out by adding the working resource URL to the version's checkout-set property.
5. Respond to the client with a 201 Created code, including a `Location` header with the URL of the working resource.

Although Figure 11–10 suggests that the working resource exists off in space, that's not necessarily true. A DeltaV server could even put the working resource inside the same collection as the VCR through which it was created.

A working resource does not have a new resourcetype value. It's not a new kind of resource, it's just a resource that happens to be checked out. If the client has a URL to some resource and needs to know if it's a working resource, the client must examine other properties. A working resource is required to have all the same properties as a regular checked-out resource.

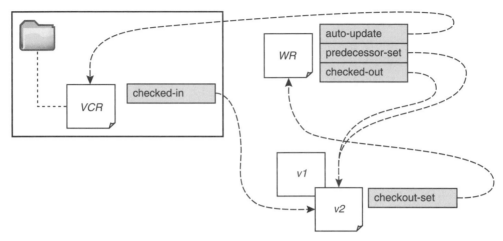

Figure 11–10 Working resource relationships.

The auto-update property is unique to a working resource, but it doesn't always exist, so that's not a reliable property to look for. Instead, a client can try to look at the supported-method-set property. If the resource supports UNCHECKOUT, it can't be a working resource, because only a checked-out VCR supports UNCHECKOUT.

Working Resources without Simultaneous Checkouts
Some pre-DeltaV versioning servers effectively have working resources (edits are made in a server location not normally visible to other users) but do not allow simultaneous checkouts. In these servers, a checkout acts as if it locks the resource so it can't be checked out by other clients. It's not clear whether this model can be implemented in a DeltaV server that must interoperate well with standard DeltaV clients.

11.8.2 Editing a Working Resource

When a client checks out to a working resource, write operations are sent to the working resource, rather than the VCR that is not checked out. While the working resource exists, it is a complete stand-alone resource. For example, it may be locked or unlocked independently of the VCR it was created from.

 A GET operation on the working resource will return the latest changes to that resource, whereas a GET operation on the checked-in VCR will still return the contents and dead properties of its target version. If any other users have permission to view the working resource, these users can see the results of any write operation to the working resource.

DeltaV does not specify whether other users can view or edit working resources. Certainly the user creating the working resource ought to have permission to view and edit it.

Perhaps the working resource should be limited so that only that user can view and edit it, or perhaps the working resource should inherit its permissions from the permissions of some other appropriate resource such as the VHR. If the server supports the WebDAV Access Control specification, it may even be possible to change permissions on the working resource and explicitly allow new principals to edit it.

 Before checking in, the client should set the comment property and make sure the predecessor-set value is appropriate, considering whether the checkin will create a fork and whether the server will allow the fork to be created. (Check the checkin-fork property on the checked-out version.)

11.8.3 CHECKIN a Working Resource

When a working resource is checked in, the state of the working resource is used to create a new version and the working resource is deleted. Since the working resource is deleted when it is checked in, a working resource never exists in the checked-in state.

For interest's sake, we'll assume that the predecessor-set of the working resource names a version that already has a successor, so this checkin will create a fork. The client has checked the value of checkin-fork on the version that was checked out, and its value is discouraged. However, the user has confirmed that creating a fork is the intended outcome of this checkin, so the client includes fork-ok in the CHECKIN body (see Listing 11–10).

Listing 11–10 CHECKIN working resource.

```
CHECKIN /wr/docs/index1.html HTTP.1.1
Host: www.example.com
Content-Type: text/xml; charset="utf-8"
Content-Length: 1234
↵
<?xml version="1.0" encoding="utf-8" ?>
<D:checkin xmlns:D="DAV:">
   <D:fork-ok/>
</D:checkin>

HTTP/1.1 201 Created
Location: http://www.example.com/his/vers1/35.html
↵

GET /wr/docs/index1.html HTTP.1.1
Host: www.example.com
↵

HTTP/1.1 404 Not Found
↵
```

This interaction shows a checkin to a working resource, which creates a new version, and the new version's URL is returned. The checkin was intended to create a fork, and it may have; the server does not specify whether a fork has been created in the response. The GET request and 404 Not Found response are shown to illustrate that the server has cleaned up the working resource.

When the working resource is checked in, the server performs the following steps:

1. Examine the successor-set property of the checked-out version to see if a fork will be created. Make sure the checkin-fork property of the checked-out version allows a fork to be created.
2. If the checkin is allowed to proceed, create a new version with the contents and dead properties of the working resource, and copy the value of predecessor-set from the working resource.
3. On the checked-out version, change the successor-set property to include the URL of the new version. Remove the live property checked-out.
4. If the auto-update property contains a VCR URL, change the checked-in property of that VCR to contain the URL of the new version (and make sure its contents and dead properties are the same as those of the new version).
5. Delete the working resource. Respond to the client with the Location header and the URL of the newly created version (see Figure 11–11).

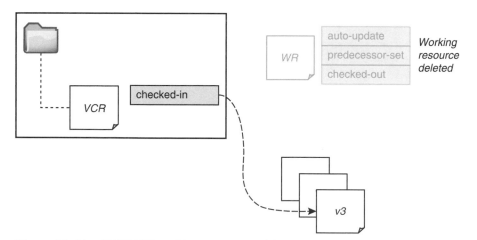

Figure 11–11   CHECKIN working resource—deletes working resource.

The client may not use UNCHECKOUT with a working resource but may DELETE a working resource. This operation cancels the changes and deletes the working resource. The server cleans up the version that was checked out, to reset to its previous state (no checked-out property).

If the working resource is never checked in and never deleted, the working resource exists indefinitely. DeltaV has no provision for a working resource to expire. The version would also remain checked out, which may prevent other checkouts if checkout-fork prevents forks.

11.8.4 Working Resources Create Forks

Working resources make it very easy to create forks, accidentally or intentionally. Here are some of the ways forks can be created:

- Check out a version that already has a successor. Leave the predecessor-set of the working resource alone. Check in.
- Check out a version that does not have a successor, but change the predecessor-set of the working resource so that it points to a version that does have a successor. Check in.
- Check out a version that already is checked out. If both are checked in (without altering the predecessor-set), the two checkins will create new versions with the same predecessor.

There is no way for the client to ensure it doesn't create a fork. The client can check out a version without a successor, edit the working resource, and just before checking in, make sure that the checked-out version still does not have a successor. Then, just before checking in, another user could update the version history such that the checked-out version now has a successor. There is no way for the client to indicate to the server that it does not want to create a fork on checkin. There is also no way for for the client to prevent other checkins for a time. The client could lock the VCR to try to protect it from being updated; however, it may not be possible to prevent working resources from being created, and as shown in the next chapter, there may even be multiple VCRs.

11.8.5 Checking Out Other Versions

Other versions, not just the current target version, can be checked out too. A CHECKOUT request addressed to a version URL also creates a working resource (however, the auto-update property must start out empty). This can be a useful shortcut if a user wants to work from the content of a specific version other than the target version. The working resource is initialized with the requested version's content, not the target version's content (see Listing 11–11).

Listing 11–11 CHECKOUT of a version creates a working resource.

```
CHECKOUT /his/vers1/32.html HTTP/1.1
Host: www.example.com
⏎

HTTP/1.1 201 Created
Location: http://www.example.com/wr/docs/index2.html
⏎
```

Listing 11–11 shows a CHECKOUT of a specific version and the server's response indicating that a working resource was created. The server must perform these steps:

1. If the requested version has a successor, make sure the value of checkout-fork allows a fork to be created.
2. Create a working resource where the checked-out property points to the target version. Initialize the contents and dead properties of the working resource from the contents and dead properties of the version. Add a checked-out property that points to the requested version.
3. Mark the version checked out by adding the working resource URL to the version's checkout-set property.
4. Respond to the client with a 201 Created code, including a `Location` header with the URL of the working resource.

Note that the auto-update property is not added to the working resource, although it was in the steps outlined in Section 11.8.1.

The server must perform the same steps on checkin outlined in Section 11.8.3, except that if the auto-update property is still absent, there is no need to update any VCR's checked-in property.

11.9   Checkout Determinism

DeltaV servers can be very different from each other. For example, some may allow a property like predecessor-set to be changed, which can allow the client to do a merge or prevent a fork. There's no way for a client to find out the server's policy on this. A server may even have different behavior for different resources in the same collection. With many DeltaV operations, it's hard or impossible for the client to predict what will happen.

Predicting Success

Clients often need to determine what actions will be allowed. It isn't enough for the client to try the operation to see if it fails. In a learnable and rich UI, the user is only presented with actions that are allowed. If a resource can't be checked out, the UI doesn't allow the user to initiate a checkout. To implement this kind of UI, the client must have some idea what actions will be allowed.

It's not necessary to be 100 percent accurate in this. Timing, edge cases, and errors can all make requests fail that otherwise would succeed. However, when policy forbids an action, the client should be able to find that out before trying it.

In particular, DeltaV doesn't make it easy for a client to know when to allow checkout and checkin. It's hard to know whether a resource is already checked out or whether a second checkout will be permitted. It's hard to know whether a checkin will be allowed and whether it will create a fork. Some answers can be determined in advance, and this section explains how to get as much of that information as possible.

11.9.1 How to Tell If a Checkout Exists

At this point, we have all the pieces to be able to tell if a VCR or any of its versions are checked out. Recall that if a VCR is checked out in place, the checked-out property appears on the source URL. If a checkout to a working resource exists, the version that was checked out has the check-out-set property with the URL of that working resource.

Thus, to find out if there are any checkouts relating to a resource, the client software must look for both kinds of checkouts. This is done most efficiently with a PROPFIND to the VCR to get the checked-out property and a REPORT method to the VCR to get the version-tree report including the checkout-set property.

If there is already a checkout relating to a resource, a user may choose not to check out that resource again, even if the server supports multiple simultaneous checkouts.

11.9.2 How to Tell If a Resource Can Be Checked Out

If a checkout exists, it may not be possible to do another CHECKOUT relating to the same version history. To find out if a resource can be checked out, the first step is to find out if it's already checked out. If it's not checked out, the client is probably able to check out the VCR or create a working resource (subject, of course, to access control). However, if the VCR or a working resource is already checked out, the client must look a little harder to see whether the server will allow another checkout.

Recall that the properties checkin-fork and checkout-fork are required on every version. These properties can be empty (action allowed) or take the value `forbidden` or `discouraged`. If checkout-fork is allowed, then a client may check out a version that already has a successor or is already checked out. If checkin-fork is allowed, the client may do a checkin that would create a fork.

Therefore, if a checkout exists, how can the client software find out if another checkout will be allowed, and if it is allowed, will it create a fork? (See Figure 11–12.)

If the version is already checked out and forking on checkout is allowed but forking on checkin is forbidden, it's hard to know what to do. The client could create a second checkout of the same version, but only the first CHECKIN will be allowed normally. The second CHECKIN request will fail unless the client is allowed to edit the predecessor-set property to prevent the fork. Because the client can't know in advance which CHECKIN request will happen first and whether the predecessor-set is editable, the client can't predict whether the CHECKIN will be allowed.

11.10 DeltaV Special Mechanisms

DeltaV introduces some new WebDAV mechanisms that are useful even outside of versioning. Some of these mechanisms have already been reused in other WebDAV-based specifications.

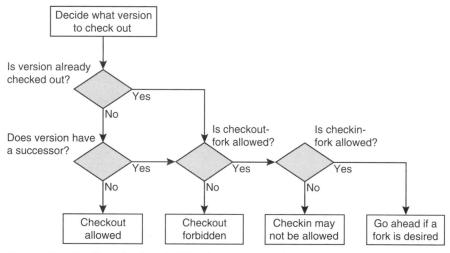

Figure 11–12 Flowchart to decide whether to check out.

11.10.1 REPORT Method

The REPORT method is a general-purpose request for the server to compile a useful set of information (perhaps with some input provided in the client request) and return the information as one response. There is no standard for requesting a report (the format of the body can vary), the kind of information returned in the report, or how the report response is formatted. This is defined independently for each kind of report.

A REPORT request typically addresses some resource that is essential to the report results. For example, in the version-tree report, the request is addressed to the VCR for which the version-tree is needed.

The REPORT request has a body where the root element names the report being requested. Inside the root element may be some more information used in compiling the report. In the version-tree report, the body specifies the property values to return for each version.

The complete list of reports DeltaV defines is:

- **version-tree**: Lists all the versions belonging to the same version history, along with selected property values.
- **expand-property**: Similar to version-tree but more powerful.
- **compare-baseline**: Determines how two baselines differ and compiles the differences.
- **latest-activity-version:** Tells the latest version in a version history that belongs to the named activity.
- **locate-by-history**: Collects the URLs of all the VCRs in this collection that are related to one of the specified version histories.
- **merge-preview**: Shows what the result of a merge would look like before it's done.

The REPORT mechanism is so broadly useful it is already used by some other standards such as the access control proposal.

11.10.2 Error Reporting

DeltaV introduces more detailed error reporting. The response codes 403 Forbidden and 409 Conflict have been extended to contain additional error information. For example, when a client attempts to check out a resource that is already checked out and that may not be checked out again, the server uses the 409 Conflict code plus a specific error element must-be-checked-in (in the DAV: namespace, of course) in the body (see Listing 11–12).

Listing 11–12 DeltaV error response.

```
HTTP/1.1 409 Conflict
Content-Type: text/xml; charset="utf-8"
Content-Length: xxxx
⏎
<?xml version="1.0" encoding="utf-8" ?>
<D:error xmlns:D="DAV:">
   <D:must-be-checked-in/>
</D:error>
```

The DeltaV specification introduces nearly 150 such error codes. In the draft, they are labeled "precondition" and "postcondition." Either a precondition or a postcondition code may be used in either the 403 Forbidden or the 409 Conflict response body, at the discretion of the server. Implementors must read the precondition and postcondition sections very carefully because they also contain the normative information about how an operation must behave or the state the server must be in for an operation to be legal.

Many of the precondition error codes are actually ways for the server to indicate that the client has attempted to use a feature the server does not support. Some features cannot be advertised in the OPTIONS response, so only the error is available to indicate that the feature is not supported. For example, if the server does not support deleting versions, it uses the no-version-delete error code in a response to a DELETE request to a version. Clients may have to attempt the operation and see if it fails to find out if that feature is supported. This leads to poor client GUI design, as discussed in Section 11.9.2. The situation is even worse if a server supports deleting versions in some situations but not in others. Thus, if the server uses the no-version-delete error code, the client must assume that *this particular version* can't be deleted. The client can't assume that versions can never be deleted.

Other status codes besides 403 Forbidden and 409 Conflict continue to be appropriate exactly as already defined. For example, 400 Bad Request should still be used if a header is badly formatted.

11.10.3 Feature Discovery by OPTIONS Body

DeltaV introduces a body in the OPTIONS request to find out additional information about the system as a whole. The body is only returned if the client asks for it by using a specific type of XML body in an OPTIONS request. The body contains the `options` element, and the `options` element contains one or more of the following elements:

- `version-history-collection-set`: The server returns the set of collections (or reserved namespaces) the server uses to store version-history resources.
- `workspace-collection-set`: The server returns the set of collections where workspaces may be created.
- `activity-collection-set`: The server returns the set of collections where activities may be created.

The successful 200 OK response from the server contains a body, and the body contains an `options-response` root element. The `options-response` element can contain any or all of the previous three elements, depending on which ones the client asked for, and each contains as many `href` elements as necessary to list all the special collections.

11.10.4 Feature Discovery Properties

DeltaV uses OPTIONS in the regular way to determine whether various named features are supported. Various feature strings may appear in the DAV response header to indicate support for those features.

Another way to discover functionality is to look for three new properties that must exist on any resource in a repository supporting DeltaV:

- supported-method-set
- supported-live-property-set
- supported-report-set

The OPTIONS response already lists a supported set of methods in the HTTP/1.1 Allow header (Section 3.7.2), so the supported-method-set property is redundant. One advantage to the supported-method-set property is that its value can be retrieved for a number of resources at once with the PROPFIND request and a Depth header. An OPTIONS request can only address one resource at a time, so the client would have to send OPTIONS once per resource to catalog the set of supported methods.

These properties make it possible to indicate support for some DeltaV features that can't be advertised in any other way. For example, if the server supports deleting versions, it should list the DELETE method in the supported-method-set property of a version.

There remain some features that cannot be advertised by the server or discovered by the client. For example, to see if the server supports automatic versioning, it's not sufficient to see if the auto-version property is present or supported in live-property-set, because it may be present yet its value may be fixed at empty (no auto-versioning). Instead, the client must attempt to set the auto-version property to see if the server is capable of handling the various defined automatic versioning options. If the client can't set this property, it proves little, because the server might only allow auto-versioning to be configured through administration tools and not via PROPPATCH.

11.10.5 Live Property Requirements

Live and dead properties were defined in Section 4.4.1. Live properties are any properties for which the server controls the semantics or syntax. All properties defined in DeltaV are live properties, including the comment property, even though the client controls its value.

Configuration Live Properties DeltaV defines some live properties that the user may be able to modify to change the behavior of the resource over subsequent operations. The server controls the syntax and values of these properties because the values are used as configuration information. DeltaV does not specify what error message should be used when the client attempts to set one of these properties to an illegal value. A generic 400 Bad Request response would be appropriate but not very informative.

Supporting Unsupported Live Properties DeltaV requires that when a DeltaV server does not support a DeltaV live property, the server must prevent that live property from being given a value by clients. Otherwise, other clients will believe this is the server-generated value for that live property

Allprop Semantics Changed The DeltaV RFC effectively changed the semantics of the PROPFIND allprop request. If a server supports DeltaV, it *must not* return all live properties in response to even an allprop request—it must return only the live properties defined in RFC2518 and the dead properties. Instead, to get the names of live properties, the client may issue a propname request or get the supported-live-property-set property. Then, the client can issue a more specific PROPFIND response to get the values of those live properties.

The propname request continues to list all property names whether live or dead or DeltaV. In addition, dead properties continue to be returned in PROPFIND requests, along with the live properties defined in RFC 2518.

A side benefit here is that for the first time, the client can tell the difference between live and dead properties. If the server supports DeltaV, and it returns a property in response to propname that is not returned in response to allprop, it's a live property. If a DeltaV server returns a non-RFC2518 property in response to allprop, it is very likely to be a dead property.

This redefinition for allprop is accepted outside of DeltaV as well because it reduces performance costs for servers.

11.11 Summary

DeltaV extends the WebDAV data model to include versioning concepts. DeltaV adds a number of new methods and many new live properties to WebDAV.

The core components of any DeltaV system are regular resources together with VCRs and versions. A version-controlled resource or VCR is any resource that is associated with a version history and that may be checked out, edited, and checked in again to create a new version. A version is an unchanging snapshot of a VCR. A new version is created whenever the VCR is checked in.

CHECKOUT, CHECKIN, and UNCHECKOUT give the client control over when to create new versions. CHECKOUT puts a resource in the checked-out state. The checked-out property marks the resource that is checked out. A checked-out VCR may be changed as often as desired during the checkout. CHECKIN releases the checkout and makes a single new version, the successor to the previous version. A VCR that is not checked out has the checked-in property. UNCHECKOUT releases the checkout and does not make a new version, discarding changes if necessary.

Some features are optional for servers, but a different set of features is optional for clients. Clients must understand version trees, including forks and merges. Clients should also recognize when a resource is checked out or checked in. The UPDATE, version history, and working resource features are optional for both client and server.

Multifile Versioning

So far, we've only considered versioning scenarios in which the versioned file is independent from all other versioned files. Versioning gets much more complicated when multiple files with relationships to each other may be checked out and checked in.

Let's imagine a simple Java program for finding employee information, department information, and which employees are in which department. The program requires only two source files, Employee.java and Department.java, and each file corresponds to a Java class. The Java object for a Department references a number of Employee objects when the code runs. Thus, Department.java must reference the other file when it is compiled. If Department calls a method getID() on Employee, then the method getID() must exist in Employee.java for the code to compile (see Figure 12–1).

When Department.java and Employee.java are first created as files, they compile successfully into executable code. Thus, version 1 of Department.java and version 1 of Employee.java are related. Then some changes are made to Department.java, creating version 2, which still compiles with version 1 of Employee.java.

When a developer decides to work on a feature (adding the ability to find the manager of an employee or department) separately from the main effort, the developer forks each version-tree. On the new branch, v5 of Department.java compiles with v4 of Employee.java. However, development continues on the main branch: v4 of Department.java compiles with v5 of Employee.java. The versions on the different branches don't compile with each other, so the latest version of Employee.java (v5) doesn't compile with the latest version of Department.java (v5).

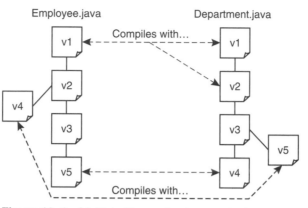

Figure 12–1   Multiple-file version tree example.

How can the developers of this project keep track of which branch they're working on across a number of files? How can they check out versions that compile together? How can they look back in time and identify sets of versions that compile together? These are the kinds of problems solved by multiple-resource versioning features.

In this section, we'll examine those features. However, in the interest of not putting you to sleep, this chapter doesn't describe features in detail. Still, the chapter is pretty dense and complicated. Many applications don't involve dependencies between resources and thus don't require these features, so probably many readers can skip this chapter.

12.1   Workspaces

Chapter 11, *Versioning*, introduced the concept of a working resource (Section 11.8). A working resource is a server-provided location or "sandbox" for editing content from a single VCR such that the changes are not automatically seen by users downloading the VCR.

It's possible for a developer in the multifile scenario to use working resources. The developer asks the server for a working resource for Employee.java and a working resource for Department.java. Now the developer can upload changes to each of these files. If the developer needs to work on a new machine, the software on the new machine can download each working resource and compile them. However, there's no way for the system to indicate that these two working resources belong together, so the developer would have to manually configure the software to make sure everything compiles together.

To make this process easier, **server-side workspaces** provide a location where VCRs being edited, VCRs not being edited, and even regular resources can exist in the same place. When they are all available in the same place, it's easier to make sure that cross-references work and that they all compile together before checking in changes.

A workspace can contain collections, regular resources, and VCRs. Within the workspace, resources can be changed, renamed, moved, deleted, or created. None of these changes is visible outside the workspace until the client checks in part or all of the work in progress.

A user may have a workspace that belongs to him for his development use. Alternatively, a user could have multiple workspaces to use or could share a workspace with other users. New files can be added to a workspace before being checked into the main repository. This provides a handy way to make sure the new file is integrated correctly and imported or referenced in all the other files that need to link to it, before making changes that could affect all other users.

12.1.1 Workspace Model

The main purpose of a workspace is to contain a number of VCRs, each of which points to a VHR. Many other workspaces may point to the same VHR. A VCR may be created from scratch (using PUT and VERSION-CONTROL) in the workspace, in which case the server creates a new VHR to manage versions. Alternatively, the user can choose to create a VCR that links a pre-existing VHR into the workspace.

The Meaning of Version History Resources

Now it becomes clearer how crucial VHRs are to the DeltaV data model. The VHR is the official location and URL for the content reflected in its versions. Any operation that adds a version can affect any VCR that points to those versions. VCRs may be moved, renamed, or deleted, but VHRs last forever with the same name. Any version that was ever saved on a repository can be found in a single VHR.

Regardless of whether the VCR was created from scratch or based on an existing VHR, what appears in the workspace is a real VCR. The user can check out the VCR in place to make changes within the workspace, independently of any editing going on in other VCRs. When the VCR inside the workspace is checked in, a new version is created in the version history.

Figure 12–2 shows two VCRs linked to the same VHR. One VCR is in the shared /docs/ repository, and the other is in Alice's workspace. While the VCR in Alice's workspace is checked out, Alice can edit the resource without affecting the main repository. The VCR in /docs/ could even be checked out independently.

Even when Alice checks in the document, creating v3, the other VCR is not directly affected. The content at /docs/index.html continues to reflect the content in the first version. Only an UPDATE request will make the VCR in the main repository show the latest version. It's the same thing with any other workspace: For Bob to see the latest versions in his workspace, his client must send an UPDATE request for each VCR that has new versions.

 When a server supports workspaces, *every* WebDAV resource has a workspace property containing an href element to indicate what workspace it is in. The main repository is a workspace, too. The data model is very consistent in treating workspaces exactly alike, with no difference in treatment of the main repository or primary namespace.

The value of the workspace property on a nonworkspace resource must be the same as the value of the property on the resource's parent. A collection can be identified as a workspace if its

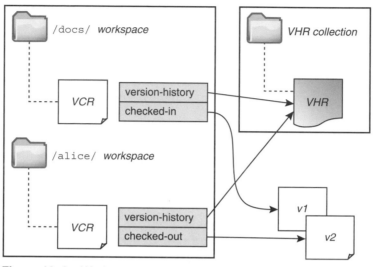

Figure 12–2 Workspaces.

workspace property points to itself. DeltaV does not specify whether it's legal for the workspace property to be empty. Since every collection is a workspace or inside of one, it's pretty safe to assume that this property should never be empty.

Once the conceptual model for workspaces is understood, the mechanics are fairly easy. Clients can find or create workspaces, link in resources, and change resources within the workspace.

12.1.2   Finding or Creating a Workspace

First, the user needs a workspace to work in. The user can select a workspace to use in a couple of ways:

- The client may simply be configured by the user with the URL of the workspace to use.
- The client can browse workspaces and allow the user to select one.
- The client may create a new workspace for the user.

To browse workspaces, the client sends a special OPTIONS request to any resource supporting DeltaV. The body of the OPTIONS request contains an XML element `workspace-collection-set`. The server returns a set of collection URLs such as `http://www.example.com/wksp/`. Now the client can browse these collections to see what workspaces exist, and the user selects one.

To allow clients to create new workspaces, DeltaV defines a new method MKWORK-SPACE. It works much like MKCOL. No body is required on the request. The `workspace-collection-set` OPTIONS request must be used again to figure out where to put the new workspace.

12.1.3   Linking Resources into Workspaces

The first step in editing a resource in a workspace is often to link the resource into the work-space. In this case, the client is simply creating a VCR based on a pre-existing VHR, so the method is the same as that used to create a VCR from a nonversioned resource: the VERSION-CONTROL method, this time with a body. The Request-URI identifies the workspace and VCR to create, and the body of the request identifies the VHR that will be linked to. The server creates a new modifiable VCR with the Request-URI, linked to the VHR if it exists.

The user might select existing VCRs in the main repository and tell the client to work on those files in the workspace. To do this, for each existing VCR the client must:

- Find out the VHR of the existing VCR with PROPFIND to the existing VCR.
- Decide what to call the new VCR. It must be inside the workspace or a subdirectory of the workspace, so the URL must contain the workspace name. The client must choose a final segment or file name. This might be the same as the name of the existing VCR.
- Send a VERSION-CONTROL request to the URL just constructed, where the body of the request specifies the URL of the VHR. This creates a new VCR linking to an existing VHR. This is Step 2 illustrated in Figure 12–3.

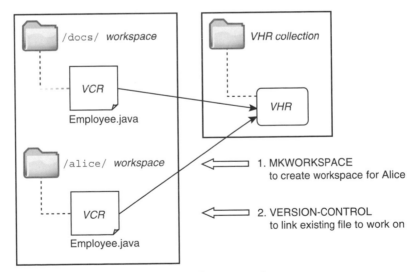

Figure 12–3   Linking existing VHR into a workspace.

12.1.4   Working in Workspaces

Now the workspace is set up to begin working on files. From here, the set of steps is the same as modifying a regular VCR. For example, if the client wants to send explicit CHECKOUT and CHECKIN requests:

- Send a CHECKOUT request to `/wksp/bob/index.htm` to check it out to edit in place.
- Send PUT and PROPFIND requests to `/wksp/bob/index.htm` to update it.
- Send a CHECKIN request to `/wksp/bob/index.htm` to create new version `/vers/index.html.3` for the VHR `/vhrs/index.htm`.

Ordinary resources can be created with PUT, MOVE, COPY, or MKCOL. Nonversioned resources can be replaced with VCRs using the VERSION-CONTROL method as described in Section 11.2.6. In general, resources behave the same way they do inside the main repository.

12.2   Change Sets

A developer changing multiple files may prefer to check them all in at the same time or not at all. If there are problems checking the files in, the developer prefers to fix the problems and then try again with the entire batch. This allows entire projects to remain consistent with versions that work together.

Many source code systems already have this concept of the **change set** to allow multiple files to be checked in together. Sometimes it's just a matter of committing several files together (e.g., in the Concurrent Versions System or CVS, *www.cvshome.org*).

DeltaV defines an **activity** to group changes together for checkin. An activity is a new resource type. The resource itself is very simple: It has only a few live properties defined and no body or dead properties defined. To commit a number of files together, the client makes sure that all the files are listed in the activity-checkout-set property and then checks in the activity resource. This checkin operation is illustrated in Figure 12–4.

When the server checks in the activity, it must check in all the checked-out resources identified by the activity or fail. After a successful checkin, the activity's activity-checkout-set property is empty.

12.2.1   Checking Out to an Activity

One way of setting up an activity with a number of checked-out files is to declare the activity when checking out each resource. The client does this by including the `activity-set` element and the URL of the activity in the body of a CHECKOUT request. Listing 12–1 shows how to check out one resource to the activity; the client has to do this for all the resources that will ultimately be checked in together.

In this example, the `Employee.java` file is checked out with `apply-to-version` so that it will create a working resource, and the working resource will be part of the fixbug4321 activity.

The client also has to check out and edit every file that is involved in the change. The client can do this bit by bit, adding each file to the activity as it is checked out. DeltaV also allows the client to add a resource that is already checked out, by editing the activity-set property of the checked-out resource. This causes the server to modify the activity-checkout-set of the activity to add the URL of the checked-out resource to keep consistency.

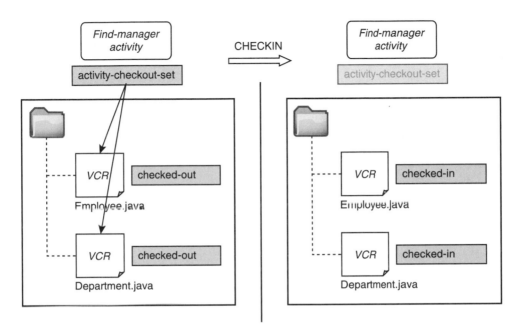

Figure 12–4 CHECKIN of an activity commits a change set, before and after.

To check in a change set, the client sends a single CHECKIN request to the activity URL. The server must check in all the resources identified in the activity-checkout-set property together or fail the request and check in none of them.

Listing 12–1 CHECKOUT of a VCR to an activity.

Request:
```
CHECKOUT /dev/Employee.java HTTP/1.1
Host: www.example.com
Content-Type: text/xml; charset="utf-8"
Content-Length: 1234
⏎
<?xml version="1.0" encoding="utf-8" ?>
<D:checkout xmlns:D="DAV:">
   <D:apply-to-version/>
   <D:activity-set>
      <D:href>http://www.example.com/_act/fixbug4321</D:href>
   </D:activity-set>
</D:checkout>
```

Response:
```
HTTP/1.1 201 Created
Location: http://www.example.com/wr/docs/index1.html
⏎
```

12.2.2 Creating Activities

A new activity can be created with a new method, MKACTIVITY. The server will advertise one or more collections where activities can be created. To get this list of activity collections, the client uses a special OPTIONS request where the body asks for the `activity-collection-set`. When the activity is first created this way, it will have empty properties. The user can start associating files with the activity by checking out files to the activity.

A new activity may also be created on-the-fly as a file is checked out. This is accomplished with special syntax in the CHECKOUT request to a file. The server creates the new activity with some server-selected name, and the checked-out resource is associated with the new activity.

12.3 Branches

DeltaV allows files to be forked, allowing some developers to work on one fork and other developers to work on the other. How do developers identify which fork to work on? How do they ensure that they are working on the correct fork across a large number of files? How do they identify a set of historical versions that belong together in the same area of work? A common term for a number of versions in the same line of descent is a **branch**. A single branch can be handled with mechanisms introduced so far, but it becomes difficult to manage multiple branches without some way of naming them.

Imagine that two developers need to work on an experimental feature to add the ability to find an employee's manager or a department manager. The feature must be developed without affecting developers working on the main functionality. That makes it complicated for the two developers on the experimental feature to coordinate their work. To make this process easier, the two developers need to be able to identify a branch as the find_manager branch across a set of files. The developers ought to be able to examine each version and see what branch it is on. Conversely, it's nice to be able to examine a branch and see what versions are in it.

Somewhat confusingly, branches are also implemented using activities. DeltaV allows activities to identify multiple versions in the same branch of a version tree. Each version in the branch belongs to the same activity. Once the activity is established in this manner, it self-perpetuates: Subsequent versions in the same branch automatically are added to the activity.

Let's say Alice creates the activity initially by checking out v4 of `Employee.java` and v3 of `Department.java` in the find_manager activity (using the body of the CHECKOUT request), as illustrated in Figure 12–5. Subsequent actions all take place within the context of this activity:

- When Alice checks in v5 of `Employee.java`, the new version is automatically in the find_manager activity.
- When Bob checks out v5 of `Employee.java` with a simple CHECKOUT request (no body), the checked-out resource is automatically part of the find_manager activity.

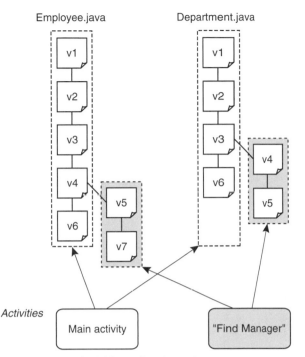

Figure 12–5 Activities select branches.

- When Bob checks out v4 of `Department.java`, it is also automatically part of the find_manager activity.
- When Bob checks in these two resources either separately or together (by checking in the activity), the new versions he creates (v7 and v5) are automatically part of the same activity.

12.3.1 Switching Activities

Activities allow a developer to keep track of more than one work item. Bob is working on the find_manager feature and may change a number of files. Then, before completing his work and checking it in, Bob is interrupted by the sudden need to fix a bug. The changes required to fix the bug are not the same changes as the feature changes, but they involve the same files.

If Bob tries to work on the changes required to fix the bug in the context of the find_manager activity, then the find_manager work will have to be checked in along with the bug fix. That will delay the bug fix because the find_manager work isn't done yet. It might be better for Bob to work on the bug fix without using an activity, except that he could find a new bug with even higher priority, and so must track the low-priority bug fix changes separately from the high-priority bug fix changes.

The solution is to use a different activity. Each bug fix and each feature task can be in a separate activity. Now the changes involved in each activity can be reviewed, put aside, continued, or checked in as necessary, independently from other activities.

A workspace can have a default activity. When any developer checks out any resource in that workspace, the server automatically adds the resource to the activity's checked-out resource list. This default activity takes precedence over the activity of the version that was checked out.

In systems with heavy use of activities, every checkout may be associated with some activity.

12.3.2 Combining Atomic Checkin with Named Branches

It may be necessary to name branches with an activity but then do an atomic checkin (of a change set) with a subset of the versions the activity identified. Since atomic checkin is done with an activity and so is naming branches, DeltaV defined a way to relate two activities: One is a **subactivity** of the other.

The change set of checked-out resources is an activity that belongs to a particular branch of a number of resources. (The two must be consistent, of course.) The change set is the subactivity, and therefore the branch is the parent activity. For example, if multiple developers are working on the find_manager branch, Bob could create one subactivity to do an atomic checkin on that branch, and Alice could create a different subactivity to do another set of changes on the same branch. Each subactivity can be checked in as long as the checkins do not create forks. In general, whenever an operation is done on an activity, the operation is also done on the subactivities in this set.

The subactivity-set property is the way a branch activity keeps track of the atomic checkin subactivities it may contain. A server can leave the property value empty and never allow subactivities to be created by forbidding this property to be modified.

12.4 MERGE

Recall from the previous chapter that you can do a single-file version-tree merge by changing the predecessor-set property of a checked-out working resource or VCR so that it points to two versions. When the new version is created at CHECKIN, the server keeps the predecessor-set value on the new version. Modifying the predecessor-set works great for single files, but with multiple files, there needs to be a way to coordinate the modification. The MERGE operation is specified in DeltaV to provide a convenient way to merge version trees from multiple files. Activities are used again to relate the files.

In addition to merging the version trees, some DeltaV servers may be capable of merging the content of versions. If the server cannot merge content, then the client must do so and upload the contents of the new versions. Regardless of how the content is merged, the server is responsible for updating the version trees to show the merge.

12.4.1 Merge Rules

The MERGE operation checks out a VCR. Thus, the MERGE method takes the place of CHECKOUT when the client wants to begin a merge process. The client uses PUT, PROPPATCH, and finally CHECKIN to complete the process. Multiple files are involved if the client selects a number of VCRs in the same activity and checks each of them out with MERGE or CHECKOUT.

During a merge, the merge-set property on the VCR acts like a "to-do list." It contains the list of versions that will be merged into the checked-out VCR. The predecessor-set property is the list of versions that have already been merged into the checked-out VCR.

Either the server or the client may integrate the contents of the merge-set versions into the VCR. Whoever does the integration must move the version URL from the merge-set to the predecessor-set to show what has been accomplished. The next sections cover the details of what happens when the client performs the actual integration as well as when the server does the integration.

12.4.2 Client-Managed Merge

When the client is 100-percent responsible for merging content, all the server does is a normal checkout, checkin, and then construct the version tree where the latest version has two predecessors.

Figure 12–6 shows the two major steps of a client-managed merge. First, the MERGE method is used to check out the resource, replacing CHECKOUT. In this step, the client identifies both a **merge source**, which is a version, and a **merge target**, which is a VCR and its target version. Then the client must PUT the results of the integration between the merge source and merge target and PROPPATCH the merge-set and predecessor-set to show that it has done this. Finally, the client does a CHECKIN to complete the operation.

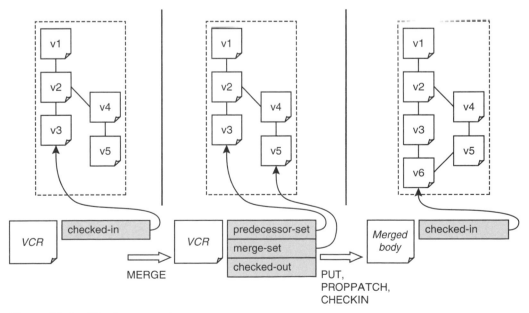

Figure 12–6 Client-managed merge.

The actual details of this process are slightly more complicated because the client can select multiple merge sources, which means that more than two branches are merged. Furthermore, the server does some of the property manipulation and verification. Here are the details:

1. Client sends the MERGE request to a VCR, making it the merge target. The body of the request contains a `source` element with at least one merge source URL and the `no-auto-merge` element to tell the server not to attempt the merge automatically.
2. Server checks out the VCR and adds the merge source URLs to the merge-set property. Server updates the predecessor-set property on the checked-out VCR to the target version, which is the merge target.
3. Client combines the content of a merge source with the VCR contents and uses PUT to update the VCR with the combined content.
4. Client uses PROPPATCH to remove the merged version's URL from the merge-set property and add it to the predecessor-set property. Repeat Steps 3 and 4 as necessary until merge-set is empty.
5. Client may use CHECKIN to finish the operation.
6. Server checks in the VCR and creates a new version with two predecessors indicated by the value of the predecessor-set property of the VCR.

12.4.3   Server-Managed Merge

The server-managed merge operation results in the same state and follows nearly the same process, but the server actually attempts to integrate the content of the merge sources with the merge target. The server gives the client/user a chance to verify that this was done correctly before checking in to commit the merge.

As Figure 12–7 shows, when the server has integrated the content from a merge source during the MERGE operation, the URL of the merge source appears in the auto-merge-set property instead of the merge-set property. The auto-merge-set is a different kind of to-do list because it shows that the server has already done most of the work. The client can check each merged resource out and if it approves of the way the server did the integration, then it moves the URLs from the auto-merge-set to the predecessor-set.

Again, the details get a little more complicated:

1. Client sends a MERGE request to a VCR. The request body contains the `source` element with the merge source URLs.
2. The server checks out the VCR. If the server can combine any merge source into the merge target, it does so and adds the merge source URL to the auto-merge-set property. The content of the checked-out VCR is initialized to the result of the integration. If the server cannot combine a merge source (e.g., it encounters an unknown file type), it adds the merge source URL to the merge-set property to signal that the client must do this part.

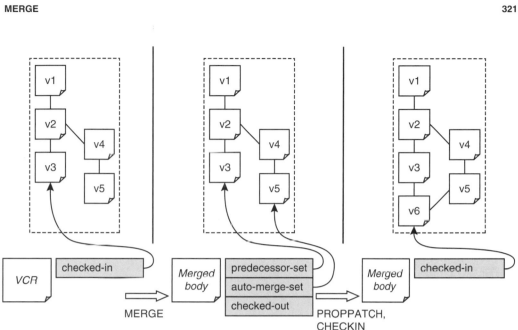

Figure 12–7   Server-managed merge.

3. Client checks the value of the auto-merge-set property. If it contains URLs, the client should check that the contents of the VCR are consistent. If they are, the client should use PROPPATCH to move the URLs from the auto-merge-set to the predecessor-set.

4. Client checks the value of the merge-set property. If it contains URLs, the client must do the merge for those source versions. Client uses PUT to update the VCR with the results of the client's merge and then uses PROPPATCH to move the merged URLs from the merge-set to the predecessor-set.

5. When both merge-set and auto-merge-set are empty, client may CHECKIN.

6. Server creates the new version with the content and predecessor-set of the VCR and checks in the VCR.

12.4.4   How Content Is Combined in Merges

DeltaV does not specify how versions are to be combined by either the client or the server. Either client or server could use any algorithm. There is no provision for the server to include merge "conflict" information inside the body of the merge result, as CVS does when there are problems during the merge.

 DeltaV does not specify how dead properties are to be merged at all. If two dead properties on the two versions have the same name but different values, then it's impossible to know which value to choose or whether the values can be combined. In addition, DeltaV does not specify whether the server will merge dead properties when the server merges contents. If the client cares about dead properties, it's safer for the client to do the merge itself.

There is no way to find out in advance whether the server can actually integrate the contents of two versions. The client must be prepared to do the integration itself or cancel the checkout with an UNCHECKOUT operation if the server fails to merge the content.

If the two versions being merged are on the same branch, then the later version is assumed to have the correct content, and the content from the later version is used. It's only when two versions are on different branches that the server or client is supposed to combine the content from both versions.

12.4.5 Merging, Activities, and Workspaces

Merge is quite useful in conjunction with activities and workspaces. The workspace may contain many changes to resources, the activity selects which of those changes to apply, and the merge feature helps apply those changes to another workspace. For example, the latest checked-in versions can be merged into a user's workspace so that the user has the latest content in his or her workspace.

Since an activity can be checked in, a multifile atomic merge is done by checking out a number of files to the same activity, following the merge steps for each, and checking in the activity.

12.5 History of Multiple Resources

One of the most complex parts of versioning with multiple files is looking back in time. Imagine that a mistake was made recently in the development of a software project and hasn't been fixed yet. The build team wants to be able to rebuild the software project from a point before the error was made. Imagine that this point is called "build 148," because the build team numbers builds sequentially. How does one identify which versions of every file to use in build 148? How does one identify which points in time are interesting checkpoints?

A rather unsophisticated approach is to copy an entire versioned repository to create a checkpoint. If a project reaches Beta 1, the administrator might create a directory somewhere and copy the entire version-controlled repository or just the latest versions of each file in the repository to the Beta 1 directory. Either way, this takes up an enormous amount of space. Another drawback is that the files in the Beta 1 directory must be carefully managed so that they cannot be accidentally altered. In any case, because of the costs of this approach, the project won't likely have many such checkpoints.

Another naive approach is to use timestamps to determine checkpoints. Every version has a creationdate property. Pick the point in time for build 148, and select the last version of each file that was created before that point. However, this approach has problems because files can be moved. If a VCR is moved into the software build area of the repository from some other area of the repository, it may have a history that predates build 148, even though it was moved into the project afterward and should not be included in build 148. Another problem is that it's difficult to recall at exactly what point build 148 occurred.

The final naive approach is to use labels. After some changes have been made, an automatic process can use the LABEL method on the current version of every VCR to label this instant as "build 148." Unfortunately, while the automatic process is applying this label to all the current versions, somebody could be in the process of adding new versions on files that the process hasn't labeled yet. The resulting set of versions selected by the "build 148" label may not be consistent. Labels could still be used if the repository is locked during labeling, but this isn't ideal. Also recall that labels can be changed, thus changing the set of versions that makes up our checkpoint: We ideally want the flexibility of labeling a set of versions but also the reliability of a fixed, unchangeable checkpoint.

So far, our requirements are that a checkpoint must be unchangeable and that it archives the state of a set of resources at a point in time. This is starting to sound just like a version, only for a set of resources instead of just one resource. Perhaps if we had a different kind of container resource that captured the state of multiple resources, we could then track the version history of that set. This new container resource exists in DeltaV, and it is called a **configuration**. A configuration is rooted at a collection, and it includes all VCRs inside the collection. The configuration is different from the collection because it includes VCRs within subcollections too, but it does not include any other kind of resource besides VCRs.

A configuration changes when any of its VCRs change. A configuration is a VCR, too. The configuration can be checked out and checked in to create a new configuration version. A configuration version is called a **baseline**.

The term for the collection where the configuration is rooted is a **baseline-controlled collection** because all VCRs within that collection have their collective state captured in baselines.

12.5.1   Baselines

Although baselines look very complicated, the function they serve is rather simple. Baselines select one version from all the VCRs in a configuration. When the baseline is created, the current version of each VCR in the configuration is referenced in the baseline. Only one version from each VCR may be in any baseline. However, the same version may appear in many baselines (see Figure 12–8).

Once the baseline is created, its membership never changes. VCRs that were added to the configuration after the baseline was created do not appear in the baseline. VCRs that were deleted from the configuration after the baseline was created are still represented through their version links in the baseline.

It is possible to customize the state of the VCRs in a configuration to create a baseline with specific versions of those VCRs. To do this, UPDATE VCRs as necessary so that the target version is the version that is wanted for the baseline, and then create the baseline by checking in the configuration. However, it is not possible to create a baseline that does not include every VCR in the configuration at the instant the baseline is created.

The exact mechanism by which a baseline lists a number of versions is with the aid of a **baseline collection**. A baseline collection may contain subcollections and VCRs, where each VCR has the same checked-in version it had when the baseline was created. It's the list of members and their target versions that is the important data in a baseline collection.

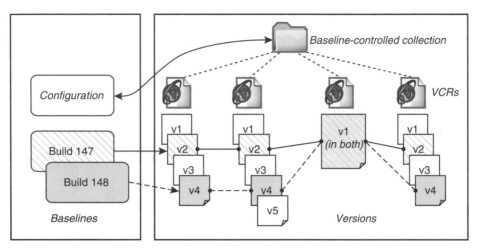

Figure 12–8   Baselines identify sets of versions.

There exists one more new resource tied to baselines, the **baseline history resource**. A baseline history resource is just a VHR used to track baselines instead of versions. Otherwise, it behaves identically to a VHR tracking versions.

Baselines, baseline-history resources, configurations, baseline-controlled collections, and baseline collections have all been introduced rather quickly. Here's the big picture, literally (see Figure 12–9).

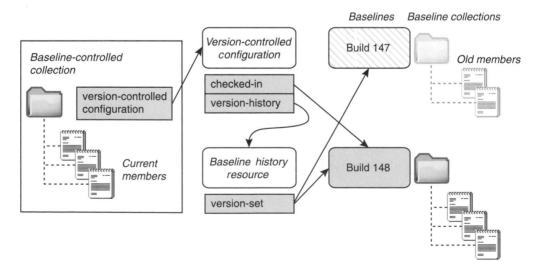

Figure 12–9   Baselines, configurations, and baseline history resource.

In Figure 12–9, we have one baseline-controlled collection in the main repository. It contains three VCRs. The collection was put under baseline control with the BASELINE-CONTROL method, and that request created the version-controlled configuration, the baseline-history resource, the first baseline, and the first baseline collection. Whenever the version-controlled configuration is checked out and checked in again, a new baseline and a new baseline collection are created to capture the changed state.

12.5.2   Configurations and Subconfigurations

A configuration is rooted at a collection, and normally the configuration refers to all VCRs inside that collection (recursively). However, configuration membership can be customized if **subconfigurations** exist. If a collection /hr has a configuration, and its subcollection /hr/recruiting also has a configuration, then the recruiting configuration is a subconfiguration of the HR configuration. The HR configuration refers only to the set of resources inside /hr that are not included in a subconfiguration (see Figure 12–10).

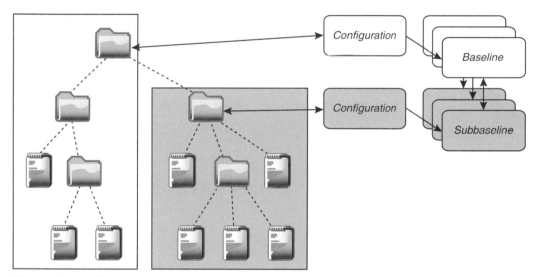

Figure 12–10   Resource tree showing configuration membership.

When baselines are created, each baseline only includes versions of VCRs from the configuration, not versions of VCRs from the subconfiguration (and vice versa). Each baseline has links to the subbaselines to which it is related, so it's possible to reconstruct the state of an entire repository, even when the repository is broken up into several configurations for easier management.

12.5.3   Collection Membership Versioning

Tracking the combined history of multiple resources involves a few problems that aren't solved by baselines. If a resource is added to a collection and then removed in between creating baselines, it's hard to tell that the resource ever existed in that collection. In fact, if the resource wasn't a VCR, there may be no record of its existence.

DeltaV defines **version-controlled collections** to solve this problem. One way to understand version-controlled collections is to compare the concept to baselines:

- Baselines are only created on request. Versions of version-controlled collections are created whenever the collection changes.
- A configuration covers a set of VCRs that are not all in the same parent collection. A version-controlled collection only keeps track of its direct children.

A version-controlled collection is much like a VCR, having a VHR and versions and changing when content and dead properties change. The content of a collection is its membership list. Every change to the collection's direct membership (every added, deleted, or renamed resource) could create a new version of the collection if autoversioning is supported. The collection can also be checked out and checked in to create new collection versions.

Figure 12–11 shows that a collection version is much the same as a regular version. It doesn't have a body or contents, however. Instead, it has a version-controlled-binding-set property that lists the name (and VHR, not shown in the diagram) of each member of the collection.

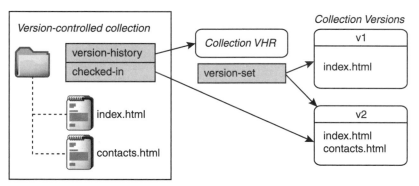

Figure 12–11   Version-controlled collection and its versions.

Version-controlled collections don't track nonversioned resources at all. That's too bad, since baselines don't track nonversioned resources, either. These can slip through the cracks in a versioning system, untracked, untrackable, leaving no mark that they ever existed in any baseline or collection version. Serious versioning systems generally make every resource version-controlled.

Version-controlled collections are briefly specified in DeltaV but are still very complex because of the many interactions.

12.5.4 Working Collections

Just as a working resource exists for a regular VCR, a working collection can exist for a version-controlled collection. To create a working collection, CHECKOUT a specific version of a version-controlled collection. You can make changes in the working collection, and a new collection version is only created when the working collection is checked in. Since a working collection is a kind of a working resource, the same rules that apply to a working resource apply to a working collection. For example:

- The resource type of the working resource is always the same as the resource type of the version that was checked out. For a working collection, that type is a collection.
- A working resource only exists in checked-out mode. It is destroyed when checked in, or it may be deleted. The same is true for a working collection.

A working collection contains unversioned resources and VHRs but never VCRs. Thus, resources inside a working collection cannot themselves be checked out and checked in. New resources created with MKCOL and PUT are created as unversioned resources. If a working collection is checked in while it contains nonversioned resources, the nonversioned members are converted to versioned resources.

To add a nonversioned resource to a versioned collection and keep the new resource nonversioned, a working collection can't be used, because when it is checked in, unversioned resources are converted to versioned resources. Add the new nonversioned resource to the version-controlled collection (which can be done without checking out the collection at all).

 It's hard to tell if working collections are incompletely specified in DeltaV or if they are simply a complicated concept to begin with. For example, the DeltaV mailing list archives have quite a few confused questions related to moving versioned resources between version-controlled collections when the version-controlled collections are checked out to working collections. I have a terrible time understanding this part of the specification, as well as the answers on the mailing list, which leads me to believe that the feature may be particularly complex or underspecified. Here are some of the issues:

- DeltaV seems to allow MOVE of a VCR into a working collection. However, a working collection can't contain VCRs, only links to VHRs. One way to handle this MOVE would be to find the associated VHR and link that into in the working collection instead. However, VHRs have no target version. When the working collection is checked in, resulting in a moved VCR in the version-controlled collection, it's not clear what the target version of the moved resource should be.
- DeltaV seems to allow MOVE of a VHR from inside a working collection. However, VHRs cannot normally be moved, according to the definition of a VHR.
- Taking the previous two points together, there may be no way to move a resource from one working collection to another. The client could use COPY (which should work the same way as PUT) and then DELETE the source for more reliable behavior.
- If a server does allow a resource to be moved from one working collection to another, and then the first working collection is checked in and the second is deleted, the moved resource may not exist anymore. Some have argued that this is the client's fault and

may result in the resource being deleted from the version-controlled collection in which it originally appeared.

12.6   Other Feature Interactions

Baselines and configurations, subbaselines and subconfigurations, activities, workspaces, and version-controlled collections—all these new kinds of resources potentially interact with each other and with every DeltaV method. Many of these interactions and relationships haven't been explained or pointed out in this chapter. Some examples:

- The target baseline of a configuration may be changed with UPDATE.
- Version-controlled configurations have version trees. Version trees may have branches and merges. Thus, forking and merging may be possible on configurations.
- Version-controlled configurations are VCRs and therefore have all the same auto-version semantics and functionality as regular VCRs.
- Baselines are versions; therefore, they can be labeled.
- A workspace can contain baselined collections, which point to version-controlled configurations.
- A workspace may be under baseline control.
- A workspace may be under version control, turning it into a version-controlled collection.
- A version-controlled collection may also be a baseline-controlled collection. To add members, the version-controlled configuration as well as the version-controlled collection would have to be checked out.
- Version-controlled collections may contain version-controlled collections.
- Version-controlled collections can be auto-versioned so that they don't have to be checked out to have changes made.
- The target version of a version-controlled collection may be changed with UPDATE.
- Version-controlled collections have version trees. Version trees may contain branches and merges. Thus, forking and merging are possible on collections.
- Versions of version-controlled collections may be referenced in baselines.
- Branches of version-controlled collections may be identified by activities.

This chapter only provides an overview of advanced DeltaV features to provide a framework for the reader. To go beyond the framework, the DeltaV specification must be read very carefully. DeltaV defines some of the interactions, but many are left to be deduced according to the definitions of each method, property, and resource.

12.7   DeltaV Features and Packages

In DeltaV, the functionality that can be offered is divided into named **features**. Support for each feature can be advertised in the OPTIONS response by including the feature name in the DAV: header. There are 11 named features, and only one (the version-control feature) is required.

The DeltaV authors realized that the abundance of optional features presented a problem: No client could be expected to interoperate with all the possible variations of server functionality (there are 2^{10} theoretical combinations of advertised features). In an attempt to deal with this issue, several **packages** were defined; a package is a set of features. None of the packages can be advertised (in OPTIONS response or elsewhere), so the client must look for each feature involved in a package to see if the server supports the package. DeltaV only requires that the server "should" support one of the defined packages, so supporting a package is not strictly required.

 In addition to the advertised features, major functionality differences can be inherent in how servers allow and forbid operations and property values. For example, if the server never allows the auto-version property to be set to a value, that implies that the server does not support automatic versioning at all. Another example is that if the server forbids checking out a version that already has a successor, the server does not support branches. These variations in supported functionality can only be discovered through trial and error and much examination of property values.

Certain features are arbitrarily defined in the DeltaV specification as "Basic" features. The "Advanced" features are supposed to add functionality for parallel development and configuration management, yet the workspace feature is Basic and the merge feature is Advanced.

12.7.1 Basic Features

The **version-control** feature is the minimal feature set required by a server claiming to support DeltaV. It exposes the DeltaV data model, including a simple way of checking out and checking in a resource. All the other Basic features are optional, and they all require the version-control feature (see Table 12–1).

Table 12–1 Basic Versioning Features and Concepts

version-control	How to make a nonversioned resource into a VCR. How to automatically create new versions of VCRs when they are changed. • Resource: VCR, version • Methods: VERSION-CONTROL, REPORT • Reports: version-tree, expand-property
checkout-in-place	How to check out a VCR, make several changes, and check in a single new version. How to indicate forking support. • Methods: CHECKIN, CHECKOUT, UNCHECKOUT
version-history	How to collect a related set of versions, no matter how many VCRs point to that set of versions and even if all VCRs pointing to that set have been deleted. • Resource: Version-History Resource • Report: locate-by-history

Table 12–1   Basic Versioning Features and Concepts *(Continued)*

workspace	How to collect several related works-in-progress into a single place (the work-space). How to add a new item to the workspace (VERSION-CONTROL). • Resource: Workspace resource • Method: MKWORKSPACE
update	How to change the target version of a VCR. • Method: UPDATE
label	How to identify versions. • Method: LABEL • Header: Label
working-resource	How to create a single resource on the server, to serve as a place where a work-in-progress can be edited in private. • Methods: CHECKOUT (on a version), CHECKIN, UNCHECKOUT (on a working resource) • Resource: Working Resource

12.7.2   Advanced Features

The advanced DeltaV features are related to configuration control (see Table 12–2). Since a configuration is a set of related VCRs, configuration control is how you manage those files. In other words, configuration management solves the problems encountered in multifile versioning. Configuration control is uniquely found in source control systems, where many code files must work together. Configuration management is done through baselines, activities, and version-controlled collections.

Table 12–2   Quick Reference of Concepts Introduced in Each Advanced Feature

merge	How to combine changes made in a workspace's resources with the original source resources. • Method: MERGE • Report: merge-preview
baseline	How to identify the set of related versions of a number of version-controlled resources. • Resources: baseline, baseline history, version-controlled configuration • Method: BASELINE-CONTROL • Report: compare-baseline

Table 12–2   Quick Reference of Concepts Introduced in Each Advanced Feature *(Continued)*

activity	How to track a single logical change affecting multiple resources (such as adding a new feature to a software project involving multiple source files). How to merge this activity (logical change) into the main repository. How to branch a version-controlled resource. • Resource: activity • Method: MKACTIVITY • Report: latest-activity-version
version-controlled-collection	How to track changes to collections (their list of members) as a history of collection versions. • Resource: Version-controlled collection, collection version, working collection

12.7.3   Core Versioning Package

The **core versioning package** is just the version-control feature. Although it may seem extremely limited by the lack of explicit checkin and checkout ability, a versioning-aware client can gain a modest amount of control over the way versions are created by knowing how LOCK and UNLOCK interact with auto-versioning. A versioning-aware client can also create VCRs and can easily explore past versions of existing VCRs.

12.7.4   Client Workspace Package

The **basic client workspace package** assumes that most of the development and coordination of content takes place on the client machine. The basic client workspace package consists of:

- version-control
- working-resource
- update
- label

The client workspace package is for systems where the general assumption is that ongoing changes are saved only on each developer's machine. During this time, other users don't see the changes in progress. Other users see the modifications only when the files are checked in.

To make this model work, clients create working resources with every checkout. The client can actually upload the contents at any time, but since working resources generally don't appear to other users, the changes aren't seen until checkin. Thus checkout-in-place is not part of this model, even though it might be useful to handle non-DeltaV clients.

A well-known source control system with approximately this model is CVS. However, the terminology used in CVS is rather different from that used in DeltaV. For example, a CVS "checkout" is an operation that downloads initial copies of all the VCRs from the server to the client and is only done once, when a user starts working on a new CVS module. In DeltaV, this is done with GET. A CVS "update" downloads and merges new content (for a module that has already been "checked out" in the CVS sense). In DeltaV, this is done with GET and PROPFIND (and the client is responsible for doing merges locally). Finally, a CVS "commit" operation uploads one or many changes to the server, creating a new version of each changed resource. In DeltaV, this is done with CHECKOUT, PUT, PROPPATCH, and CHECKIN for each changed resource. The terminology differences don't prevent DeltaV from being used as a framework for standards-based access to a CVS-style server.

DeltaV also defines an **advanced client workspace package**, which adds all the advanced features (merge, baselines, activities, version-controlled collections).

12.7.5 Server Workspace Package

In the basic server workspace model, clients are expected to do their work largely on the server. Many more PUT and PROPPATCH operations will be expected. The **basic server workspace package** includes:

- version-control
- workspace
- version-history (required by workspace)
- checkout-in-place

Server workspaces have several advantages over client workspaces. First, with a client workspace, there may be a greater chance that work in progress will be accidentally lost, because the client machine is likely to be less reliable than the server repository. Second, the author may find it inconvenient to store work-in-progress on the client machine if the author ever has to use another machine, because the work-in-progress isn't automatically transferred between one client machine and another. More rarely, multiple users may want to collaborate on a file in a workspace. Server-side workspaces are sometimes supported in order to achieve the benefits of workspaces without the disadvantages of storing them on the client machine. However, a slow server or slow connection can make this model less usable.

DeltaV also defines an **advanced server workspace package**, which adds all the advanced features (merge, baselines, activities, version-controlled collections).

12.7.6 Feature Dependencies

The DeltaV specification points out some feature dependencies. For example, it's impossible to construct a workspace without VHRs, so the workspace feature requires support for the version-history feature. In addition, there are near-dependencies, where one feature isn't very useful without another. For example, the merge feature isn't very useful unless version trees have forks, and forks aren't common unless the server supports either working resources or workspaces.

> ### Workspace and Other Features
>
> Workspaces are much more useful with the merge and update features supported as well, yet workspace is part of the basic server workspace package, and merge and update aren't.
>
> Merge is the primary mechanism to make work from one workspace appear in another workspace. Update is also useful because when a VCR inside a workspace is checked in, this won't automatically affect the checked-in property of the other VCRs that point to the same VHR. The client must send an UPDATE request to the VCR in the main repository to make that VCR point to the newest version created through the workspace.

Figure 12–12 shows the official dependencies noted in DeltaV with solid lines and practical dependencies with dashed lines.

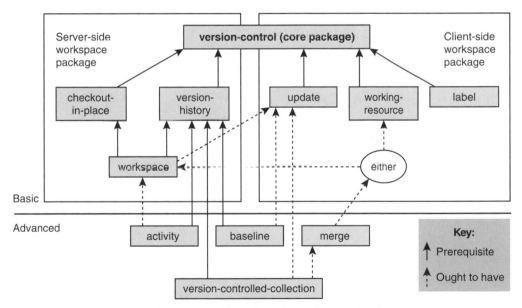

Figure 12–12   Versioning features and how they depend on each other.

12.8 Summary

This chapter introduced the DeltaV features used in managing versioning when multiple files with interdependencies are involved.

Workspaces allow multiple developers to independently change multiple files in different areas of the repository. Activities and merges are used to coordinate between developers and synchronize between workspaces. An activity can encompass a number of changed files that are checked in together atomically, or an activity can identify a number of versions in branches of multiple files that belong in the same line of work. Either way, an activity is conceptually what a developer is working on.

Configurations and version-controlled collections allow the histories of multiple files to be correlated. A configuration does this by acting as a versionable resource representing a repository or a project. Each time the configuration is revised, a new baseline is created to represent the project at that point in time. A version-controlled collection is a collection whose membership is under version control.

DeltaV offers packages of recommended features. Servers can support one of these packages in order to offer a useful combination of functionality:

- Core Versioning package
- Client Workspace package
- Server Workspace package
- Advanced Client Workspace package
- Advanced Server Workspace package

CHAPTER 13

Access Control

J ust because a document is on a Web server doesn't mean that every-body can read and write it. Web pages on many public sites can be read by everybody but written only by authorized authors. The process of allowing some access to some users and not others is called **access control**. Administrators can configure Web servers with lists of what requests to allow, from whom, and to what resources. These lists are called **access control lists** (ACLs); they contain **access control entries** (ACEs). The WebDAV ACL proposal (in the final stages of standardization as of fall 2003) defines how a WebDAV client can interact with the server and potentially define the instructions in the server's ACLs.

WebDAV was originally standardized without access control because there was enough work to do simply standardizing the material in RFC2518. Access control is very hard to stan-dardize. To start with, existing Web servers had completely incompatible access control models and couldn't make a change that would be incompatible with their deployed base.

In practice, lack of standard access control hasn't harmed the deployment of WebDAV too badly. ACLs are often set out-of-band by administrators rather than by users. When this is the case, administrators don't need WebDAV protocol elements or standards to set access controls. Instead, in most current systems, administrators use some direct interface to server software.

However, standardized access control is quite useful in many WebDAV scenarios. Intranet file sharing is more efficient when users can grant access to their resources without having to bother the administrator. Web site authoring benefits even more from the ability to set access control from remote standardized clients.

This chapter explains the ACL model and all the concepts from the ACL draft, but it doesn't describe all the details of the syntax. The syntax may still change slightly if ACL requires more modification to become a standard, but the model looks pretty firm. Some server and client implementors, including SAP and Xythos, already support the ACL proposal and have achieved mutual interoperability.

13.0.1 Prior Approaches

Before WebDAV ACLs were standardized, WebDAV servers had various approaches to setting ACLs on resources. For example, Xythos WebFile Server has a server-hosted, Web-based GUI so that users can change their own resource ACLs using a Web browser. Microsoft IIS 5.0 allows remote Web authors to change ACLs using SMB (the local file-sharing protocol), which restricts non-Windows users from managing permissions. Exchange 2000 used a WebDAV property to allow all users to read and write the ACL for a mailbox, calendar, or resource, but only Windows-based software could easily parse the format of the property value.

If all WebDAV servers had a Web-based GUI for setting access control, one could imagine declaring that the standard. The only thing client software would need is some way to know the link to the Web-based GUI, display that GUI to the user, and allow the user to change ACLs that way. With this approach, the server could present any list of privileges, any model for access control, and any interface it chose. This is the "dumb client," or thin client model.

The thin client model already exists in Web-based user interfaces and can hardly be called a standard. It is unacceptable to implementors of rich clients. Rich clients need control over the presentation to have a consistent and usable user interface. The thin client model is also extremely unwieldy for handling bulk changes. The WebDAV Working Group knew of these problems and started working on standardizing ACLs even before the WebDAV RFC was published.

WebDAV ACLs are designed to be roughly compatible with NFS version 4 [RFC3010] and Windows NT File System (NTFS) access controls. A server implementation ought to be able to store files and set permissions directly in any NTFS or NFS-compatible file system and expose this system interoperably over WebDAV.

13.1 What Is Access Control?

The most basic form of access control, found in almost all file systems, is *a way to grant a long-term privilege to access a resource to a user or group*. That description can be taken as the problem statement for WebDAV access control. Let's look at each part of this problem statement and the features commonly or rarely found in existing repositories, particularly file systems.

Access is granted to resources in the repository. If a file exists named index.html, it's generally possible to grant privileges specifically for index.html. When the resource is a directory, the privileges may also apply to resources inside the directory. Granularity to the level of properties, however, is rare. The server enforces access control for all resources in the repository.

Access to resources is granted to users or groups. Access control information must identify users and groups in order for the server to grant permission to the specified principals. The server must be able to authenticate users and know enough about group membership to decide whether to grant access based on group membership.

Roles and certificates are advanced authorization features not commonly seen in shared file systems.

Authentication

User authentication is typically handled separately from access control. WebDAV supports the HTTP user authentication mechanisms [RFC2617]. Both standard HTTP mechanisms offer a way to identify the user (with a user name and optionally a realm). The access control specification assumes that the server has some way to authenticate users and uniquely identify them, although this may be some nonstandard mechanism such as NTLM authentication for HTTP or session cookies.

Let's see what information a simple ACL contains in a quick example before proceeding. Assume there is a group called `hr-group` with members Alice, Bob, and Carl. The access control information for `index.html` includes the following permissions and ownership:

```
Grant administer to the owner
Grant write to hr-group
Grant read to all
The owner is Alice
```

With this list of permissions, a write operation with authentication from Alice, Bob, or Carl will be allowed, but not from any other user. Alice owns and thus can administer the

---

Locks and Access Control

WebDAV locks can be likened to a temporary revocation of write permission for all users except the lock owner. Although locks do cause write operations to be forbidden, this comparison fails to describe important parts of lock functionality.

- Locks are held not just by a user but also by a specific WebDAV client process. The lock protects the document from other software authenticated as the same user.
- You can lock a resource, change its permissions, and unlock it again, since locking and access control are independent. In fact, I recommend locking resources while changing permissions.
- Locks time out.
- Locks identify who is currently changing the resource and hopefully even what client software package holds the lock. In contrast, write permission may be granted to many principals who may not currently be editing the resource.

resource, although we're not yet sure what that might mean. The **all** user is not a real user, it's a special principal name that encompasses any user (sometimes called "public" or "guest"). Thus, the server will allow read requests from any user, with or without authentication.

13.1.1 Access Control Model

The access control model for WebDAV resources was very consciously derived from existing file system practice, with slight adaptations to handle properties.

Access is divided into several well-defined **privileges**. The most common privileges are the right to **read** a file and the right to **write** it (change or update it). Other possible privileges are:

- The ability to delete the resource (may be covered by the write privilege)
- The ability to read properties or metadata (may be covered by the read privilege)
- The ability to write properties or metadata (may be covered by the write privilege)
- The ability to read the ACL
- The ability to alter the ACL
- The ability to view the contents if the resource is a collection (sometimes this is covered by the read privilege)

When a privilege is not **granted** to a user (directly or as a member of a group), that type of operation is not allowed.

A resource may have an **owner** who is treated specially for access control. The owner of the file can have irrevocable privileges, such as the privilege to change access control settings. If all privileges could be taken away from everybody, the resource could be put into a state where nobody can do anything on it, including changing privileges. If the owner has the irrevocable privilege to set access control, then the owner can always fix up the resource and grant privileges to those who should have them.

Each resource has one ACL. (The acronym ACL, pronounced "ackle," is also used to refer to the functionality provided by access control in general.) The ACL contains a number of ACEs. On simple systems, a resource's ACL contains all the privilege information relating to that resource.

Each access control entry identifies a single **principal**. A principal can be a named user or a named **group** (a group is a collection of named users). The principal can also be a special kind of role or characteristic identifier such as *all users* or *all authenticated users*. Each entry in an ACL names a principal using a **principal ID**.

Within an ACE, multiple privileges can be granted or denied to a single identified principal. That means that each principal named in the access control list must have its own entry. For example, if read access on `index.html` is granted to "all" and write access is granted to "hr-group," this must be two access control entries, which together form an ACL.

13.2 Getting Access Control Information

The WebDAV ACL specification defines how to retrieve and interpret ACL and principal information, as well as how to modify some of that information. We begin with the task of retrieval and interpretation. That will provide a framework to understand how to modify access control information.

13.2.1 Principal URLs

In WebDAV ACL support, principal IDs are in the form of an HTTP URL. In fact, the principal URL is the address for a WebDAV resource that represents a user and can be queried with PROPFIND. Principal resources exist inside principal collections, which are also WebDAV resources. This is just an easy way to represent principals in a familiar way so that clients can access them easily.

Not much can really be done with principal resources. It's not expected that clients will be allowed to copy, move, delete, or create new principal resources. A principal resource must of course have all of the standard WebDAV resource properties, plus a special property displayname. Thus, a client can easily retrieve an appropriate string for displaying a principal in the UI: Send a PROPFIND request to the principal URL and ask for the displayname value.

Groups are also represented as principal resources. A group isn't the same thing as a principal collection, which just exists as a collection containing principals. A principal resource will likely exist in one principal collection only but be a member of several groups. To represent members, a group resource has a group-member-set property containing the principal URLs of its members. A principal (user or group) also has a property called group-membership listing all the groups that the principal is a member of.

The collections containing groups and users can be organized a number of ways. One simple way is to identify one collection for all users and another for all groups.

```
http://www.example.com/principals/users/
http://www.example.com/principals/groups/
```

13.2.2 Identifying a Resource Owner

If each resource has an owner, it's pretty important to see who that owner is. The owner property on a resource contains the principal URL of the user who owns and can administer the resource. The principal URL appears inside an href element, which is a standard WebDAV syntax for an HTTP URL.

The client can use PROPFIND to request the owner property. The response contains the owner property value, as shown in Listing 13–1.

This PROPFIND response fragment shows that the user identified by http://www.example.org/principals/ids/alice is the owner of the hr/ collection. This HTTP URL is the principal ID, but it's also a real WebDAV resource address. As I'll show in Section 13.4.5, that URL can also be used to query the resource it names, to retrieve a minimal set of information about the user it identifies. The URL that uniquely identifies a user or any other principal is called the **principal URL**.

Listing 13–1   Owner property in partial PROPFIND response.

```
<D:response>
   <D:href>http://www.example.com/hr/</D:href>
   <D:propstat>
      <D:prop>
         <D:owner>
            <D:href>http://www.example.com/principals/ids/alice
            </D:href>
         </D:owner>
      </D:prop>
      <D:status>HTTP/1.1 200 OK</D:status>
   </D:propstat>
</D:response>
```

The owner property may be a rather widely available piece of information, depending on a system's policy. Users who can read a file sometimes need to see who the owner is to ask that the permissions be changed. It's common for this property to be visible to any principal who can read the resource.

13.2.3   Getting ACLs

Since each resource has a single ACL, retrieving the ACL is done through a simple PROPFIND for the acl property. Each acl property contains a number of ace elements, one for each principal to whom access privileges are granted or denied (see Listing 13–2).

Listing 13–2   Example value for acl property.

```
<D:acl>
   <D:ace>
      <D:principal>
         <D:href>http://www.example.com/principals/ids/hr-group/
         </D:href>
      </D:principal>
      <D:grant> <D:privilege> <D:write/> </D:privilege> </ D:grant>
   </D:ace>
   <D:ace>
      <D:principal>
         <D:all/>
      </D:principal>
      <D:grant> <D:privilege> <D:read/> </D:privilege> </ D:grant>
   </D:ace>
</D:acl>
```

In this example, the `hr-group` (and all its members) may write the resource, and all principals may read the resource. That means that members of the `hr-group` can also read the resource. Although the read privilege can be explicitly granted to the group, it need not be.

13.2.4 Privileges Vary

Not all systems have privileges as straightforward as "read" and "write." In fact, read and write aren't that simple themselves. Does "read" mean that the user can read the resource body? Can the user read the resource properties? Can the user read the acl property? On some systems, the answer would be yes, but on most systems, access to the acl property is not granted to all users with access to the resource body.

The ACL designers quickly realized that with privileges, one size does not fit all. Nobody could agree on a single list of privileges with well-defined meanings. Some systems had as few as three or four privileges on a resource, while others had closer to 20. Some pure WebDAV implementations had already exposed access control through some nonstandard method such as Web-based administration pages. Other WebDAV implementations were built to expose a pre-existing file system, complete with its ACL information. For example, Apache permissions have always been respected by mod_dav, and MS IIS5 exposed resources in NTFS with NTFS ACLs. There is necessarily a semantic gap between any standard list of privilege definitions and the "real world" as found in various file systems and repositories.

If a WebDAV resource is an object that can be exposed through other protocols as well (FTP, SMB, CIFS), it's very important that the permissions be consistent across all protocols. It's already hard enough to administer permissions correctly without having variation in what permissions are granted through different protocols.

The complexity of existing systems leads to the requirement for a very flexible system for specifying what privileges can be granted. Thus, the privilege list on a server can be defined by that server and published so that client software can see what privileges may be granted or denied on that server. The ACL specification can attempt to define a standard list of privileges, but some implementations will deviate from the standard list.

13.2.5 Standard Privileges

The WebDAV ACL specification does define a list of standard privileges, because if a server *can* support the standard list, client interoperability with that server should be easier.

A standard list of privileges can be very simple and coarse; for example, `read`, `write`, and `administer`. At the other extreme, a standard list of privileges could attempt to be more granular than any actual implementation by defining a large number of extremely specific privileges. The WebDAV ACL specification took the Goldilocks approach, attempting to come up with a reasonable list of privileges, not too coarse and not too granular.

- `read`: Read a resource body, or if a collection, list its children, or read ordinary properties.
- `write-properties`: Change value of ordinary properties of the resource.

- `write-content`: Write a resource body, or if a collection, change its list of children by adding, removing or renaming a child.
- `write`: Both `write-properties` and `write-content`, and including also `lock resource`.
- `unlock`: Remove a lock without having to be the owner of the lock.
- `read-acl`: Read the acl property.
- `read-current-user-privilege-set`: Read the current-user-privilege-set property.
- `write-acl`: Use the ACL method to modify the acl property.
- `all`: All of the above privileges.

Note that two of these standard privileges contain others. That's because it might be syntactically and semantically possible to grant `all` but deny `write-acl`. The `all` privilege is a shortcut to make setting access control easier. The "'write" privilege contains both `write-properties` and `write-content`.

Writing Properties

The entire set of properties is covered by a single `write-properties` privilege. It's rare to have separate write privileges apply to individual properties on a resource. However, it is still possible for the server software to enforce a different server policy on certain properties. For example, the server can prevent the creationdate property from being changed by anyone. That kind of policy doesn't require a specific privilege or ACE for that property. It is a protected property and "immune" from access control. Similarly, some properties could be restricted by policy only to be written by the resource owner. To help interoperability, any custom or dead properties should be directly governed by the standard `write-properties` permission.

13.2.6 Privilege Composition

The standard list of privileges can also serve as a basis for understanding a custom list of privileges. A custom list of privileges probably has at least some relationship to standard concepts like "read" and "write." Therefore, the WebDAV ACL specification defines a way to show these relationships. Servers can advertise how their custom ACL model maps to the standard privileges.

Information for Rich and Automated Clients

A "dumb" client might simply present the server's list of custom privileges to a user and give the user no assistance in selecting or understanding those privileges. That's not acceptable to rich client designers, and it's impossible for automated clients to use. For these reasons, custom privileges are defined in terms of standard privileges.

Based on the WebDAV standard privileges, which are not too coarse and not too granular, there are four basic approaches for a server implementation:

- The most obvious and interoperable approach is for a WebDAV ACL implementation to expose exactly this list of privileges. The server advertises to clients that it supports exactly the standard meaning of each standard privilege. That makes it easy for WebDAV clients to display and change ACLs.
- If a server implementation must have custom privileges that are more coarse than the standard privileges, the server can advertise a set of privileges that are composed of the standard privileges. One custom privilege can tie together two standard privileges. A client implementation can still deal with this in a number of ways. Possibly the client would show all the standard privileges, but when the user grants one privilege that is tied to a second, the client automatically shows the second privilege as being granted as well.
- If a server implementation must have custom privileges that are more fine-grained than the standard privileges, the server can advertise its custom privilege as a subset of the standard privilege. Two custom privileges can both be subsets of the same standard privilege. Again, a client implementation can deal with this in a number of ways. Possibly the client would show all the standard privileges. When a user attempts to grant a standard privilege, the client would grant both of the custom privileges that map to the standard privilege.
- Finally, it's possible that a server implementation will have some custom privileges that are more coarse and others that are more fine-grained than the standard privileges. If the previous two models are supported, this could also be supported. The custom privileges are advertised as either subsets or compositions of the standard privileges.

Since the server must advertise what privileges it supports and how its custom privileges relate to standard privileges, WebDAV ACLs define a property to advertise this information. The property with this information is the supported-privilege-set property. It can have a different value on each resource in a repository because the repository may have different privileges defined for collections, regular resources, or other resource types.

The supported-privilege-set property contains a tree of `supported-privilege` elements, including every one of the standard privileges. The tree is a way of showing hierarchy.

- If a standard privilege contains one or more custom privileges, then the custom privileges are subsets, or more granular.
- If one or more standard privileges are contained by a custom privilege, then the custom privilege is a composition, or more coarse.
- The `all` privilege must be at the root of the tree.

 Even if the standard privilege is not directly supported, it must appear in the tree. To show that the standard privilege is not directly supported, it is marked as "abstract." The server will not permit clients to directly grant or deny an abstract privilege. If a server defines a standard privilege as abstract, then it must define at least one custom privilege that is either a composition or a subset of that standard privilege.

If a custom privilege is a composition including an abstract standard privilege, then that standard privilege can only be granted by granting the custom privilege. This also grants whatever else that concrete privilege entails. For example, a server may define `read-acl` as abstract, and define the concrete privilege `administer` as a superset of `read-acl`. From this definition of `administer`, the client can understand that granting the `administer` privilege will include the permission to read ACLs.

If an abstract standard privilege contains custom privileges, then the custom privileges are a subset of the standard privilege. To get the effect of granting the standard privilege, grant all the concrete privileges that it contains. For example, a server may define `read` as abstract, and define the concrete privileges `read-content` and `read-comments` as subsets of the `read` privilege. From this definition, the client can understand that in order to grant `read`, it must grant both `read-content` and `read-comments`.

Listing 13–3 is a full example value for the supported-privilege-set property. This example illustrates a server implementation with very simplistic and limited permissions, only supporting `read`, `write`, and the custom privilege `administer`. Most of the standard privileges are declared as `abstract` or not directly supported.

Listing 13–3 Example value for supported-privilege-set.

```
<supported-privilege-set xmlns="DAV:">
   <supported-privilege>
      <privilege> <all/> </privilege> <abstract/>
      <supported-privilege>
         <privilege> <read> </privilege>
      </supported-privilege>
      <supported-privilege>
         <privilege> <write/> </privilege>
         <supported-privilege>
            <privilege> <write-properties/> </privilege> <abstract/>
         </supported-privilege>
         <supported-privilege>
            <privilege> <write-content/> </privilege> <abstract/>
         </supported-privilege>
      </supported-privilege>
   </supported-privilege>
   <supported-privilege>
      <privilege><C:administer xmlns:C="http:// www.example.com/"/>
      </privilege>
      <description xml:lang="en">Administer the permissions and
         locks of this resource</description>
      <supported-privilege>
         <privilege> <read-acl/> </privilege> <abstract/>
```

Listing 13–3   Example value for supported-privilege-set. *(Continued)*

```
        </supported-privilege>
        <supported-privilege>
            <privilege> <write-acl/> </privilege> <abstract/>
        </supported-privilege>
        <supported-privilege>
            <privilege><read-current-user-privilege-set/>
            </privilege> <abstract/>
        </supported-privilege>
        <supported-privilege>
            <privilege> <unlock/> </privilege> <abstract/>
        </supported-privilege>
    </supported-privilege>
</supported-privilege-set>
```

Note that all privileges are abstract except `read`, `write`, and the custom `administer` privilege. The custom privilege is defined in the `http://www.example.com/` namespace, not in the `DAV:` namespace. Here's an English explanation of this example:

- The `all` abstract privilege encompasses everything else, but it's not directly supported.
- The `read` privilege is a standard privilege that is supported normally.
- The standard `write` privilege is also directly supported.
- The `write-content` and `write-properties` privileges are not supported, so they're declared abstract, and shown as subsets of `write` because that's how they're defined in the specification.
- The custom `administer` privilege includes the permission to read ACLs, write ACLs, and unlock other users' locks on the resource. Thus, four more standard privileges are shown as `abstract` to show that they are not directly supported.

Figure 13–1 is another way to view the same supported-privilege-set property value. The `read`, `write`, and `administer` privileges—the only privileges that can be granted—are shown in bold. All of the privileges in the model are directly from the ACL standard except the `administer` privilege, which is custom.

Based on these relationships, a client ought to be able to take the user's intent, and as long as it's not more complicated than the model allows, translate that intent into privileges the server supports.

- If a user wants to grant the `write-content` privilege, the client can't grant that privilege directly. It can only offer the ability to grant the `write` privilege, in which case the `write-properties` privilege is also granted.

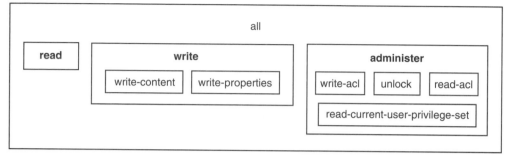

Figure 13–1   Privilege containment.

- If a user wants to grant the `read-acl` privilege, the client must grant `administer` privilege, which also grants the ability to do `write-acl` and `unlock` as well.
- If a user wants to grant all privileges at once, the client must separately grant `read`, `write`, and `administer`.

Thus, standard ACL clients can still use the server with this limited set of privileges. The simple permission model maps clearly onto the standard WebDAV ACL privilege set, and this mapping can be explained by showing how concrete privileges encompass abstract privileges.

Text Description of Custom Privileges

The supported-privilege-set property has optional descriptions for each privilege. The client has the option to show the user the server's description (choosing the most appropriate language option available from the server), and hope the user can figure it out.
The text description is most useful when the custom permissions are more granular than the standard permissions. For example, a server could define two custom privileges called `read-content` and `read-properties` inside `read`. The client software can't know what these custom privileges mean, but with a description, a human may be able to figure it out.

Because this mechanism for defining privileges allows so much flexibility for server implementation, there is added risk that interoperability will suffer. Client implementors may decide that the privilege model hierarchy is too complicated to parse and understand. We'll see how it plays out as client implementations develop and mature.

13.2.7   Finding Current User's Permissions

Typically, users are not allowed to read the entire ACL for a resource owned by somebody else. Sometimes this is a security precaution to limit users from finding out who they would have to impersonate to gain more access. Still, it would be pretty convenient for the client software to see what privileges are granted before attempting operations. A smart client wouldn't attempt operations known to be forbidden. In fact, a smart client would not even present those operations to the user. (Typically in GUI clients, operations that are forbidden are shown gray and are unclickable, to prevent the user from attempting an operation that will fail.)

It's easy to resolve this dilemma, because there is no security concern if the client can find out what the current authenticated user is allowed to do. (The client could find this out anyway through trial and error.) The current-user-privilege-set property contains this information, in the form of a list of privileges granted. This property must be supported on any resource that supports ACLs (see Listing 13–4).

Listing 13–4 Example value for current-user-privilege-set property.

```
<D:current-user-privilege-set>
   <D:privilege> <D:read/> <D:write/> </D:privilege>
</D:current-user-privilege-set>
```

This value is shown for the same resource used in Listing 13–2 to show the ACL property value. The current user is authenticated as a member of the group hr-group, so the write privilege granted only to members of hr-group is granted to the current user. The current user can do read and write operations, but not view or change the ACL for the resource.

Servers supporting ACLs should return this property with a value even when it's requested by an unauthenticated user. Thus, if the user is unauthenticated and the resource is publicly readable, the privilege set would include read.

13.3   Setting Access Control Information

If a user has permission to write the acl property on a resource, the client should be able to modify the ACL and govern how the resource may be accessed.

Although there is a standard mechanism to change the ACL, there is no standard way to change the owner of a resource. The owner property is a protected property and must be changed through administrator software access to the repository, not through WebDAV.

13.3.1   Setting ACL

PROPPATCH is not used to change or set the ACL for a resource, even though PROPFIND is used to retrieve it. A couple of issues led to this choice:

- The server may parse the ACL, reorder it, or otherwise change the value, based on what the client submits. In other words, even if the client's request to change the ACL succeeds, the value of the acl property may not be exactly what the client sent. This doesn't correspond to the general model for PROPPATCH.

• The PROPPATCH method is used to change all kinds of metadata, most of which is not nearly as sensitive as the ACL. By using a separate method to set the ACL, the design allows firewalls to easily block attempts from outside to change WebDAV access control information.

The ACL request is simple enough: It takes a body with the proposed value of the acl property. It should not use the Depth header; it is defined only for one resource (see Listing 13–5).

Listing 13–5   ACL request to set access control for a resource.

Request:
```
ACL /hr/index.html HTTP/1.1
Host: www.example.com
Content-Type: text/xml; charset="utf-8"
Content-Length: xxxx
Authorization: xxxx
↵
<?xml version="1.0" encoding="utf-8" ?>
<D:acl xmlns:D="DAV:">
   <D:ace>
      <D:principal>
         <D:href>http://www.example.com/principals/groups/hr-group/
         </D:href>
      </D:principal>
      <D:grant>
         <D:privilege> <D:read/> </D:privilege>
         <D:privilege> <D:write/> </D:privilege>
      </D:grant>
   </D:ace>

   <D:ace>
      <D:principal>
         <D:property> <D:owner/> </D:property>
      </D:principal>
      <D:grant>
         <D:privilege> <C:administer/> </D:privilege>
      </D:grant>
   </D:ace>

   <D:ace>
      <D:principal> <D:all/> </D:principal>
      <D:grant>
         <D:privilege> <D:read/> </D:privilege>
```

Listing 13–5   ACL request to set access control for a resource. *(Continued)*

```
      </D:grant>
    </D:ace>
</D:acl>
```

Response:
```
HTTP/1.1 200 OK
Date: Mon, 27 May 2002 15:23:19 GMT
⌐
```

This example shows the read and write privileges being granted to the group `hr-group`, the `administer` privilege granted to whoever the owner is, and the `read` privilege granted to all principals. Whatever the ACL was before this request, it is replaced with this after the request.

13.3.2 Semantic Complications

The ACL supplied in Listing 13–5 is fairly easy to understand in isolation. However, the reality of granting permissions can be much more complicated. WebDAV servers may use inheritance, ACE ordering, or other optional advanced features that can subtly affect the permissions algorithms. To understand these advanced features, both client and server implementors need to read the WebDAV ACL specification carefully. A brief overview:

1. Not all servers parse ACEs in the same order or apply the same precedence rules. The acl-semantics property gives the client a hint how the server will order and parse ACEs. Most of the time, simple ACLs such as the previous one will be handled the same way by every server implementation. The complications only matter when the ACEs may overlap; for example, privileges are granted and denied to both users and groups containing those users. These options may be restricted in the next version of the draft.

2. Servers can protect some ACEs. The client cannot remove ACEs protected by the server. The client may not know which ACEs are protected until it attempts to remove one of them.

3. Servers can allow privileges to be denied in addition to being granted. The server must declare this in the acl-semantics property. All clients must be able to handle denied privileges as well as granted privileges when displaying ACEs to users, because it makes a big difference to the user whether a privilege is denied, granted, or neither.

4. A server may support dynamic ACL inheritance. If a resource inherits ACLs, it processes access control rules not just from its own ACL but also from other locations. Because this inheritance is dynamic, changes in ACLs at those other locations may affect operations immediately on the original resource. The specification defines a property on resources that can point to those sources, so they can be examined as well. However, a user may not have permission to see all the ACLs that would be required to

figure out what is allowed and what isn't. This feature is underspecified because it doesn't allow the client to figure out exactly what permissions are inherited or how to make permissions inheritable.

13.4 Principals

As we've seen in ACLs and owner property values, each principal is uniquely identified by a principal URL. That URL is not just an opaque string, because it must be the address of a Web-DAV resource that represents that user. The WebDAV resource representing a user or a group is called a **principal resource**. The principal resource for a user can be used to find more information about the user, particularly the user's displayname.

Although the principal URL will not often be displayed to users, it is the official identity of the principal and must be used whenever a principal must be uniquely identified.

13.4.1 Finding Principal Information

Once we have a principal URL for Alice, what can we do with it? In the WebDAV Access Control specification, a principal is a very simple WebDAV resource. Thus, we can ask that resource for its properties. Listing 13–6 shows a request for all of the properties that are defined by ACL on a principal resource. The response has values for all these properties, naturally.

Listing 13–6 PROPFIND request and response with principal properties.

Request:

```
PROPFIND /principals/ids/alice HTTP/1.1
Host: www.example.com
Content-Type: text/xml
Content-Length: 200
Depth: 0

<?xml version="1.0" encoding="utf-8" ?>
<D:propfind xmlns:D="DAV:">
<D:prop>
   <D:resourcetype/><D:displayname/><D:principal-URL/>
   <D:alternate-URI-set/><D:group-membership/>
</D:prop>
</D:propfind>
```

Response:

```
HTTP/1.0 207 Multi-Status
Content-Type: text/xml; charset=UTF-8
Content-Length: 654
Date: Mon, 27 May 2002 17:23:25 GMT
Server: Tomcat Web Server/3.3.1 Final (JSP 1.1; Servlet 2.2)
```

Listing 13–6   PROPFIND request and response with principal properties. *(Continued)*

```
<?xml version="1.0" encoding="utf-8" ?>
<D:multistatus xmlns:D="DAV:">
   <D:response>
      <D:href>http://localhost/xythoswfs/principals/ids/alice
      </D:href>
      <D:propstat>
         <D:prop>
            <D:resourcetype><D:principal/></D:resourcetype>
            <D:displayname>Alice Wetherill</D:displayname>
            <D:principal-URL><D:href>
               http://www.example.com/principals/ids/alice
            </D:href></D:principal-URL>
            <D:alternate-URI-set>
               <D:href>ldap://ldap.example.com/ cn=Alice%20Wetherill, ↵
                  dc=example,dc=com</D:href>
            </D:alternate-URI-set>
            <D:group-membership>
               <D:href>http://www.example.com/principals/groups/↵
                  hr-group</D:href>
            </D:group-membership>
         </D:prop>
         <D:status>HTTP/1.1 200 OK</D:status>
      </D:propstat>
   </D:response>
</D:multistatus>
```

The principal resource has a resourcetype of `<D:principal/>`. This principal resource has a displayname property value of `Alice Wetherill` and is a member of the group `hr-group`.

The official principal URL is shown in the principal-URL property; it's the same URL used to query the principal properties. Principal resources can appear elsewhere (e.g., inside a group collection), in which case the principal URL becomes useful to point to the official URL for querying principal properties.

The alternate-URI-set property is used to show if there is more information about the principal that can be looked up elsewhere. This could be an address to a Lightweight Directory Access Protocol (LDAP) [RFC2251] directory entry. If the company in our example had a SunONE directory server [LDAP03] (previously the Netscape directory server [LDAP02]), the URL to the directory entry corresponding to Alice might look something like it does in Listing 13–6.

13.4.2   Finding Group Membership

Group principal resources have some of the same properties as user principal resources: displayname, resourcetype, and alternate-URI-set. In addition, groups have a group-member-set property to list the principals within a group. This property has the same format as the group-membership property: It contains any number of `href` elements, and each `href` element contains the URI of a principal. A PROPFIND to a group resource principal, asking for the group-member-set property, would return a value as shown in Listing 13–7.

Listing 13–7   PROPFIND request and response with principal properties.

```
<D:group-member-set>
    <D:href>http://www.example.com/principals/ids/alice</ D:href>
    <D:href>http://www.example.com/principals/ids/bob</D:href>
    <D:href>http://www.example.com/principals/ids/carl</D:href>
</D:group-member-set>
```

13.4.3   Shortcut for Displaying Principals from ACLs

The principal URL is great for uniquely identifying principals, but it isn't very friendly for displaying to users. Section 13.4.1 showed how to query a principal resource to find out the properties of a principal, like the display name. That's great for one principal, like the principal found in the owner property. However, it will be very common for a client to want properties (like displayname) for all the principals listed in an acl property, and it's not very efficient to have to issue one PROPFIND for each principal.

To make this more efficient, there is a special report, **acl-principal-prop-set**, to query the server for information on all the principals named in an acl property. The REPORT method for retrieving reports is defined in DeltaV (introduced in this book in Section 11.10.1), and the ACL specification defines four new reports that servers must support. The acl-principal-prop-set report allows the client to quickly retrieve properties for all the principals referred to in an ACL.

The REPORT method is defined so that the REPORT request is addressed to a particular resource supporting that type of report. In this case, any resource that has an ACL should support this report. In the body of the REPORT request, the client may specify what properties to return. The response is a multi-status, in exactly the same format as a PROPFIND response with one `response` element for each principal resource. Listing 13–8 shows only the request, in which the client asks for the displayname property for every principal listed in the ACL.

Listing 13–8   REPORT request for acl-principal-prop-set report.

```
REPORT /index.html HTTP/1.1
Host: www.webdav.org
Content-Type: text/xml; charset="utf-8"
Content-Length: xxxx
↵
```

Listing 13–8 REPORT request for acl-principal-prop-set report. *(Continued)*

```
<?xml version="1.0" encoding="utf-8" ?>
<D:acl-principal-prop-set xmlns:D="DAV:">
<D:prop><D:displayname/></D:prop>
</D:acl-principal-prop-set>
```

13.4.4 Who Am I?

The **principal-match** report (which also uses the DeltaV REPORT method) is a multipurpose report. First, it allows the client to find what principal matched the user's authentication credentials. It also allows the client to make many more general queries based on the current user's principal URL. Basically, the report looks for resources in a certain scope, where a specified property contains the current user's principal URL. The REPORT request identifies the scope by addressing a collection and specifies the name of property to examine.

Depending on what collection is addressed and what property is examined, this report can be used for a couple of things:

- Find out "who am I logged in as?" or in other words, "what is the principal-URL for my user authentication context?" This is done by addressing a principal collection in the request-URI of the REPORT request and by specifying the principal-URL property. If there are multiple principal collections, the client might have to ask each one.
- Find out "what groups am I in?" by addressing a collection of groups and specifying the group-member-set property.
- Find out "what resources do I own in this collection?" This is done by addressing a regular collection in the request-URI of the REPORT request and by specifying the owner property.
- If a custom property authors appeared on every resource and contained principal URLs, the report could theoretically be used to find out "what resources am I an author of?"

The principal-match report must be requested for a collection, but it can be any kind of collection (collection of principals, groups, or regular resources). The chosen property is specified in a simple XML body.

Before the client can query a principal collection to find out "who am I," the client must find out the name of a principal collection. This is done by querying a regular resource, using PROPFIND, to find out the value of the principal-collection-set property. Let's assume that this property value returns only one principal collection URL: `http://www.example.com/principals/`, so only one REPORT request is needed to find out who is the current user.

Note that reports are always requested with a `Depth: 0` header or no depth header, even if child collections are searched as part of the report processing (see Listing 13–9).

Listing 13–9 Principal-match report used to find out "who am I?"

```
REPORT /principals/ HTTP/1.1
Host: www.example.com
Authorization: Digest username="alice", realm="example.com",
    nonce="...", uri="/hr/", response="...", opaque="..."
Content-Type: text/xml; charset="utf-8"
Content-Length: xxxx
Depth: 0
↵
<?xml version="1.0" encoding="utf-8" ?>
<D:principal-match xmlns:D="DAV:">
    <D:principal-property>
        <D:principal-URL/>
    </D:principal-property>
</D:principal-match>

HTTP/1.1 207 Multi-Status
Date: Mon, 27 May 2002 17:19:21 GMT
Content-Type: text/xml; charset="utf-8"
Content-Length: xxxx
↵
<?xml version="1.0" encoding="utf-8" ?>
<D:multistatus xmlns:D="DAV:">
    <D:response>
        <D:href>http://www.example.com/principals/ids/alice</D:href>
        <D:status>HTTP/1.1 200 OK</D:status>
    </D:response>
</D:multistatus>
```

Listing 13–9 shows how the question "who am I?" is answered. A PROPFIND request to the principal resource would be required to find out more information, such as the user's full name.

In the body of the REPORT request, the `principal-match` root element must contain a `principal-property` element. The `principal-property` element must contain the name of a property that is known to contain principal URLs.

Since the principal-match report can match any property known to contain principal URLs, the report could be used for any number of purposes. However, only two such purposes are mentioned in the ACL specification. The first is to find out the current user, and the second is to find out what resources the current user owns. The specification doesn't say which properties the server must support with this report, so the client can only try naming the property and see if the report works. A server could neglect to implement the report for the group-member-set property, for example.

The request to find out what resources Alice owns is very similar. The client addresses a regular collection (not a principal collection) and asks the server to match the owner property (see Listing 13–10).

Listing 13–10 Request for principal-match report to find out resources owned by current user.

```
REPORT /hr/ HTTP/1.1
Host: www.example.com
Authorization: Digest username="alice", realm="example.com",
   nonce="...", uri="/hr/", response="...", opaque="..."
Content-Type: text/xml; charset="utf-8"
Content-Length: xxxx
↵
<?xml version="1.0" encoding="utf-8" ?>
<D:principal-match xmlns:D="DAV:">
   <D:principal-property>
      <D:owner/>
   </D:principal-property>
</D:principal-match>
```

The successful response to this request is a 207 Multi-Status response, where there is a `response` element and URL for each resource under /hr/ that Alice owns.

13.4.5 Browsing Principals

We've shown how to alter ACLs on resources but not how to figure out what principals can be granted privileges or how to identify them. WebDAV ACLs defines two basic ways to do this: browsing and searching.

The client can browse collections of principals the same way regular collections are browsed; the client can issue PROPFIND requests to navigate starting from the root principal collection. The structure of the principal collection is up to the server implementation. It's likely that many implementations will put users into one collection and groups into another collection (both within the principals root collection) but the names for these collections are left up to the server. A server implementation could also divide the user collection into subcategories. For example, a university may choose to put professors, staff, and students each in separate principal collections for ease of administration.

13.4.6 Searching Principals

When many principals exist (some companies have hundreds of thousands of employees and a similar number of groups in the company directory), browsing becomes less feasible, even after users are divided into subcollections. Although the server must still allow browsing, it may allow searching for principals as well. In WebDAV ACLs, the client requests searches with the principal-property-search report, after getting the principal-search-property-set report to figure out what kinds of searches are allowed.

If a complete standard existed for searching WebDAV resources based on property values, this report would not be needed. A proposal is in the works, but it was still some way from standardization when WebDAV ACLs were submitted for RFC status.

First, the client uses the principal-search-property-set report to find out what properties may be searched. The server's response might look like Listing 13–11.

Listing 13–11   Body of response to principal-search-property-set report.

```
<?xml version="1.0" encoding="utf-8" ?>
<principal-search-property-set xmlns="DAV:">
   <principal-search-property>
      <prop><displayname/></prop>
      <description xml:lang="en">Full name</description>
   </principal-search-property>
   <principal-search-property>
      <prop xmlns:a="http://www.example.com/"><a:title/></ prop>
      <description xml:lang="en">Job title</description>
   </principal-search-property>
</principal-search-property-set>
```

In Listing 13–11, the server advertises search support only for principals' full names and job titles. Note that it's not clear whether the server could support different properties for different kinds of principals. For example, the job title property described here might be supported for searching on users, but it surely wouldn't return results on groups.

Now that the client knows what properties it can search on, it can submit the search request (see Listing 13–12).

Listing 13–12   Search for principals by matching substrings.

```
REPORT /principals/ HTTP/1.1
Host: www.example.com
Content-Type: text/xml; charset=utf-8
Content-Length: xxxx
↵
<?xml version="1.0" encoding="utf-8" ?>
<principal-property-search xmlns="DAV:">
   <property-search>
      <prop> <displayname/> </prop>
      <substring>alice</substring>
```

Listing 13–12   Search for principals by matching substrings. *(Continued)*

```
</property-search>
<prop> <displayname/></prop>
</principal-property-search>
```

Note that the displayname property is named twice in Listing 13–12. The first time, it specifies what property to search on: The displayname property will be searched for the substring alice. The second time, it specifies what property to return. The client wants the full displayname value for every principal matching the caseless substring search. We know from previous examples that Alice Wetherill will be one of the values, but any other Alice will also be returned, along with principals whose name contains "alice" in the middle (like "Eduardo Valicenna"). Group display names may also match this search expression. For example, if Alice has a group called "Alice's direct reports," that group would be returned in the same principal search.

The server's response is the multi-status PROPFIND response, with one `response` element per principal resource, so we won't show it here.

13.5   Standardization Challenges

Standardizing access control has been particularly difficult. It was known to be a difficult problem from the start. Dan Connelly asked the mailing list in July 1996, "This has been an open problem in distributed systems for tens of years. We don't expect to solve this long-standing problem, do we?"

It's not that the basic functions for changing access control settings are that complicated. They are rather simple. There are significant barriers to defining an interoperable system because of the way existing systems work. Existing systems can't be ignored when it comes to access control, because WebDAV is often built on top of or to extend existing systems, and it's important for access control information to be consistent and consistently enforceable.

13.5.1   User Databases

Every company with more than a handful of employees has some kind of user directory or user database, if only a set of Unix accounts on a server. Many secondary user databases exist as well. Popular Web sites such as *The New York Times* require users to log in to access certain pages. An access control system for WebDAV must not ignore these user information databases.

LDAP servers are increasingly being used as a central and authoritative repository to store and retrieve principal information for an organization. LDAP was designed to provide lightweight access to a directory of users, groups, and other entities. An LDAP directory has a number of entries, some of which may correspond to principals.

Although LDAP is a standard protocol, the LDAP data model can vary. There may not be a standard list of attributes (those are LDAP's analog to properties) that a common object such as a "group" must have. An Informational IETF standard [RFC2798] defines standard attributes for a user object, and this standard seems to be gaining adoption at Microsoft and Sun.

LDAP URLs are standardized [RFC2255]. An LDAP URL begins with the `ldap` scheme, identifies the host and the port just as HTTP URLs do, and then contains the distinguished name for the directory entry. This definition of an LDAP URL isn't complete, but it's enough for us to be able to name principals with LDAP URLs. For example:

```
ldap://ldap.example.com/cn=Alice%20Wetherill,dc=example,dc=com
```

In this example, the common name (cn) for the entry is `Alice Wetherill` (note that the space character is commonly escaped as `%20`) and the domain is `example` within the domain `com`.

Because of the way WebDAV ACLs require user and group information to be exposed as WebDAV resources with WebDAV properties, client software doesn't have to support LDAP (or any other protocol besides WebDAV) to do basic access control operations. This is critical to keeping the standard simple enough so that client software can implement it.

A WebDAV server may connect to an LDAP server and retrieve information on behalf of clients, transforming LDAP attributes into WebDAV principal resource properties. In fact, a WebDAV server could theoretically expose any user directory that way.

13.5.2 Multiple Access Protocols

WebDAV is usually not the only way that resources in a repository can be accessed. In Web servers such as IIS 5.0 and Apache, resources are primarily available over HTTP and Web-DAV. However, the same resources can also be accessed directly on the file system. In an intranet, files shared on the Web are often shared on a networked file system at the same time. In the Internet, files may be accessible via HTTP and FTP at the same time. Exchange 2000 supports a handful of ways to get to each resource: An email may be available through Web-DAV, MAPI, SMB, and IMAP.

Such multiprotocol support is wonderful for end users who have the freedom to choose the most appropriate client software for each task. However, it's a nightmare to administrators and implementors who must ensure that access is consistent for each protocol. If access to the resource is denied, it must be denied over all access protocols; otherwise, access control becomes quite unmanageable. It's too complicated to set access control separately for each access protocol, because the models may be different and it's too easy to make mistakes, allowing an operation on one protocol when the corresponding operation is denied on other protocols.

The IIS 5.0 approach to unifying access control over several protocols is to use the underlying file storage system to control access. The file `index.html` may ultimately be stored as a file somewhere on the C:\ drive of a Windows-based server, and Windows access control can be used to prevent unauthorized client access. Then every service that allows any remote or local access to `index.html` (the FTP server, the Web server, and SMB) must use those permissions. The service authenticates the user to identify them, and then provides that identity to the file system.

The file system must trust the server software to do this securely and honestly. This also requires that each principal needing access has an identity known to the file system.

If multiple protocol access is not a goal, then it's possible to lock down WebDAV resource access much more tightly, as Xythos WebFile Server does. When only one service controls access to files, then access control policy is more likely to be consistent. If files are stored encrypted on the file system or in a database, then even local access to the computer where the files are stored may be possible without compromising the security of the WebDAV resources.

An intermediate model is illustrated by mod_dav. Files and collections are stored as files and folders in the file system, and metadata is also stored as files in the file system. File system ACLs may be very restrictive. The administrator is expected to lock down the file system access so that even though those files are theoretically accessible via NFS, other processes can't readily alter Web content or metadata. Instead, mod_dav obeys Apache permissions stored in configuration files. To support access control, mod_dav might expose the Apache permissions through the WebDAV ACL model and modify the permissions on disk.

Because multiple protocol access is a reality in many situations, the designers of WebDAV ACLs had to define a flexible set of privileges, shown in Section 13.2.4. Theoretically, the privileges defined can be customized so that the underlying operating system can enforce the privileges if that model is chosen.

13.6 Summary

WebDAV access control extends WebDAV to provide two major related pieces of functionality: the ability to retrieve and change access control settings and the ability to identify and search for principals to name in access control settings.

Access control settings are exposed through properties on a resource. The primary property contains an ACL. The ACL property contains a number of access control entries, each of which names a principal and a number of permissions granted or denied. The ACL property is not directly writable; instead, the client must use the ACL method to change the value.

The set of permissions supported may not be the same on every server. Instead, the WebDAV ACL standard provides a way to map custom permissions to a known set of standard permissions.

Each principal is assigned a WebDAV URL for identification. The principal URL space provides a minimal way to find, list, and identify principals, which can be users or groups. The principal URL is used to identify principals in the ACL property, as well as in other WebDAV access control properties that require a principal.

CHAPTER 14

Custom WebDAV Applications

When WebDAV is used for an application that includes but goes beyond simple distributed authoring, it is a custom WebDAV application. The application can be as simple as a few business rules acting on custom property values or as complex as Exchange 2000. This chapter discusses the advantages of using WebDAV for custom applications, the issues involved, and some examples.

Before the ubiquity of the Web, custom applications typically involved custom client code. That meant that client software had to be installed on users' computers. Users don't like installing software, but a client application is sometimes the only way (even today) to present a usable interface with required functionality. If the custom application ever requires added functionality after initial deployment, then the difficulty and cost of upgrading the deployed base of client applications is huge.

With the Web, many more custom applications can be designed to use server-side code alone. Many user interfaces can be done entirely in HTML, with HTML form submissions when the user needs to perform an action. Web-based custom applications are now very common, featuring many useful tools to cut down on development and deployment costs. However, many Web-based custom applications are also slow, suffering from poor user responsiveness, poor scalability, or both.

The development of client-side scripting helped Web applications designers cut costs and improve the usability of a custom Web-based application. Client-side scripting improves performance when it reduces the number of requests that need to be made. Although the client must download the script in addition to the Web page, if the script reduces roundtrips at all, performance is improved because that's where the real costs are incurred. If you've designed Web applications to use client-side scripting, then you're aware that scripting requires careful design, making decisions about what gets done where.

In many of the same ways, WebDAV can be another valuable tool to cut Web application costs. As a bonus, WebDAV is far more standardized than client-side scripting!

This chapter discusses first how to use WebDAV to augment an existing application without writing any client-side code (not even a browser-run script) and very little server-side code, in the context of an online photo album or other picture storage repository. Second, a more complex example shows how WebDAV was integrated into Exchange 2000. Among other things, this example shows how browser-executed script can use WebDAV to host an application that is faster than customer Web-hosted applications where the browser downloads server-generated pages without client script. Because so many client applications already support WebDAV, neither of these custom applications requires any software to be installed by the user.

The third example in the chapter is instant messaging. That example includes some suggestions where *not* to use WebDAV as well as some ideas how WebDAV can happily integrate with other protocols. Finally, a problem-solving environment for research organizations shows how much more flexible a WebDAV property schema is than traditional database-backed custom application schemas.

14.1   Online Photo Album

Now let's examine how we would implement a hypothetical Web service using WebDAV. As digital cameras have become more popular, a number of Web sites have emerged to allow people to share, manage, and print their digital images. These services are generally called **online photo albums**.

14.1.1   Application Overview

An online Web-based photo album is a Web service that hosts collections of photos for many users. The service provider can offer the service for free, support it via advertisements, or charge for this service. The site could contain mostly people's travel and family pictures, professional photographers' portfolios, or images collected by a publisher for use in books. We'll assume that the users are regular computer users with no special software-related expertise, so the service has to be easy to use.

Images can be created in many applications. Digital photos can be created directly on the user's computer from a connected camera, downloaded from a portable camera, or scanned in. Applications like Adobe Photoshop are used to create enhanced photos. Most likely, the image is stored at some point on the user's computer (see Figure 14–1).

Uploading files is a special-case function on the Web. Browsers must protect users' privacy. In the upload case, this means ensuring that unauthorized Web sites cannot select and upload users' files from their hard drives. Consequently, Web browsers have security blocks built

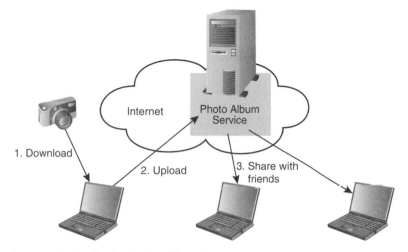

Figure 14–1 Photo-sharing life cycle.

in specifically so that when the server suggests a file upload (through an HTML form), the user must be involved to select a single file and agree to upload it.

Frequently users have several images to upload at the same time. It is possible to use an HTML form to upload multiple files, but it's not exactly easy to use. Only one file can be selected for each file upload input slot. To upload five files, the user must select each file independently in its own input slot and then submit the HTML form (or worse, submit the HTML form five times). It's not possible with ordinary HTTP Web browsers to upload five files by selecting them all together.

To solve the multiple-file upload problem, Shutterfly (a public Web photo album service) implemented a special plug-in for Web browsers. This plug-in is very nice, but not only did Shutterfly have to develop it and maintain it, but each user had to agree to terms of use and download and install this component.

Once images are uploaded to the server, they may be arranged according to how or when the pictures were taken, the subject matter, or some other scheme. In any case, users must be able to organize images according to their own plan. It would be nice if it were possible to reorganize images too, to be able to move them from one collection to another.

Once the images are uploaded, other users can view the images. In most public Web photo services, anybody can view the images, so security is rather minimal. For example, a photo collection may have a password, which every viewer needs to know. Another possibility (as in Shutterfly) is that the album may only be viewable by users who have an account with the Web service. Note that the user must be able to set permissions at the granularity of an album at least, if not on individual pictures.

When sharing photos, users like to give their images names and comments. Some systems might allow more detailed information, such as who took the picture and when it was taken. In addition, the photo albums or collections of photos need to be named.

14.1.2   Existing Architecture

An online photo album service can be implemented using only a Web server with an extensibility model (e.g., Apache with CGI scripts). However, the result would be rather hard to implement, be difficult to use, and perform poorly. We can reconstruct how a theoretical Web-based photo album service would be implemented, and consider the challenges:

- The implementation would take a lot of time because every function has to be implemented from scratch. For example, Web servers don't have native ways to allow the client to move a Web resource (like an image) from one place to another, so the Web service has to be programmed to do that.
- The Web user interface would be difficult to use, particularly for uploading multiple photos, but also for moving, renaming, and deleting photos. Users may be accustomed to using a tool like Windows Explorer to move, rename, and delete files, but they can't use these skills with a plain Web interface, because the interface features aren't rich enough.
- The service would perform poorly because all the work of collating data and preparing the presentation must be done on the server. The server is the bottleneck for all client access tasks, and because the server does all the heavy lifting, this becomes a very narrow bottleneck indeed.

Figure 14–2 shows a simple Web service architecture that could be used to run a photo album service or many other kinds of data-backed Web service. This architecture is characterized by a completely server-controlled and server-processed presentation layer on the front end and a tight dependency on the data schema on the back end.

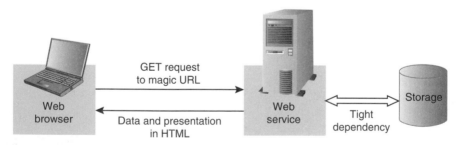

Figure 14–2   Simple Web service architecture.

14.1.3   WebDAV for Photo Authoring

How can WebDAV help in this scenario? What if users could:

- Use a familiar interface, like Explorer, to upload several photos at once?
- Use a familiar interface to move, copy, rename, and delete photos on their collections on the server?

- Use Photoshop or any image-processing application to edit photos from the server and save the photos directly back to the server?

WebDAV offers these features by making photos available as WebDAV resources organized in WebDAV collections. Web Folders and Photoshop natively support the WebDAV protocol and can store files directly on a WebDAV repository. Editing documents directly on a Web repository (without having to download, edit, and upload as three separate steps) is a unique feature of WebDAV and is extremely difficult to provide through HTTP alone.

A photo album service could easily be based on WebDAV from the ground up. This architecture has additional benefits that end users aren't aware of, but these benefits would be important to an Internet startup on a shoestring budget:

- New WebDAV tools are automatically supported. For example, if camera software had WebDAV functionality added, users could save to the Web service right from their camera. Less development is required.
- The server-side presentation layer can be easily separated from the data layer. More data is served directly from the data layer, with less presentation processing required by the server. Fewer servers are required.
- The data layer automatically handles a rich permission model. The Web service implementors can use as much or as little of this model as desired. Permissions are guaranteed to be consistent.
- It is trivial to make the service richer by adding features based on properties. For example, a "style" property (baby album, wedding album, trip album) could be added to each collection simply by using a new WebDAV property. Costly data re-architecture (such as database schema modification) is unnecessary; the programmers can focus on the features.
- It is trivial to extend the service by allowing multiple people to share authoring responsibility for a photo album. With WebDAV locks and permissions, this feature works properly.
- Performance improves because the most frequent type of request (a simple download of a single photo through a GET request) is handled by commercial software that has been tuned to do this quickly.

How Properties Are Exposed

When a Web application uses WebDAV properties, standard Web browser software can't automatically view those properties. Some code is still required to pull the property values into a Web page, format, and display them. Today this is most commonly server-side code such as JSP or ASP pages. However, there are higher-performance alternatives in which the processing and presentation is offloaded to the client, as discussed in Section 14.2.4.

This model assumes that the application is designed with WebDAV in mind, such that WebDAV can be the primary storage model for all the information stored through the Web service. This requires some familiarity with the WebDAV data model to choose how to represent application data most effectively (see Figure 14–3).

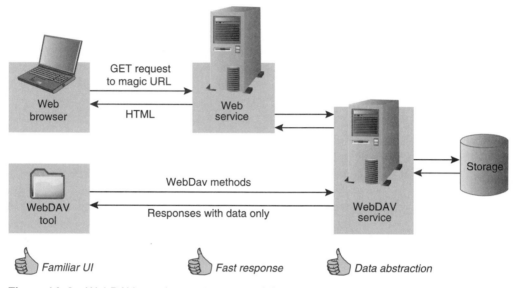

Figure 14–3   WebDAV as primary storage model.

WebDAV is an appropriate technology to use for this purpose, because photos can be simple WebDAV resources and photo albums can be WebDAV collections. Any additional information can be associated with either an individual photo or a collection, using WebDAV properties.

14.1.4   Gateway Model

If the photo album service has already been deployed without WebDAV support, is it worthwhile transitioning to WebDAV? A full transition can be difficult and time consuming. Another model is to expose the existing service through a WebDAV gateway. This could provide the end user benefits of WebDAV access to photos and albums without having to rewrite core architecture.

A WebDAV gateway would not likely be an out-of-the-box solution in this case, but that doesn't mean that the Web service implementors would have to do all the work. For example, the mod_dav module can plug into a custom data layer using a simple data access interface (see Figure 14–4).

14.1.5   Lessons Learned

Why does WebDAV provide such convenience and benefits for a photo album service? To generalize this example, it's useful to see what characteristics made the photo album application so

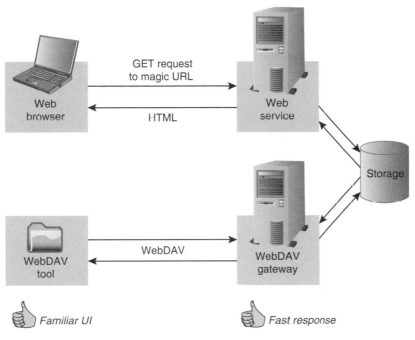

Figure 14–4   WebDAV gateway with existing data storage.

easy to map to WebDAV. Conversely, some of these lessons point out the WebDAV characteristics that make it so useful in this situation.

A Web-Based Service   The Photo Album service was conceived as a Web service from the start. WebDAV extends HTTP, so it fits well into this model. Rather than route every JPEG and GIF through the custom code of the Web service, browser requests for photos can be handled directly by the WebDAV repository. The custom code in the Web service can focus on the presentation of thumbnails, browsing albums, and showing banner advertisements—all the value-added functionality, that is, rather than the basics.

Authoring Applications Natively Supported   Photos are authored as well as simply uploaded and viewed. End users benefit from being able to use authoring applications (Photoshop, PowerPoint, Illustrator) to directly access files on the server. A photo stored on the server can be touched up with Photoshop quite simply: The user opens the photo, makes changes, and saves it back to the server.

Flexible Metadata Support   Photos and albums require metadata to be coordinated into a rich Web presentation. Since a WebDAV repository must already support metadata, the photo album service implementors don't have to do a lot of work to add properties to photos. Even better, there's no fixed schema for properties, so the implementors can add functionality as they go along. That's much easier than knowing the schema, field names, and data types at the beginning of the project. These properties can be static (defined when the photo is updated), calculated live by the server, or even created by the end user.

Document-Oriented Storage   The Photo Album service naturally conforms to storing documents in folders. It works much better when using WebDAV to handle this document storage than when using a database, where storage of large "blobs" is not always easy (photos can be several megabytes in size). Even if the Photo Album service were architected to use regular Web server file storage for the photos and use a database only for storing metadata, the database is inferior for this purpose because the metadata has to be associated with each photo using custom code. Using a WebDAV server means that metadata is already associated with each photo, so that whenever a photo is moved or copied, its metadata goes with it.

Native Support for Document Management   For the online Photo Album service, the simple document management features WebDAV provides (moving, locking, synchronizing) are quite useful. WebDAV provides a way for users to organize and upload their photos without requiring custom code on the part of the service providers. Savvy users can use a tool like sitecopy to keep their online photo album synchronized with a local copy of all the photos.

14.2   Email and Calendaring

Exchange Server, Microsoft's email and collaboration server product, stores and handles users' email messages, calendar appointments, contacts, and news postings.

Before the Web and the explosion of Internet protocols, Exchange Server had only a few standards to support (RFC822 for message format and SMTP for message exchange). These standards were only supported for communicating with the outside world. To allow client access to server-stored email and calendaring information, Exchange Server instead supported Messaging API (MAPI).

Exchange MAPI

MAPI is an API that both clients and server extensions use to work with Exchange Server. It's a proprietary interface exposing functions used to create, manipulate, transfer, and store email messages. Confusingly, MAPI is also a protocol used over the wire between Exchange clients and servers or applications designed to be compatible with Exchange (see Figure 14–5).

In addition to Exchange and Outlook, Microsoft has had several other email clients, servers, and services—including MSN mail and Hotmail. To achieve greater interoperability among its own products and services, Microsoft adopted a standard protocol (WebDAV) with a custom schema and proprietary extensions. This section focuses on how and why WebDAV was integrated into Exchange Server 2000.

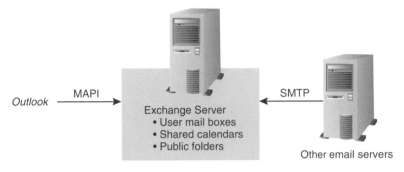

Figure 14–5 Exchange Server communication in early releases.

14.2.1 Web and Internet Standards In Exchange

By the time Exchange Server 5.5 was released, Exchange supported quite a few Internet standards:

- RFC822 for message formatting
- SMTP for message exchange
- POP3 (Post Office Protocol) for client retrieval of email
- IMAP (Internet Mail Access Protocol) for client access to email stored on server
- NNTP (Network News Transport Protocol) for client access to news posts shared among users
- HTTP for browser access to a Web UI, for users who do not have client software installed (e.g., kiosk users)

Exchange Server 2000 (the release after 5.5) needed to do a better job of both Web support and Office 2000 support. According to the Exchange file-sharing vision, every user ought to have Office 2000 (with Outlook) and an email account on an Exchange server. Therefore, Exchange Public Folders were recommended as a central location for sharing documents among Office users. To achieve this vision, Office 2000 users needed to be able to save Office documents directly to an Exchange Public Folder.

Public folders have some advantages over using a simple file system folder to share documents. Public folders can contain news postings, contacts, and emails, as well as Office documents, text files, and so on. Items in the folders can have metadata. Resources in public folders can be locked by a remote user. In other words, a public folder is a lot like a WebDAV collection (see Figure 14–6).

How was Office 2000 going to do remote authoring in public folders? POP3 and IMAP were out of the question because those protocols are limited to email usage. MAPI was rejected because the Office 2000 development schedule was tight and MAPI support would have been a lot of work for not enough benefit. HTTP was a better option, but as we know, HTTP alone doesn't solve remote authoring issues. The development schedule for Office 2000 already

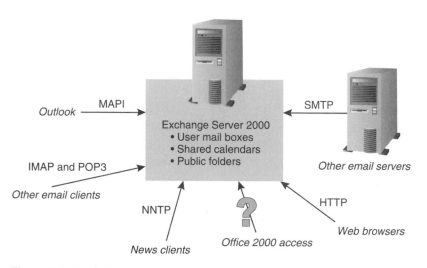

Figure 14–6   Exchange server supporting how many protocols?

included plans for WebDAV support, so client implementors encouraged Exchange Server planners to add support for WebDAV as well.

The biggest question was how all the objects in an Exchange server (Office documents, email, calendars, appointments, contacts, and news postings) would be represented with WebDAV. Calendars and all folders were exposed as WebDAV collections. Emails, appointments, contacts, news postings, and Office documents were exposed as regular WebDAV resources, but each had special properties. For example, an email object needs properties such as "from" address, "to" address, date sent, date received, and subject. Thousands of custom WebDAV properties were defined to hold all the metadata that can be found in an Exchange repository.

14.2.2   "Webifying" Exchange 2000

One of the planned new features for Exchange 2000 was direct Web access to its folders and resources. Although at first blush it doesn't sound exciting to do a GET to an email, this functionality was useful for a number of reasons and, in fact, consistently requested by Exchange customers.

First, URLs, particularly HTTP URLs, have become universal addresses. A URL is extremely portable because it includes not just the location of the resource within a repository but also the server name and even the protocol to use to access the resource. Exchange resources didn't have addresses of any kind, so HTTP URLs would be particularly useful, providing universal and interoperable addressing. HTTP URLs allowed information in Exchange to be linked into the World Wide Web. Customers were demanding this feature, with the obvious implication that if Exchange did not provide URLs, customers would have to remove important information from their Exchange servers and put that information somewhere on the Web.

The Exchange designers thought even bigger than this. They aspired to make Exchange the first place users and application writers would think of storing all shared information. Often, shared information is in the format of Web pages (HTML files) and images, and these are now expected to have URLs. HTTP support allows application software developers to easily write code to add and retrieve information from a server (it's much easier than supporting MAPI). HTTP dramatically lowers barriers to custom software. For example, a cell phone that already had some HTTP support would find it relatively easy to download data from a user's calendar and automatically remind the user of appointments.

Finally, customers were also demanding a Web-based GUI front end for Exchange so that users at kiosks and on the road could have full access to their inbox, navigate mail folders, send and reply to email, and delete messages. In response, Exchange developed **Outlook Web Access** (OWA).

14.2.3 OWA

OWA was the first Microsoft client application to access Exchange 2000 data over WebDAV. (In fact, it shipped with Exchange 2000 [Microsoft00].) OWA is a Web server application that can run either directly on the Exchange server or on a separate server. It allows users at kiosks, or any computer that doesn't have a mail client installed (including Unix and Linux clients), to use a Web browser to get to their Exchange mailbox content. It's also useful when I use a computer configured to view somebody else's mail and I don't want to change the configuration. For example, when I'm at a remote site and borrow a friend's Internet-connected workstation to check my mail, I can use my friend's Web browser to do so without changing the configuration or settings of her machine.

To present its Web-based GUI, OWA must of course dynamically generate Web pages that contain some of the data from a user's mailbox—just enough to fill a screen, so the download is quick and the interface feels responsive to the user. This can be a lot of work for a Web application server, because as soon as the user pages down to view more email or deletes an email, the whole page must be regenerated. At least, that's how it works with IE 5.0 and earlier, as well as with Netscape clients. With IE 5.5, OWA can make the client use WebDAV.

14.2.4 How OWA Uses WebDAV

When OWA builds a dynamic Web page for IE 5.5, it doesn't put the data in the page. Instead, it includes scripted routines for doing WebDAV PROPFIND requests to the user's mailbox. The script uses a component called XMLHTTP. As soon as IE 5.5 receives the page, it executes the script and gets the PROPFIND response. The script also includes instructions for using an XML stylesheet to convert the PROPFIND response body in XML to nicely formatted HTML. Appendix A has a much-simplified example of this kind of code.

Why PROPFIND?

OWA could have used GET requests to dynamic resources, to ask for property sets and get answers formatted in XML. Instead, PROPFIND was used because it was already well defined and specified and included almost all the functionality required (the ability to request a specific range of responses was added). A dynamic GET solution would have had to redesign some of the same solutions.

Furthermore, Exchange Server already had to support PROPFIND in order to support WebDAV for Office 2000 authoring, and PROPFIND already had to be optimized to respond quickly. The OWA designers wanted to take advantage of the functionality already implemented and optimized.

To get the first view of a page such as a mailbox listing, the client has to make three requests instead of one:

- A GET request for the page framework and script
- A PROPFIND request for the listing data
- A GET request for the stylesheet to format the data

However, once these pieces are in place, every time users scroll down in their mailbox or delete an email, the script in the page tells the client how to do another PROPFIND request to fill in the new data. With the same page framework and the same stylesheet, the new data is inserted in the page. Since all of this client processing happens faster than the full HTML could be downloaded, users see their data faster.

Although OWA supports browsers that do not have XMLHTTP, it is much more efficient when XMLHTTP is available to separate data from presentation. Stylesheets can do the presentation part of the job, but there must be a way to download the data only, and that's where XMLHTTP comes in. The server running OWA sends client script code invoking the XMLHTTP object. This script causes the browser to make WebDAV requests (usually PROPFIND) to get the data in compact form in XML. Since fancy Web pages are 90 percent presentation, this can result in much more efficient browsing when the presentation is reused.

A good example to illustrate this concept is the way OWA displays the user's inbox. The screen shows about 20 messages at a time. To scroll down or resort the listing of emails, Internet Explorer 4.0 has to ask the server for a whole new Web page, complete with all the presentation information, even though only a few data fields change. In contrast, Internet Explorer 5.0 is instructed to use the XMLHTTP component to make a PROPFIND request to get the first 20 emails in the inbox and then download a stylesheet to present the PROPFIND response body. When IE 5.0 users scroll down, a new PROPFIND request is made that only retrieves the new data; since the stylesheet is cached locally, it is reused.

OWA servers do less processing when handling WebDAV requests, compared to integrating data into a HTML presentation. That means that OWA servers can handle many more IE 5.5

clients (and later IE versions, too, of course) than other browser versions. A data sheet on OWA performance states that before IE 5.0 features were available, "the effective number of users per server was limited by the overhead needed to support interpreted scripts in ASP and to run MAPI sessions within ASP." With IE 5.0, WebDAV, XML, and DHTML are used to increase performance. With IE 5.5, stylesheets improve performance even more (see Figure 14–7).

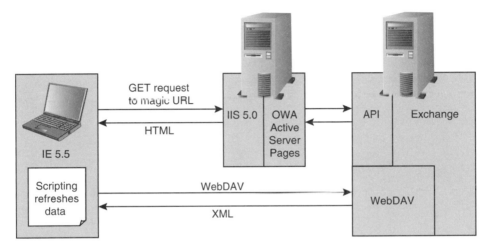

Figure 14–7   OWA architecture.

Because IE 5.0/5.5 users consume fewer server resources, not only is their experience faster, but the server can also handle more of them.

Apple iCal

Microsoft is not the only company to use WebDAV for calendaring. In 2002, Apple introduced iCal using WebDAV to publish calendaring information to the Web. However, its schema is likely quite different.

14.2.5   Hotmail and Web Infrastructure

At the time when Exchange developers were considering all these Web features, Microsoft had recently acquired Hotmail, and the Exchange and Hotmail teams were planning how to move closer together in terms of technology and platform.

Hotmail was entirely dependent on the Web from day one. The Web allowed an email service to potentially make money by showing ads to its users, which IMAP and POP3 didn't do. The Web also allowed a service like Hotmail to traverse firewalls. If a public email service were configured to use a proprietary protocol, it would never get through corporate firewalls and onto employee computer desktops. Most computer users are not savvy enough to telnet out of their corporate firewalls to a Unix telnet host and run a command-line email client to read their non-work-related email, but that's how I had to view email that arrived at my student account during work terms. The Web changed that (see Figure 14–8).

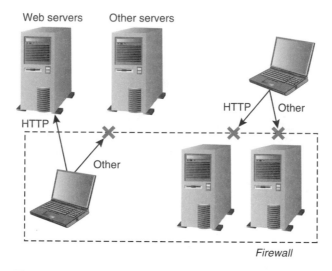

Web servers   Other servers

HTTP   Other

HTTP

Other

Firewall

Figure 14–8   Firewalls allow outgoing HTTP traffic but almost nothing else.

Many firewalls simply block traffic through almost every port, but very few firewalls block port 80 entirely. Because the Web is so key to communication, firewall administrators are forced to allow HTTP requests from inside the firewall to reach Web servers outside the firewall. HTTP responses to return through the firewall must return over the same connection.

The Hotmail acquisition thus provided even more reasons to add HTTP support to Exchange server. Users became accustomed to access their email even if they were behind a firewall, and HTTP support via Outlook Web Access allowed them to do that.

14.2.6 Outlook Express

Exchange Server supported another client in addition to OWA and Outlook, and that was Outlook Express. Outlook was designed primarily for corporate use and it had to be purchased as part of the Office suite. Outlook Express was designed to be a free consumer email client, so it had much simpler functionality than Outlook. However, Outlook Express was still a real client-side application, which the user could download, install and configure, and use offline. To make it even easier to obtain, Microsoft included Outlook Express as part of Internet Explorer. In fact, since Internet Explorer shipped with Windows, Outlook Express came preinstalled for many users buying Windows computers.

Outlook Express was frequently used to access MSN and Hotmail email accounts. Because Outlook Express is not a thin client, like OWA, it needs to use a data-oriented protocol so that it can populate its own GUI with data, rather than accept the formatting the

---

Handling Intermediaries That Block HTTP Requests

WebDAV extends HTTP, so WebDAV benefits from nearly the same treatment at the firewall. WebDAV does not attempt to subvert security, however—in theory, it can be blocked by a slightly more sophisticated firewall that filters HTTP requests based on method.

However, there are two ways to work around firewalls that block methods. First, a protocol can always tunnel through POST. A custom client or gateway can send POST requests, with a custom header that names a WebDAV method. (This technique is also useful to bypass Web application servers that ignore non-HTTP methods.) Second, the server can simply provide SSL/TLS access. Some firewalls are configured to allow any opaque SSL/TLS connection on port 443 [RFC2818] through the firewall, but WebDAV methods are blocked on port 80. Even using port 80, it may be possible to use the CONNECT method [RFC2817], which essentially tunnels an opaque channel through the firewall.

Firewalls and applications using tunneling protocols are sometimes seen to be engaged in an arms race. The firewall can always look deeper into the guts of the message, but the tunneling application can always embed its information more deeply in seemingly innocuous messages. Eventually, the tunneling application can encrypt its messages in a stream, and the firewall's ability to filter on syntax is completely forestalled.

---

server provides. MSN used IMAP as a data protocol, but Hotmail never did. Instead, to support Outlook Express, Hotmail added very basic WebDAV support. Since WebDAV used the same port, protocol, and infrastructure as HTTP, it was much easier to add and served the purpose at least as well as IMAP.

Some users who had not purchased Office or who simply preferred the simplicity of Outlook Express wanted to use Outlook Express to access their Exchange-hosted email as well as email from MSN, Hotmail, or other services. WebDAV support was needed in Exchange to handle Outlook Express, too.

14.2.7 Scalability

A final pressure on Exchange Server developers was continual performance and scalability improvements. Customers found that in order to support 2000 to 3000 users, they had to buy two Exchange Server licenses. The real cost wasn't so much in the licensing fees but in the system administration costs to link two Exchange servers, share user addresses, manage delivery of incoming mail to the correct server, and share Public Folder content across both.

HTTP/WebDAV offered the promise of handling more users than IMAP and MAPI. Both IMAP and MAPI are connection-oriented protocols, so while a user is online and has his or her email client running, the email client tries to maintain a connection to a server. Even when data isn't being exchanged, the connection is still open and the server has to remember the context for each open connection. In contrast, HTTP allows the server to respond to a request for data and close the connection. The server can quickly move on to the next request. HTTP makes it easier to load-balance client requests across a number of identical application servers (a model that was integral to the scalability of Hotmail).

However, OWA requires the server to do all the presentation as well as data hosting. OWA servers could handle half as many simultaneous users as a regular IMAP/MAPI Exchange server because of the high cost of producing and transmitting presentation information. Any time the server can delegate presentation to the client and serve only data, the server should be able to move more quickly to the next client and handle more users. With WebDAV requests scripted from the OWA pages when viewed in IE and formatted by the client using stylesheets, OWA was able to delegate some of the presentation to the client and handle more IE users.

14.2.8   Integration Challenges

One problem with implementing email and calendaring in the request/response model is that in some cases it would be very convenient for the server to be able to send the client a notification: "You have new mail" or "You have an appointment in 15 minutes." IMAP already does this perfectly well, but the approach chosen by the Exchange team was to do notification over HTTP/WebDAV and over port 80 instead so that the client didn't have to maintain a constant IMAP connection to the server. In WebDAV, frequently updated information may be retrieved through frequent PROPFIND requests, but this polling technique is prohibitively expensive in terms of server performance costs [Fielding98].

A true notification model would be much better, if the client has an address where it can be contacted with notifications. It's also possible to design a cheaper polling technique than PROPFIND, in which the client tells the server the kinds of changes it's interested in and polls to see if changes have been flagged. Clearly, WebDAV doesn't solve the notification problem adequately.

Other problems were more or less easily addressed. Some examples:

- A search framework had already been proposed within the WebDAV Working Group. Exchange used this framework with SQL syntax searches to provide fully equivalent search functionality.
- Some email folders (Sent Items and Deleted Items for many users) are extremely large. The client doesn't need to display everything in the folder, however. There ought to be some way to request a range of resources from a large WebDAV collection and to get simple properties to quickly show how many resources are in the collection altogether. This functionality was added rather simply with a range header definition for PROPFIND along with custom properties.
- Calendaring properties weren't always easy to map to the WebDAV flat property list model. For example, the recurrence pattern of a recurring appointment is hard enough already, and on top of that the server and client must be able to express exceptions to the recurrence pattern.

14.2.9 Lessons Learned

Once again, the characteristics that made Exchange Server and WebDAV suited for each other teach us lessons for similar applications.

Web Addresses Since every object in the Exchange repository became an HTTP resource, every resource had a Web address. Web addresses are useful as universal links, easy to pass around in email and insert into files. This linked information in Exchange into the World Wide Web.

Lower Application Development Costs Exchange found that OWA and other applications were cheaper to develop once the Exchange repository supported HTTP.

Web Infrastructure HTTP and WebDAV support allowed the Exchange server to take advantage of existing Web infrastructure. Users can use Outlook Web Access or a WebDAV client to access their Exchange Server information despite firewalls.

Another benefit of the Web infrastructure comes from caching proxies. Since OWA includes images (e.g., in the toolbar), a client could download images from a cache without even hitting the OWA server.

Not all resources are cachable, though. When a resource is subject to access control, the server must prevent caching to avoid breaches of confidentiality.

Document-Oriented Storage Like the Photo Album service, email and calendaring already have a natural document-oriented storage model. It wasn't hard to adopt WebDAV as a standards-based mechanism to move, copy, and delete objects and manipulate properties that already fit the data model.

Flexible Metadata Support Even more than the photo album example, WebDAV's flexible metadata support was important in Exchange 2000. Several thousand properties were defined for contacts, appointments, emails, postings, forms, events, tasks, and notes, and more were defined for special folders like mailboxes, calendars, and address books. Although the underlying store already existed (and the implementation already had similar metadata support), WebDAV was a useful tool to access metadata. Using the XMLHTTP component to run PROPFIND requests, Exchange administrators and developers of custom applications can easily script Web pages to display any metadata from the store. Chapter 15 has more information on this component.

XML Stylesheets Work with WebDAV Exchange OWA uses XML data from Web-DAV responses together with stylesheets to delegate presentation to the Web browser. Exchange isn't the only application to use this trick. Tamino XML server and Tamino WebDAV server provide a platform based on this model.

Support for Remote Document Management To copy, move, delete, or rename Exchange resources or create folders or resources, previously a custom application had only a couple of options. It could run on the Exchange server and use server-side APIs, but that requires administrator approval, which is difficult at sites where the servers are carefully managed or already nearing their top capacity just handling ordinary usage. The application could run remotely and use MAPI, but MAPI is complicated. Support for WebDAV greatly simplified development of remote applications, which could now put together simple HTTP requests to do many operations on resources on an Exchange 2000 server.

Support for Multiple Authors   Email and calendaring applications are not typically designed from the ground up for multiple authors, but in fact there are quite a few scenarios in which multiple author support is necessary. Personal email folders and calendars are often shared between executives and their assistants. Group calendars may need to allow events to be authored by a number of users. WebDAV supports multiple authors, so it was able to handle even these scenarios.

Stateless vs. Connection-Oriented   HTTP's stateless design is a contributor to a Web server's ability to scale to handle a great number of users. Every HTTP request contains all the context needed to be able to handle the request. Every HTTP request can be dealt with by sending a single response. Once the response is sent (and potentially some data is saved), the Web server can "forget about" the event that just happened. With a connection-oriented protocol such as IMAP, the server has to maintain a connection for every active user, remember what the user is doing, and use previous messages as context for new messages. On similar machines, an HTTP server can typically handle more active users than an IMAP server can.

14.3   Presence and Instant Messaging

Now let's look at an application that doesn't benefit as clearly or directly from WebDAV. **Instant messaging**, together with presence information, is a relatively new Internet application. Instant messaging is the ability to send a short message to another person while he or she is online and have that person respond immediately, forming a conversation more than a correspondence. An instant message doesn't get stored for delivery later. Presence information is deeply embedded in instant-messaging applications because the instant message isn't composed, sent, or delivered unless the recipient is online. "Buddy lists" has become a common phrase to describe the lists where people can quickly see which of their contacts are online and decide whether to send an instant message to any of them.

The difference between instant messaging and email isn't very clear and may blur more because email has become nearly instant, and instant messages may be stored like email. Part of the difference seems to be the user interface, which in instant messaging is lightweight and sometimes playful.

Instant messaging has quickly grown to include participation from a large proportion of the Internet population. The application appeared and grew suddenly, and the slow protocol standardization process is only catching up now. Part of the problem in developing standard protocols for this application is that it is complicated. The application involves many different facets, complicated security models, and high-performance requirements.

I'll outline the different pieces of the puzzle first, paying particular attention to how the application is used, because in this case the details of how it is used are especially important in choosing a model for a solution. I'll compare and contrast to existing protocols because in five years of designing instant-messaging protocols, I've heard dozens of people with prior protocol experience say, "Why not just use X?" where X is the existing protocol with which they have experience (including WebDAV but also SMTP, IRC, and others). It's not that simple.

14.3.1   Instant-Messaging Requirements

These are some of the problems and requirements for sending instant messages.

Sending Instant Messages   Users send instant messages to only a small group of "buddies." Contrast this to email, where my contacts list contains 104 entries, and there are easily 100 more people I might send email to in a given month. My buddy list contains only 25 buddies and I only send messages frequently to about 10 of them. To have a satisfactory experience sending an instant message, it must be trivial for me to choose a user and send a quick, informal, and small message. It shouldn't be necessary to go to another application and find an address. Thus, all the instant-messaging clients I've used allow me to choose a user and send an instant message with two mouse clicks (no scrolling if the target is in the top of my buddy list).

Instant messages must be received pretty much instantly. Because it's text (not speech), a delay of a couple of seconds (a fairly large Internet latency for a short message) is acceptable. However, a delay of five seconds or more is unacceptable because it noticeably impedes a back-and-forth conversation. Compare this to SMTP store-and-forward design, where a one- or two-minute email delivery time (over the Internet) is considered fast.

File Sharing   When users discuss and share files, the easiest way to transfer the file (or a link to a file) is with the same application used to discuss the file. That's why email attachments are ubiquitous. However, sending files directly over an instant-messaging protocol can be problematic. The most worrying concern is viruses, but there are also problems with denial-of-service (DoS) attacks, against the server or directly against instant-messaging clients. The current AOL Instant Messaging (IM) client allows users to transfer files directly to one another, but it warns users that before allowing a buddy to send a file—even before deciding whether to open the file—they should have trust in that buddy. That's because the file transfer reveals the recipient's IP address and opens that system up for an attack. However, the AOL system surely doesn't want the file transfers to pass through the servers, because that would put a large load on servers that have plenty of fast traffic to handle. MSN Messenger also handles direct file transfer to buddies. File sharing is difficult yet necessary. At home, IM users want to share images, sounds, and movies. At work, IM users want to collaborate on and discuss documents.

Multiple Clients   Users want to have IM functionality available at home, at work, at school, and sometimes even on the road. Some cell phones and PDAs interact with instant-messaging systems. Laptops with wireless connectivity frequently have IM clients installed. This leads to a couple of requirements:

- The user needs a server to help synchronize or manage IM addresses, rather than re-enter addresses on many client devices. Many email servers do this today for email clients.
- In addition, the server must help synchronize or enforce permissions. Email doesn't typically involve "white lists" and "black lists" where certain users are forbidden from sending mail—but modern IM applications always have this feature.

14.3.2 Presence

Sending an instant message is only worthwhile if the recipient is there to see it. Otherwise, people choose email, which gets stored until the user sees it. Thus, successful instant-messaging applications have been coupled with a way to find out who is online. It's most convenient to see at a glance who is online, rather than query one by one for different buddies. It's also most convenient if I can see immediately when somebody comes online (many client applications notify you with a sound like a chime ringing or a door opening) in case I've been waiting to send somebody a message. The entity getting presence information updates is called a **watcher**.

Sensitivity of Presence Information   The information about whether I'm online is sensitive information, not for everybody to know (think Internet stalkers). Presence functionality requires a way for the user to decide which watchers can receive their presence information. When a watcher wants to see my presence information for the first time, the system withholds that information until I approve that watcher. If I don't approve of a watcher, the system pretends that I'm always offline (to that watcher). This decision is typically made for the long term: Once I approve a watcher, the system continues to feed that watcher my presence information until I change my mind.

Notice that the ability to hide my presence information from some watchers implies the need for a server. Peer-to-peer instant-messaging applications have been designed and deployed but haven't met with the same success. One reason is that when my client machine is responsible for being a peer in the communication net, publishing my online status directly, forbidden watchers can find out some information based on the reachability of my client machine. If the client machine responds "she's offline" and doesn't respond at all other times, that's too much information. A presence server can do a much better job of pretending, to a watcher I don't like, that I'm completely unreachable all the time. This also implies the need for a server location to help synchronize or manage presence access control information for multiple clients.

Buddy Lists   Now that we've looked at the need to send messages quickly to a small group of people and the need to find out conveniently if those friends are online, the "buddy list" concept seems obvious. My buddy list always shows up in my instant-messaging application, with only a glance required to see who is online and only two mouse clicks required to send an online buddy a message.

Recall the requirement that users can do instant messaging on any device. This implies three important requirements for buddy lists:

- The buddy list should be stored somewhere centrally available, so all my devices can use the same buddy list.
- As a user, I should have a consistent address, so all my buddies can still see my presence even when I change devices.
- It should not be obvious that I've switched devices. If I leave for lunch and my PDA takes over from my PC to receive instant messages, that should not affect how my buddies see my presence or how they send messages (unless I choose to provide that information).

14.3.3   Could WebDAV Do Instant Messaging?

In theory, WebDAV could be used as the basic protocol to provide an instant-messaging service (and this idea has been seriously suggested to me several times in the past). However, instant messaging would have to be painfully shoe-horned into the WebDAV model for this to work. I'll lay out a straw man proposal:

- A special collection on a WebDAV server is designated to be an instant-messaging inbox (as Exchange does with email inboxes). The address of this collection is the IM address for both presence and message delivery.
- A set of properties on that collection could advertise my presence status, which other users would query with PROPFIND.
- Messages can be delivered to this inbox with PUT.
- Properties such as sender and recipient can be added to messages with PROPPATCH.

In theory this sounds reasonable: A WebDAV server is likely to be always online, so it can always advertise the user's presence. However, there are a number of problems:

- How are Web proxies and caches expected to handle these messages? Could they cache instant messages, or does every instant message have to be tagged to prevent caching? There's also a risk that firewalls would block incoming HTTP PUT requests, assuming them to be attacks on internal Web sites.
- How do instant messages get from the user's server to a client application? Would the client application have to be a WebDAV server too, in order to receive PUT requests from their server? WebDAV isn't meant to be lightweight on the server side, so this could be a serious burden for a PDA to be a WebDAV server.
- Using PROPFIND to get a user's presence information works fine the first time, but users want to be notified every time a buddy's status changes. WebDAV has no provision for a live constant connection, for notifications from server to client, or for subscriptions to changing information.
- Once an instant message is sent, the sender should have no ability to change the message. Therefore, the sender can't use PROPPATCH to put the appropriate metadata on the message.

- How are MOVE and COPY useful? There is an expectation that any WebDAV server must be a full WebDAV server, supporting at least MKCOL, MOVE, COPY, PROPFIND, and PROPPATCH, in addition to HTTP methods GET, PUT, POST, and so forth.

Surely another protocol, designed more for lightweight messaging and a trusted connection between a presence/messaging client and server, would have many better characteristics. However, while designing a new protocol for presence and instant messaging, there still seems to be a role for file sharing. WebDAV can usefully be a small piece of a much larger picture.

14.3.4 Appropriate Use of WebDAV

Here are some problems related to instant messaging where WebDAV may be appropriate but only to solve these specific problems and not as a general transport. The benefit to this reuse is that the instant-messaging protocol can specialize in the tasks that are truly special and important to the whole character of instant messaging, without solving all of the file-sharing problems that WebDAV has already solved.

Storing Buddy Lists and Access Control WebDAV might be a useful way for a number of client devices to share and synchronize the same buddy list and access control lists. The buddy list can be one resource or several resources, as can the ACLs. This model could be used even if the server enforces access control restrictions.

WebDAV locking is surprisingly useful here, to avoid having one client device overwrite the buddy list changes of another client device. Other configuration information, in addition to buddy lists, could be stored centrally in the same collection.

File Sharing Should files be sent between users by storing them temporarily on a Web-DAV repository? With an intermediary like that, some of the security problems of direct file transfer can be mitigated, and it certainly makes the instant-messaging protocol simpler.

Storing Offline Messages Some instant-messaging servers can store messages for the user while the user is offline. When the client reconnects, the offline messages are all delivered. WebDAV could be used as a storage location for these offline messages so that the instant-messaging client can retrieve the offline messages at leisure. However, offline messages really start to resemble email, so probably an email protocol would be even better for solving this problem.

14.3.5 Lessons Learned

Only Clients Make Requests in WebDAV WebDAV is more useful for applications where the client is making the requests. There is no standard way for the instant-messaging server to initiate communication to deliver messages to the client instantly. The WebDAV model would require it to wait until the client asks for instant messages. WebDAV is best used for those applications, or those components of applications, where it's most appropriate for the client to initiate requests and receive responses.

While one could imagine turning every WebDAV client into a WebDAV server so that it could also receive incoming messages, this is a complicated approach and probably not worth it for the application of instant messages. First, WebDAV has more functionality than an instant-messaging receiver needs to receive messages, so a simpler protocol might be better. Second, if the instant-messaging sender and receiver can both make WebDAV requests and handle WebDAV responses, then WebDAV has no way of managing or correlating this parallel traffic.

WebDAV Can Be a Component of a Solution   WebDAV has functionality that can solve some parts of the instant-messaging problem. For example, we can choose to store buddy lists on a WebDAV server and transfer files via intermediate storage on a WebDAV server. In contrast, a lightweight connection-oriented messaging protocol can be optimized to handle the delivery and reception of instant messages. The WebDAV component can behave independently of the other parts of the solution—there is no need for the messaging protocol to be aware of or interact with the WebDAV component. Breaking down problems like this, reusing existing solutions where most appropriate, is an excellent way to simplify.

Similarly, other protocols can integrate with WebDAV to provide benefits in WebDAV-based applications. For example, Jabber (now being standardized through the IETF as XMPP) is an instant-messaging protocol that can be extended to provide all kinds of subscription/notification services to a custom application [Shigeoka02].

The Storage Model Is a Necessary Feature of WebDAV   Although an instant-message delivery protocol that looked a lot like WebDAV could be written, it would be difficult to make it interoperable. WebDAV applications that PUT WebDAV resources expect them to be there, and be readable, and be the same content that was just placed there. A store-and-forward or drop-box model, where the messages are PUT into a black hole and can't then be retrieved by the sender, may not be a good use of PUT.

Compliance Means All Methods   To be a standards-compliant and interoperable WebDAV server, a server must implement the following functionality:

- All of HTTP, including GET, PUT, POST, HEAD, DELETE, OPTIONS. Also remember HTTP requires ETags (entity tags), ranged requests, and conditional headers.
- All of WebDAV level 1 (everything except locks).

If the server doesn't support all of these, then many existing WebDAV clients won't be able to interoperate. The client may attempt a method to connect to the server and then give up if the server doesn't seem to support WebDAV properly.

Clients can get away with a smaller set of functionality because clients can always choose not to initiate a request that they don't want to have to deal with, but there is still a heavy implementation burden to bear.

14.4   Pacific National Laboratories

The last example is a real case study like the Exchange 2000 discussion, not a hypothetical case. This case study shows how WebDAV can be used to design a custom application and make it extensible and scalable.

14.4.1   Overview

Pacific National Laboratories (PNL) designs problem-solving environments (PSEs) for government research groups. PSEs allow researchers to share and update documents. Researchers author many papers together, even forming teams that cross national boundaries. The final papers are made very widely available, perhaps publicly available on the Web. In contrast to normal multiple-author scenarios, researchers annotate documents more often, adding properties to make searches work better. The information in this chapter is from PNL papers [Schuchardt02a], [Schuchardt02b].

In addition to authoring and publishing papers, researchers now need to share their raw data and semantic data on the Web. For example, a researcher might construct an XML file representing the structure of a specific molecule and publish that semantic data together with raw data from a number of tests involving that molecule. Other researchers can interact with the data and use it more easily than when study results are distributed in paper journals. There are already standard file formats to make data sets or molecule structure information transferable, but there's no standard to share these files.

PSEs have been developed to try to unify these data-sharing functions into one flexible application. The traditional approach to storing information in a PSE has been to store documents in database **Binary Large Object** (BLOB) tables and to store the metadata in related tables. Then the PSE presents a custom view of those documents and metadata, possibly by generating dynamic Web pages. However, this approach leads to overly rigid schemas because it's difficult to plan in advance precisely what metadata will be used. Fixed table schemas for database storage make it difficult to update the system when researchers need to change the way they refer to documents.

PNL researchers designed a new approach to PSEs that involved a number of separate repositories and a flexible schema. Each repository can extend the base metadata schema in different ways. In their design, no one data store or component needs to know the entire schema. Thus, it's much easier for each repository to evolve to serve the needs of its main users (the researchers directly contributing to that repository) while still allowing access to a large readership.

WebDAV is an ideal protocol for this problem. It defines the syntax for this extensible metadata schema (property names and XML namespaces) as well as the access protocol.

14.4.2   Example Problem-Solving Environment

An example of one of the specific problem-solving domains is molecular science and complex chemical systems. PNL has a Molecular Science Software Suite, including software with advanced computational chemistry techniques, project management assistance, and calculation engines. It allows scientists to construct models of complex molecules, enter research results and analyze them, and launch distributed server-side execution of their computational models for speedy completion.

One component of this suite is called "Ecce," and among other things, Ecce needs to store its data and modify the data at later stages. Originally (1994–2002), Ecce used an **Object-Oriented Database** (OODB) to store data represented internally as objects. In 2001, Ecce had 70 different kinds of objects it could store in the database, such as Molecule, Task, Experiment, Calculation, and File. Although this approach was successful for years, eventually it began to reach its limitations.

- Any database schema used by multiple parties requires agreement on all aspects of the schema, and the implementors of the different modules in Ecce found the agreement process arduous.
- The choice to use OODBs unexpectedly created a dependency on a specific vendor. Although there are some standards in the area, each OODB may have a proprietary binary document storage format and different ties to programming languages.
- OODBs are not easily and tightly linked to the Web for wide publishing.
- OODB clients are "fat," not "thin." OODB clients must know the specific data schema in order to consume data in OODBs. Compare this to the Web, where thin clients accept whatever data the Web server is capable of formatting and simply display the data for the user.

Now that Ecce is adding support for molecular dynamics, the problems of the underlying store may be magnified. Database schemas become more and more complex as the system grows to handle more and more kinds of data, and eventually the system becomes quite unmanageable. Although PNL could have addressed some of these problems by spending more money on OODB software and related software, Ecce's designers chose to investigate other technology, such as WebDAV/database interface software.

14.4.3 Solution Requirements

PNL required a solution to meet the following requirements:

- Allow direct access to raw data. Data should be accessible in its raw format, not just through the libraries that impose an object model on the stored data.
- Metadata schemas should be discoverable and extensible, rather than fixed in advanced.
- The storage layer should not have to be aware of the nature of each application object (each document or object that has to be stored). This layer separation allows the metadata schemas to evolve independently of the features of the storage system.
- A standard protocol should be used to do data management operations, yet this standard protocol should still not have to be aware of individual schemas.

The solution also had to be deployable in a widely distributed manner, with data stores in many locations and managed independently by different groups.

14.4.4   Solution Choices

PNL chose HTTP, XML, and WebDAV as a solution. HTTP provides extremely broad access. XML is an ad hoc and extensible way to marshal object data. WebDAV combines the two, making Web servers capable of storing XML properties on arbitrary documents. The documents themselves are not restricted to the XML format but can be images or raw data sets. New document types and properties can be added at any time, and each application can use whatever set of properties happens to be needed and understood by that application.

PNL selected mod_dav 1.1 as its WebDAV server and data storage implementation. The Apache module was free and easy to extend, and Apache 1.3.11 provided the required security features. PNL used mod_dav's ability to plug in a new repository layer to replace the existing property storage capabilities with a vastly more scalable property storage solution, allowing very large property values (and large numbers of properties per document) to be reliably stored and retrieved. PNL's replacement property storage layer used a hash table in a database manager formatted file. The Gnu DataBase Manager version 1.8 was used to handle the property storage files (one property storage file exists for each WebDAV resource). The Apache Xerces 1.3 XML engine was used to parse and generate XML.

The system was used to create properties as large as 100MB and documents as large as 200MB without problems, sizes that exceeded the expected typical usage.

14.4.5   Mapping Database Schemas to WebDAV Storage

The designers of the new system decided that each data piece that a domain scientist would recognize as a separate object would be stored as a separate WebDAV resource. The designers also considered combining a number of objects inside one WebDAV resource, but this would force clients to download large files and then parse the document body to extract each object. The more granular approach also means that each different object can be annotated individually with metadata of its own. For example, a Molecule object would be stored as a single WebDAV resource with its own properties.

The WebDAV hierarchical storage model was useful in the new system. For example, although each task object in a calculation is a separate WebDAV resource, all the tasks involved in a single calculation can be stored in the same WebDAV collection. This is convenient when using a regular WebDAV browser to look at the repository. However, since each task is tied to each other task in a specified order, there are dependencies or relationships between resources. The implementors planned to represent such relationships between resources through additional property values.

Where data format standards existed (like Molecule representations in Protein Data Bank format), the implementors chose to comply with the data format standard by keeping that data together in one resource body or property value. Otherwise, the implementors broke down metadata into small chunks to maximize flexibility. Many other researchers are working on standard data formats and MIME types for chemistry information, and these standards are easily integrated into the WebDAV data model.

A namespace was defined for all Ecce properties, and the same namespace was used throughout. However, the implementors envisioned that once the basic system was established, extension work would begin in multiple areas independently, and these extensions would define and use their own namespaces.

14.4.6 Results

The Ecce implementors decided that their new design did alleviate the schema sclerosis that was affecting the old system. With a more flexible XML-based schema, changes in one area of the PSE did not affect other areas as much. The entire system involved fewer up-front costs (in paying for commercial software), as well as allowing for more rapid feature development.

Since WebDAV, HTTP, and XML are such open standards, much more powerful and cheaper middleware software and infrastructure can now be used to deploy a PSE. The system benefits from additional independent layers (storage, transport, data format, data manipulation, and semantics) because most layers can now be constructed out of standard and replaceable software components.

The researchers were happy to report that after Ecce was redesigned to use cheaper middleware, deployment costs became low enough that Ecce was able to reach a wider user base.

14.4.7 Lessons Learned

Higher Performance The implementors of this solution did performance tests to compare the new solution to the network performance of the original OODB-based solution, which had used FTP to transfer files after pulling them out of the database. The file upload performance on the server tested was as good as FTP. The implementors were concerned that the Ecce software modules might perform worse after conversion, and their goal was modest: to avoid a significant performance decrease in these objects. However, overall performance improved, exceeding expectations.

Additional performance optimizations, including HTTP pipelining, multiple TCP connections, and bundling requests, could still be implemented.

Greater Disk Space Required The basic cost of the flexibility in the new system appears to be storage size. Disk requirements increased by up to 25 percent when files and database property files replaced blobs and tables. Part of the bloat, however, was due to the Gnu DataBase Manager software used to store properties: Each property database file has a minimum size of 25KB, even if most of this space is empty. PNL could replace or reconfigure the property database software to improve disk usage. Since the disk storage tests were run with small average resource sizes, the property storage requirements were a significant fraction of the total storage. In a usage scenario with larger documents, the property storage would involve a smaller relative increase in storage space required.

The PNL system could also be optimized to use less storage if the server software used techniques like compression or avoiding file duplication. These kinds of optimizations can be added without disrupting the way the WebDAV repository is used.

Lower Cost Than OODB   The implementors also found significant cost benefits resulting from the new architecture. Apache and mod_dav were not only free but also cheaper to maintain than OODB systems, even if each department had to have its own storage server. With WebDAV, departments can share storage servers without having to manually harmonize their schemas, so costs are reduced even further. The departments and laboratories could even contract the WebDAV repository hosting to a third-party generic WebDAV hosting service.

Support for Web Access   Since all the Ecce data is on the Web, it is now possible for researchers to access their data directly through a Web browser or WebDAV explorer, indirectly through Web server extensions that manipulate the data (results viewed in a Web browser), or through specialized tools.

Note that basic support for Web access means that the system is naturally compatible with MIME and XML standards. Many researchers use text or XML data formats, and there are specific MIME types for many kinds of science-related data files. Chemical Markup Language and Chemical Structure Markup Language, the Math Markup Language, and the Extensible Scientific Interchange Language all use XML. Since they all use XML, they can easily be stored as property values, as well as file bodies. Any format that has a MIME type is automatically labeled and handled by a WebDAV repository.

WebDAV Is Easy to Work With   The Ecce developers found that the new architecture was much more conducive to debugging. Web browsers and WebDAV explorer tools became debugging tools, enabling the developers to independently verify the sizes, locations, and names of resources stored and accessed by Ecce. Raw XML data can be inspected in text editors or in XML editors.

Security Was Maintained   HTTP security is mature, flexible, and scalable. In addition to meeting the minimum security requirements, the Apache-based system supports many alternative security features. New security features are frequently implemented for Apache, allowing the system to keep pace with recent developments in security functionality.

No Transaction Support   The PNL implementors felt that the lack of transaction support in WebDAV was a drawback. Although it did not block deployment in this case, other custom applications could find otherwise.

Continual Improvement Possible   A database-backed solution has a certain lack of flexibility. It's a slight pain to add columns to existing tables, and it's more difficult to change columns when data must be upgraded. When functionality changes are large, it's extremely hard to reengineer a set of interrelated tables to handle the new functionality. In comparison, WebDAV makes it easy to change what properties exist on which resources and where those resources are stored.

WebDAV also makes it possible for clients and servers to be improved and upgraded independently. The core WebDAV engine can be upgraded to a new version that will provide backward compatibility for client requests. The custom rules and logic on the server can be updated. New properties can be added to certain types of files, and because of the way PROPFIND is designed, client software that is already deployed will still be able to view those files and retrieve the known properties.

14.5   Other Application Ideas

Finally, here are other ideas for applications or services that could conveniently and usefully incorporate WebDAV:

- Résumé and cover letter database with comments from résumé reviewers
- Special-purpose image libraries (e.g., medical imaging) with rich image metadata
- Class or course resources (syllabus, books, articles, links)
- User and group directories, such as student "e-lockers"
- Online storage services
- Group calendars, event calendars
- WebLog or "blog" server, needing interoperable authoring support
- Virtual safety-deposit boxes
- Publishing and document-related workflow servers
- Wcb publishing process incorporating contributions, review, approval
- Contract or invoice approval and archiving with simple workflow based on properties
- Collaborative FAQ writing (submit questions, add answers, add further detail)

14.6   Summary

WebDAV provides a number of interesting benefits to different vertical or horizontal client-server applications.

A data-backed Web service can use WebDAV to offer more usable authoring to its content contributors. This kind of application was illustrated with the online photo album example, where users can edit and submit their photos using WebDAV-enabled applications like Adobe Photoshop. The Web service retains control over presentation to users browsing photos over the Web.

A server offering a set of application features like Exchange 2000 can use WebDAV to unify access to application data. WebDAV can be used to model many different kinds of documents and data structures. This also makes the application data available securely over the Internet, reusing Internet infrastructure such as firewall support, SSL/TLS, and HTTP authentication.

WebDAV can be used as a component, even when it's not suitable as the core communication protocol. The instant-messaging and presence example showed that while WebDAV is not a suitable protocol basis for instant messaging and presence subscriptions and notifications, it can still provide associated pieces of functionality.

A vertical or custom data-oriented application can use WebDAV to improve flexibility and lower costs. WebDAV typically introduces a greater level of flexibility into schema management because it is much easier to define custom properties in WebDAV than in OODB systems. Deployment flexibility increases because WebDAV separates the storage layer from the storage management layer and from the server custom logic layer, allowing each layer to be swapped out to improve system functionality.

CHAPTER 15

Designing WebDAV Applications

This chapter is intended to be useful to application designers who have already decided to use WebDAV. It discusses some decisions that you must make early on and provides a range of options that you might not otherwise have considered.

The chapter is organized according to the timeline for developing a custom application. Early modeling and framework decisions come first, followed by implementation decisions and finally tips on deploying and maintaining WebDAV applications.

15.1   Metadata Usage

A large part of a custom application (like the problem-solving environment described in Chapter 14, *Custom WebDAV Applications*) can be the properties: the data they contain and the way they are organized. A little thought up front can be a benefit to making the application work better. It's not necessary to determine the entire schema up front, though—one of the benefits of WebDAV is that a resource's metadata is flexible and can easily be extended or altered later.

15.1.1   Choosing a Namespace

Choose at least one unique namespace. No other group should define elements or properties in this namespace unless there's some strong mechanism for coordination. To ensure this, use a domain name for which your group or your company retains rights. For example, Xythos Software, Inc., uses `www.xythos.com` as part of its namespaces, or the WebDAV resources site could use `www.webdav.org`. Only Xythos should use `www.xythos.com` namespaces unless some other software implementor is specifically adding compatibility for properties defined by Xythos. Domain names work very well for ensuring uniqueness, because a domain name registry exists and because any legal URL is a legal namespace. Turn the domain name into a namespace by filling out the URL with a protocol scheme and perhaps a category or product name. For the Xythos WebFile server, the namespace used is `http://www.xythos.com/namespaces/storageServer`.

15.1.2 Property Names

If the namespace is well chosen, it should be easy to pick a property name that does not conflict with any other property. This is just like naming variables inside code: Choose a name that communicates what the property stands for.

Note that a valid XML name can only begin with a letter or underscore character, although the name can contain letters, digits, hyphens, and underscores. Thus, a property name of 800number is illegal, but toll-free-number and numberin800code are valid.

15.1.3 Property Values

Recall that one of the benefits the Pacific National Laboratories researchers found (see Section 14.4 in Chapter 14) was that WebDAV is easy to debug, in part because it is all text. A tracing tool can be used to capture a WebDAV request and response, and frequently a bug can be found simply by examining the text of that request and response. Keep this benefit working for you in properties by using human-readable property names and property values. Exchange 2000 did not do this for all properties, and one of the challenges of interoperating with Exchange 2000 servers is to figure out what oddly named or formatted properties might mean.

Complex Values   Some data modeling involves a heavy use of hierarchy. Try to flatten the hierarchy because it is easier for a client, when using WebDAV, to ask for individual properties and get single values. However, when some property substructure is required, this can also be handled using XML values. For example, a value for a userFullName property might be:

```
<x:userFullName xmlns:x="http://www.example.com/namespace/">
    <x:first>Thomas</x:first><x:last>Poole</x:last>
</x:userFullName>
```

XML elements inside property names should also have namespaces to help guarantee uniqueness and extensibility.

15.1.4 Property Location

Properties can be added to any collection or file. However, the location of the property matters because clients need to address a particular resource to find out the value of a property. If the client can get more needed properties with fewer requests, the system performance will be better. For example, Exchange 2000 puts properties on folders such as the number of children and the number of unread children. Even though the client can calculate the number of child resources and unread child resources (by asking for the unread property on every child resource), the server keeps track of those counts to improve performance.

Sometimes a resource must be used to hold properties that semantically apply to some other concept, such as a user or a repository. For example:

- The root collection on a repository might be used to hold properties applying to the whole repository (rather than duplicate that property value on every resource in the repository).
- Both Xythos WebFile Server and Apple's iDisk service use properties on the user's home directory to maintain information such as the user's quota for storage usage.

One consideration in determining the location for properties is performance. If a number of properties will be requested as part of a common client action, these properties ought to be retrievable in a small number of requests.

15.1.5   Group Resources in Collections

It can be hard to decide what collections to put resources into. The choice is important because it governs how users browse collections and how fast or large PROPFIND responses are when used for browsing.

How would resources such as résumés be grouped into collections in a résumé repository replacing a résumé database? A natural semantic grouping is the job type the résumé submitter was seeking. However, semantic groupings can break down. Can a résumé belong both to "development" and to "user education?" Does it have to be copied from one collection to another?

The other extreme is not to choose—to put all resources in a massive collection. If a résumé repository tosses all résumés into one collection, the application interface can still allow résumé searching and selection via other mechanisms. Still, this may not work very well on all WebDAV servers—performance may suffer, and user browsing certainly will.

Another option is to sort documents into collections according to some type of information that isn't ambiguous and doesn't change. For example, résumés could be put into subcollections according to the month of the year they were received. Metadata can be used, rather than collection membership, to indicate that a résumé was submitted for "development," "user education," or both.

15.1.6   Use WebDAV for Global Information

Consider one of the problems of traditional database-backed custom applications. One of the most common ways to deploy a custom client/server database-backed application is to design a database architecture, write client software that uses SQL to access the database, and deploy the client software.

A major problem with that kind of solution, common though it is, is the need to upgrade. For some simple upgrades, the database architecture could be enhanced in one step and the enhanced client software deployed in the next step. However, when more extensive database architecture changes were made that the client wasn't prepared to handle, the database upgrade and deployment of new versions of client software had to be carefully and expensively coordinated.

Designers of these systems came up with all kinds of tricks to minimize the need to upgrade. For example, imagine that the client software needs to present a drop-down list for "Operating System." If the values are hard-coded into the client software, then every time a new value comes up, the client software must be upgraded. Well, that's just so painful that a better solution was quickly found. A table on the database would be created called "OS_TYPES" and it would be populated with values like "Windows 98," "Windows ME," and "Macintosh OS 9." When Apple ships Macintosh OS X, the new field can be added to the server, and all the clients pick up the new value with a simple SQL query.

WebDAV can enable the same trick. Rather than create a table, the repository can provide a property on some globally readable resource. That property can contain all the values for some drop-down selection widget. Alternatively, a file (such as an XML schema) stored on the server can serve the same purpose.

This kind of approach makes it even easier to have rich clients and custom applications that are easy to improve and upgrade.

15.1.7 Handling Multiple Document Schemas

WebDAV already handles custom applications involving documents with various MIME types. For the photo album example design described in the last chapter, the situation is simple: Browsers already know how to display images based on file name extension (.gif, .jpg) or content type. All pictures in a photo album have the same set of properties (title, date taken, display order), so there's little need to distinguish between document schemas.

On the other hand, consider the email and calendaring example. Modern email and collaboration applications frequently handle many kinds of objects, and these different objects have very different sets of properties. Email messages have "to" and "from" properties; appointments have "start-time" and "end-time" properties. However, these objects could all be represented with XML bodies and properties and share the same MIME type. Where the objects really differ is in their metadata schema (whether it's formally defined, as in a DTD, or informally defined). For an application like this, here are the questions that need to be answered:

- Are documents with different metadata schemas going to appear in the same folder, or will they be segregated (e.g., invoices go in the invoice folder, receipts in the receipt folder)?
- If documents with different schemas appear in the same folder, how are they identified so that the client knows what properties to display for that resource?

- If documents are segregated by their schemas into different folders, how are the folders identified or labeled so that the client knows what kind of resource is inside? (Hint: Don't use the name of the folder. This is likely to change for localization or other reasons. Use a property on the folder instead.)

In extreme cases, repositories can have a large number of different schemas (invoices, receipts, applications, resumes, expense reports) and these can change over time. A very flexible and extensible approach to this problem is to have a special location somewhere on the repository for referring to schemas [Lee00]. Note that a schema is never needed for WebDAV properties, but the schema can sometimes provide helpful additional information to clients. The client may be able to intelligently deal with properties that have never been seen before.

The schema approach typically involves a property on the resources, which points to the most appropriate schema to use for interpreting that resource. The schema might provide extra information about properties, such as data type, maximum value, or minimum value. It could indicate which properties should be displayed in listings or which properties are content-indexed and can be searched with text-search forms and can include property descriptions for human consumption.

15.2 Performance Considerations

Whenever the WebDAV repository will be accessed over the Internet or by a large number of users, performance considerations are important. Many tricks that improve performance also improve scalability and vice versa, so don't ignore one if the other is important.

Improving server performance is an art, but it's an art that depends more on programming choices (language, thread and memory management, and data lookup and caching) than on protocol usage choices. In other words, designing a high-performance WebDAV server is a lot like designing any other Internet server. Besides, not many implementors will write their own WebDAV server from scratch. So I'll ignore the server implementation performance considerations and refer readers to language-specific resources like [Bulka00].

The usual WebDAV performance problem isn't slow servers, it's inefficient clients. Clients that make more requests and more roundtrips than are needed not only slow their own performance, but they also make demands of the server that may affect other clients and the server's performance overall. There's very little the WebDAV server implementor or administrator can do about a client that makes more requests than it needs to.

WebDAV was designed to minimize roundtrips because the latency of an HTTP request across the open Internet is high enough to get quite painful if repeated. Early Web browser designers discovered this once Web page authors started putting a dozen small images (icons, bullets, logos) in a Web page [Padmanabhan95]. If the Web browser downloads the HTML document, then makes a request for the first image and waits for a response before asking for the second image, the document takes at least $2 \times (n + 1) \times L$ seconds to load, where n is the number of images and L is the latency, or number of seconds it takes for a short message to arrive at its destination. Some HTTP mechanisms were designed to alleviate the latency cost.

15.2.1   Minimizing Unnecessary Requests

There are a number of ways to reduce roundtrips, and one of them is simply to think carefully whether each request is really required, or whether multiple requests can be combined.

- *Use the* Depth *header wisely.* A request that can be used to apply to one resource can frequently be used to apply to many resources. For example, a client can build a full picture of the directory hierarchy more quickly with a PROPFIND depth infinity than by issuing a separate PROPFIND for every directory. There's always a tradeoff between sending many separate requests and asking for more information than is needed in one request. Servers may forbid depth infinity PROPFIND requests, but it should always be possible to get the properties of a collection and its children in one request.
- *Cache authentication information.* I've seen traces of WebDAV interactions where the client makes every request twice. The first time, the client attempts the request without authentication, and the second time it authenticates. It seems insane for the client not to continue sending the authentication information with each request after the initial authentication challenge, at least for a while.
- *Go directly to the target resource.* Web Folders (IE 6.0 and Windows XP) provides a counter-example of this principle. When connecting to a URL like http://www.example.com/alice for the first time, Web Folders sends an OPTIONS request to the root directory as well as an OPTIONS request to /alice (see the sidebar, *Web Folder Creation: Eight Roundtrips*). Most WebDAV servers respond the same way to an OPTIONS request for both a folder and its parent. The extra OPTIONS request for the parent costs a roundtrip. It could at least have been done asynchronously rather than force the user to wait for both OPTIONS responses.
- *Don't keep pinging the server.* Web Folders seems to do this as well. At each step of creating a Web Folder, it sends an identical PROPFIND (depth 0, allprop) request to the URL (see the sidebar).
- *Ask for exactly the properties that are needed.* This would have avoided a roundtrip in the Web Folders interaction shown in the sidebar, because the PROPFIND allprop request doesn't return all the properties the client needs. In addition, this saves the server from having to calculate or look up values for properties that the client is going to ignore anyway.

15.2.2   Keeping Connections Alive

Recall that TCP also adds roundtrips to interactions whenever the TCP connection is terminated and needs to be restarted. HTTP has developed two tools to minimize TCP connection restart costs:

- **Connection "keep-alive"** is an HTTP/1.1 header that asks the server to keep the TCP connection open if it can. With a potentially open connection, the client can now

---

Web Folder Creation: Eight Roundtrips

When creating a new Web Folder for `http://www.example.com/alice/`, the client code generates the following requests:

   a. OPTIONS /
   b. OPTIONS /alice
   c. PROPFIND /alice (depth 0, allprop, unauthenticated)
   d. PROPFIND /alice (depth 0, allprop)
   e. PROPFIND /alice (depth 0, asks for specific properties)

Now the client prompts the user to choose a name for the Web Folder. When the user chooses the Next button:

   f. PROPFIND /alice (depth 0, allprop)

Now the client prompts the user to finish. When the user chooses Done:

   g. PROPFIND /alice (depth 0, allprop)
   h. PROPFIND /alice (depth 1, asks for specific properties)

Finally, Web Folders pops open an Explorer window with the contents of the folder.

---

pipeline requests or wait for responses normally, but the TCP connection setup cost may be saved.

- **Pipelining** spreads the roundtrip cost across many requests. The client sends multiple idempotent requests on the same connection, without waiting for each response. The server still handles each request in order. Many sets of operations, such as downloading all the images in a Web page, can benefit from pipelining.

15.2.3   Multiple Connections

Some clients initiate many parallel HTTP requests using multiple TCP connections. This is often done to download all the images in a Web page. As soon as the image names are known, the client requests each of them, each in its own connection. This generally improves perceived performance for the user.

TCP connection startup costs are unavoidable when the client chooses to do this. An extra roundtrip is required to set up the connection. TCP slow start [Stevens98] makes the new connection less efficient at first.

Transport layer security (SSL or TLS) makes the situation only slightly worse because these protocols offer a connection resumption feature once initial shared secrets have been established. The place where SSL/TLS demands an unavoidably high cost is in setting up the very first connection and its security context, but users are accustomed to a startup cost the very first time they connect to a server.

Because multiple connections are definitely higher load for the server, a considerate client implementation would only use multiple connections if the benefits outweigh the cost. For example, the client might initiate separate connections only for downloading or uploading large resources and use the original connection for all requests that are likely to be quick.

15.2.4 Minimizing Server Load

Another consideration, which sometimes conflicts with the goal of reducing roundtrips, is that many operations have a high server load. Some of these have been discussed on the WebDAV mailing list:

- Any `Depth: infinity` operation, potentially
- PROPFIND `allprop` requests, particularly if some properties are calculated dynamically
- Searches
- `lockdiscovery` is expensive on some servers
- Locks of many resources may be expensive

A general recommendation is to use `Depth: infinity` PROPFIND requests only when they are a clear communications improvement, not just a programming shortcut. If roundtrip reduction is the reason that the client is doing a `Depth: infinity` request, even though not all the information returned is being used, consider doing pipelined requests for the information that will be used.

An even stronger recommendation can be made in the case of `allprop`: Don't use it. WebDAV servers may have resources with many properties, even hundreds of properties. Even if a client retrieved the values for all properties on a resource, what would it do with the ones it was unfamiliar with? Thus:

- If discovering what properties exist is the goal, use PROPFIND with the `propname` tag.
- If retrieving property values is the goal, use PROPFIND with the names of the desired properties.

15.3 Security Considerations

WebDAV is very likely to meet the security requirements of a custom application, thanks to the security solutions that already exist for HTTP. HTTP/1.1 supports several authentication schemes; these are used in exactly the same way with WebDAV. Encryption is typically provided with SSL or TLS.

Basic Authentication   Basic authentication uses plain-text passwords. These are only sufficient for the most insecure applications, unless the entire connection is protected with transport layer encryption.

Digest Authentication   Digest is not considered to be quite secure, although it's so vastly preferable to basic, there's little reason not to use it. Since Digest authentication requires extra roundtrips, it does slow down a protocol interaction, so implementors frequently choose the option to reuse "nonces" for the duration of a session. As long as an old nonce is used, Digest is subject to replay attacks: Attackers can copy the digest header from somebody else's message to authenticate themselves improperly to the same server.

SSL and TLS   SSL and TLS can easily be used to provide many important security features for WebDAV. In particular, encryption, message integrity, and certificates to verify server credentials are all easily provided. It's a little more complicated to set up SSL to authenticate client requests (e.g., for access control), because the client must have a certificate, and certificate distribution is not yet widespread. Instead, Basic authentication is used once the connection is secure. Most Web servers, as well as most Web browsers support SSL now, although WebDAV applications may not.

Authorization and Access Control   Authorization involves granting to specific users the authority to do specific operations. Even without supporting the Access Control specification, a WebDAV server can provide detailed and fine-tuned access control. The only problem is that administering access control must be done through some out-of-band mechanism. For instance, a Web-based interface could be built to allow management of access control by many users, or administrative tools could allow management of access control only by administrators.

15.4   Technology Considerations

Most of the work in writing a custom WebDAV application has really been done already—that's the whole point, after all. These are components that already have been written. Open-source or otherwise free components exist for each of these categories:

- WebDAV implementations, either standalone clients or servers or APIs for either
- XML engines to parse and generate XML, and tools to transform and display XML
- Web servers, application servers, and Web security modules
- Script engines for browser scripting

This section provides a little help choosing components and technologies.

15.4.1   Choice of Framework Software

When choosing WebDAV client or server software, consider your functional needs early on. The first question to ask is whether an application or an Application Programming Interface (API) is required. A custom WebDAV application may extend or use an existing WebDAV client or server. Some clients and servers offer extensibility APIs that allow a wide range of changes to be made to the repository or interactions. Other APIs are simply libraries without stand-alone programs. Choosing the right piece of software is especially important in either case (see Table 15–1).

Table 15–1   Feature Considerations

Client	Server
Metadata Considerations	
Does the client allow you to view (and edit) the metadata that your application will use? Web Folders and Office 2000 do not.	Does the server allow the quantity of metadata your application will use? If your application relies heavily on metadata retrievals, is it fast? Apache with mod_dav has metadata size and performance limitations unless the metadata store is replaced with a custom storage layer.
Locking Considerations	
Does the client reliably lock files it is working on and then release them? This is particularly a concern for drive mapping clients, where users may forget they are working on a shared file.	Most servers support locking, but does the server guarantee lack of conflicts if you need locking? IIS 5.0 supports resource locking but not collection locking. In addition, IIS 5.0 locking may fail if the data is being accessed via other protocols.
Web Folders attempts to lock files for only two minutes at a time. The server needs to be able to handle this if Web Folders is being used.	
Versioning Considerations	
Does the client support versioning? Does it support the packages you need? Most clients do not support versioning yet.	Do you need particular versioning packages? Do you need auto-versioning?
Searching Considerations	
Does the client support searching at all? Does it allow searching on custom fields? Can it do a "client-side" search if the server doesn't offer searching?	Do you need metadata searching? Do you need the ability to search the body of text-based resources? If so, do you need indexing for faster searches?
Most clients do not support resource searching yet.	Apache with mod_dav doesn't support searching, but the open-source mod_dav extension Catacomb may add sufficient search functionality for your application.
	Searching isn't quite standardized, so consider whether the implementation supports a recent draft of the DASL proposal or has gone a different way entirely.

Table 15–1   Feature Considerations *(Continued)*

Client	Server
Access Control	
Do you need the client to be able to view and set access control, or is it enough for the server and its administrators to set it?	Do you need the server to support the DAV ACL specification, or is it enough for it to offer custom access control functionality?

15.4.2   Choice of XML Parser

WebDAV implementations are greatly affected by the choice of XML parser because WebDAV uses XML namespaces, and not all XML parsers do namespaces equally well. Microsoft's XML parser (version 4.0 and later) works with COM (Visual Basic and C/C++). IBM and Apache have XML parsers that work with Java. James Clark's "expat" nonvalidating XML parser library for C is recommended for its high performance. This library can be found at *sourceforge.net/projects/expat/*.

Some parsers do validation, comparing the XML document to a DTD to ensure that the document follows all the rules of the DTD. However, few, if any, WebDAV servers take advantage of validation, because WebDAV request and response bodies may be extended. (Read Appendix 3 of the WebDAV RFC to familiarize yourself with the special requirements of WebDAV.) RFC2518 requires that any element that is unrecognized by the recipient must be ignored along with everything inside it. Thus, the only advantage of doing validation is to reject messages that do not contain required elements in the right places; validation must not reject messages that contain extra elements. The XML DTD in RFC2518 cannot be directly used in validation because it does not show all the places where there may be extra elements.

Many sites are dedicated to XML and you can find many comparisons of XML parsers. This information changes faster than a printed book can reflect. Instead, try *PerfectXML.com*, O'Reilly *XML.com*, or devx (*www.xml-zone.com*) for reviews. The XML pages at the W3C site (*www.w3.org/XML/*) have extensive software listings.

15.4.3   Libraries and APIs

WebDAV APIs exist for several languages and platforms.

Java   IBM Alphaworks hosts the WebSphere DAV for Java API (*www.alphaworks.ibm.com/tech/DAV4J/*). It's an API designed to simplify client application development, and it supports Java Remote Method Invocation (RMI).

The Jakarta Slide project consists of a number of modules that work with each other over the Internet using WebDAV. The content management system includes a Java API for server-side operations, supporting WebDAV Class 1 and 2 (including locking), access control, versioning, and searching. The client components include HTTP and WebDAV libraries as well as WebDAV-enabled Swing (Java GUI) components.

Xythos WFS includes a Java API for customizing server operations. The entire Web-based GUI included in the product is available as sample code using the API. Functionality exposed through the API includes WebDAV Class 1 and 2, access control, versioning, searching, quota, and tickets.

The Java servlet API can be used to implement a WebDAV server. Although it doesn't natively support WebDAV methods or operations, its HTTP method support (e.g., parsing headers, handling requests and responses) can easily be adapted to handle WebDAV methods. Note that the iPlanet application server blocks WebDAV methods, so it's only possible to use that server if some trick is used to bypass the blocking logic (e.g., by moving the method name to a header).

Python   Both client and server WebDAV libraries exist for Python. The Python davserver is a set of Python classes that implement a WebDAV level 1 server. It was written for groupware software but can be used for general-purpose servers. The documentation is as yet rather light but may improve by its 1.0 release. A Python DAV client interface will be part of Python 2.0 when it ships, as an adjunct to the HTTP classes already present in Python.

There's some argument that Python is the best language to use here if the choice of language is wide open. Three Python WebDAV servers have already been written, including one written as a master's thesis (by Christian Scholtz). In terms of general characteristics, many believe that Python has many features and resources that make it good for all sorts of Web applications. It comes with:

- XML parsers and other XML tools
- URL parsing and construction tools
- SSL support
- A rather capable and customizable HTTP server implementation

Perl   PerlDAV is an HTTP and WebDAV client library. It supports SSL and Digest authentication and all the basic WebDAV methods.

15.4.4   XML Stylesheet Language and Transformations

The eXtensible Stylesheet Language (XSL) is a language for expressing transformations, including stylesheets. The transformation algorithms are built using XSL Transformations, resulting in a document with processable instructions on how to transform one kind of element into another kind of element or text. XML Path Language and XSL Formatting Objects are also part of XSL. These tools help build more powerful transformation algorithms or stylesheets.

In general terms, a stylesheet is a template for transforming data into presentation. Any data that fits the stylesheet's requirements can be handled by that stylesheet. A frequent example is to translate a list of books with information on authors (expressed in XML) into a HTML table displaying those books and authors.

Transformations are even more general than stylesheets. A simple translation could convert an XML document listing each book with its authors to another XML document listing each author with his or her books. In addition to generating HTML and XML, transformations can even convert XML into very dissimilar text formats such as PDF.

Stylesheets may be easier to write in many situations than text manipulation code, and they are certainly more portable.

Displaying PROPFIND Results Because the results of a PROPFIND request are expressed in a standard XML format, a stylesheet can be used to display the successful PROPFIND results as HTML. This means that "dumb" clients, which have no knowledge of what kind of resource is being viewed or what its properties are, can still do a good display job by downloading the stylesheet that goes along with that resource. The stylesheet for an "appointment" resource in a calendar folder could do the following:

- Transform date/time elements from the transfer format (20010420T10:06:49) to a display format (10:06 a.m, Sunday, April 29, 2001).
- Display the title, location, start time, and end time at the top of the display space, in bold, attention-getting fonts.
- Display the description of the appointment further down in smaller font, with a scroll bar if necessary.

Transforming Incoming Documents Documents submitted to a repository can be transformed using XSL. This allows old or competing formats to be converted with a minimum of effort. Transforms can even be used to split a single incoming document into multiple documents, to filter out information that was only useful in transit, or to filter out information that for security reasons should not be stored.

15.4.5 XMLHTTP

Internet Explorer 5.0 and later versions of Internet Explorer support XMLHTTP, a component that was designed with WebDAV in mind. For IE, XMLHTTP together with XSLT allow an ordinary browser to be scripted to efficiently browse and interact with a very rich repository. This was used in Exchange 2000 Outlook Web Access, as discussed earlier in this chapter. More information on XMLHTTP, including sample code, is included in Appendix A, *Microsoft and Windows Tips*.

Note that even though IE is the only browser to support XMLHTTP (or an equivalent tool) at this time, there is no requirement for the server hosting pages for IE to be based on Microsoft technology. Any Web server can host pages including client script using XMLHTTP. A Java-based server may be particularly suited to host XML data, XML stylesheets, and dynamic Web pages (using Java Server Pages) with client script, because so many tools exist for development of XML- and HTTP-based applications in Java [Avedal00].

15.5 Deployment Considerations

Some WebDAV tools or proven approaches can be used to deploy a new WebDAV-based application or to maintain an existing WebDAV system.

15.5.1 Migrating Existing Repositories

Many custom applications evolve from previous systems. Over time, these systems tend to become out of date or strain at the seams, and eventually the system may need to be redesigned to take advantage of new technology such as WebDAV.

There are three major variations in this kind of task. The simplest is a pure migration, where all the data is moved to a WebDAV system, and the old access methods are no longer available. When a pure migration is not feasible because the old access methods must still be available, there are two choices. First, the data can be moved to a WebDAV-based system and the new repository exposed using the old access method. Second, the data can remain in the non-WebDAV repository, and a WebDAV "wrapper" or access layer can be added.

Migrating Data   If it's feasible to migrate data to a WebDAV solution, the job ought to be simpler in the long run. The migration can be challenging, but the resulting system is less complex and should be easier to maintain than a dual-access system.

Content can be migrated to the WebDAV repository all at once, but it doesn't need to be. A large insurance company used WebDAV for its new underwriters repository. Because the existing repository was so large, in-house developers wrote some migration tools to transfer documents "on demand" (see Figure 15–1).

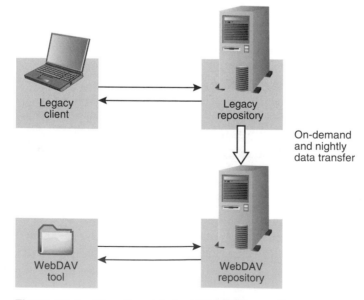

Figure 15–1   Migrating data to a WebDAV repository.

When the WebDAV system was asked for a document, if it hadn't already been migrated the requested document was immediately moved to the WebDAV system so the request could be answered. When the system had some spare cycles, unused documentation was also moved to the WebDAV repository. The old access methods continued to work, and the gateway provided old-style access to documents that had already migrated to the WebDAV repository.

Wrapping an Existing Repository This can be the hardest and the least reliable method, but sometimes it's the only choice. The reason it's so hard is that existing repositories rarely have compatible functionality to support WebDAV, if the functionality is there at all. It may only be worth doing if there are compelling reasons to support WebDAV authoring applications.

If the old access method (e.g., FTP, HTTP, proprietary protocols, or APIs) must still be available but WebDAV locking must also be supported, the data must be in a repository that truly supports locking. Otherwise, locks are hard to make work correctly through a gateway (see Figure 15–2).

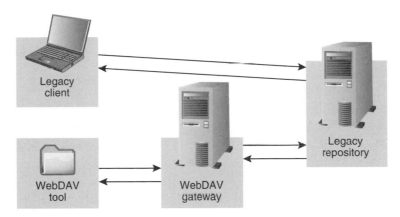

Figure 15–2 WebDAV shim or gateway.

Here are the major challenges:

- *Properties/metadata.* Most existing repositories do not have unlimited space, if any, allocated for metadata. Most existing Web servers could quickly support DAV level 1 (no locking) if it weren't for the lack of metadata storage. Even if metadata storage is available, WebDAV can easily bump up against the limitations of that storage. The amount of storage may be limited, or access could be slow.
- *Locking.* If the existing repository does not support locks or has a different locking model, it can be difficult to support WebDAV locks. It can be fairly disastrous if WebDAV clients rely on locks but the old access method is allowed to circumvent locks.
- *Versioning.* If the existing repository does support versioning, and if versioning will be exposed using WebDAV and DeltaV, make sure the models are compatible, particularly checkin/checkout.

• *Access controls.* If the existing repository has poor access control or simply a different model, it may eventually become a serious security problem. A WebDAV layer that does support access control will be unable to enforce security for protocols that bypass WebDAV. It's hard to make users sufficiently aware of this complexity to use the system in a secure manner.

15.5.2 Synchronizing Sites and Collections

Some deployment and maintenance scenarios involve duplicating a large number of files one time or repeatedly synchronizing a large number of files:

• A new repository is being deployed. Synchronization may be used to transfer content. When the synchronizing software reports no differences between the repositories, the old repository can be phased out (made read-only, taken offline, or content deleted).

• A Web site developer works on a local copy of a large Web site. Files are changed and tested locally, and then when the Web pages are all consistent, local versions are synchronized with the server.

• A Web server used for development and verification (a "staging" server) may be synchronized with the public Web server when new pages go live.

• Two WebDAV servers host the same data but in two remote locations. Because users access the data frequently at both sites, the same data needs to be stored in both locations to be accessed quickly from each. However, changes are only made at one location, so the read-only location can synchronize from the master location.

• A one-time copy, import, or export (e.g., when a bunch of file system data is being loaded into a WebDAV repository for the first time) can behave like a synchronization task. The data is synchronized once, and then when the WebDAV repository is running, the file system copy of the data can be deleted or archived.

Often these situations can be handled nicely with simple synchronization software (made relatively easy by WebDAV servers' support for ETags and last-modified datestamps). Some of the tools that do synchronization include sitecopy for Linux and Xythos WebFile Client for Windows.

15.6 Summary

Information design is a crucial part of application design. Much of the decision making is simply how to format and express each piece of data. WebDAV properties encourage small pieces of information in a flat list. However, WebDAV properties are perfectly capable of expressing complex and hierarchical information in XML.

Reduce roundtrips through careful client interaction design. Since in WebDAV, clients choose what to ask for and what to cache, a naive client implementation can easily reduce performance by a factor of two or three. A careful client implementation that does more caching and planning can minimize its load on the server and improve responsiveness for the user.

Security requirements should be determined up front. This is always a good idea in application design. Many security requirements can be met with out-of-the-box software that is designed to make HTTP secure.

Many tools and components exist to contribute to rapid application development. These include client APIs, XML parsers, server storage layers, servlet-based APIs, and extensible WebDAV servers.

An existing repository can be migrated to a WebDAV repository at once or over time. Software tools exist to synchronize two WebDAV sites. Custom software can be written to migrate data from an old site to a new one over time.

Microsoft and Windows Tips

Since so much of the deployed base of end-user operating systems is Windows, applications designers naturally may take Windows tools into account more than others. There seem to be more WebDAV-related tools somehow related to Microsoft or Windows than otherwise. In any case, some of this information can be adapted to other platforms with a little research.

This appendix provides some random tool information, tips, and tricks to help administrators, application developers, and tech support.

A.1   Supporting Legacy Windows Applications

Some users are stuck using older applications that don't (and never will) support WebDAV. Yet they may need to use these applications to edit documents stored on the repository. There's an alternative to taking multiple steps (download, then edit, then upload), and that's to use a drive-mapping client application. Chapter 10, *WebDAV Products and Tools*, discusses two drive-mapping clients for Windows (Xythos WebFile Client and South River Technologies' WebDrive). In addition, there's a free tool to map a WebDAV repository to a disk drive on Linux (the open-source DAVfs Linux file system driver).

Note that third-party software is not necessary to map a WebDAV repository to a drive letter on Windows XP, because it has native support for mapping to WebDAV repositories. On Mac OS X, the best WebDAV mounting tool is the operating system itself.

A.2   Internet Explorer Tips

Internet Explorer comes with a couple of small features that make it easier to work with Web-DAV. One feature is simply a way to mark a link as a WebDAV collection, which allows the user to browse collections very naturally starting from Web pages. A more substantial tool is XMLHTTP, a component designed to make it easier to script HTTP requests and XML document handling within a Web page in IE.

A.2.1   Open Web Folders with Link in IE

There's a little-documented way of telling IE to open a WebDAV collection as a Web Folder, rather than doing an HTTP GET request as is normally done with links. The advantage to launching a Web Folder is that the user can immediately manage the contents of the folder, deleting, moving, copying, or renaming resources. Because the Web Folder opens as an Explorer window, the user can also drag and drop files to or from the Web Folder and other Explorer windows.

This is done with a style declaration that grants the behavior `AnchorClick` to an anchor (this is just a regular link, represented with an "a" element). The `AnchorClick` behavior causes the browser to navigate to a Web Folder when a link with that behavior is clicked. However, since the link is still just a link, any Web browser can understand the link normally.

The style element can be placed just after the opening body tag of an HTML page or anywhere else it's legal to define styles. The link can go anywhere in the page. The link contains two URLs: The `folder` attribute declares the URL of the Web Folder, and the regular `href` attribute declares an alternate URL.

```
<html>
<STYLE>A {behavior:url(#default#AnchorClick);}</STYLE>
<a href="http://example.com/hr/"
    folder="http://example.com/hr/">Link</a>
</html>
```

When this link is clicked, IE opens /hr/ as a Web Folder using a PROPFIND request and displays it as a folder, allowing the user to immediately move, copy, rename, or edit Web-DAV resources. Browsers other than IE (or earlier than IE 5.5) will open the URL http://example.com/hr/ with a HTTP GET request instead, showing a static HTML page with a list of links to the resources in the collection, and the user has no direct ability to author those resources.

Another way to use this feature is to put two different URLs in the attributes of the link. The alternate page could be an error page, so browsers that ignore the folder attribute display an error instead.

```
<STYLE>A {behavior:url(#default#AnchorClick);}</STYLE>
<a href="http://example.com/unsupported-browser.html"
    folder="http://example.com/hr/">Link to Web Folder</a>
```

With this link, browsers other than IE (or earlier than IE 5.5) will instead open a specific error page, rather than try to open the collection with a GET request.

The Web page containing this kind of link doesn't have to be stored on a WebDAV server itself. It could be a page hosted on a regular Web server, containing a link to a WebDAV collection on a WebDAV server.

The AnchorClick behavior is documented in MSDN Online [Microsoft03a]. It is intended for use with the anchor element only.

A.2.2 Open Web Folders with Script in IE

Another way to use IE to open Web Folders is to use a client-side script to launch a Web Folder. This has the advantage that the target for the Web Folder can be determined dynamically. Here's an example of a Web page that can be put in any WebDAV collection. When IE displays this Web page and the user clicks the button, IE shows the contents of the parent collection as a Web Folder.

```html
<html>
<head><title>Web Folder Scripting</title></head>
<body>
<STYLE>
   .hfolder{behavior:url('#default#httpFolder');}
</STYLE>

<SCRIPT>
function openFolder(){
   var sFolder=location.href.substring(0,
      location.href.lastIndexOf("/"));
   oViewFolder.navigate(sFolder);
}
</SCRIPT>

<P>This page is hosted in a WebDAV collection. Push the button
to view the parent collection using a WebDAV PROPFIND query.
</P>
<form>
<input type="button"
      onclick = "openFolder()" value="Go Up To Collection"/>
</form>

<span ID=oViewFolder CLASS = "hFolder"></span>

</body>
</html>
```

When the page is loaded, the STYLE element grants the httpFolder behavior (the ability to navigate to a Web Folder) to anything defined as class hFolder. The span at the bottom of the page is defined as class hFolder. Normally, a span element doesn't have the ability to navigate to a Web Folder, but style declaration gives it that ability. The form contains a button, and the button is the trigger for the `openFolder()` script. The `openFolder()` script dynamically determines what WebDAV collection to view, and tells the span to navigate to that collection.

The `httpFolder` behavior is documented in MSDN online as well [Microsoft03b]. It is much more flexible than the `AnchorClick` behavior because it can be used with many types of HTML elements, including "span" and the anchor or link element.

A.2.3 XMLHTTP in Web Page Scripts

MS IE versions 5.5 and later come with a component called XMLHTTP. It allows simple client-side code to build HTTP requests and parse HTTP responses, particularly if the request or response bodies are XML documents. The component can be used in many situations, but so far it has found wide use in Web pages with VB or JScript code to run the request through the component and handle the response.

XMLHTTP can be used in interesting ways inside Web pages. Because of its combination of XML and HTTP capabilities, the component makes it easy to script WebDAV requests. That means that the script downloaded from the server instructs the client how to make the WebDAV request, and then when the response is received, what to do with it.

Mozilla has a couple of modules that achieve nearly the same functionality as XMLHTTP. However, Mozilla supports more standardized W3C-defined approaches like the XML-DOM recommendation [Le Hors00] for XML processing. To handle scripted HTTP requests and responses, Mozilla supports the JavaScript XMLHTTPRequest object [Arvidsson02]. I recommend *webfx.eae.net* for information on using XML in browsers in general.

A.2.4 VBScript and XMLHTTP

Visual Basic Script (VBScript) is one of the IE scripting languages that can use the XMLHTTP component. VBScript only works with IE, but then again, so does the XMLHTTP component.

VBScript is syntactically much like Visual Basic (VB). Thus, this example can easily be adapted to apply to a VB application that needs to make WebDAV or HTTP requests.

The example is a page that does a PROPFIND request on a directory selected by the user. The code builds a PROPFIND request, sends it, and handles the response. The meat of the example is the Web page script, a single VBScript subroutine that loads a XMLHTTP object, sets it up, and sends it.

Listing A–1 shows a VBScript routine or **subfunction** that makes a PROPFIND request to the server and handles the response.

Listing A–1 VBScript subfunction to do PROPFIND.

```
Sub cmdDoPropfind
   Dim strDdirectoryName, propfindRequest, xmlDoc
```

Listing A–1 VBScript subfunction to do PROPFIND. *(Continued)*

```
    strDirectoryName = directoryForm.text_directory.value
    Set propfindRequest = CreateObject("Microsoft.XMLHTTP")
    propfindRequest.Open "PROPFIND", strDirectoryName, FALSE
    propfindRequest.send("")
        Set xmlDoc = propfindRequest.responseXML

    div_results.innerHTML = _
        xmlDoc.transformNode(transformPROPFIND.documentElement)
End Sub
```

Here's what this method does:

1. First, the function declares its local variables.
2. Then it initializes the local variable `strDirectoryName` to the name typed in by the user. As we'll shortly see, `directoryForm` is the name of the form, and `text_directory` is the name of the field, where the user types in the directory name to view.
3. The next local variable, `propfindRequest`, is created as an instance of the XMLHTTP object.
4. Now, `propfindRequest` is configured to send a synchronous PROPFIND request to the directory name ("FALSE" means not asynchronously, or in other words, synchronously).
5. The request is sent and the response returned synchronously (the Web page may freeze while this is happening).
6. Since the code waits until the response returns, the variable `xmlDoc` can immediately be set to the value of the response XML returned.
7. Finally, the `div_results` element (which appears inside the page as a placeholder for the table we're going to create) is given a bunch of text to display, consisting of the response XML transformed via the `transformPropfind` stylesheet.

This code referenced four objects outside the scope of the subfunction:

- The form named `directoryForm` inside the main Web page
- The field named `textDirectory` inside that form
- The `div_results` HTML element inside the main Web page
- The stylesheet named `transformPropfind`

To see how this routine works in the context of a Web page, Listing A–2 shows the entire Web page, repeating the VBScript routine and showing the stylesheet and HTML framework.

Listing A–2   Web page with VBScript, PROPFIND, and stylesheet formatting.

```
<HTML>
<HEAD>
  <TITLE>Simple PROPFIND formatted with stylesheet</TITLE>
</HEAD>


<!-- The script does a PROPFIND request and formats the response
     using the stylesheet. -->

<script language="vbscript">

Sub cmdDoPropfind
   Dim strDdirectoryName, propfindRequest, xmlDoc

   strDirectoryName = directoryForm.text_directory.value
   Set propfindRequest = CreateObject("Microsoft.XMLHTTP")
   propfindRequest.Open "PROPFIND", strDirectoryName, FALSE

   propfindRequest.send("")
   Set xmlDoc = propfindRequest.responseXML

   div_results.innerHTML = _
      xmlDoc.transformNode(transformPROPFIND.documentElement)

End Sub

</script>

<!-- The body of the Web page itself is very short. The form
     allows the user to select a directory to propfind. The 'div'
     element is where the output of the script is written. -->

<BODY>

   <form id="directoryForm">
      <input type=TEXT value="http://localhost:8080/hr/"
         id="text_directory" size="50">
      <input type=BUTTON value="Show" ONCLICK="cmdDoPropfind">
   </form>

   <div id="div_results"></div>

</BODY>
```

Listing A–2 Web page with VBScript, PROPFIND, and stylesheet formatting. *(Continued)*

```
<!-- The stylesheet is in an xml island.
    It produces a table with one row for each 'response'
    element in the PROPFIND multistatus response. Each 'select'
    attribute contains a XML Path statement that selects an XML
    fragment from the XML response body. -->

<xml id="transformPROPFIND">
   <xsl:template xmlns:xsl="uri:xsl" xmlns:d="DAV:">
      <table cellspacing="2" border="1">
         <tr>
            <th>Resource</th>
            <th>Creation Date</th>
            <th>Last Modified Date</th>
         </tr>
         <xsl:for-each select="d:multistatus/d:response">
         <tr><td>
            <xsl:value-of select="d:propstat/d:prop/ d:displayname"/>
         </td><td>
            <xsl:value-of select="d:propstat/d:prop/ d:creationdate"/>
         </td><td>
         <xsl:value-of
            select="d:propstat/d:prop/d:getlastmodified"/>
         </td></tr>
      </xsl:for-each>
      </table>
   </xsl:template>
</xml>
```

The page itself doesn't look terribly exciting because the example was kept simple and short. When the user types in a WebDAV collection URL and clicks Show, all the resources inside the collection are displayed in a table (see Figure A–1).

Note that in this example the script, HTML body, and stylesheet components are all static. The client only needs to download these components once. The client can then do as many fast PROPFIND requests as needed without reloading the stylesheet or the Web page itself. Typically, this reduces server load and increases perceived user responsiveness.

The script, the HTML formatting, and the stylesheet can all be stored and downloaded in separate files. For example:

- `dopropfind.vbs` for the VB function
- `displaypropfind.xml` for the stylesheet
- `viewfolder.html` for the rest

Figure A–1   VBScript example (after clicking Show).

Multiple files can be useful when the subroutine and stylesheet are reused in more than one Web page. Each page imports the script file containing the correct subroutine and the XML file containing the relevant stylesheet. If the script file and stylesheet file are imported in more than one page, the client only has to download each file once and then cache and reuse them for a while.

A.2.5   JavaScript and XMLHTTP

XMLHTTP also works with JavaScript. It functions the same way, only the syntax is different. Listing A–3 is a trivial JavaScript function that does a PROPFIND to a URL.

Listing A–3   JavaScript and XMLHTTP.

```
<SCRIPT language="JavaScript">
function GetData(url)
{
   var objHTTP = new ActiveXObject("Microsoft.XMLHTTP");
   objHTTP.open("PROPFIND", url, false);
   objHTTP.send("");
   return objHTTP.text;
}
</SCRIPT>
```

A.3   Microsoft WebDAV

Microsoft implements a number of useful extensions to WebDAV in their WebDAV servers. Some are rather difficult to use, but some have simple syntax and straightforward usage.

A.3.1   Microsoft Row Extension to Range Header

The Range header (described in Chapter 3, *HTTP Mechanics*) is an HTTP/1.1 header that can be used to limit the number of bytes the server will return in response to a method such as GET. The Range header is quite useful for clients to resume interrupted download requests. A quick example to recall the format of this header:

```
Range: bytes=0-1000
```

Since WebDAV PROPFIND requests can also produce long responses, it could be quite useful to have a similar mechanism for PROPFIND. However, there's a better way to limit the size of the response, and that is to ask the server for a limited number of resource responses, rather than a limited number of bytes. The resource responses are analogous to rows in a table, so the Microsoft-defined custom Range header syntax calls them rows. For example:

```
Range: rows=0-24
```

With this header on a PROPFIND request, some Microsoft WebDAV servers (Exchange 2000, Sharepoint, perhaps others) will return only 25 response elements in the PROPFIND response. Even if the collection contains hundreds of resources, properties are returned for only 25 of them. If this is sufficient to fill up a screen in a client UI, then there's no need for the client to immediately download more information than is required to fill up the screen. Later, the client can ask for "rows = 25 – 100" to get more responses if necessary. Note that this assumes that the server applies some type of consistent ordering to PROPFIND responses, although it doesn't say what ordering that must be.

The complete syntax of the rows extension to the Range header is the same as that for bytes (e.g., the last 100 rows can be requested with "rows = 100 –").

A.3.2   Property Name and Namespace Concatenation

Many existing Microsoft tools have been adapted over the past few years to integrate with WebDAV. One of the popular ways to do this is to use the Microsoft OLE DB Provider for Internet Publishing, a.k.a. MSDAIPP (I'm not responsible for the acronym having little to do with the full name, that's just what the DLL is called). MSDAIPP is a client library providing an OLEDB interface for the application to use and translating requests to WebDAV to send to the server. One challenge in implementing this component was that OLEDB doesn't have the concept of namespaces. The implementors needed a way to handle namespaces and property names together so that the OLEDB layer could translate a request for a property into the full WebDAV PROPFIND format complete with namespaces.

The rules for namespace/name concatenation are useful in other places as well, such as in the SQL SEARCH statements, where SELECT and WHERE clauses need to name columns. The property namespace/name combination is used as a column name in SQL requests.

1. If the namespace name ends with a :, \, or / character, concatenate the property name directly onto the namespace name. For example:

   The displayname property
      in the `DAV:` namespace
      becomes `DAV:displayname`

   The rank property
      in the `urn:schemas.microsoft.com:fulltextqueryinfo:` namespace
      becomes `urn:schemas.microsoft.com:fulltextqueryinfo:rank`.

2. If the namespace name ends with another character, concatenate a # character onto the namespace before adding the property value. Thus:

   The Title property
      in the `urn:schemas-microsoft-com:office:office` namespace
      becomes `urn:schemas-microsoft-com:office:office#Title`.

3. This transformation is reversible. To decompose a concatenated property string into its namespace name and property name, look for the last instance in the string of any of the characters :, \, /, or #. That is the separator character. If the separator character is #, remove it; otherwise, keep the separator character as part of the namespace name, and the rest of the string is the property name.

A.3.3 SQL SEARCH Syntax

Microsoft implemented an HTTP method called SEARCH in its Exchange 2000 and Sharepoint servers. Although a couple of IETF Internet Drafts have proposed SEARCH methods and syntaxes, Microsoft's implementations do not conform to any of these proposals. (Note that none of the proposals were made into standards at the time and still aren't standardized at the writing of this appendix.)

The Microsoft SEARCH method syntax simply embeds a SQL statement inside an XML body in the SEARCH request:

```
<?xml version="1.0"?>
<DAV:searchrequest>
   <DAV:sql>
      sql-select-statement
   </DAV:sql>
</DAV:searchrequest>
```

In addition, the SEARCH request requires a couple HTTP headers in order to work completely. The headers required for Sharepoint are covered in Sharepoint documentation, which can be found online.

Like the Internet Draft SEARCH proposal, the Microsoft SEARCH format is intended to be able to search property values on WebDAV resources as well as the bodies of those resources. Thus, SQL SELECT statements and WHERE clauses must be able to name property names. The mapping between WebDAV property names and SQL statement column names is pretty straightforward, even though strictly speaking there's no such thing as a "table" with "columns" in a WebDAV repository. The concatenation trick described in the previous section allows the property namespace to be included as well as the property name.

Building SQL Statements   Once we know how to build property and namespace concatenated strings, we can use those in the SQL statements in SEARCH requests. The property strings are quoted. If we want to find the displayname property value for every resource of size greater than 10000 bytes within /hr/, this is the SQL statement to use.

```
SELECT "DAV:displayname"
    FROM SCOPE ('DEEP TRAVERSAL OF "/hr/"')
    WHERE ("DAV:getcontentlength" > 10000)
```

Notice the FROM clause names a WebDAV collection and a scope or depth. This scope overrules the Depth header value, which is ignored.

To put this SQL statement inside the XML body of the SEARCH request, the characters &, >, and < must be escaped first. The body of the SEARCH request will be:

```
<?xml version="1.0"?>
<DAV:searchrequest>
   <DAV:sql>
      SELECT "DAV:displayname"
          FROM SCOPE ('DEEP TRAVERSAL OF "/hr/"')
          WHERE ("DAV:getcontentlength" &gt; 10000)
   </DAV:sql>
</DAV:searchrequest>
```

Finally, the SEARCH method takes a couple of headers that may modify how the server responds. The same range rows header that works for PROPFIND works for the SEARCH request:

```
SEARCH /hr/ HTTP/1.1
Host: www.example.com
Range: rows=0-39
Content-type: text/xml
Content-length: xxx
```

The Microsoft Developer Network (MSDN) has further information on this and other special Microsoft request methods and headers.

HTTP Status Codes

All response status codes used and defined by WebDAV are listed here. Many of the HTTP/1.1 codes are used as is by WebDAV without attaching any additional meaning. For completeness, all HTTP/1.1 codes are described here, because all WebDAV clients must also be HTTP clients and can expect to see any of these codes from a server.

Each status code is listed with a brief gloss of its meaning or use and a reference to the specification in which it is first defined. Status codes are ordered numerically, since the first digit provides some guidance as to the kind of status being reported.

Current and in-progress WebDAV extensions do not define new numerical codes. It's difficult to define and use numerical codes without risk of collision with other HTTP extensions. Instead, DeltaV, ACL, and other WebDAV extensions use the most appropriate numerical error code and then in the body of the error response include an XML error code. Those XML codes are not covered here. Clients must still be able to get a general idea of the class of failure from the numerical code, even when most of the information is in the XML error code.

B.1   Informational Status Codes

Status codes from 100–199 are classified as "Informational." They are not successes, failures, or redirections.

B.1.1   100 Continue

The 100 Continue response indicates that the server is ready to receive the body of the request. This is only used if the client asked for confirmation before sending the body, by using the `Expect: 100-continue` header in the request, as explained in "Predicting Success for

Lengthy Requests" in Chapter 3, *HTTP Mechanics*. Servers must handle this feature, but clients aren't required to. As an example, a client might use the `Expect` header together with the `Content-Length` header in a PUT request to confirm that the server is willing to handle a file of a given size. If the server cannot, it should send 417 Expectation Failed.

> Defined in HTTP/1.1.

B.1.2   101 Switching Protocols

101 Switching Protocols indicates that the server will now begin communicating using a different protocol. This is only used when the `Upgrade` header is sent in the request and the server decides to switch.

> Defined in HTTP/1.1.

B.1.3   102 Processing

102 Processing is used by a WebDAV server to indicate that it is working on a time-consuming request. For example, a `depth infinity` MOVE request to a large collection could take some time to complete. Clients may time out lengthy requests under the assumption that the request was ignored or dropped somehow. This status code allows the server to let the client know that it shouldn't time out the request, that the server is still working on the real response. Clients *must* support this response code, since the server can return it in any time-consuming operation. Servers are not required to use this response code.

> Defined in WebDAV.

B.2   Success Status Codes

The status codes in the 200–299 range are all success responses of some kind or another. Not all successes are equal, however, and often clients need to know exactly how a request succeeded.

B.2.1   200 OK

200 OK is the basic success code for responses that are accompanied with a body. Whenever a basic GET request is successful, this code is used to return the resource's body.

> Defined in HTTP/1.1.

B.2.2   201 Created

201 Created is used to indicate that the server created a new resource as a result of the request. PUT, MKCOL, LOCK, and COPY all return 201 Created when a new resource is created. This status response does not typically have a body, but it may.

> Defined in HTTP/1.1.

B.2.3 202 Accepted

202 Accepted was defined for operations that are requested now but may not take place until later, such as documents submitted to an acceptance process that takes human intervention. Neither HTTP nor WebDAV commonly uses this.

Defined in HTTP/1.1.

B.2.4 203 Non-Authoritative Information

203 Non-Authoritative Information can replace 200 OK when the server might not be responding with the most up-to-date and correct resource body or headers. This is not frequently seen in practice.

Defined in HTTP/1.1.

B.2.5 204 No Content

204 No Content is a basic success code, like 200 OK, but the response has no body. This could be the case, for example, where a GET request is issued for a resource that exists but has an empty body. It is used more commonly in WebDAV, for success responses to methods like COPY and MOVE, where there is no information to be returned in the body.

Defined in HTTP/1.1.

B.2.6 205 Reset Content

205 Reset Content is intended to be used when a server has accepted some input on a resource and the client should refresh its view of that resource as a result. It could theoretically be very useful in submission of Web forms, but it is not used in practice.

Defined in HTTP/1.1.

B.2.7 206 Partial Content

200 Partial Content is used very much like the 200 OK status code, except that it is used when not all the available information was returned. For example, the client could request only the first 1000 bytes of a page using the `Accept-Range` header, and this response would indicate a successful fulfillment of that partial request.

Defined in HTTP/1.1.

B.2.8 207 Multi-Status

207 Multi-Status responses indicate that the response contains one or more response codes inside its body text. These response codes may refer to multiple resources, with the URLs to those resources also inside the body text. This is most useful in responding to requests that address multiple resources.

Many WebDAV servers return 207 Multi-Status even when only one status code is in the body. For example, the server may consistently prepare 207 Multi-Status bodies for every PROPFIND response, in case there is a need for more than one status code. Even when only one status code is required, the 207 Multi-Status response is already prepared and might as well be sent.

Defined in WebDAV.

B.3   Redirect Status Codes

The status codes from 300 to 399 are intended to redirect the client to the right URL at which to make the request. These can be problematic in WebDAV. Although all clients are supposed to support redirects, they may choose not to follow redirects, and this has caused interoperability issues.

B.3.1   300 Multiple Choices

300 Multiple Choices indicates that there are actually several related entities or resources available at the requested URL. The response includes a body with information on how to pick one of those entities. This status code is not commonly used.

Defined in HTTP/1.1.

B.3.2   301 Moved Permanently

301 Moved Permanently is a basic redirect response for a single URL to a single new URL. This is used commonly on the Web, when a popular Web page must move to a new server address (e.g., to a server with more power to handle all the requests). It can also theoretically be used in response to WebDAV methods. The client will frequently just repeat the same request to the new URL.

Defined in HTTP/1.1.

B.3.3   302 Found or 302 Moved Temporarily

302 Found is also known as 302 Moved Temporarily. The first wording is the official one, found in RFC2616. However, the other version can frequently be found on the Web. Either way, this code is used when the resource can temporarily be found at a different URL. This response can theoretically be used with any WebDAV request.

Defined in HTTP/1.1.

B.3.4   303 See Other

303 See Other is used to redirect to another resource, which is not a replacement for the originally requested resource. This code is intended to be used when a Web client submits a form to one URL, and the server wants to tell it to display the results of a GET to another URL now that the form has been submitted.

Defined in HTTP/1.1.

B.3.5   304 Not Modified

304 Not Modified is used only in response to a method with an `If-Modified-Since` header. The `If-Modified-Since` header is used to make a request conditional on the last-modified time of the requested resource. It is frequently used with the GET method to download a resource only if it has changed since the last time it was downloaded, when the client has a cached version. The client shouldn't need to support this status code if it doesn't use If-Modified-Since.

> Defined in HTTP/1.1.

B.3.6   305 Use Proxy

305 Use Proxy was intended to be used by firewalls to reroute clients to a proxy server. It can theoretically be used in response to any HTTP/1.1 or WebDAV method.

> Defined in HTTP/1.1.

B.3.7   306 (Unused)

This status code is reserved in HTTP/1.1.

B.3.8   307 Temporary Redirect

307 Temporary Redirect is defined almost identically to 302 Found. I can't tell the difference.

> Defined in HTTP/1.1.

B.4   Client Failure Status Codes

The status codes in the 400–499 range are all client failure responses, or at least the server thinks the client is at fault. The request could be badly formatted, sent to the wrong place, illegal, or unauthorized.

B.4.1   400 Bad Request

400 Bad Request means that the server thinks the request is poorly or illegally formatted. This could include use of a method that the server does not support, a header with an illegal value, or a request body with incorrect syntax. It can be returned in response to any method.

> Defined in HTTP/1.1.

B.4.2   401 Unauthorized

401 Unauthorized means that the client cannot perform the request it is making with the current authentication credentials. The implication is that if the client had different credentials, the request could be successful.

Usually, when clients receive this response and have not previously sent authentication information, the client will display a "log-in" dialog to get authentication information from the user. Thus, the response code should only be used when that approach may help. Compare to 403 Forbidden, for actions that wouldn't be allowed no matter how the user authenticated.

Defined in HTTP/1.1.

B.4.3   402 Payment Required

Similar to 401 Unauthorized, this response implies that if the client or user followed some payment procedure, the request could succeed. Unfortunately, no common payment protocols have arisen to fill this void, so in practice there's nothing clients can do when this error is received.

Defined in HTTP/1.1.

B.4.4   403 Forbidden

403 Forbidden is usually used for methods that are not allowed under any circumstances. In WebDAV, this is used frequently, and even more so in DeltaV. Some example situations:

- A property is read-only, and the client is trying to edit it.
- A MKCOL request is made in a location where a collection cannot be created.
- A MOVE or a COPY request is made when the source and destination URLs are the same (that is, it is forbidden to move or copy a resource over itself).
- A request is made for a depth-infinity lock, but the server doesn't allow that kind of lock.

Defined in HTTP/1.1.

B.4.5   404 Not Found

404 Not Found indicates the resource identified by the request URL could not be found on the server. Note that some servers may use this when the requesting user does not have permission to see the resource.

Defined in HTTP/1.1.

B.4.6   405 Method Not Allowed

405 Method Not Allowed is used when the resource identified in the request URL does not support the method in the request. In WebDAV, this status code is used when a MKCOL request is made to a resource that already exists. MKCOL is only allowed on URLs that do not map to existing resources.

Defined in HTTP/1.1.

B.4.7   406 Not Acceptable

406 Not Acceptable has a very specific meaning; it doesn't just mean that the server didn't like the request. It is related to the "Accept" family of headers that the client may send in the request.

If the client sends one of these headers (e.g., `Accept-Language` or `Accept-Encoding`) with values such that the server cannot pick or format an acceptable response, this error is returned. Thus, this status code should never be used unless the client used one of these headers in the request.

Defined in HTTP/1.1.

B.4.8 407 Proxy Authentication Required

407 Proxy Authentication Required is similar to 401 Unauthenticated, but the client must authenticate the user to the proxy server, not the content server.

Defined in HTTP/1.1.

B.4.9 408 Request Time-out

408 Request Time-out is used when the client's request is taking too long to finish and the server must cancel. This status code is intended for use when the client's request is incomplete or not even started, not when the server processing is taking too long.

Defined in HTTP/1.1.

B.4.10 409 Conflict

409 Conflict is defined as "the request could not be completed due to a conflict with the current state of the resource." This is ambiguous enough to make this error code very attractive as a general-purpose error code. However, the HTTP/1.1 specification is very clear that this should only be used when there is a reasonable expectation that the client could fix the state of the resource, resubmit the same request to the same resource, and have it work.

WebDAV makes frequent use of this status code to indicate that an operation cannot succeed because the expected parent resources do not exist yet. For example, a request to create a collection called `/chris/public/photos` cannot succeed if `/chris` and `/chris/public` do not exist yet. However, the client can clearly detect this, create those collections, and make the `photos` collection successfully.

If there is no way the client can make the request succeed, use 403 Forbidden or some other status code.

Defined in HTTP/1.1.

B.4.11 410 Gone

410 Gone means the resource used to exist here but doesn't any longer. It may have been moved, but there is no new address. This could theoretically be used in response to any method.

Defined in HTTP/1.1.

B.4.12   411 Length Required

411 Length Required may be used if the client's request did not have a `Content-Length` header. This indicates a serious client error because the server simply has no way of knowing when the body ends without a `Content-Length` header.
Defined in HTTP/1.1.

B.4.13   412 Precondition Failed

The 412 Precondition Failed status response must only be used when specific headers are in the request. In this case, it's used if the conditions specified in any conditional header do not hold true. Conditional headers in HTTP include `If-Match`, `If-None-Match`, or `If-Unmodified-Since`. WebDAV adds the `If` header to this list.
Defined in HTTP/1.1.

B.4.14   413 Request Entity Too Large

413 Request Entity Too Large is pretty self-descriptive. The server can refuse to handle a request that is too large, by the server's definition. This is rarely a problem in practice; some Web servers can handle PUT request with file bodies that are hundreds of megabytes long.
Defined in HTTP/1.1.

B.4.15   414 Request-URI Too Large

414 Request-URI Too Large is similar to 413 Request Entity Too Large: It's at the server's discretion to refuse a request if it thinks the Request-URI is problematically large. In Apache, the limit appears to commonly be 8190 bytes [Gossamer02].
Defined in HTTP/1.1.

B.4.16   415 Unsupported Media Type

415 Unsupported Media Type refers specifically to the format of the request body. For example, an HTTP/1.1 server is quite likely to refuse to handle a POST method with a body such as a GIF or an XML file. WebDAV servers may also use this status code when a request method isn't expected to have a body at all, but the client sends a body with the request.
Defined in HTTP/1.1.

B.4.17   416 Requested Range Not Satisfiable

This error is used in response to requests with the `Range` header. If the `Range` header is in the proper syntax but the range is invalid or otherwise not obtainable, this is the error to use.
Defined in HTTP/1.1.

B.4.18 417 Expectation Failed

This error is used in response to requests with the `Expect` header. It is related to 100 Continue. When the client sends an `Expect: 100-continue` header, it waits for the server to respond before sending the body of the request. If the server doesn't want to handle the rest of the request, it should use this error code.

Defined in HTTP/1.1.

B.4.19 418-421

These status codes were not defined in HTTP. WebDAV skipped over these status codes due to a potential conflict with other HTTP extensions that had been proposed.

B.4.20 422 Unprocessable Entity

An "Unprocessable Entity" is a request body that the server cannot parse. For example:

- The client used a MIME-type that the server just does not support.
- The client sent a MIME-type that the server supports, but the body does not meet the requirements of that MIME-type (e.g., invalid XML body).

Defined in WebDAV.

B.4.21 423 Locked

423 Locked means that the resource (or one of the resources inside it) is locked, and therefore the operation requested cannot be performed. The operation requested could be a LOCK request for a new lock on an exclusively locked resource, or a request to perform a write operation on a write-locked resource.

Defined in WebDAV.

B.5 Server Failure Status Codes

The range of status codes from 500 to 599 indicates that some error occurred on the server. It may be a temporary condition, but more often it's fairly permanent.

B.5.1 500 Internal Server Error

500 Internal Server Error is often a server coding error. A WebDAV server implemented in C might include "asserts" for conditions that the programmer believes should not occur. Code that deals with unexpected asserts or exceptions should usually construct a 500 Internal Server Error response and send it to the client as part of the cleanup.

Defined in HTTP/1.1.

B.5.2   501 Not Implemented

501 Not Implemented means that the server does not support the method used. For example, a LOCK request to a server that only implements WebDAV Level 1 should result in a 501 Not Implemented response. Similarly, a typo or case mismatch in the method name (e.g., "PRO-PATCH" for "PROPPATCH") would result in this response.

    Defined in HTTP/1.1.

B.5.3   502 Bad Gateway

502 Bad Gateway is most frequently returned by a proxy that fails to reach the destination Web server at all and can't complete the request.

    It's possible that a destination Web server could return this status code, too. A client could send a COPY request with a `Destination` header naming a target on another server. Since WebDAV doesn't support copying a file to another server, the appropriate response might be 502 Bad Gateway. Even within what appears to be a single repository (a namespace exposed through a single consistent domain name), there may be clustering or multiple database backends, and imperfect reliability in integrating these components may sometimes result in a 502 Bad Gateway error.

    Defined in HTTP/1.1.

B.5.4   503 Service Unavailable

This code is returned when the server is temporarily unavailable to handle requests. This could happen when the server is being reconfigured, upgraded, or is simply too busy.

    Defined in HTTP/1.1.

B.5.5   504 Gateway Timeout

This response code indicates that the responding server was able to contact another Web server to complete the request, but that other Web server took too long to finish. Like 502 Bad Gateway, this would frequently be used by Web proxy servers that timeout in their requests to destination Web servers.

    Defined in HTTP/1.1.

B.5.6   505 HTTP Version Not Supported

The server does not support the HTTP version of the request.

    Defined in HTTP/1.1.

B.5.7   507 Insufficient Storage

507 Insufficient Storage response code is used to indicate that the server has run out of memory or persistent storage. It can also be used to indicate that the user has some kind of quota that has been reached.

    Defined in WebDAV.

References

Much of the information that was filtered into this book came from difficult-to-cite sources: working group meetings, hallway conversations, discussions with co-workers, and the copious traffic on the various WebDAV mailing lists. Meeting minutes are available online through the IETF archives (*www.ietf.org/proceedings/directory.html*). The official WebDAV standards development mailing lists and their archives can be found through the WebDAV Working Group's home page (*http://ftp.ics.uci.edu/pub/ietf/webdav/*). Various development-related mailing lists also have extensive archives, most notably dav-dev (*http://dav.lyra.org/mailman/listinfo/dav-dev*).

[Adobe01] "A Manager's Introduction to Adobe eXtensible Metadata Platform." November 2001. (*www.adobe.com/products/xmp/pdfs/whitepaper.pdf*)

[Alliance01] *ASLabs-2001-01: Multiple Security Problems in eEye Secure.* IIS Alliance Security Labs. May 2001. (*http://archives.indenial.com/hypermail/ntbugtraq/2001/May2001/0014.html; www.cotse.com/mailing-lists/ntbugtraq/2001/May/0014.html*)

[Amsden99] *Goals for Web Versioning.* J. Amsden, C, Kaler, and J. Stracke. Internet Draft proposed to DeltaV Working Group. June 1999.

[Arvidsson02] "XML Extras." Erik Arvidsson. May 2002. (*http://webfx.eae.net/dhtml/xmlextras/xmlextras.html*)

[Avedal00] *Professional JSP.* Karl Avedal et al. 2000. Wrox Press.

[Berners-Lee00] *Weaving the Web.* 1999. Tim Berners-Lee and Mark Fischetti. San Francisco: Harper

[Biron01] *XML Schema Part 2: Datatypes.* Paul V. Biron, Ashok Malhotra. May 2001. (*www.w3.org/TR/2001/REC-xmlschema-2-20010502/*)

[Box00] *Simple Object Access Protocol (SOAP) 1.1*. Don Box. DevelopMentor. David Ehnebuske, Gopal Kakivaya, Andrew Layman, Noah Mendelsohn, Henrik Frystyk Nielsen, Satish Thatte, Dave Winer. May 2000. (*www.w3.org/TR/SOAP/*)

[Bray99] *Namespaces in XML*. Tim Bray, Dave Hollander, Andrew Layman. January 1999. (*www.w3.org/ TR/REC-xml-names/*)

[Bray00] *Extensible Markup Language (XML) 1.0*, second edition. Tim Bray, Jean Paoli, C. M. Sperberg-McQueen, Eve Maler. October 2000. (*www.w3.org/TR/REC-xml*)

[Bulka00] *Java Performance and Scalability Volume 1: Server-side Programming Techniques*. Dov Bulka. 2000. Addison-Wesley.

[CGI96] *The Common Gateway Interface*. NCSA, March 1996. (*http://hoohoo.ncsa.uiuc.edu/cgi/*)

[Clemm02] *WebDAV Access Control Protocol*. Geoffrey Clemm, Anne Hopkins, Eric Sedlar, Jim Whitehead, WebDAV Working Group Internet Draft. July 2002.

[Clemm03] *Binding Extensions to WebDAV*. G. Glemm, J. Crawford, J. Reschke, J. Slein, E. J. Whitehead, WebDAV Working Group Internet Draft. February 2003.

[Delio02] *Rooting Around Site With Intent?* Michelle Delio. *Wired*. October 30, 2002. (*www.wired.com/ news/politics/0,1283,56079,00.html*)

[Dick03] *XML: A Manager's Guide*. Kevin Dick. 2003. Addison-Wesley.

[Dürst02] *Character Model for the World Wide Web 1.0*. Martin J. Dürst, François Yergeau, Richard Ishida, Misha Wolf, Asmus Freytag. Tex Texin. April 2002. (*www.w3.org/TR/charmod*)

[Fielding98] *Web-Based Development of Complex Information Products*. Roy T. Fielding, E. James Whitehead, Jr., Kenneth M. Anderson, Gregory A. Bolcer, Peyman Oreizy, Richard N. Taylor. *Communications of the ACM*. 1998.

[FrontPage02] "Frequently Asked Questions About FrontPage," Microsoft, 2002. (*www.microsoft.com/ frontpage/faq.htm*)

[FrontPage03] "Ready-to-Run Software's UNIX support for Microsoft® FrontPage® 2002 Server Extensions and Microsoft® FrontPage® 2000 Server Extensions." © 2003. (*www.rtr.com/fpsupport/*)

[GeoCities02] "Free Web Host Features: Geocities." April 2002. (*www.helpwithhosting.com/ geocities_features.html*)

[GeoCities03] "Yahoo! PageWizards Help." © 2003. (*http://help.yahoo.com/help/us/geo/builder/pbwiz/*)

[Gossamer02] "Request-URI Too Large." Discussion on *Gossamer Threads*. April 2002. (*www.gossamer-threads .com/archive/mod_perl_C1/asp_F3/Request-URI_Too_Large_P1463/*)

[Gourley02] *HTTP the Definitive Guide*. David Gourley and Brian Toddy with Marjorie Sayer, Sailu Reddy, and Anshu Aggarwal. 2002. O'Reilly & Associates.

[Hopmann98] *Additional WebDAV Collection Properties*. A. Hopmann and L. Lippert. Internet Draft proposed to WebDAV Working Group. December 1998.

[Ito01] *Ticket-Based Access Control Extension to WebDAV*. Keith Ito. Internet Draft proposed to WebDAV Working Group. October 2001.

[Kim02] *mod_dav_dbms: A Database Backed DASL Module for Apache*. Sung Kim, Kai Pan, Elias Sinderson. March 2002.

[Korver03] *Quota and Size Properties for DAV Collections*. Brian Korver, Lisa Dusseault, Clark Warner. Internet Draft proposed to WebDAV Working Group. March 2003.

[Krishnamurthy99] *Key Differences between HTTP/1.0 and HTTP/1.1*. Balachander Krishnamurthy, Jeffrey C. Mogul, and David M. Kristol. 1999. Elsevier Science.

[Krishnamurthy01] *Web Protocols and Practice: HTTP/1.1, Networking Protocols, Caching and Traffic Measurement*. Balachander Krishnamurthy and Jennifer Rexford. 2001. Addison Wesley.

[LDAP02] *Administrator's Guide, Netscape Directory Server*. January 2002. (*http://enterprise.netscape .com/docs/directory/601/ag/url.htm*)

[LDAP03] *Tips for LDAP Users: LDAP· & LDAPS URLs*. Online Sun Tutorial, 2003. (*http://java.sun.com/ products/jndi/tutorial/ldap/misc/url.html*)

[Leach98] *UUIDs and GUIDs*. Paul Leach and R. Salz. 04 IETF Internet Draft. February 1998.

[Lee00] "Designing Knowledge Management Solutions with a Web Storage System." Walson Lee, MSDN Online. October 2000. (*http://msdn.microsoft.com/library/default.asp?url=/library/en-us/dndotnet/ html/designkmsols.asp*)

[Le Hors00] "Document Object Model (DOM) Level 2 Core Specification." Arnaud Le Hors, Philippe Le Hegaret, Lauren Wood, Gavin Nicol, Jonathan Robie, Mike Champion, Steve Byrne. November 2000. (*www.w3.org/TR/2000/REC-DOM-Level-2-Core-20001113/*)

[Martin00] *Programming Collaborative Web Applications with Microsoft Exchange 2000 Server*. Mindy Martin. 2000. Microsoft Press.

[Microsoft00] *Outlook Web Access in Exchange 2000 Server*. Microsoft White Paper, March 2000.

[Microsoft03a] "anchorClick Behavior." MSDN Online: Microsoft Corporation. © 2003. (*http://msdn.microsoft .com/library/default.asp?url=/workshop/author/behaviors/reference/behaviors/anchor.asp*)

[Microsoft03b] "httpFolder Behavior." MSDN Online: Microsoft Corporation. © 2003. (*http://msdn.microsoft .com/library/default.asp?url=/workshop/author/behaviors/reference/behaviors/httpfolder.asp*)

[Mozdev03] "UserAgent Spoofing." MultiZilla Documentation. March 2003. (*http://multizilla.mozdev.org/ docs/spoofing.html*)

[Nielsen99] *Detecting the Lost Update Problem Using Unreserved Checkout*. Henrik Frystyk Nielson, Daniel La Liberte. May 1999. (*www.w3.org/1999/04/Editing/*)

[Padmanabhan95] "Improving HTTP Latency." *Computer Networks and ISDN Systems*. 28(1/2):25–35. Venkata N. Padmanabhan and Jeffrey C. Mogul. December 1995.

[ODMA97] *Open Document Management API Version 2*. September 1997. (*www.infonuovo.com/odma/ downloads/#ODMA-20-Specification*)

[Owen03] *Cross-site tracing attacks*. Tom Owen. © 2003. (*http://lwn.net/Articles/21364/*)

[Reschke03a] *Datatypes for WebDAV Properties*. J. Reschke. Internet Draft proposed to WebDAV Working Group. March 2003.

[Reschke03b] *WebDAV SEARCH*. J. Reschke, S. Reddy, J. Davis, A. Babich. Internet Draft proposed to WebDAV Working Group. February 2003.

[Rescorla01] *SSL and TLS: Designing and Building Secure Systems*. E. Rescorla. 2001. Addison Wesley.

[Schuchardt02a] "A Web-Based Data Architecture for Problem-Solving Environments: Application of Distributed Authoring and Versioning the Extensible Computational Chemistry Environment." *Cluster Computing*. 5(3):287–296. K.L. Schuchardt, J.D. Myers, E.G. Stephan. 2002.

[Schuchardt02b] "Ecce—A Problem-Solving Environment's Evolution Toward Grid Services and a Web Architecture." *Concurrency and Computation: Practice and Experience*. 14:1221–1239. K.L. Schuchardt, B.T. Didier, G.D. Black. 2002.

[SecuritySpace03] "Apache Module Report." *E-Soft*. May 2003. (*www.securityspace.com/s_survey/data/ man.200302/apachemods.htm*)

[Servertec03] "Servertec Performance." *Servertec*. January 2003. (*www.servertec.com/products/iws/docs/ performance.html*)

[Shigeoka02] *Instant Messaging in Java: the Jabber Protocols.* Iain Shigeoka. 2002. Manning.

[Simone00] "GoLive 5.0 Unites the Adobe Family." Luisa Simone. *PC Magazine.* November 2000.

[Stein99] "WebDAV: Distributed Authoring and Versioning." Greg Stein. Adobe Technical Seminar Series. May 1999.

[Stein00] *WebDAV and Apache.* Paper for ApacheCon 2002. Greg Stein. 2000.

[Stevens98] *TCP/IP Illustrated: Volume 1.* W. Stevens. 1998. Addison Wesley.

[Vidstrom03] "The Use of TCP Port 445 in Windows 2000." Arne Vidstrom, 2003. (*http://ntsecurity.nu/ papers/port445/*)

[Whitehead01] "DeltaV: Adding Versioning to the Web." Jim Whitehead. WWW10 Tutorial, 2001.

IETF Documents: RFCs

[RFC524] A Proposed Mail Protocol. J. White. 13 June 1973.

[RFC793] Transmission Control Protocol. J. Postel. 01 September 1981.

[RFC959] File Transfer Protocol. J. Postel, J. K. Reynolds. 01 October 1985.

[RFC1738] Uniform Resource Locators (URL). T. Berners-Lee, L. Masinter, and M. McCahill. December 1994.

[RFC1864] The Content-MD5 Header Field. J. Myers and M. Rose. October 1995.

[RFC2026] The Internet Standards Process—Revision 3. S. Bradner. October 1996.

[RFC2045] Multipart Internet Mail Extensions (MIME) Part One: Format of Internet Message Bodies. N. Freed and N. Borenstein. November 1996.

[RFC2046] Multipurpose Internet Mail Extensions (MIME) Part Two: Media Types. N. Freed and N. Borenstein. November 1996.

[RFC2246] The TLS Protocol. Version 1.0. T. Dierks and C. Allen. January 1999.

[RFC2251] Lightweight Directory Access Protocol (v3). M. Wahl, T. Howes, S. Kille. December 1997.

[RFC2255] The LDAP URL Format. T. Howes, M. Smith. December 1997.

[RFC2277] IETF Policy on Character Sets and Languages. H. Alvestrand. January 1998.

[RFC2388] Returning Values from Forms: Multipart/form-data. L. Masinter. August 1998.

[RFC2396] Uniform Resource Identifiers (URI): Generic Syntax. T. Berners-Lee, R. Fielding, and L. Masinter. August 1998.

[RFC2518] HTTP Extensions for Distributed Authoring—WebDAV. Y. Goland, E. Whitehead, A. Fazi, S. Carter, and D. Jensen. February 1999.

[RFC2616] Hypertext Transfer Protocol—HTTP/1.1. R. Fielding, J. Gettys, J. Mogul, H. Frystyk, L. Masinter, P. Leach, and T. Berners-Lee. June 1999.

[RFC2617] HTTP Authentication: Basic and Digest Access Authentication. J. Franks, P. Hallam-Baker, J. Hostetler, S. Lawrence, P. Leach, A. Luotonen, E. Sink, and L. Stewart. June 1999.

[RFC2798] Definition of the inetOrgPerson LDAP Object Class. M.Smith. April 2000.

[RFC2817] Upgrading to TLS Within HTTP/1.1. R. Kharen and S. Lawrence. May 2000.

[RFC2818] HTTP Over TLS. E. Rescorla. May 2000.

[RFC2965] HTTP State Management Mechanism. D. Kristol and L. Montulli. October 2000.

[RFC3010] NFS version 4 Protocol. S. Shepler, B. Callaghan, D. Robinson, R. Thurlow, C. Beame, M. Eisler, and D. Noveck. December 2000.

[RFC3061] A URN Namespace of Object Identifiers. M. Mealling. February 2001.

[RFC3066] Tags for the Identification of Languages. H. Alvestrand. January 2001.

[RFC3120] A URN Namespace for XML.org. K. Best and N. Walsh. June 2001.

[RFC3143] Known HTTP Proxy/Caching Problems. I. Cooper and J. Dilley. June 2001.

[RFC3229] Delta encoding in HTTP. J. Mogul, B. Krishnamurthy, F. Douglis, A. Feldmann, Y. Goland, A. van Hoff, and D. Hellerstein. January 2002.

[RFC3339] Date and Time on the Internet: Timestamps. G. Klyne and C. Newman. July 2002.

Microsoft Support Articles

Microsoft Support articles can be found online through *http://support.microsoft.com*. The Knowledge Base contains articles indexed by ID but can also be searched using text search queries. The dates in these references are taken from the article's "Last Reviewed" date.

[q195851] How to Install and Use Web Folders in Internet Explorer 5. *http://support.microsoft.com/default.aspx?scid=kb;en-us;195851*. October 2002.

[q221600] Working with Distributed Authoring and Versioning (DAV) and Web Folders. *http://support.microsoft.com/default.aspx?scid=kb;en-us;221600*. December 2001.

[q289871] HOWTO: Use MKCOL in WebDAV to Create a New Folder. *http://support.microsoft.com/default.aspx?scid=kb;en-us;289871*. October 2001.

[q293885] How to Search a WebDAV Directory with XML. *http://support.microsoft.com/default.aspx?scid=kb;en-us;293885*. April 2001.

[q296126] HOW TO: Create, Modify and Delete Contact Items Via WebDAV (PROPPATCH). *http://support.microsoft.com/default.aspx?scid=kb;en-us;296126*. October 2001.

[q296713] HOWTO: Send a Message from Visual Basic by Using WebDAV. *http://support.microsoft.com/default.aspx?scid=kb;en-us;296713*. July 2002.

[q298637] No Option to Install Web Folders When You Install Internet Explorer 6. *http://support.microsoft.com/default.aspx?scid=kb;en-us;298637*. August 2002.

[q304133] FP2002: Errors Appear if You Use an Office XP Program to Save Content. *http://support.microsoft.com/default.aspx?scid=kb;en-us;304133*. April 2002.

[q308373] HOWTO: Send a Meeting Request Using WebDAV. *http://support.microsoft.com/default.aspx?scid=kb;en-us;308373*. October 2001.

[q317891] HOW TO: Add an Access Control Entry to a Folder Item in Exchange 2000 Web Storage System by Coding in Exchange 2000 Server. *http://support.microsoft.com/default.aspx?scid=kb;en-us;317891*. November 2002.

INDEX

A

abstract privileges, 343–345

Accept-Charsct hcader, 75

Accept-Encoding header, 75

Accept-Language header, 48, 75, 226

Accept-Ranges header, 73, 74, 109

access control entries (ACEs), 335, 338, 349

access control lists (ACLs), 335
  current user permissions, 346–347, 353–355
  dynamic inheritance of, 349–350
  owner identification, 339–340
  parsing of ACEs and, 349
  principal URLs and, 339, 350–351
  retrieving, 340–341
  setting, 347–349

access control for buddy lists, 381–382

access control, WebDAV, 10, 251, 335–359, 399
  denial of privileges, 349
  development of standardized, 335–336, 357–359
  LDAP servers and, 357–358
  locks vs., 101–102, 337
  Microsoft Exchange and, 256
  multiple protocol support and, 358–359
  pre-standardization approaches to, 336
  principal resources and, 338, 339, 350–357
  privileges and, 338, 341–346
  protection of ACEs and, 349
  retrieval and interpretation of ACLs, 339–347
  setting ACL information, 347–349

acl-principal-prop-set report, 352–353

acl-semantics property, 349

activities, DeltaV, 314–316
  atomicity and, 318
  branches and, 316–317
  merges and, 322
  subactivities, 318
  switching, 317–318

activity-checkout-set property, 314

activity-collection-set element, 306

activity-set property, 314–315

administer privilege, 345, 346

Adobe products, 19, 26, 248, 252

Advanced Client Workspace Package, DeltaV, 332

Advanced Server Workspace Package, DeltaV, 332

AFS. *See* Andrew File System (AFS)

all privilege, 342, 345

Allaire's ColdFusion, 3

Allow header, 74, 109

allprop element, 159–160, 220, 307, 396

alternate-URI-set property, 351

Amaya browser, 27, 31

AND logic, token lists and, 186, 191, 196

Andrew File System (AFS), 24, 37

AOL, 4
  AOLPress, 27
  AOLPress Extensions, 29–30
  AOLServer, 27–28

informIT

www.informit.com

YOUR GUIDE TO IT REFERENCE

Articles

Keep your edge with thousands of free articles, in-depth features, interviews, and IT reference recommendations – all written by experts you know and trust.

Online Books

Answers in an instant from **InformIT Online Book's** 600+ fully searchable on line books. Sign up now and get your first 14 days **free**.

POWERED BY

Catalog

Review online sample chapters, author biographies and customer rankings and choose exactly the right book from a selection of over 5,000 titles.